A Promise
and a Way of Life

Also by Becky Thompson

Mothering without a Compass: White Mother's Love,
  Black Son's Courage

A Hunger So Wide and So Deep: A Multiracial View of Women's
  Eating Problems

Names We Call Home: Autobiography on Racial Identity
  (coedited with Sangeeta Tyagi)

Beyond a Dream Deferred: Multicultural Education and
  the Politics of Excellence (coedited with Sangeeta Tyagi)

Becky Thompson

A Promise

white antiracist activism

and a Way of Life

University of Minnesota Press   Minneapolis / London

The University of Minnesota Press gratefully acknowledges permission to reprint the following. Lines from "For the White Person Who Wants to Know How to Be My Friend," by Pat Parker, from *Movement in Black* (Ithaca, N.Y.: Firebrand Books, 1978), reprinted courtesy of Firebrand Books; copyright 1978 by Pat Parker. Lines from "Some Advice to Those Who Will Serve Time in Prison," by Nazim Hikmet, from *Poems of Nazim Hikmet,* translated from the Turkish by Randy Blasing and Mutlu Konuk (New York: Persea Books, 1994), reprinted by permission of Persea Books, Inc. (New York); copyright 1994. "Thirteen Springs," by Marilyn Buck, first published in *Sojourner: The Women's Forum,* vol. 29, no. 9 (May 1999); copyright Marilyn Buck and reprinted by permission of Sojourner Feminist Institute. "Autobiograph" and "To the Woman Standing behind Me in Line Who Asks Me How Long Is Black History Month" are unpublished poems by Marilyn Buck; reprinted by permission of Marilyn Buck.

Published by the University of Minnesota Press
111 Third Avenue South, Suite 290
Minneapolis, MN 55401-2520
http://www.upress.umn.edu

Library of Congress Cataloging-in-Publication Data

Thompson, Becky W.
    A promise and a way of life : white antiracist activism / Becky Thompson.
       p.   cm.
    Includes bibliographical references (p.) and index.
    ISBN 0-8166-3633-8 (hardcover alk. paper) — ISBN 0-8166-3634-6 (pbk.: alk paper)
    1. Civil rights workers—United States—Interviews. 2. Whites—United States—Interviews. 3. African Americans—Civil rights—History—20th century. 4. Minorities—Civil rights—United States—History—20th century. 5. Civil rights movements—United States—History—20th century. 6. Whites—United States—Politics and government—20th century. 7. Racism—United States—History—20th century. 8. United States—Race relations. I. Title.
    E185.98.A1 T48 2001
    323.1'09—dc21   2001001489

Printed in the United States of America on acid-free paper

The University of Minnesota is an equal-opportunity educator and employer.

11 10 09 08 07 06 05 04 03 02 01   10 9 8 7 6 5 4 3 2 1

To David Gilbert,
Susan Kosoff,
and my grandmother, Beth Fillmore

willows in the wind

Contents

List of Abbreviations

AAUW   American Association of University Women

ACE   AIDS Counseling and Education

ADX   Solitary confinement, sensory deprivation section of a prison

AFDC   Aid to Families with Dependent Children

AIM   American Indian Movement

BLA   Black Liberation Army

CEED   Community Education for Economic Development

CESA   Committee to End Sterilization Abuse

CISPES   Committee in Solidarity with the People of El Salvador

CLUW   Coalition of Labor Union Women

CORE   Congress of Racial Equality

CRECE   Central American Refugee Center

DARE   Dykes against Racism Everywhere

ERAP   Economic Research and Action Program

FALN   Puerto Rican Armed Forces of National Liberation, Fuerzas Armadas de Liberación Nacional Puertorriqueña

FAN	Feminist Action Network
FEMA	Federal Emergency Management Agency
GROW	Grass Roots Organizing Work
HUAC	House Un-American Activities Committee
IMF	International Monetary Fund
INS	Immigration and Naturalization Service
IRA	Irish Republican Army
IWWDC	International Working Women's Day Committee
LUNA	Lesbians United in Nonnuclear Action
MANA	Mexican American Women's National Association
MFDP	Mississippi Freedom Democratic Party
MOVE	A spiritual and political Black activist organization from Philadelphia
NAACP	National Association for the Advancement of Colored People
NaCOPRW	National Conference of Puerto Rican Women
NAFTA	North American Free Trade Agreement
NBFO	National Black Feminist Organization
NOW	National Organization for Women
NWRO	National Welfare Rights Organization
NWSA	National Women's Studies Association
NYWAR	New York Women against Rape
OHOYO	A national network of American Indian and Alaska Native Women
PEPA	Prisoners' Education Project on AIDS

SANE A nuclear freeze organization

SCAR Statewide Correctional Alliance for Reform

SCEF Southern Conference Educational Fund

SCLC Southern Christian Leadership Conference

SDS Students for a Democratic Society

SLA Symbionese Liberation Army

SNCC Student Nonviolent Coordinating Committee

SOC Southern Organizing Committee for Economic and Social Justice

SPARC Sparking Powerful Anti-Racist Collaborations

SSOC Southern Student Organizing Committee

TPS Temporary protected status

UNO National Opposition Union

VISIONS Vigorous Interventions in Ongoing Natural Settings

WARN Women of All Red Nations

WITCH Women's International Terrorist Conspiracy from Hell

ZANU Zimbabwe African National Union

Introduction

In the Silences, the Stories Are Told

During the past five years I have been traveling around the country doing interviews—driving, walking, taking the forever-late train, and flying—meeting white people who consider racial justice the center of their lives' work. During this time, I have marveled at the diversity of those I have interviewed: people in their early twenties to people in their late eighties; Jews and Buddhists and some JewBus, as my friend Maury Stein would say; Italian Catholics and staunch atheists. So staunch, in the case of one ex-Communist, Herman Liveright, that he referred to a young woman who might be called his "goddaughter" as his "citizen daughter"—a label he used more than once during our time together with a completely straight face. I interviewed people who came up through the Communist Party and young antiracists first introduced to feminism through Cherríe Moraga and Gloria Anzaldúa's *This Bridge Called My Back*.[1] I interviewed single mothers and people in extended families; a wealthy woman who lives with her husband in a fancy house in Sudbury, Massachusetts; a couple living in a row house in a working-class, mostly white neighborhood in Baltimore; and a lesbian raised in South Africa who now lives in a mixed-class, mixed-race neighborhood in Oakland, California.

There are also ideological differences among those I interviewed, based on conflicts about essential questions for progressives: the role of violence in liberation struggles; unfinished conversations about the fall of the "beloved community"; the emphasis that should and should not be placed on process in social movements; ongoing conversations about "theory in the flesh" and its connection to identity politics;[2] and the balance that activists continue to strive for in the 1980s and 1990s between "fighting the power" and creating multiracial communities. The different frameworks reflect conversations among those white antiracists who referred to themselves as "revolutionary" in the late 1960s and again in the 1990s in their work with political prisoners, and conversations among twenty-something activists who consider "revolutionary" an outrageously ancient term.

This book offers a social history of white antiracist activism from the 1950s to the present in the United States by using in-depth interviews as the basis of analysis. The first chapter describes how people got started as activists. Chapters 2 through 7 chronicle white antiracists' positions within the early Civil Rights Movement, the Black Power Movement, and early and late second-wave feminism. Chapters 8 and 9 focus on Central America solidarity work in the 1980s and antiracism in prison activism, in nonprofit multiracial organizations, and by educational trainers. The last chapter reflects upon what antiracist culture feels and looks like for white people at the turn of the twentieth century.

The title of the book comes from Bonnie Kerness, whose activism in the Civil Rights Movement and since then has taught her that antiracism is both a "promise" she made to herself and others and "a way of life." The book explores the steps people take toward racial consciousness, the limits of white activism, and the richness of antiracist culture—the multiracial ways of living that people create along the way.

At a time when many of us believe the clock is turning backward in terms of racial justice, my passion for the project comes from knowing that many white people struggle to do antiracist work but lack road maps to draw upon in that struggle. Similarly, many people of color are interested in who white allies are and why cross-race alliances both falter and succeed. We do not need to look far to see white identity that is rooted in bigotry and domination. The elimination of affirmative action in many locations throughout the country and the upsurge of white supremacist activity and its increasing infusion into local and national politics underscore the need to learn from white people who actively oppose racism. Although at no period in U.S. history has there been a sufficient number of white antiracists to constitute a critical mass, in the last fifty years white activists have been intimately involved in progressive, race-conscious social struggles.

My hope has been to excavate a usable history of people who do not consider the term "white antiracist" an oxymoron. A spate of recent books offer nuanced and careful analyses of the destructiveness of white culture, of its arrogance, its overemphasis on individualism, its determination to control people of color.[3] I am concerned, however, that most of the recent writing on whiteness by white scholars focuses on racism and virtually ignores antiracism. Whether they state it or not, these writers seem to have little belief in the possibility of subversive action among white people. I am left asking what it means that the story of racism in this country, the story of white dominant culture, is told more often by progressives than is the story of white antiracist activism. What is at risk in treating antiracism as a historical reality and a current possibility?

Might the attention to racism rather than antiracism serve as a form of beating up on the collective self that fosters a kind of immobility, a way out of the hard work of naming how each of us is implicated and how we collectively might create a culture that is different from the one presently surrounding us? What is even more troubling about the dearth of attention to white antiracism is that it renders invisible organizing by activists of color. It is the centuries of activism against racism by people of color that has largely nurtured white antiracism.

For me, studying antiracist activism historically—its conflicts, successes, and limitations—is an antidote to despair. It is also a way to counter a long history of historical amnesia about progressive social change in this country in general. What I did not know when I started, however, was that the invisibility of antiracism is part of the very nature of doing antiracist work. Yes, the absence of all but a frightfully few white antiracists in U.S. history is partly why their history is so unknown. Yes, the history books and media have substantially ignored the white antiracist activism that has existed. Yes, scholars need to do their part to provide a comprehensive history of this area of inquiry. But antiracists have perpetuated their own invisibility as well, a reality that I took a while to understand. Getting to the heart of this self-imposed invisibility and the silences that feed it have made it possible to understand white antiracism across the decades.

The most obvious manifestation of this invisibility is in the activists' hesitation to name their work as "antiracist activism." Most of those I interviewed express deep skepticism about using the term "antiracist activist" to describe themselves. The skeptics even include those antiracists whose work is nationally known: David Wellman, who wrote the landmark 1977 book *Portraits of White Racism* and was involved in the Civil Rights Movement in Detroit and California;[4] Howard Zinn, who is the author of several volumes on race and class in U.S. history;[5] and Dorothy Stoneman, who is the president of YouthBuild USA, a youth action program that has won federal appropriations of more than $300 million that is used for local YouthBuild programs.

Their reasons for skepticism vary, which is revealing in itself in terms of political generation and political efficacy. For example, Bonnie Kerness received most of her education as an activist over the years from Black people, first in a settlement house in New York City in the 1950s, then in Tennessee and Florida during the Civil Rights Movement. Her most important mentors in the Movement were Black. Over the last thirty years, through her work with Vietnam Vets against the War, tenants' rights activists, welfare rights organizers, and her prison activism, her teachers have primarily been African American. Like most white people involved in civil rights during the 1960s, Bonnie referred to herself as part of "the Movement"—a term used by both Black and white people. Furthermore, none of the Black people who have been her teachers and peers described themselves as "antiracist." Since they have been her reference point, it would not have occurred to her to use the term "antiracist" as a self-description. Dorothy Stoneman agrees: "The term 'antiracist' is a basically white invention" that she remembers first hearing used in the late 1970s by white people who were not particularly grounded in a Black community. Dorothy came of age as an activist in the 1960s through the East Harlem Block Schools and other projects that were initiated and led by Latinos and Blacks. For both of these women, not using the term "antiracist" speaks to the formation of their racial identities as white people that developed alongside of, and in many ways through, African Americans and Latinos.

Although many white antiracists identified themselves collectively as part of the Civil Rights Movement through the mid-1960s, by the late 1960s such identification had become more complicated. The step from integrationist politics to Black Power meant white people needed to work within their own communities. This decision signaled the end of an era in which Black and white people used the same term to describe their work against racial domination.[6] White antiracists who were born in or after the late 1950s may have grown up hearing about "the Movement," but they were too young to be part of it. This generational difference may explain why the younger people I interviewed, though hesitant to describe themselves as "activists," did not voice complications about identifying themselves as "antiracist," as did most of the older people.

Women whose activism first developed through multiracial feminism represent a different trajectory than do activists born in the 1940s and earlier. For many feminists of the late 1970s and early 1980s, the label "antiracist" *is* an explicit point of reference, but only with the constant clarification that race cannot be considered separately from such issues as homophobia, sexism, and classism. Taking their cues largely from lesbians of color who were producing a remarkable collection of writings on the "simultaneity of oppressions," white lesbians and straight feminists came to understand that any attempts to work in coalition with women of color required seeing women's multiple identities.[7] "Antiracist" is a term these white women use, but only with several other political identifiers. The emblematic song of the 1960s, "We Shall Overcome," sung together by Black and white people on the picket lines and in paddy wagons following arrests, is a far cry from the equally symbolic title of Lorraine Bethel's late-1970s poem, "What Chou Mean 'We,' White Girl?"[8] That title served as a telling warning from African American feminists and womanists about the dangers of white women's attempts to conflate or falsely compare white and Black women's perspectives.

Several people also hesitate to identify themselves as antiracist activists because of their painful belief that radicals of the 1960s were unsuccessful in much of what they tried to accomplish. Naomi Jaffe, who has been organizing against racism for more than thirty-five years (including several years' membership in a militant anti-imperialist and antiracist group), is careful to clarify that this failure was not primarily a consequence of internal weaknesses—of sexism and racism within the Movement, splits over militant versus mass-based strategies, and instances of antidemocratic decision making. Although all of those limitations did exist, Naomi is quick—and right—to emphasize that activists of the 1960s were up against the most powerful nation in the world: "They had the guns, the prisons, the jobs, the houses, the access to health care."[9] And the government infiltrated progressive organizations with such tenacity that activists found it virtually impossible to do what they planned to do: make a revolution. Despite activists' knowledge that they faced formidable odds and that self-blame cannot be the final conclusion, their anger, sadness, and rage over the gains they never made or have subsequently lost continue to mean that, at best, claiming the term "antiracist activist" is bittersweet.

Another complication with the term "antiracist" involves concern that it implies a political stance that simply cannot exist. In Naomi Jaffe's words, "Before I speak as an authority on anything, I need to speak about how I got there. The trap I see is that it is tricky for white people to define antiracism. A lot of people go around thinking they are antiracist, but issues of race are very difficult for white people to get right. You never want to think that you have got it, because it is a trap. I am wary of being defined as an authority on antiracism because I know how many traps and pitfalls there are, and I know how far I am from where I need to be, and I have heard too many white people be too glib about it, and I am trying to figure out how not to be one of them. I am overwhelmed by the temptation to be one of them." She adds, "It is not an identity I don't want. It is an identity that I don't think can be fixed that way. It is not something you ever get. It is something you spend your whole life working on."

Like Naomi, Dorothy Stoneman was willing to be interviewed, since she has been doing antiracist work almost all of her life. But she has never used the term "antiracist" before and doesn't intend to in the future. As she explains, "I don't talk about it. I just do it." She says that she has a "certain aversion to talking about it," largely because identifying or labeling it runs the risk of drawing attention to it, when "you certainly don't want to suggest that you are doing anything special or out of the ordinary." She sees calling herself an "antiracist activist" pretentious: pretending to do more than she really is and then wanting to get credit for it as well. That, she explains, will definitely render one suspect by people of color. Doing the work requires not asking for credit or recognition.

Almost to a person, those I interviewed, especially the older activists, are humble and understated. They understand deeply that their work deserves no special congratulations. It is simply a way of trying to be human. Their recognition that racism is endemic and systemic feeds into a sense of themselves and their work as a drop in the bucket in eradicating racism. The humble assessments of their work sustain these people's activism over the long run; they simply could not do this work without this philosophical stance. Without a collective way of identifying these older activists, however, young activists find few ways to track them, and seasoned activists may have little sense of their work as part of a larger intergenerational community.

If part of antiracists' understated ways of being in the world are a consequence of coming to understand the enormity of racism, then their humility may also signal a knowledge that they do not respond to so much that they see. Political prisoner David Gilbert explains that being in prison means he witnesses injustices daily that he cannot try to stop. If he intervened every time, he would constantly be put in isolation, which would make it impossible for him to continue his AIDS work. But David says one potential consequence of his inability to respond is self-hatred. In his conceptualization, self-hatred is fueled by not being able to protect *others*—an understanding dramatically different from the common notion that self-hatred results from anger and hostility aimed at oneself.

For white people in a racist society, then, confronting self-hatred becomes an ongoing process, since we see and feel racism every day. Doing antiracist work requires struggling against the self-hatred that exposure to and complicity in racism engenders. Antiracists' apologies and clarifications help explain psychological dynamics of living in a racist society, dynamics that are, in turn, structurally enforced. Toni Morrison and James Baldwin write of racism as a sickness of white people's souls; I am left believing that the psychological dynamics of self-hatred are ones we must reckon with carefully and persistently.[10]

The complications of accepting "antiracism" as a political identity speak to the need to create collective identities that are not rooted in denial and avoidance, that say as much about what white activists are against as what they are for. This requires grappling with a number of complicated questions. What does a white identity and politic based on undermining itself look like? Once domination, exploitation, and unearned privileges are accounted for, is there anything left to whiteness? What, outside of someone's class, ethnicity, sexuality, skin color, or religion, constitutes whiteness? Does standing against the racial order for white people require self-annihilation? If whiteness is nothing beyond an invented system of domination, then where does the power come to undermine it from the inside?

Contemporary writers on whiteness have developed two distinct perspectives on these issues. For some, well represented in the work of legal theorist Barbara Flagg, becoming antiracist depends upon developing what she calls a "positive white identity."[11] She does not mean "positive" in any kind of glorified or romanticized way. Instead, she asserts that dealing with race in this country requires that all people, including white people, understand that they are raced. For Flagg, race itself is not the problem. Racism is. The task is to develop a white identity that is not based on subjugating others.

Ian Haney Lopez, a critical race theorist, disagrees with Flagg, positing that any attempt to find goodness or acceptance of whiteness in this country is problematic. He writes, "Given the inextricable relationships of meaning binding white and Black, it is impossible to separate an assertion of White goodness from the implication of Black badness. . . . For Whites even to mention their racial identity puts notions of racial supremacy into play, even when they merely attempt to foreground their Whiteness."[12] Lopez asserts that the only acceptable white identity in the United States is one bent on destroying whiteness, on becoming what has increasingly been called a "race traitor."

An example of this approach is seen in the Boston-based periodical *Race Traitor: A Journal of the New Abolitionism,* which is published under the slogan "Treason to whiteness is loyalty to humanity."[13] The basic ethic of this periodical is that a race traitor is someone who "is nominally classified as white, but who defies the rules of whiteness so flagrantly as to jeopardize his or her ability to draw upon the privileges of white skin."[14] The editors of this journal, Noel Ignatiev and John Garvey, explain the logic behind this approach through analogy. They ask, "How many counterfeit bills does it take to ruin the monetary system?" Just as the presence of only a few counterfeit bills can undermine the integrity of the monetary system, white people who refuse to act and be white can undermine the integrity of whiteness as a whole. Lopez also sees race traitors as "potentially racially revolutionary" because, as he reasons, "if enough seemingly White people were to reject such differentiation by claiming to be among the 'them,' the 'us' at the base of White identity would collapse."[15]

I first encountered the term "race traitor" in antiracist activist Mab

Segrest's *Memoir of a Race Traitor*.[16] My first reaction was relief. I had finally found a term that described what I have seen many antiracists try to do. The idea that white identity needs to be overturned makes sense. The term "race traitor" also captures how life often feels for many people I interviewed. David Wellman, for example, has said that he often feels like a spy, listening in on conversations he plans on undermining in whatever ways he can.[17] Like Wellman, I am drawn to the radical connotations of the term "traitor." I see racism as something so large and all-encompassing that no response short of a national revolution will suffice.

However, I am still wary about the notion that whiteness has to be annihilated, in part because it takes many white people such a long time to stop denying their whiteness. I, for example, had to work through shame, doubt, and guilt to describe myself as white without feeling as if I were choking. And during the fifteen years I have been teaching, I have watched many white students struggle through a process of identifying themselves as white without feeling the need to apologize. Gaining a positive white identity might be part of a process people go through on their way to becoming a "race traitor." But I worry that the idea of becoming a race traitor can be a stand-in for white people to continue to hate ourselves, to look to people of color as automatic authorities, and to distrust our abilities to identify and stand against racism. For the white activists I know, becoming activists has gone hand in hand with accepting themselves as white people.

In other words, it may be impossible to do antiracist work as white people in this country without seeing ourselves as white. This reality requires getting past—or at least trying to confront—the denial, avoidance, and fear that many people feel about being white. White people's abilities to talk with each other about racism and activism depend upon dealing with the daily realities of our lives and the formative influences in our understanding of race, as well as with the complications of race that most of us have been taught never to share.

My final concern about the writing on "race traitors" is the tendency to conflate race and racism, as if the two are one and the same. In the introduction to *Race Traitor,* the editors write, "Our intention . . . is to focus on whiteness and the struggle to abolish the white race from within."[18] Their first goal—to focus on whiteness—is a crucial means of countering the academic and medical history of diverting attention away from white supremacy by focusing on Black "pathology." But the second part of the editors' assertion is troubling. Perhaps the task is not to eliminate the white race from within but, rather, to eliminate racism from within. Although the analogy is imprecise, I can argue in a parallel way that eliminating patriarchy need not mean destroying men. I am intent upon resisting sexism and recognizing the fluidity between genders (and that there may well be more than two genders). I do not want, however, for boy children to grow up thinking it is wrong to be a man, nor am I willing to reject all forms of masculinity as oppressive.

Ultimately, I agree with Howard Winant that race, as a central organizing principle in the world, is here to stay.[19] He convincingly argues against the dominant notion that the significance of race is on the decline. He sees attempts to get rid of race as unrealistic and as a way of feeding the debilitating ideology of "color blindness." His proposal is not to eliminate racial categorizing but, rather, to democratize it. As a way of organizing the world, race is not inherently oppressive. It is the ranking of racial categories as a means of upholding inequality that is the problem, not race per se.

Unfortunately, I think the continuing vacillation about identities and the search for names that effectively describe white antiracists may not simply be issues of semantics. Rather, the lack of a precise and subversive terminology speaks to the fact that white people who challenge racism have not yet created the critical mass needed to name ourselves collectively. History has repeatedly shown that effective names—names that capture the essence of a political movement—come out of struggle and collectivity. Such slogans as "Black is beautiful" and "The personal is political" and such terms as "African American" and "womanist" come out of organized political struggle. So will terms that accurately describe what it means to be white people who both acknowledge whiteness and reject the ideology of supremacy it sustains.

Listening to white antiracist activists reveals many politically astute and hard-won reasons why people often back away from a named identity. Even those I interviewed who were willing to identify themselves in some way—"woman-centered revolutionary," "racist-antiracist," or "human rights organizer"—were still quick to limit those terms. This complexity, this ambivalence, this attention to nuance, this unnaming, leaves me asking, How does one write on a subject that, to use mathematical terms, is a null set, that is, has nothing inside of it? How is it possible to write about a label, an identity, that best fits those who refuse to use it? How does one write on a subject whose time has not yet come: about a movement that has not yet happened, about a consciousness that has not yet been collectively birthed?

In the following chapters I grapple with these and a number of other questions: Does antiracist work require a repudiation of one's whiteness, or can that identity, in fact, be transformed through political commitment and alliances? How does antiracist activism require whites to, in the words of feminist historian Nancie Caraway, "think through a politics of memory which begins with the paradox of assimilating a new identity, one which holds within bounds both emancipation and shame"?[20] My wish is to build on the pathbreaking work of Ruth Frankenberg and contribute to the growing scholarship on critical whiteness studies whose intellectual roots were first developed in African American studies.[21] Most importantly, I hope this book will introduce people to a history of antiracist struggle that will help incite antiracist activity in the future.

What "Counts" as Activism and How I Found People

From the beginning, I sought out people who were well known within progressive circles in addition to people known, by choice or necessity, only within their local communities. I was especially interested in people whose activism spanned two or more social movements, since they might help me better understand historical changes. All but two of the thirty-nine people whom I interviewed requested that I use their real names, which is not often done in ethnographic research.[22] I felt strongly about honoring their decisions, particularly in order to counter widespread historical amnesia regarding progressive activism. At the same time, using people's real names made me nervous. I conducted some of the interviews almost five years ago. Even though I sent the transcribed interviews to the interviewees and revised several based on further conversations, many people have moved far beyond who they were when we first talked. My hope is that I did justice to the nuance of their interviews and that my tellings are historically accurate. Typically, I came back from interviews with multiple tapes and a lengthy reading list provided by people who saw the holes, sometimes gaping, in my knowledge. Many of those I interviewed are older than I am, and most are more experienced activists. People's intellectual generosity, kindness, and principled actions often left me in awe. I still feel that way.[23]

I sought a range of white people in terms of the communities with which they have worked: African American, Latino, Native American, and Asian American. It was easier, however, to capture the multiracial makeup of social movement history in some historical moments than in others. The story of multiracial feminism is, as the name claims, multiracial, and has been so from the beginning. This is not true of all of the movements I examine. For example, even those in the West and the North during the early Civil Rights Movement mostly framed antiracism in Black/white terms. Similarly, I began the research on the Central America peace movement assuming that activists would have had close working relationships with Latinos in the United States. Not so, to a large extent. There were times when I laid my head down on my desk, overwhelmed by the enormous gaps in my own knowledge and the limited scholarly research on antiracism from a multiracial perspective. May people write and organize way beyond the confines of this book, and quickly.

I also sought a range of people in terms of the strategies they use. Jim Corcoran grew up in North Dakota in a liberal family with populist roots. He is now a journalist who writes about hate groups, but he has never joined any activist organization. His story is dramatically different from Fran Smith's; Fran was raised in a working-class, Italian American family in the 1960s and has worked with multiple nonprofit and multiracial organizations: the Rainbow Coalition with Mel King, the Hispanic Office of Planning and Evaluation, the Urban League, the Anti-Defamation League, and the list goes on. Unlike Jim, Fran has almost no time to write and has been an organizer well known and loved in various communities since she was in high school. Jane Ariel, who grew up in a lower-middle-class Jewish family in New York, was a professional musician and lived in Israel for many years before becoming an antiracism trainer and psychotherapist in northern California. She has a strikingly different background from Suzanne Ross, who was raised in Belgium and Mozambique to escape the Holocaust before coming to the United States with her family. Like Jane, Suzanne is trained as a psychologist, but Suzanne's politics much more closely resemble "revolutionary struggle" than does Jane's nonviolent, been-living-in-California, lesbian feminist consulting work. My interest has

been to tease out the differences in people's approaches and their manifestations in various social movements.

Among those I interviewed, most would probably identify themselves as progressives or radicals rather than as liberals, although early
in the project I began to see that distinctions between liberals and progressives were insufficient to understand the range of strategies people
employ. For example, those who have used the term "revolutionary"
or "militant" tend to be careful not to speak in a devaluing or conde-
scending way about antiracist trainers. But they cannot imagine doing
that kind of work themselves. Meanwhile, the trainers tend to be careful not to label the "militants" crazy, but they do not understand how
and why a militant approach (especially armed struggle) would (ever)
be useful strategically. However, all of those I interviewed often use
what might be labeled "liberal" tactics: pushing for multicultural education, while aware that its implementation rarely goes beyond the
add-and-stir stage of curriculum development; working *with* correctional officers to confront torture in prison; and accepting federal
money to support youth work programs even though that means losing some control over program policies. Several years ago, the Reverend Katie Cannon told me that in a white-dominated institution,
there are many times when, as a Black woman, the most she can do is
make a liberal argument or take a liberal position (as opposed to a progressive or radical one). The key, in her mind, is not to berate herself
for that decision but, rather, to not confuse a liberal with a progressive
argument. My point is that a liberal/radical dichotomy does not seem
to hold true in many instances historically, especially during regressive
periods.

A final comment about the range of people I interviewed concerns
religion. The substantial number of Jews in the study (almost half of
those I interviewed) speaks to the significant influence of progressive
Jewish culture in movement organizing historically. Of those Jews I
interviewed, a few are not Jewish identified.[24] While they still "count"
as Jewish, their political work has little connection to that identity.
Most of the Jews I interviewed did connect progressive Jewish culture
directly to their antiracist politics. A few people had Jewish parents
whose activism set the stage for their own activism as adults.[25]

Of course, there is a danger in overemphasizing the position of progressive Jews in antiracist work. At the same time, the history of the
Communist Party as a locus for antiracist work is partly a Jewish story.

Many feminists engaged in antiracist work are Jewish, and many contemporary writers on racism and whiteness are Jewish.[26] There are other historical and contemporary reasons why Jews are more apt to question and then oppose racism than are Christian-raised people. In *White Man Falling: Race, Gender, and White Supremacy,* Abby Ferber explains that from the perspective of the radical right, Jews are not white.[27] Although I did not deliberately seek out Jews, because of the ways in which anti-Semitism and internalized anti-Semitism operate, identifying Jews specifically and theorizing about anti-Semitism may stand out when, in reality, the issue of making Jews invisible is the problem.

Throughout the book I also wrestle with the complicated issue of what constitutes activism. A common stereotype of activists is that of placard-carrying protesters attending rallies and demonstrations. Although protests have often been used as markers for the telling of social movement history, activists' everyday lives tend to be much less dramatic, much more mundane, and much less collective than the activist-as-demonstrator icon suggests. Among those I interviewed, there is, not surprisingly, no consensus about what constitutes activism. One end of the continuum is represented by David Wellman, who argues that it would be disrespectful and inaccurate to call himself an activist in the 1980s and 1990s, even though he speaks widely in support of affirmative action, writes about the history of multiracial union activism among longshoremen, and agitates about race- and class-biased educational policy. From his perspective, his right to call himself an activist stopped in the late 1960s, with the assault on the New Left and the Black Power Movement. Activism for him is inevitably tied to collective and organized struggle. He is also wary of the way the widespread use of the term "activist" can cheapen its meaning and power: "There are a lot of people today in the academy who were never involved in the Civil Rights Movement or the antiwar movement or any movement on any level who—and here I won't call names—who write a lot in all the right publications and call themselves activists. I guess it kind of pisses me off that these people were not involved when it was really dangerous to be, when there was really stuff at stake. When the stakes were higher, they were nowhere to be found, and now they are calling themselves activists on the basis of doing stuff they get paid $60,000 or $70,000 a year to do. That pisses me off."

From David's perspective, "It demeans me and the concept of activist which I have always seen as a kind of selfless set of activities that people did because it was the right thing to do, not because it was something they got paid to do and something they were expected to do. There are still a lot of people out there who are activists, by that standard. And I guess what I am reflecting on is how special and precious the concept of activism is to me. When I think about activists I think about my mother, who was a working-class woman who spent her whole life working, raising kids, being politically involved. When someone needed to be on the picket line, she was on the picket line. And my father, who is still going to meetings after a stroke at eighty-three. Friends of mine who died. Who were killed. It is a special concept. You were asking me earlier about the role models and heroes. People like Che Guevara, who died in a country that wasn't his for an ideal that he believed in. Gave up a career, a family, a life for an ideal."

The other end of the continuum is reflected in Ruth Frankenberg's perspective, which casts serious doubts on conceding the term "activist" solely to those who carry placards, are engaged in public protest, and are affiliated with mass movements. From Ruth's perspective, the parameters of protest against the Gulf War offered an important example of the limits of marching-down-the-street activism. Ruth remembers that "there was a huge response nationwide to the Gulf War. The majority of people in the United States were against it, so many of us took to the streets. But, one, it didn't matter because the press blanketed everything. Two, it was not true that George Bush would say, 'Oh wow, I guess you don't want this to happen. I am sorry. I'll call it off.' There was this bedrock of racism and colonial discourse that was bottled up. What was necessary was to do the work of deconstructing and unraveling it. . . . So, in other words, the Gulf War really demonstrated to me the inadequacy of taking-to-the-streets politics. That has its place, but only if other kinds of work have already been done so that we would never get to this situation." From Ruth's perspective, activism to prevent the Gulf War or to support affirmative action requires grassroots work. Teaching, then, becomes a "fundamental and crucial part of this work." Ruth believes that teaching about race and racism can be a form of grassroots organizing that does have the potential to transform consciousness and action beyond one's individual purview.

In the end, perhaps Reebee Garofalo's understanding of activism offers a bridge between the two ends of the continuum. When I asked
Reebee, who saw himself as "in the Movement" in the early 1960s and
then a "revolutionary" by the end of the decade, whether he considers
himself an activist now, he said, "Yes. You don't need a social movement to be an activist. You just need a social movement to be an effective activist. I mean it is just a lot easier when a million people are
doing it." From my perspective, both ends of the continuum are valid
and reflect differences in historical periods worthy of careful consideration. Ultimately, in writing the book, I found Bonnie Kerness's conception of antiracist activism as both a "promise" and "a way of life"
a welcome guidepost for finding my way across multiple generational
and ideological divides.

What we stand to gain by scrutinizing the complexity of white antiracism across the decades is one remedy to the divisions that literary
theorist William Pinar writes about. "We are what we know. We are,
however, also what we do not know. If what we know about ourselves—
our history, our culture, our national identity—is deformed by absences,
denials and incompleteness, then our identity—both as individuals and
as Americans—is fragmented."[28] U.S. history and culture are deformed
by what we do not know about injustice and resistance to injustice.
What antiracist activists reveal is that the story of antiracism is embedded in conflicts within social movement history. Knowing about
white antiracism can provide public iconography that might give white
people new and more humane ways of being. The history of antiracism
counters a racial script founded on divisions and hierarchy. It is a story
about the ferocious cost that racism exacts on one's mind, body,
and soul.

It is among those who have been trying to heal that split that I believe we will find some antidotes to our current despairs.

1

Getting Started:
Roots of Radical Traditions

A common stereotype of social activists is that most were born into activist families who nurtured their activism from childhood onward. Over the years I have been troubled by how this iconography fuels a sense of inadequacy among people seeking to be antiracists. I have heard many young adults who do not come from radical families speak of themselves as inadequate, saying that they do not have enough prior knowledge to get started, that they must hurry to catch up for experiences they have already missed. They also worry that if they were not born during the Civil Rights Movement or another period when there was a vibrant political movement, they could not possibly become "real" activists. This those-were-the-days conception or the I-missed-the-real-deal worry contributes to a sense of not belonging, of not being real, or of not being adequately prepared to be a genuine activist. Understanding that antiracist activists grow up in a variety of different political settings and political eras makes room for multiple origin stories and counters the notion that there is a single path to social activism.

A few people I interviewed were born into radical families: red-diaper babies, children who grew up with antiapartheid activist parents, and children who recall their first political demonstration as vividly as they remember their first birthday party. The majority, however, took much more circuitous paths toward becoming activists. For several, leaving their families of origin was essential to finding their political voices. For others, coming of age as activists meant reckoning with often-contradictory messages from family members: parents who were on the opposite ends of the political spectrum, parents who espoused a liberal racial politic while acting in clearly racist ways, parents whose politics changed radically during a child's early years.

Recognizing different paths toward radical activism highlights the often ingenious, sometimes unconscious, ways in which children and young adults become part of collective struggles. These paths also underscore multiple contradictions that young white people face as they try to understand and, in these situations, come to terms with racism. The making of an activist consciousness is rarely, if ever, linear. It always requires mentors along the way, sometimes in easy reach, most often sought out in travels far from home.

"Checked Out of the Family, into the World of Organizing"[1]

Among the most compelling accounts of becoming activists as young adults are those told by people who had to look far beyond their families and communities to begin to actively question racial domination. Several people I interviewed had no activist role models as children. For them, becoming activists meant leaving behind those they had known and, in most situations, loved.

Bonnie Kerness: "I felt like I was the luckiest person in the world."

Bonnie Kerness is a mother of six who has been an antiracist and human rights organizer since her early teens. She was born into a lower-middle-class, Jewish and Catholic family in the Bronx in the early 1940s. Although she remembers always wanting to be an organizer, she found it impossible to communicate that to her family. They expected her to marry a lawyer or an accountant, have children, and move to Long Island. If she wanted to go to school, her relatives assumed she would be a teacher. She says, "I came out of my childhood from a family where I just didn't fit in. Once in a while a kid is born into a family that just can't understand him/her. I came into the world fully decked. I already knew myself and what I am here to do in some core ways."

By the mid-1950s, when Bonnie began reading about the beginnings of the Civil Rights Movement, she was "very moved by what was going on." She continues, "The rest of my generation was listening to Elvis Presley and I developed a fascination for Pete Seeger and the Weavers and Nina Simone. Those were my first teachers, through music." In her early teens, Bonnie took a train from her Queens home to a settlement house on the Lower East Side of New York City that was organizing for fair housing and against gangs. As she explains it, "At fourteen I checked out of my family and into the world of organizing, and I haven't turned back since." At the settlement house she lied about her age to get a job as a "laundry girl" so that she could listen to all that was going on around her.

Through this work, Bonnie began meeting children from other races and comparing notes. She recalls, "We would just hang out on the stoops and talk about our different life experiences. I can remember one kid saying to me that in this neighborhood you either became a criminal or a cop. I must have thought about that for months. It was just so different from anything in my experience. Seeing children for the first time who didn't have parents to come home to. They had to come to the community center. For the first time, I was confronted with the inequities of class, and most of the inequities seemed to be race-based. I was aware that those with a darker skin hue had a different life experience; it wasn't just an observation. It was things that kids themselves told me. Children can be wonderful and very clear about their own experience." Pete Seeger lived close to the settlement house, and Bonnie got to spend time with him as she watched activists organize on the Lower East Side. She continued to work at the settlement house for two and a half years, until she finished high school.

In her late teens (the early 1960s) Bonnie moved to Memphis, Tennessee, and started learning how to be a civil rights organizer. Partly because she was a single, young, white woman who had come to the South on her own, the organizers around her made a special effort to teach and work with her. She recalls, "One of the unique things about my experience, because I did go on my own, is that most of my contacts were with people of African descent and mostly folks older than I was. I very much had a sense of being taken care of. I also had a sense of being quietly healed. It is hard to describe. The folks that I met, the ways I was handled. For the first time folks were praising my sense of what I needed to do. I didn't have that at home. My folks would tell me that I would 'glamorize' poverty. That was their famous statement. I never really understood what they meant, but I knew I wasn't doing it. For me, it was a tremendously healing experience while I was learning."

The civil rights organizers supported the questions she was asking and her passion for justice. "I was very young—nineteen and twenty years old. My thought process was not terrific at that time. I was a young person really moving instinctively, less out of an intellectual desire to help my fellow man than just an instinct that I needed to move away from my home to grow. Away from my childhood in order to grow. Just the affirmation does wonders to the internal psyche. Every one of us."

After working in Memphis, Bonnie went to the Highlander Folk School, a training center in Tennessee for activists interested in grassroots organizing and activist culture. "Everybody in the world was trained at Highlander. Rosa Parks. Stokely Carmichael. Rap Brown. Martin Luther King. I just felt like I was the luckiest person in the world in terms of who I met and how I was trained." Bonnie remembers that during that period everyone connected with Highlander seemed to be under investigation by the State of Tennessee for sedition. Being under scrutiny, they were neither able to hold organizing workshops nor to train people formally. Instead, they held music workshops. "I thought I had died and gone to heaven," Bonnie says. "People would come down from the hills and the hollows of Tennessee and sing the struggle songs about the miners in Appalachia. Seeger would come very frequently. The Civil Rights Movement was so moved through music." About the power of this music, historian Paula Giddings writes, "The music born out of the depths of history tinged with struggle and triumph provided both a common weapon and a shield. After a song, [Bernice Johnson] Reagon recalled, 'the differences between us were not so great. Somehow making a song required an expression of that which was common to us all.'"[2]

Bonnie remembers listening to a shortwave radio, trying to pick up Nina Simone, who was banned at the time from singing in the South. Under the guise of music, Highlander organizers held workshops packed with people. Through these workshops, they helped to organize the James Meredith marches and Freedom Summer (1964), and the workshops served as a meeting place for activists. At that time, Bonnie says, Highlander was "the only place in the South where people could pretty much meet comfortably in mixed cultural circumstances. There were guards that patrolled the land with shotguns because people's tires were being shot at on a routine basis. It was an actively hostile environment, probably the most actively hostile environment I have ever lived in."

As Bonnie continued to organize in Knoxville, while remaining connected to Highlander, the Knoxville Jewish community began to be concerned about her work. She had married a Jew who was working at the local Jewish community center, so she well knew how she was being perceived within that community. In many ways, Bonnie considers their discomfort understandable. "There were something like twenty Jewish families and they were, next to the people of African descent, right up there, with the 'No Jews, no niggers, no dogs.'"

In these circumstances, it seemed best that Bonnie and her family move on. Movement organizers encouraged her to move with her husband and their two children to Florida, where organizing had not been nearly as extensive as in Tennessee. As she says, "It was more deep South than the deep South." She began doing early testing to document mortgage and real estate discrimination. Bonnie would "go in as a white person, to attempt to buy a home and make sure that homes were available. And then behind me, an African American would come as a way to determine if there was discrimination. If there was, we would begin litigating."

Bonnie's story about how she began organizing is instructive on numerous levels. First, as is true for a few people I interviewed, Bonnie sensed that she had been born to seek justice, that she was already programmed internally to do the work she has been doing all her life. Another woman I interviewed, Rose Marie Cummins, spoke similarly about her path toward activism. One of eight children raised in a one-bedroom house in a segregated community in Kentucky, Rose Marie was the only child in her family who knew she wanted to live a multicultural life and work for justice. She recalls having a hunger as a young child to learn Spanish and to live in a bicultural community.

The idea that children are born with an internal plan for their lives goes against well-reasoned scientific claims that personalities are largely developed through socialization. And yet Bonnie's and Rose Marie's perspectives resonate with a spiritual sense that some people may be born already knowing what is planned for them. Rose Marie's sense that her life had a design fits with her religious beliefs and vocation as a Catholic nun. Bonnie, by contrast, does not consider herself religious. Nevertheless, their stories do suggest that some children know what they want to do at an early age and are able to thrive when they find a community to support them.

For Bonnie, the teaching and care given to her by activists in the South both helped her heal from a difficult childhood and gave her tools for organizing that she continues to use. She writes, "There was much healing afforded to me through the values of Afrikan culture that I was exposed to in the South. I have often felt that my own emerging mental health as a young person was borrowed from the many adults of color who mentored me during my early movement years. . . . You can only imagine the joy I felt in being encouraged and accepted as I was mentored and trained in my southern years. People were actually telling me to follow my heart. I had such a sense of my internal bleeding being healed."[3] Bonnie also considers herself fortunate in the timing of her involvement in the Civil Rights Movement. She thinks that "we who ended up in the Civil Rights Movement were lucky in a way because there were adults there who trained us. The Panthers had no such luxury. The American Indian Movement kids didn't necessarily have that luxury because they were almost in opposition to their elders. The times I was born into were real important to my evolution."

Bonnie's route toward activism underscores the serendipity of her seeking a justice community during a period of U.S. history when such a movement was prominent nationally. Her ability to organize in Florida, where there was less organizing, was a direct consequence of the lessons she learned within a hub of activism at the Highlander Folk School. Her ability to work consistently as an activist in the 1970s and 1980s despite the isolation she and many other activists faced due to the country's turn to the right also speaks to the energy and life force nurtured during the civil rights years. Her activism in the 1960s helped her stop the "internal bleeding" while serving as a springboard leading into the life of an activist.

Betty Liveright: "Something just woke up inside of me."

For Betty Liveright, becoming an activist also involved leaving her family of origin, both physically and psychically. An activist for more than sixty years, she has been mystified all her life by questions about what drew her toward activism. She was born in 1913 into a Christian Scientist, middle-class family in an overwhelmingly white suburb outside of Chicago. Her parents were staunch Republicans, and all of her sisters were politically and socially conservative. From an early age she "felt a constant drive to get away from my background, to get away from my hometown." Betty remembers being conscious, as young as ten years old, of wanting to get to know one of the very few Black children in her school. She says that "something just woke up inside of me" when she heard Black children talk about Booker T. Washington as having been one of the most wonderful people in the country. "I felt sort of conscious, not in an active way, but conscious of being white and other people being Black."

Betty has few answers, however, about what brought her to question the exclusiveness of white culture and the persistence of racism. She felt a need to "get away from the kind of alienation I felt with those people [her family and community]. The kind of feeling that I was different and that I wanted to get away from that." At times she has wondered if the drive to leave was unhealthy. After all, she has demanded of herself, "Why can't I just get adjusted to people?" Betty wondered why she felt a kind of relation to Black people who were alienated. "I always felt a kind of association, empathy. I could never associate with them because it was such a different world, but I felt that."

The most Betty can piece together about her need to flee from her roots relates to the contradictions she experienced around religion. As a practicing Christian Scientist during her childhood and early adulthood, Betty had an increasingly difficult time understanding how people could espouse Christian love while upholding racism and anti-Semitism. Beginning to question the contradictions in Christian rhetoric opened her up to questioning authority in general. Once she fell in love with Herman, a secular Jew who has been her husband and political partner for more than sixty years, Betty gave up religion entirely, and she joined the Communist Party in 1936. As members of the party, Herman and Betty "were educated to the fact that there shouldn't be racist behavior among political people." In fact, as Betty remembers it, "people were brought up on charges by Communist leaders if they had been racist." Through her involvement in the party, which in Philadelphia included many Black members, she saw how activists applied a class analysis to their work against police brutality, for housing, and against racism in the arts and media. The party gave them a context and community in which to work. The antireligious framework within Communist circles also gave Betty and Herman a way to work for justice while avoiding the contradictions of Christianity she had wrestled with as a child.

Betty's radicalization despite her lack of activist role models as a child is informative on a number of accounts. First, credit is certainly due to those who question racism when very young even though they do not see that questioning spirit around them. That Betty has wondered all her life about what drove her beyond the status quo also suggests one way in which people internalize the dominant narrative about race in the United States. This racial narrative teaches people that there must be a reason for questioning racial norms and that for white people to do so, especially when there are no early role models, is inexplicable. Given that many children are able to see and feel injustice from very early ages, it is painful to recognize how often they are taught not to question racism. Feeling defensive about why white people question racism as children is a bit like interracial couples feeling defensive about their mixed-race unions. The dominant narrative makes an interracial couple pathological rather than questioning what might be problematic about white people who consistently date or become partners only with white people.

Betty exemplifies the possibility of becoming an antiracist activist even without parental or community support and in repressive historical times. She was developing a race consciousness during a particularly harsh political period for Communists and those who opposed segregation. Once she and Herman had moved to New Orleans in the 1950s, they learned that the government was using anticommunist persecution to root out supposed Communists while trying to stop antiracism. Senator James O. Eastland (D.–Miss.), who headed up the Subcommittee on Internal Security of the Senate Judiciary Committee, had set up white citizens councils all through the South to investigate and terrorize the population. According to Betty and Herman, "The white citizen's council disguised their retaliation against the Supreme Court decision of 1954 by setting up committees to prosecute anyone considered to be Communist." Herman was called to testify before the Eastland committee in 1956, supposedly for importing subversive materials from Central and South America. The real reason for the charges included his commitment to integrating programs at the television station where he was program manager. When Herman was fired from his job after testifying, Betty was fired as well.

Betty's story points to the power of organizing—in progressive times, certainly, but in conservative times especially: Organizing gives people who might otherwise be completely on their own a context to get involved. Betty's marriage to Herman, their lifelong partnership as political comrades, and her involvement in the Communist Party and other left politics allowed her to develop an antiracist politic that she did not have during childhood.

Betty's work with Black Communists and other Black activists also offered her a way to revise a script written in childhood. As a child she felt empathy toward the few Black children at her school and yearned for a way to connect. But "I could never associate with them because it was such a different world." There were no bridges to cross-race communication or alliances during her childhood. Through the Communist Party, Betty found such alliances.

In truth, Communist rhetoric about antiracism did not necessarily translate into actual antiracist practice. A few histories of the Communist Party provide nuanced analyses of how the party was both racist and antiracist simultaneously.[4] Richard Wright wrote passionately about how he and other Black members were excluded and patronized despite their dedication to the party.[5] While racism within the party was on-going, given Betty's political origins—in a family of staunch Republicans—the Communist Party's race analysis was a huge step up.

Dawn Gomes: Rethinking rage

Dawn Gomes also left her family of origin behind on her way to becoming an activist. Like the others, Dawn found herself drawn to a political community that became both a social network and a political training ground. Unlike some of the others, though, Dawn believes that running from her biological family unconsciously led her to early social activism that was both politically and ethically flawed.

Dawn was raised in northern California in a working-class family amid violence and alcoholism. In 1968, when Dawn was in her early twenties, she moved to San Francisco at the height of the Black Power Movement. Her story is part of the story of, in her words, "a small group of unaffiliated leftists of the 1970s, young, idealistic, white people, who wanted to make a commitment to the revolution." From 1977 to 1982 she was a member of a white political organization that supported a Black liberation organization. Its philosophy was that white people would take direction from Black people. The mission also included taking weapons training and supporting underground organizations for the purpose of overthrowing the U.S. government. Rhetoric about needing to be completely devoted to the cause, along with other tactics, resulted in the members becoming more and more isolated from the rest of society. For example, members were discouraged from holding jobs, which would take time away from the liberation work. For most of the white people, the women especially, work revolved around fund-raising, mainly from bake sales, flea markets, and other ways of making money that would not involve paying taxes.

During her five years in this organization, including some in a leadership position, Dawn was subjected to and subjected others to expectations she now considers fascist: forcing people to isolate themselves from the larger community, creating crises and dramas among the membership and between organizations to keep people on the defensive and unable to trust each other, maintaining a party line that allowed for virtually no dissent, and being asked to support violent tactics without a democratic process. From Dawn's perspective, people were "guilt-tripped" into doing things—that is, made to feel guilty if they did not do them—that did not necessarily accomplish anything politically. There was tremendous hypocrisy within the organization, particularly regarding sexual politics and finances. Over time Dawn started to question the organization, even though such questioning scared her and made her think she could not trust anyone.

Eventually Dawn realized that she had no intention of remaining part of a revolutionary movement in order to be a "cookie girl." She began to question tactics within the organization after learning about Pol Pot in Cambodia. From the example of Pol Pot, who had headed the Cambodian government's murder of millions of men, women, and children, Dawn came to see how wrong leadership could be, even in organizations with a revolutionary platform. She found parallels between Pol Pot's extremism and the extremism in her solidarity organization. Eventually, in 1982, she found a way to leave the organization.

Since Dawn left the group she has tried to understand what drew her to be part of it, to serve as a leader, and to stay as long as she did. She has asked herself why she participated in that way in political organizing and how her participation was shaped by her own background. She now believes that she was powerfully drawn to the solidarity organization because she could identify with people's rage. The solidarity organization gave her a place to feel rage at a time when she did not yet know how to direct it at the family injuries she had faced. Although she still understands and supports the rage of activists, her own background led her to channel her rage in ways that backfired on her and on many of those around her. She sees her willingness to stick with a corrupt organization as an extension of living in her family, where she always felt on the outside. During the first few years of her work with this solidarity organization, she had no white friends, because she believed that having white friends meant "buying into the system." She referred to herself as "vehement and arrogant" during that time, assuming she was above other white people and practicing the most revolutionary approaches to political work.

Although Dawn is critical of the solidarity organization, she does not regret the lessons she learned. At the same time, she believes that the activism did not allow her to take care of herself. Of the working-class women in the organization Dawn says, "We didn't have a sense of our own self, our own low self-esteem." She sees this inability to care for herself partly as a class issue, since, as she says, "There were always ways that middle-class white people could take care of themselves in ways that I could not." For example, they had middle-class resources if they ran out of money while working for the solidarity organization; they had access to therapy to understand how their own psychological make-up interfaced with the work they were doing. Middle-class people somehow knew how to keep themselves on the agenda in a way that Dawn did not understand during that period of her life.

It's certainly true that not all white people involved in solidarity work with Black liberation groups came from troubled families. And not all of them encounter the problematic organizing strategies that Dawn did. But Dawn's story illustrates the fact that political organizations may not allow people to develop as ethical and political beings. Dawn's story offers an extreme case of political theory and practice that did not mesh. The theory—that white supremacy would only be eliminated by revolutionary overthrow of the government—was in practice sought within an undemocratic organization. In Dawn's experience, the solidarity work also fed her low self-esteem as a woman and undermined her chances to do work across race with other women. To be white in that organization required distrusting white people, including other white members. At the same time, she was told to trust African American male leadership unconditionally, even when African American women within the organization tried to intervene against hierarchical and sexualized tactics. With time, Dawn found organizations that did not replicate these tactics and activism that nurtured her multiple skills.

Stan Markowitz: Teaching history, staying class-conscious

Stan Markowitz is a professor of U.S. history who has been an anti-racist activist since the mid-1960s. His early consciousness about racism also took place despite, rather than alongside, his family and the community in which he grew up. Born in 1937, Stan was raised in a Jewish working-class family. In his neighborhood the white people lived on one side of the block and the Black people lived on the other. The unspoken assumption that the two sides would not meet bothered Stan. He always questioned injustice, a spirit he attributes to many convoluted messages about race, class, and religion in his family. When he came home with an African American friend, his mother met them by laughing at Stan. She got a kick out of the fact that Stan did not seem to notice his friend's race. *"Schvartze,"* the Yiddish word for Blacks, was used frequently in his house. Although Stan's mother used it in a more benign way than his father did, Stan felt uncomfortable with any use of the term.

Stan's parents owned a small neighborhood hardware store, where they worked very hard. His father spoke about the Black employees in disparaging terms and consistently mistrusted them. Stan liked them because they taught him skills he needed at the store. Although he did not agree with his father's attitudes, there was no room for Stan to analyze racism or whiteness, although he certainly sensed its practice.

There was talk in Stan's family, however, about being Jewish. Stan's mother thought that Jews were superior to other white people, a claim that did not make much sense to Stan. His relationship with his mother was very strained and, as his face revealed during the interview, that pain remains with him. His mother always expected him to be the "perfect," upwardly mobile, Jewish boy and eventually to become a doctor, a lawyer, or an accountant. She pushed him in school and was intent upon his making a lot of money, but he resisted her pressures. Although he went to high school, he was only interested in history. He dropped out of college and joined the army. As an enlisted man, he soon saw the horrifying ways Black men, including people he bunked with, were treated. He began to understand racism as a system of oppression, not simply isolated to his neighborhood and family but also extending to the military.

Eventually Stan went back to school and earned a doctorate in history. He then taught at Howard University, in Washington, D.C., in the late 1960s before moving to Baltimore. Although he initially left his community of origin in order to be radicalized racially, he found a way to return to a community similar in terms of race and class through his teaching at a community college. Although his doctorate in history and his steady faculty salary now put him in the middle class, his commitment to working-class students reflects the fact that he radically changed his racial politics while holding onto a class analysis. Whereas Betty and several others I interviewed who left their communities of origin never went back, Stan did. Both Bonnie and Betty were raised in middle-class families with whom they were unable to connect emotionally or politically. From middle-class backgrounds, they could move away from their families without believing they were abandoning class consciousness.

Doing antiracist work—particularly because of the lesson he learned from Black Power activists that white people's work is in their own communities—allowed Stan to stay close to his class roots. He had less success, however, in finding a positive relationship to his Jewish roots. The combination of being a secular Jew, the way leftists have historically treated religion as "the opium of the people," and the damage done to him psychically in the name of Judaism when he was a child may explain why Stan has not emphasized a Jewish identity as an adult.

Anne Braden: Liberated from "the prisons of my childhood"

Anne Braden, who was born in 1924, grew up in Alabama in a family and community that were openly supportive of segregation. As a child she remembers her father saying, "We need to have a good lynching every once in a while to keep the nigger in his place."[6] Although these and other outrageous attitudes bothered Anne deeply when she was growing up, it was not until she left Alabama as a young adult that she started to find people who felt otherwise. She moved to Louisville, Kentucky, hoping to "be a great newspaper woman. That was my goal in life." She reasoned that if she could get experience at the newspaper there, she could go to New York or Chicago and be away from the South. "I had left Birmingham running away."

Soon after moving to Louisville, she met a journalist, Carl Braden, who introduced her to the trade union movement, the writing of the socialist Eugene Debs, and other labor scholarship. As a newspaper reporter, Anne got to know some of the lawyers for the National Association for the Advancement of Colored People (NAACP), began reading about slavery and reconstruction from the perspective of abolitionists, and was introduced to antisegregation work in the city and state. Soon, "Carl would send me to union meetings when he couldn't go. You see, just meeting people who were standing up against things that had been preying on my mind all my life and where I came from. . . . Everything I had ever known turned upside down. . . . It was like looking at the world from a totally new point of view. It was a very painful process because I had to come to terms with the fact that the society I had grown up in and had been very good to me actually was just totally wrong and the people I loved, my friends and family, were wrong."

For Anne, this change of consciousness was very painful, "but it was not destructive because once you do it you are free. I changed my whole life perspective. My value system changed. I didn't want to be a great newspaper woman after all. I wanted to be part of this movement. And I basically changed my class allegiance. . . . That was harder than race, really. It is very hard to get away from the place you grow up in if you grow up in a class that controls things. Things that you take for granted are just not true. I had always thought that we had these democratic rights in this country. I found out they weren't rights at all. They were privileges I had because of the class I was born into."

During this time, Anne was falling in love with Carl, who was from a working-class background and whose father was a socialist. "I have always said that I married into the working class, which is where he grew up. It went right along with race. Race was the open sesame. Once you could see that society was wrong on race, you could see everything else too. If people cannot understand how race has shaped the country, they can't understand anything else either. Once you understand that, the rest falls like a house of cards. It happened very quickly with me. Once I accepted the fact that people in Alabama were wrong, it wasn't any jump at all to realize that people in Washington were wrong."

By 1948, when Carl and Anne were married, both were active in many progressive struggles in Louisville: to desegregate Alabama schools, to end discrimination in hospitals, and to support union organizing. Both people saw themselves as "revolutionaries. We were going to have a revolution. We didn't exactly define how it was going to happen" but there were a lot of people, both Black and white, who used the term. Anne describes Carl as "the liberator from the prisons of my childhood."[7] About their relationship, which was one of great intellectual and political partnership, Anne writes, "Over the twenty-seven years we lived and worked together, our lives had become totally intertwined like the trunks of two trees grown together. We often disagreed, we were as different as daylight and dark, but our work and our lives had always been as a team" (328). The clarity of purpose this partnership nurtured became especially important for them many times in their lives, including in 1954 when they bought a home in an all-white suburb of Louisville and then sold it to a Black family, the Wades, who then faced all manners of terror from the white community. The Bradens were arrested for sedition and faced a lengthy trial, which resulted in Carl's conviction and imprisonment.

Despite his conviction, which was eventually overturned in 1956, the Bradens never slowed down. Through the 1950s they stood strong against the House Un-American Activities Committee (HUAC), recognizing that HUAC's red baiting was often a trumped-up way of opposing antiracists. From 1957 to 1973 they were directors of the Southern Conference Educational Fund (SCEF), an interracial organization that emerged in the late 1940s to oppose segregation and that in the 1960s worked closely with the Student Nonviolent Coordinating Committee (SNCC). Throughout this activism, they remained together. Anne writes, "Carl often said that he went to prison and I wrote books and pamphlets about it" (323). In the weeks following Carl's untimely death at age sixty, Anne told herself that "I must sit down and figure out how one part of a two-person team could and would function alone. I must take time to decide, I said to myself, what I should do with 'the rest of my life.' Strange as it may seem, I never did. Too many struggles continued to rise on the horizon, too many people looked to me to do too many things. Somehow the 'rest of my life' just set its own course, and it still seems to be doing that as I look at the world from the vantage point of age seventy-four" (328–29).

Through all their political work, Anne Braden remained committed to maintaining a relationship with her parents despite their enormous differences in politics. Her parents were furious with Anne when she and Carl did not live a more "normal" life after the sedition trial ended. Anne writes, "they were constantly and excruciatingly embarrassed whenever my name surfaced in the papers in Alabama in connection with some new attack. My mother wrote me once: 'Just stay out of Alabama. You can have the rest of the country, but leave us Alabama'" (330). Still, Anne was determined to stay in touch with her family, for her own sake as well as that of her two children. She writes, "Many people, finding themselves totally at odds with family, just broke off connections. I never did that. I went to see them; I sent the children whom they adored for visits with them, often meeting in Nashville for this purpose when my parents no longer wanted to come to our house because our neighborhood had changed to almost all African American. This furtiveness must have sent very mixed messages to our children. The continuing strain on the relationship was an ordeal for us all. And yet, I still believe I was right to maintain the relationship" (330).

Eventually, Anne and her father agreed they would simply not discuss politics even though neither of them could fully stop themselves. Despite this decades-long divide, Anne writes that "there were some things I saw happen to my father in his very old age [that] were almost unbelievable" (331). When her father saw her mother's medical bill for a broken hip, which was paid for by Medicare and insurance, he asked Anne what people did before Medicare. Anne replied that Medicare was "'something that the Civil Rights Movement got for you.'. . . He thought for a minute and then replied, 'I guess you are right'" (331). A few years later, at ninety-one, Anne's father took a plane by himself to Louisville to meet his great-granddaughter. Anne writes that his great-granddaughter "is biracial, and my father knew that, but he came. He and the child, of course, loved each other, and that is not surprising. What is surprising is the fact that he came" (331). Although he never met his granddaughter's African American husband in person, he did talk with him on the phone. Upon retelling this event to Anne, he said, "'[We] had a very satisfactory conversation. At least it seemed satisfactory to me. I hope it seemed that way to him'" (332). About her father—the very man who had made the comment celebrating lynching when Anne was a child—Anne retrospectively writes, "I could hardly believe my ears. This man, with his rigid, violent views. Born in 1894, he had lived through almost a century of social change that had an impact on him personally in ways that most people of his station in life never encountered. It seemed almost like a miracle. Of course he had not changed his racist views; that would have been asking, I think, more than was possible. But he was a very kind man, and he loved his family more than anything in the world. Somehow, in the end, that made whatever they did almost all right" (332).

Anne's story offers a welcome example of a young person who found an activist community that gave her language and guidance not available to her as a child. At the same time, Anne became an antiracist activist during an era when something as basic as selling a home to a Black family resulted in fire bombings, death threats, the inability to make a living in Louisville, and a costly sedition trial. Anne's story is also representative of antiracist activists whose politics as adults are 180 degrees different from those of their parents. Yet she somehow found a way to keep a bridge between the two intact, in large part because of a lesson she learned early in her activist life: that her job was to work with and help change white people. In a period prior to increased attention in the 1980s and 1990s by white scholars and activists to how racism contorts white people, Anne writes, "Racial bars build a wall not only around the Negro people but around white people as well, cramping their spirits and causing them to grow in distorted shapes" (24).

Making Sense out of Contradictions

Among those I interviewed, some of the most complicated childhood stories belong to activists whose families offered them contradictory messages about white identity, race, and racism. These contradictions took two forms. Several activists grew up in families that supported what is generally considered a liberal racial politic. This included the lessons that everyone should be treated the same, that racism is wrong, and that educated, kind people simply are not racist. These politics also include a belief in racial progress, which was made possible through education, the courts, and government social service programs. Within this framework, racism was something that happens "out there" rather than within white families and communities. Racism was also considered an issue affecting people of color, not white people. When children witnessed racism within their families and communities and saw that people of color and white people were not being treated equally, they often felt but could not necessarily articulate these contradictions.

Several people were raised in families whose racial politics were wildly divergent: an anti-apartheid mother and a pro-apartheid father, a Democratic mother and a staunchly Republican father, a Jewish father and a Moslem mother whose methods of dealing with religious and ethnic discrimination were strikingly different. For these children, a great challenge was to make sense of these different worldviews and the tension they caused among people whom they knew and trusted. They grew up experiencing cognitive dissonance on two levels. They saw racism in the public sphere and watched it so often being minimized, ignored, or fueled. At the same time, contradictions at home left them confused or silent about how to deal with racism. These children also had to go beyond their communities of origin to begin to make sense of racial contradictions.

Bill Walsh: Cassius Clay, Muhammad Ali, and Irish fairies

Bill Walsh, who was born in 1959, grew up in a working-class, Irish and Polish family in Salem, Massachusetts, in the 1960s. He describes his racial identity developing in four stages as he moved from understanding racism on an abstract level as an evil that hurt Black people to treating it as a systematic assault on humanity. In stage one, growing up in segregated Boston, Bill first learned that racism was wrong from what he saw on the television about the Civil Rights Movement. He remembers thinking, "How could people in the South be so racist? I remember vividly watching Martin Luther King's assassination. I was about eight years old. That assassination was followed closely by Robert Kennedy's. Since we were Irish people on my father's side, the Kennedys were really iconic figures for us. I was always very proud of how Kennedy stood up in the wake of King's assassination. His dramatic gesture certainly spoke to my heart. I identified with that and saw him as a racially healing person. When he was killed, it was really a stunning thing to have these towering figures killed like that." Key to the liberal message about racism Bill received was the notion that racism came from the South, not the North, and that the government was the good guy in terms of opposing racism.

As a child Bill also learned that racism was wrong from his father, a loyal fan of Cassius Clay, later Muhammad Ali. Even when Ali faced an Irish opponent, Bill's father rooted for Ali because he felt Ali was clearly the better boxer. During the period when Ali stood up against the Vietnam War and changed his name, Bill remembers the boxer got very bad press. Nevertheless, Bill's father stood by Ali as a boxer because he had the courage to oppose the war even though it cost Ali professionally.

Bill also remembers his father as someone who broke the color line in Boston by canvassing in the Hispanic section of Salem when he was running for city councilor. His opponent took no interest in the Hispanic voters, which made little sense to Bill's father. He decided to walk the whole Hispanic ward with Bill at his side. As they walked, Bill remembers his father telling him that the Hispanics were now living in the same tenements in which the French Canadians, the other big ethnic group in Salem, had lived a generation earlier. Bill remembers, "My father found a young guy to translate the campaign brochures into Spanish. The people were afraid when my father came to the door. They didn't know why my father was there—a white guy—thinking he was either the police or the INS [Immigration and Naturalization Service]."

That his father "walked the walk" impressed Bill and "raised my expectations of what you can do and how you can do it." He recalls, "My dad pulled a good ten-twelve votes out of that precinct. He lost by thirty votes or something. He then looked back and thought that it might have been a strategic mistake, since most of the people in that precinct were not registered. He learned a lot about the sociology of the area. Because the people were not registered, they couldn't be powerful. He didn't win, but he was always proud that he won in that precinct." From that and other experiences, Bill learned that stepping out of racial norms for white people was something to be proud of and that standing up for what one believes in is important even if it is unpopular.

What he had yet to learn was that building coalitions in electoral politics cannot be done single-handedly and that confronting the racism responsible for poor voter turnout means facing racism systematically. During childhood Bill saw no one close to him, other than his father, take on racism directly. Although he was aware of the Civil Rights Movement of the 1960s, neither his family nor his community were directly involved.

During the next stage in the development of Bill's racial identity, his expectations that multiracial alliances can and do work grew as he was mentored by Black professionals and activists. While in law school, he was chosen to do an internship under Judge Leon Higginbotham in Philadelphia. As an intern Bill was surrounded by "Black people who were wealthier, smarter, more professionally developed, and more politically savvy than I had ever dreamed of being." He soon learned that Higginbotham intentionally chose multiracial groups of people to work together, including working-class white interns. In that position

Bill got early exposure to the intricacies of racism and how Judge Higginbotham and other lawyers responded to it. He also gained experience by being supervised by African Americans. In this period he moved beyond his early theoretical understanding of racism.

Bill characterizes stage three as the period in which he took a leap of faith and began using his position at Greenpeace, an international environmental justice organization, to "diversify" its staff. For him, this was the "diving in, leading-with-my-chin" stage of racial awareness. When he began working at Greenpeace, the staff in his division was entirely white. Four years later, 40 percent of the staff of this division were people of color. He applied the lessons learned under Leon Higginbotham—about taking affirmative action seriously and developing multiracial networks—to confront the old white boys' network that had historically reproduced itself within Greenpeace. Once he began to change the racial constitution of the organization, he could work closely with colleagues of color, who brought with them their own commitment to an expansive environmental agenda.

Bill associates stage four with beginning to regard racial justice as a spiritual act and as his responsibility in order to be fully human. His goal is to be an ally to people of color, a commitment that requires understanding his own privilege and being in touch with his own heritage. Through his close work with a Native American colleague, he learned that his own work against racism must include tracing his roots, which has meant taking two trips to Ireland (one with his father). On these trips he has learned much about Irish mythology and the history of Ireland's resistance to British colonialism. From these journeys he has recognized the psychic pain white people experience when they are separated from their roots. By extension he understands more deeply the pain inflicted upon African Americans and Native Americans historically through slavery and federal assaults on Native American sovereignty. He has replaced his early liberal beliefs—in the Democratic Party, that racism was a southern issue, and that racism was solely what happened to Black people—with an understanding of antiracism as a lifelong spiritual quest that requires a complete transformation of institutional priorities and people's private lives.

Through each stage of his development, his relationships with people of color have deepened. He has better understood that his life's meaning is fused with the search for racial justice, and the spiritual dimensions of his life and work have been strengthened. He also sees more clearly how antiracism separates him from his family and other white people while it requires him to explore his white roots and work closely with white people.

Although Bill has received much support over the years from colleagues, primarily people of color who share his commitment to making Greenpeace a multiracial organization, the changes in his racial consciousness have created cognitive dissonance between himself and his family. Despite his family's support, he has an increasingly hard time explaining to them how antiracism came to be so central in his life. Bill has learned that being an ally to people of color means taking racism seriously in the workplace as well as in his own family. "When you go home for Christmas," he explains, "you are not the same. You are a different person than most of your white family. You are going to hear the racist jokes, and you will have to make a decision about how much you want to fuck up your Christmas by drawing fire on this point. People know enough, perhaps, to not say racist jokes around you, and they let you know that. What being an ally means is that you are going to suffer a certain level of psychic intrusion that is different than for people of color. . . . When they go home, they are not going back to the dominant culture."

For Bill, being with his family means "voluntarily being willing to take off that mantle of privilege, and then being offered it back, time and time again. Sometimes you are just covered with it anyway." Part of Bill's challenge involves trying to talk openly and honestly about racism and about who he is, no matter how difficult that may be. In his family, Bill is the only one who is not married and does not have children. He is the only one engaged in political work. He explains, "I will be talking about my work, for example, and then all of a sudden I will start getting a lot of Indian gifts—a very nice portrait of a leading Native American elder in New England. My dad gave it to me. But it is one of the last things I want. I try to figure out if it was a painting done with the man's consent or not. Or whether the guy just drew him and is selling these paintings on the Boston Common and Slow Turtle doesn't even know that his image has been taken. I try to figure that out and explain that to my dad. The family work becomes another part of the work. It is very exhausting."

One of Bill's biggest challenges is to decide how to show appreciation of the family that raised him and still be true to his racial politics. Bill appreciates that his "family is in that stage where no one is going to tell me a racist joke. So, I have that leeway. And everybody gives me my space. One thing about my mom and dad is that I made curious choices in their eyes, especially when I went to law school and they thought I was going to have a lucrative career. When I didn't do that, they never made snide remarks, or rude remarks. I am very accepted in the subtext. There is no sense that I didn't fulfill their expectations."

At the same time, Bill has to think carefully about which issues to take on. He explains with a story: "My grandmother is eighty-five. I have a cousin who is adopted. She had a child with a Black man. They came home for Christmas. The baby was about to be born. Some of the aunts looked to my grandmother. What are you going to do about this? Are you going to the shower? My grandmother said, 'Of course. That is my granddaughter. I am going to the shower.' Still, she is very impressed that the man was well mannered when he came to the house. 'Wasn't he a nice guy?' she asks me. I said, 'Yes, he was a very nice guy.' I don't know. I respect that she, as an eighty-five-year-old, fairly uneducated, hard-struggling woman, sent the signal to her family to go to that shower. Sent the signal to her family that she is coming to the house for Christmas. And everybody better be at the house for Christmas. So, she set the pace. I don't choose to challenge her, push for a faster or better pace. Had she acted differently [not gone to the shower] I don't know what I would have done."

Bill uses the term "psychic intrusion" to describe the alienation he feels when he cannot fully explain the nuances of his politics to his family. Going home requires sitting with this dissonance and grieving about the impact of segregation on the community in which he grew up. As is true for many other antiracist activists, Bill's learning about racism took him away from his family both physically and psychically while requiring him to be part of his family—both, at the same time.

Lisa Weiner-Mahfuz: Tabouli and a Christmas tree

Lisa, born in 1972, defines herself as a "mixed-race person with white privilege" who has thought of herself as an antiracist activist since she was eighteen. She is the daughter of an Arab mother and a Jewish father, raised in New Hampshire in an otherwise all-white, Christian community. Her mother's family—first-generation immigrants—experienced much racism as the only Arab family in town. Lisa's first understanding of the need to stand up against injustice came from the stories she heard around the dinner table about the discrimination her Arab relatives faced as immigrants and the anti-Semitism her father's family faced in Europe and in the United States.

Although the pressures to assimilate were not explained to her when she was a child, Lisa knows now that pressures on her family to minimize their ethnicity were intense. After her Arab grandparents suffered racial violence, they stopped celebrating Ramadan and changed their names. Lisa's grandfather became "Fred" rather than "Fuad"; her grandmother became "May" instead of "Amina." Her family ate hummus and tabouli at Christmastime while a Christmas tree was set up in the living room window. "This was such a paradox," she says, "a rack of lamb on the table and the Christmas tree that was a facade. A way of letting folks know that we had assimilated, that we were just like them. On the inside, we very much honored Arab traditions and culture." Her grandparents spoke Arabic. Lisa's mother continued to raise the children to be both Jewish and Moslem, but her father insisted the children develop a solid sense of who they were, which in his mind meant raising the children solely as Jews. Her parents argued about this until the children were mitzvahed. Lisa's mother eventually converted to Judaism after a long series of conflicts.

The emphasis in her nuclear family on downplaying her Arab background contributed to Lisa's self-image until her midtwenties as solely Jewish and white rather than of mixed heritage. Meanwhile she grew up with two grandfathers—one Jewish, one Moslem—who got along famously and loved each other, a reality that gave Lisa an early model of the two cultures coexisting rather than being in opposition. She recalls, "As a kid, I sat in my grandmother's living room, and both sides of the family would be sitting around the table. We would have Jewish and Arab food. They would play poker together. There would be heated, passionate dialogue about coming to this country, about what it was like back home, sharing cultures. Much debate. It was never angry debate. It was passionate dialogue. I was two years old, absorbing all of this." Lisa also went to temple and learned much about the Holocaust. From a very early age she responded viscerally to this atrocity. In high school she was introduced to the history of slavery in the Western Hemisphere and remembers having a similar response.

By the time Lisa became a women's studies major in college, she began to find a "both/and" model for understanding her own identity. After reading Audre Lorde's *Sister Outsider*,[8] about how oppressions are interrelated, "all the walls came tumbling down" for Lisa. Reading Lorde gave her a framework for grasping connections among oppressions—anti-Semitism, racism against African Americans and Arabs, and patriarchy. Lorde's writing also helped Lisa see that she could be Arab, Jewish, and antiracist at the same time.

Lisa's learning differences and physical disability also helped her understand the politics of oppression. As a child she was severely dyslexic and also had a genetic back disorder. Because of her dyslexia, fellow students and teachers made fun of Lisa mercilessly. In third grade she had to sit with her back turned away from all of the students after the teacher told her that she would never understand the way the other children could. During adolescence she endured surgeries to correct the back problem, which involved spending three years in full-body back braces. With the dyslexia, severe back pain, and immobilization, Lisa said she "vacated" her mind and body. Only as an adult has she begun to live inside herself again.

This experience taught Lisa how horrible it is to be ridiculed for simply being who one is and showed her the damage done by physical, spiritual, and emotional immobilization. As an adult she has used these lessons in workshops about oppression. She brings an understanding of the importance of listening and being present with each other. These experiences taught her to be watchful of issues and people who are ignored or silenced in conversations.

In early adulthood Lisa began to find ways to integrate her mixed heritage in her work against racism. At the heart of this task is what she has termed the "radical logistics" of negotiating as a white, Arab, Jewish, Moslem woman. She has learned that when participating in political meetings, she often cannot identify herself in all of this complexity without the tension in the room skyrocketing. Being up front about her mixed heritage strikes at the heart of Black/white dualism and strikes different chords for whites, Blacks, and Latinos. In conversations with Black people she needs to establish herself as an ally and to recognize her own white privilege. At the same time, she still wants to challenge Black people to resist the Black/white dichotomy that too often excludes communities of color that are not Black. Lisa also shares no automatic affinity with Latinos, who either mostly identify with or were raised in communities of color. Lisa understands that many Latinos feel conflicted and pained about being part white. Although many Latinos and Arabs in the United States have this in common, their stories are not the same.

Lisa also tries to challenge white people to understand their own privileges as well as her own. As she says, "I don't want to be a back door—I don't want to provide an excuse for white people to not understand white privilege." At the same time, she increasingly feels restricted by identifying herself solely as white. Only by piecing together how the pressure toward assimilation shaped her parents' decision to raise her Jewish and white could she claim her mixed heritage while still working against white privilege.

Lisa's creation of what she calls sound bites for dealing with the complexity of her identity enables her to avoid being a "suicide bomber": By anticipating how different communities respond to her, she can present her complex identity while recognizing people's different vantage points. Lisa also tries to fill gaps in understanding about Arab culture. At the same time, continuing to learn about her own family's complex history has required her to grieve about "the way my family went down" because of hidden histories and anti-Arab racism, as well as her parents' eventual divorce, linked, in no small part, to their conflicts about religion.

Lisa's story exemplifies how wrestling with racial contradictions from childhood enables powerful and forthright strategies to emerge for activists as adults. Lisa was raised to downplay her Arab background and to identify herself as white and Jewish because of her family's awareness of anti-Arab racism. Her understanding of racism, anti-Semitism, and white privilege early in life gave her the experience she then drew on in helping to found Sparking Powerful Antiracist Collaborations (SPARC), a community-based organization that trains people to organize against racism in white communities. Through SPARC Lisa has worked primarily to help white people understand white identity and racism. By seeking out more people of mixed heritage, including those who are very light skinned, as friends and political allies, she has developed an antiracist politic able to hold in place these seemingly contradictory identities: being both white and of color.

Susan Burnett: "Tears streaming like a windshield with no wipers"

Susan Burnett was raised in an upper-class family in Mexico, Brazil, and the United States in the 1940s and 1950s. Her father was a "stuffed shirt" who held a top position at General Motors in Mexico. Her mother was anything but "stuffed." In Susan's house "there were people like Trotsky and Diego Rivera and Frida Kahlo." The woman who cared for Susan was the granddaughter of Emiliano Zapata—a Mexican revolutionary leader. As Susan recalls, "In our house, there was this super capitalistic, paternalistic father alongside the grandchildren of one of the greatest revolutionary heroes of Mexico. . . . There was always this political tension between my parents. My mother was always a humanist and constantly struggling against classism, whereas my father liked classism."

During World War II Susan was sent to Texas to live with her grandparents, who enrolled her in an exclusive Catholic school. Susan's grandmother "hated" Chicanos and was enraged when she realized she would have to hire a Chicana to care for Susan, since Susan spoke no English and her grandmother spoke no Spanish. At school Susan was ostracized. As she relates, "Even though I looked like Shirley Temple, I spoke like a wetback, and I was discriminated against in the schools." Eventually Susan rejoined her parents, who had by then moved to Brazil. Her mother refused to enroll her in American schools because they were supported by the United Fruit Company, which her mother considered an imperialist company. Susan went to a local Brazilian school instead, although she did not speak Portuguese.

By the time Susan was ten, her family had moved to "a white, Anglo-Saxon, Protestant, planned community with absolutely no cultural diversity on Long Island." Susan went to the town public school. As a member of the PTA, her mother began talking openly about how an all-white community jeopardized her child's education. Susan recalls, "My mother was asked to serve on a panel for the PTA where she said that the children are underprivileged. The whole PTA group went crazy. She explained that her child never sees anything but clones of herself. They never get to see a Levy or a Ling or any other ethnic group. It is like living in pabulum all of your life. They never solicited her for PTA membership after that." Soon after, school officials called Susan's mother and said, "We are very concerned. Your daughter doesn't seem to fit in." Susan's mother said, "Thank God" and sent her to a school that had some ethnic and class diversity.

By the time Susan was in high school, Enola Butler, a young African American woman from the South, had come to live with her family. Enola had been exploited while working as an au pair for a white family in the community, so Susan's mother suggested she move in with the Burnetts. Susan and Enola had many conversations about the racial politics of the time. They argued about the politics of Malcolm X and Martin Luther King Jr. Enola talked with Susan about southern politics and what it meant to have witnessed a lynching when she was a child.

However, it was not until Susan and Enola were adults and living on their own that they could talk about how racism played itself out between them. Susan says, "She made me face certain things about myself I didn't want to face." Susan remembers a time when they were arguing and Susan backed off, unwilling to hold her ground in the disagreement. Enola asked her to leave and "take her racism with her." Susan "was nineteen and arrogant, and I thought I knew everything." She was stunned when Enola accused her of racism. Susan remembers Enola saying, "Look. Don't patronize me. You either accept me as an equal—and if you do, that means you would be willing to argue and dialogue with me—or get out of my house. But don't ever patronize me because that is what white people do to Black people. They don't accept them as intellectual people."

After the argument Susan drove away from Enola's house, "tears streaming like a windshield with no wipers." She sobbed all the way home, wondering how someone she considered her sister could accuse her of racism. With time and further conversations with Enola, she began to understand that Enola was right. And she was able to talk with Enola about her jealousy. Susan recalls, "I always said that my mother loved Enola more than she loved me. There was a lot of sibling rivalry between me and Enola. On my part. Not on her part." As Susan remembers the conversation, Enola told her, "Your mother is a wonderful human being, and I love her like my own mother. But let me tell you this. You could be the royal bad seed child of the world and you'll always have a place in that family. But if I didn't know my place and know how to keep it, I would have been out. You could be the brattiest brat, but if I acted like you did, believe me, I wouldn't have been in that house overnight."

Once Susan began to understand condescension and unrecognized white privilege as key elements of racism, she was better able to evaluate the complicated relationship between her parents' divergent racial politics and its relation to their class standing. Although Susan's mother had given her an alternative to her father's unabashed racism and classism, her mother's attitude was still fundamentally problematic. Susan says, "This is something I have learned. When you come from a privileged class, from any society, both in race and class, you have the privilege . . . you can afford to reach out to anybody, because you are coming from a very strong position of power. If you are middle- or working-class and you are trying to work your way up, you have to be very careful who you associate with. Once you are up there, you can bring the gardener into your dining room and nobody is going to say anything. As a matter of fact, many aristocrats did that. . . . my mother married and was from a position where her reaching out to all kinds of people came from her being in a safe place where she could do it. No one could touch her."

Although Susan's mother's work in Harlem meant Susan was familiar with the city—and could find her way there to hear Malcolm X and other Black activists—her mother's orientation toward Blacks was part of "the community service society" approach to racism. On the other hand, during her childhood, when Susan wanted to talk about the 1955 killing of Emmett Till or when she spoke after first hearing Billie Holiday sing "Strange Fruit," Susan's father refused to engage on any level.

These complicated contradictions ultimately propelled Susan away from both conservative and liberal responses to race. As she sees it, the defining moment in her young adulthood and as a human being occurred after she saw the films *Judgment at Nuremberg* and *Mein Kampf* about Hitler and the concentration camps. Susan remembers being "physically moved and trembling with fear about *Mein Kampf*. I called my father at work and said, 'Dad, we need to have lunch.' We were estranged at the time, so he was glad to comply. I met him downtown, and asked how our relatives in Germany could have allowed that to happen. He said that they just didn't speak up. It was like a thunderbolt. I realized from that moment on that I had to speak up or I was as guilty as those people who ran the concentration camps. Nothing really dramatic, but it was the definitive moment. And I realized that, as a white person, especially coming from the class that I came from, that it was my job more than anybody else's. It was my responsibility. Not in the 'carry the white man's burden' situation, as Kipling would have us believe. But from a sense of self-survival on a spiritual level. If I did not do this, I was going to be fucked spiritually. This was for me. Not anybody else."

After this revelation Susan was not sure of her next step. She "checked out" for a while and became a "ski bum." But, as she describes it, "You can only check out for so long, if you are a person with any kind of inner life. How long can you live on whipped cream? Sour whipped cream, at that?" It was not long before she was arrested during a sit-in in Birmingham, Alabama. During that period she also heard Malcolm X talk again and was able to speak with him. Again, she heard that fighting against racism required that she understand she was fighting for herself, not to save or fix others. About Malcolm X, Susan remembers, "He was one of the most powerful influences in my life. His charisma, his truth, his spirituality. When you were in his presence, you really understood that he was a spiritual person. I remember speaking with him once and I was going on about my class background and my father was a this and my mother was a that and I was going to reject them all. I am here to be a sojourner, a revolutionary. He stopped me in my tracks and said, 'Susan, you are making a big mistake. You have to understand who you are and where you are from. If you reject your past, you are rejecting 90 percent of who you are. You are here, in this theater, doing the blues for Mister Charlie because of a lot of what your parents gave you. If you throw them out, as being bad, then you are throwing a lot of yourself out as being bad.'. . . What he was basically saying is don't be a little kid and rebel against your parents." From Malcolm X, Enola Butler, and later relationships with her husband, Ali Bey Hassan, and others, Susan was coming to believe the work ahead was much bigger than a rebellion against her past—as complicated and contradictory as that had been.

It's in the Milk

A small minority of the people I interviewed got their start as antiracist activists through lessons they learned from radical parents and other relatives. They learned very early that being an activist can be a rich and integral part of one's life, and that it does not require leaving one's family behind. This radicalization also meant that as children they learned that being white does not necessarily mean doing nothing or denying racism. They learned that they were raced, that being white was not an empty category. They were never taught to be "color-blind." Understanding their position within the racial hierarchy served as a foundation for how they responded once they became activists. By contrast, those who left their families before becoming activists found only later in life a paradigm for understanding race outside of color blindness or racial superiority.

The early lives of those who grew up in radical families also show why linear racial identity models are sometimes inadequate. Some white people never go through or have to get over what is typically considered the first stage of white racial identity: naïveté and obliviousness about the politics of race.[9] Their stories exemplify how exposure to social activism can catapult people into racial consciousness at an early age. Many people who were raised in antiracist families go through stages of racial identity that may more closely resemble stages evident among people of color. Their stories also suggest the need for racial identity models that account for social movements, that see racial identity as formed by both psychology and history. A model of racial identity that makes room for the lives of antiracist activists must account for how mentoring by people of color influences development, how family dynamics shape people's paths, and how progressive struggles shape consciousness.

David Wellman: "We weren't treated like white people. We were the Reds."[10]

David Wellman, who was born in 1940, is currently a professor of community studies and a research sociologist with a focus on labor history. His first memories of his parents' activism go back a long way. Both his mother and father were working-class Communists who raised their children in a predominantly Black neighborhood in Detroit. His father was a truck driver who organized his first union at the age of fifteen. His mother was a waitress and a member in the Shoe and Boot Workers' Union. David emphasizes, "It is very important in understanding how I view myself and my relationship to antiracism . . .

that race was very much a part of growing up in Detroit in a Communist family. I knew Black people all of my life, from a little child on. Many prominent Black Communists came to our house. Many non-prominent Black Communists came through our house. An all-white gathering would have been abnormal."

David can remember going as a child to Save Willie McGee meetings; McGee, a Black man in Mississippi, was falsely accused and convicted in 1945 of raping a white woman and was eventually executed. As a child David attended Free Hayward Patterson meetings; Patterson was one of the Scottsboro Boys, nine young Black men who had been accused in 1931 of raping two white women in Alabama. Eight of the nine were sentenced to death, although through activism, including that of the Communist Party, none were executed. David recalls, "Hayward Patterson had escaped from a chain gang in Alabama and come to Michigan, where the cops found him. They were going to extradite him back to Alabama, but the Communists organized several important meetings to block that." David remembers being taken to meetings where Paul Robeson sang and to meetings where W. E. B. Du Bois spoke. David says, "In Detroit in the 1940s and 1950s, there was a very large Black population and an already important relationship between Blacks and Communists, because the Communists had played an important part in organizing the Ford factory. At that point of history, Blacks were in the foundries and had pretty rough jobs. So there was a level of comfort between the Communists and Black people in Detroit. There was a lot of back and forth."

Growing up, David did not think of himself as white. Rather, he understood himself as "red." This identification might suggest an avoidance of dealing with white privilege common to those raised within a liberal, "color-blind" tradition. But I think a more accurate reading of David's early racial identification as "red" reflects a historical period when, for white people, being an active Communist meant that one risked harassment and persecution in some ways similar to that faced by many Black people. David learned early that his parents' Communist politics assumed an antiracist stance. Furthermore, antiracism was not only what people organized for publicly but was also about who people considered family.

When David reached adolescence, he rebelled against his parents in the only way that a child of Communists could: by declaring himself apolitical in all regards. He recalls, "I was much more interested in being a little gangster on the street and hanging out with my buddies and getting into low-level trouble." He fondly refers to this as his James Dean period. But as soon as he went away to college in 1960, he quickly became involved in the Civil Rights Movement and later was a supporter of the Black Power Movement.

David's background suggests that an analysis of power relations first acquired in childhood—specifically the power of the state to restrict protest and progressive social change—gave him a framework for understanding his own relation as a white person to the Civil Rights and the Black Power Movements. His exposure to Black Communists and Black women in the neighborhood enabled him to approach antiracism from a position of saving himself and those he loved from an impending race war rather than from the abstract, missionary-like position that characterized the orientation of some white activists. His background as a child of Communists from the working class allowed him to keep up with the times politically as white activists moved from being "in the Movement" to "confronting white privilege."

Jeanine Cohen: "Children have a natural sense of justice."

Jeanine Cohen, a Jewish lesbian filmmaker who currently lives in Oakland, California, grew up in the 1950s with actively antiapartheid parents in Johannesburg, South Africa. Of all those I interviewed, Jeanine knew the earliest that she was white and that racial categorizations dehumanized her and all those around her. This early racialization makes sense; she was born into a highly politicized family in a country that was as racially polarized as any in the world.

Jeanine identified positively with her parents' political positions from an early age. As she explains, "The conditions of apartheid are extremely ugly, and I believe that children have a natural sense of justice." Because she was part of a multiracial community, she visited the townships frequently and heard and witnessed violence against Black people. Black people she knew and loved were being violated by white people. She spoke of "being in the township and watching the police harass people around their passes and being very violent." From what she witnessed as a child, Jeanine felt confused about her position as both white and a witness to the violence being done to people she loved.

In 1960, when Jeanine was seven years old, both of her parents were imprisoned and then forced upon release to go into hiding. Although she believed that her parents were doing the right thing, their imprisonment traumatized her. Jeanine experienced her parents as mostly absent from her life—a reality for many children of activists. In *Long Walk to Freedom,* Nelson Mandela wrote that being away from his children while they were growing up was the most devastating regret and loss he had faced in his life.[11] The frequent absence of Jeanine's parents, along with her father's sexual abuse of her, meant she turned elsewhere for tenderness and comfort: toward the Black women who cared for her. "The people who nurtured me and gave me the things I really needed to survive in life were Black people. There was a way in which [the Black people] were my safety." Jeanine adds, "The fact that my parents were white, they were engaged in resisting apartheid, and absent on some level, meant that I felt unimportant, like my needs weren't important. Then I was being violated at the same time. It was full of contradictions. At the same time, Black people were taking care of me emotionally, were giving me the love and nurturing I needed that made me the sane human being that I am."

Even though Jeanine knew she was a white child, she identified most with the Black people around her. "I saw myself aligned with them and as them, of them. They were where I wanted to be really." What this meant is that Jeanine had a difficult time coming to terms with her own whiteness. She would go to a township and see how other people lived, and she knew that it was different from how she lived. When Jeanine and the Black woman who raised her went to the post office, the woman could do business on the white side only because she was with Jeanine. "When I think about it I cringe inside, and I would cringe inside then. That is how I would feel."

For Jeanine, the bind of being a white girl growing up under apartheid meant she eventually began to separate herself from other white people. "I would feel appalled by where I was placed, and I didn't want to be placed there. When I think about myself as a racialized subject, that is where that happened. And the sense of deep shame and rejection that came up for me. I didn't want to be identified with that side. Even though my parents were engaged in the struggle and I identified myself differently, one of the strategies I developed to cope with that contradiction was to feel like I was better than other people, that I knew more. Better than other white people."

Jeanine psychically separated herself from other whites. She decided that, "I was cool and they were stupid. . . . I think that is how I got through the feeling of shame about who I was. I kind of, almost deliberately . . . placed myself on the margins in relation to dominant culture." The superiority she felt toward other white people was also her way of protecting herself from being treated as an outsider. White children made fun of her parents' being arrested, having their names printed in the newspapers, and being referred to openly and in print as criminals. Jeanine was left to protect herself from the taunting while she "took the children on when they would talk about Black people in a derogatory way." She "desperately wanted to impact the way the children saw the world" but had little chance to change the children's minds or get support for her actions in the process.

A second racial contradiction Jeanine faced as a child took place after her parents moved from South Africa to England. She was excited about going to England, partly because she thought that civil rights for people of color existed there, unlike in South Africa. Jeanine quickly saw that having civil rights legislation did not guarantee its enforcement, a reality that squashed her innocent hope of finding a society free of racism. Once in England, her parents became less directly involved in the antiapartheid struggle. As they started to prosper financially, they adopted a more conservative lifestyle. As a consequence Jeanine felt her parents had betrayed her with their "bourgeois lifestyle, particularly because of their activist roots." The contradictions in their politics also made her feel ashamed.

Meanwhile she felt herself being targeted as a Jew for the first time in her life, and she received no support from her family about how to deal with it. South Africa had a fairly substantial eastern European Jewish population, so Jeanine did not feel like an outsider as a Jew. Her grandparents were immigrants who had escaped the pogroms in eastern Europe. Raised by a father who had been imprisoned as a Jewish Communist in Russia, Jeanine's father related culturally to being a Jew. Jeanine's mother became involved in the antiapartheid movement to some extent in reaction against her Orthodox Jewish roots. From Jeanine's mother's perspective, the Orthodox Jews in South Africa were perpetuating the same injustices toward Blacks that Jews in eastern Europe had suffered.

Although Jeanine's mother and father came to antiapartheid activism as Jews from different vantage points, neither engaged actively in resisting anti-Semitism in England. Retrospectively, Jeanine believes that she picked up a lot of internalized anti-Semitism from them, including the notion that Orthodox Jews were by definition politically regressive people. As a consequence, once she became a target for anti-Semitism in England, she had no skills to deal with the assaults and did not believe she had the right to be protected from them. Jeanine always felt that "my issues were not as important as other people's issues." In Jeanine's mind, she was being ostracized as a Jew, but what "happened to other people was much worse."

In the 1980s Jeanine's involvement in multiracial feminism and her work as an antiracist trainer helped her understand her complex racial and religious identity. In the process she began to confront the paradox of feeling both ashamed of being white and superior to other white people. She moved from shame to "embracing the fact that I was a white person engaged in an antiracist struggle. I could embrace my whiteness because I could see that historically, I had taken antiracist stances." The psychological dynamic Jeanine describes—of feeling superior to other white people while being treated as an outsider—was clearly a form of psychic survival in the midst of unstated racial contradictions. As an adult, however, this protective stance has required much work to sort out. The superiority she felt in relation to other white people as a child became a block for her in adulthood when she sought to understand her relation to women of color and white women.

Her change in consciousness affected every aspect of her life. Whereas she had previously separated herself from other white women, now she began to seek out antiracist white women who, like herself, were trying to do justice work and sustain friendships and political alliances with people of color. With other white women she created a performance piece called *White Food*, which draws a parallel between the homogenization of food, particularly white foods—white flour, white sugar—with the way white people have lost their ethnicities in order to benefit from whiteness. For Jeanine, reclaiming her ethnic roots meant coming to terms with why she had denied being Jewish. By understanding herself as white, Jewish, and antiracist, Jeanine felt more patience working with other white people. Her feeling of being superior to other white people gave way to more compassion and less judgment. At the same time, she was better able to work with the desperation about injustice she had felt all her life.

Stepping through the Door

By examining racial identity among activists, it is possible to chart the psychological complexities of childhood and adolescence through a racial lens. Many people I interviewed experienced tremendous confusion and alienation about race when they were growing up. For those who had to leave their families in order to become activists, this alienation took the form of feeling, deep down and from a young age, that they were going to have to "go it alone." Cooper Thompson, who grew up in an all-white, Christian, upper-middle-class town in New Jersey, spoke about being a very "worried kid." He was worried about the state of the world and knew that there was something "drastically wrong." But he could not seem to find anyone around him who could make sense out of his worry. Cooper remembers as an adolescent driving with his father on a freeway in New Jersey, past the flames coming from what he later found out was a riot. He saw an entire neighborhood burning and knew something was wrong. And he knew race was somehow involved. But no one in the car spoke as they drove past the flames. The silence was deafening.

People who grow up witnessing racism but lack the language to understand its origins or causes are frequently left with a nagging sense that something is terribly wrong. Too often they have no way of translating that feeling into action. The worry that big trouble is looming often translates into a kind of silence and withdrawal during childhood and a kind of inertia in early adulthood: They become ski bums, drop out of school despite being very smart, or feel so alienated in their families that there are no words to describe the loneliness.

In "The Ethnic Scarring of American Whiteness," legal theorist Patricia Williams tells a story of an upper-class white family on a train whose conversation veered from a discussion of investments, Japanese wood-joinery, and photography to redneck jokes. When the eight-year-old asked what a redneck was, their explanation quickly educated her about her family's class biases. Williams concludes the story with a telling reminder: "That little girl will have to leave the warmth of the embracing, completely relaxed circle of those happy people before she can ever appreciate the humanity of someone who drives a pickup, who can't afford a dentist. 'Rednecks' were lovingly situated, by that long afternoon of gentle joking, in the terrible vise of the comic, defined by the butt of a joke."[12]

For many white people who become antiracist activists, the journey toward racial consciousness requires leaving "the warmth of the embracing, completely relaxed" family once it is clear the humanity of others is put at risk in the process. In Patricia Williams's words, "hate learned in a context of love is a complicated phenomenon. And love learned in a context of hate endangers all our family" (263).

For activists who grew up in activist families, the risks of living a racially conscious childhood are different. They, unlike children from conservative families, are graced with adults who practice the art of collective organizing as a way of sustaining one's humanity. Those commitments, however, do not come without costs. Of living with Communist and antiracist parents in a home that was potentially under FBI surveillance, David Wellman wrote, "We lived in absolute terror of being overheard, being seen, being physically attacked by them. If we [his sister or parents] had something important to say, we went outside on the street to say it. I slept with a baseball bat under my bed. We were taught how to speak on the phone, how to recognize someone without verbally acknowledging them. We learned to never speak names on the phone. (I still don't.) We were told to distrust anyone we didn't know. (I still do.) We were not permitted to display emotions in public. (I still don't.) When we were too candid or about to spill a secret Peggy and Saully [David's parents] would put an index finger to their mouths signaling us to be quiet. 'The walls have ears,' they would say, gesturing about the room. We were experiencing and internalizing state terror, an American version of totalitarianism."[13]

For Jeanine, having activist, antiapartheid parents meant being able to identify in a positive way with her family's values from a young age. Their activism gave her a political education that will always be with her. At the same time, Jeanine was only seven when her parents were imprisoned. She was shuffled from family to family, unsure, in the shuffle, about her worth as a child.

Ultimately, what children who become activists have to reckon with—whether as children or later in life—are the risks involved in moving beyond the racial status quo. Adrienne Rich's "Prospective Immigrants Please Note" metaphorically captures the psychic risk involved when young people walk through a door—in this case, when they question racism—when they do not yet know whether there will be anyone on the other side to catch them.

The risks of going through the door—of going toward racial consciousness—are many. For Cooper Thompson, who was raised in a politically conservative family, the "risk of remembering your name"[14] required coming to terms with a family history that includes the ownership of slaves in previous generations. For some who grew up in conservative families, going through the door also required giving up religious traditions—Judaism, Christian Science, Mormonism. In doing so, they were not only questioning a set of religious principles. They were also contemplating stepping away from a culture.

However, when the people I interviewed found a doorway out, there was community on the other side. Although initially "the door itself makes no promises"[15]—part of what makes questioning racism so scary—stepping through the door brought them to new places, often more secure and whole than the places they left. Time and time again, those I interviewed spoke of people, most of whom were people of color, who had extended themselves graciously as teachers, mentors, friends, and family along the way.

part i

Civil Rights and the 1960s

Civil Rights and the 1960s

There may be no period in U.S. racial history as volatile and transformative as the years from 1955 to 1970, a time when white people's position within the struggle for racial justice made dramatic shifts. Initially, from 1955 through the early 1960s, whites involved in the Civil Rights Movement were few and far between. As Bonnie Kerness remembers, the strategy was to spread the whites out at the marches and rallies so that the media could see that there were, in fact, white allies. By Freedom Summer in 1964, when two thousand young white people from the North traveled south to work with civil rights activists, concerns about highlighting the few whites who were involved in the Movement had been replaced by careful planning to incorporate whites while maintaining the Movement's southern-led and Black-centered roots. White and Black activists sang, ate, worked, and often lived together—not without struggle, not without tensions, but together, nevertheless.

By 1966 the emergence of Black Power brought another organizing principle to the forefront at a time when self-determination for Blacks typically meant separate groups for Black and white activists. Having been raised with a multiracial feminist politic in which all-white groups were by definition suspect, I initially wondered how activists either rationalized or explained participating in all-white groups during this period. When I asked Naomi Jaffe about this, she replied, with exasperation at my naïveté, "What were we going to do? Join the Panthers?" During that period in history, to be a white ally by definition meant accepting the politics of racially distinct groups—a development that was a far cry from the "spread-out-the-whites" approach Bonnie Kerness grew up with in the late 1950s. Embedded in whites' changing positions within the Movement is the story of the mistakes they made and the lessons they learned.

In chapter 2 I trace white people's position within the first decade of the Civil Rights Movement (1955–1965), with particular emphasis on the philosophy of integration developed by the Student Nonviolent Coordinating Committee (SNCC). Founded under the guidance of Ella

Baker in 1960, SNCC based its racial ideology on two fundamental principles: one, that Blacks and whites could stand together to oppose racism and support integration; and two, that such a project of integration depended upon Black leadership at every level of engagement. From their work with SNCC, white activists got the chance to be under the leadership of and maintain peer relationships with Black activists, learn from the constant dialogues and struggles at the heart of a democratic decision-making process, understand the necessity of building initiatives from the ground up, and feel in their minds and hearts what it was like to be part of a "beloved community." Although SNCC's main work focused on the South, it offered a model for race consciousness that was studied and adopted across the country.

By the mid-1960s, however, many civil rights activists had become skeptical about whether education and nonviolent protest could, in themselves, destroy racial apartheid in the United States. Despite the historic Civil Rights Act of 1964, Black people were denied the right to represent themselves at the Democratic National Convention, were barred from access to public schools and higher education, and were gunned down on the streets, on the picket lines, and in their beds. The assassination of Malcolm X in 1965 reflected a war on Black leadership across the country that escalated to the point where hundreds of Black activists were intimidated, killed, or imprisoned. As the Civil Rights Movement spread north, Martin Luther King Jr. and other civil rights leaders recognized the need for an expansive politic that could respond to the Movement's increasing scope, from a southern-based movement focusing on voting rights, bus boycotts, and desegregation to a national movement to end racism, poverty, and the Vietnam War.

The expansion of the civil rights agenda taxed the Movement as never before, requiring a rethinking of integrationist politics. Although King and many other civil rights leaders held on to an integrationist ethic, SNCC and other groups began to examine the limits of an interracial organization, which ultimately resulted in their decision in 1967 to become an all-Black organization while keeping close contact with white allies.

During this transition, some white antiracists got lost in the shuffle, only to regain their footing later. Many, however, moved forward, determined to find ways to oppose racism in white communities as well as in coalition with Black organizations. Contrary to the common notion that white people were kicked out of the Movement, many white activists firmly supported a transition from integration to Black Power. Not surprisingly, these white activists often included those who had known persecution by the government during the McCarthy period, a perspective that helped them see that the government was willing to do whatever it took to destroy the Movement. White activists took with them into the next phase of the Movement a political consciousness born from working in Black-led organizations and a sense of collective struggle that can and did move mountains.

From the mid-1960s forward, white activists could be found working in the free speech movement; in the most prominent white New Left organization, Students for a Democratic Society (SDS); in antipoverty programs; in activities against the Vietnam War; and in white-led militant organizations. Each of these arenas had an antiracist agenda, but all failed to keep antiracism central. In chapter 3, I analyze why these initiatives had difficulty keeping antiracism front and center. White antiracists learned, for example, that having antiracist intentions as a welfare worker was not enough to counter the racism embedded in welfare policies. They learned that making the soldiers the enemies while protesting the Vietnam War drove a wedge between the largely middle-class, white protesters and the enlisted men, a disproportionate number of whom were Black, Latino, or working class. Standing against imperialism in a faraway country became, in many ways, an easier and less threatening agenda than dealing with racism within white left organizations, a reality that further separated the white left from Black Power initiatives. Sexism within New Left organizations clipped the wings of many women activists, including those with experience in Black-led groups. Ironically, although women increasingly protested the male dominance in New Left groups, the whiteness of these groups went largely unquestioned.

By 1968 struggle about strategy and philosophy in SDS was threatening to break it into many pieces. Out of the conflicts within SDS emerged militant, white-led organizations, the most visible of which was the Weather Underground. The Weather Underground believed that white people needed to be willing to take the risks, including the risk of dying, that Black, Latino, and Native American activists had long assumed. Through the late 1960s and early 1970s, as the government stepped up its mission to harass and kill Black, Latino, and Native

American leaders, many white people who adopted a militant stance were imprisoned. Many are still in prison, where they continue their antiracist work.

White radical activists' retrospective accounts help fill a gaping hole in this period of movement history. Militant organizations' need to go underground in response to the government's assault on its members have made it decidely difficult to document their accomplishments and limitations. The imprisonment of many of their members has further stifled their stories. And yet their work was an integral piece of a white antiracist agenda during the late Civil Rights Movement and is instructive for many still, thirty years later.

2

Will the Circle . . .

Five mysteries hold the keys to the unseen: the act of love, and the birth
of a baby, and the contemplation of great art, and being in the presence
of death or disaster, and hearing the human voice lifted in song. These
are the occasions when the bolts of the universe fly open and we are
given a glimpse of what is hidden; an eff of the ineffable.

Salman Rushdie, The Ground beneath Her Feet

On a warm June day in 1997, at the end of a workshop held during a
two-day conference, Race and Racism in the 1990s: Teaching Social
Justice, Living Social Justice, one of the participants suggested we conclude the meeting in song. Everyone drew together, in that kind of be-
labored, shy way people do when they want to embrace but have had
little experience with each other in doing so. People looked around at
each other, and there was a pregnant pause as the hundred or so people
waited for someone to start us up in a song that, I am guessing, everyone
hoped would sing us through the end of this session. There were members of the Freedom Singers of the 1960s in the room, including Mat-
thew Jones, as well as people who had been active in Central America
solidarity work in the 1980s. There were people who had come of age
as activists in the feminist and lesbian movements, people who had
been involved in civil disobedience in the South during the 1960s, as
well as people who came of age as activists in the 1990s.[1] The conference had been tough to organize for financial, logistical, and ideological
reasons. It had been a working conference; a conversation between the
generations and across race that had not been easy, but one that most
participants seemed to think had been worth having.

When the moment came for a song, for the tune that would carry us
forward, the silence was long. There were searching faces and waiting

ears until finally someone started "We Shall Overcome."[2] The first line, many voices sang, but with little spirit; the second line, fewer voices. By the third line the melody was failing as people looked around, many not knowing the words. Most drifted away from the embrace. Eyes held questions only later spoken out loud: Who is the "we" in "We Shall Overcome"? What are "we" overcoming? And then, in silence, people drifted out of the room, ostensibly in search of food and drink, but on a deeper level, in search of the song that could somehow draw together, in the 1990s, generations that no one term has defined.

The organizers had pulled together a conference that drew activists from across the nation and from the 1950s to the present. The group was multiracial, but not as multiracial as the 1990s required. It was an intergenerational group that had somehow kept sexuality, class, and gender on the agenda without sidelining attention to racism in the process. But still, there was no song that could do it for us in that moment. "We Shall Overcome" had an integrationist, nonviolent feel to it that did not resonate with many young people in the room, young people whose schools and neighborhoods had been as segregated as those of the children of the 1950s. Sister Sledge's "We Are Family," which I remember being sung at many a multiracial demonstration in the 1980s, felt out of date somehow. I remember reasoning to myself, in the silence, that no *one* song need be chosen. Many songs would do. But none of the many that might have done was offered in that room that day.

This workshop, as much as any single event in the last several years, raised a number of questions for me about social justice activism from the 1950s to the present. To what extent did the enormous demands and stresses placed on civil rights activists and the necessary differentiation of agendas between Black and white activists in the late 1960s contribute to the songlessness? To what extent has the increasingly multiracial character of social justice activism not yet been fully addressed or accounted for? How might the stories of activists who sang "We Shall Overcome" in the 1960s and those who have become activists since help explain why that song did not work at an antiracism conference in the 1990s? What responsibilities do young activists have to those who came before them? What might the changing position of white activists in the 1960s reveal about songs of solidarity still waiting to be sung?

" 'In the Movement' Years"

In the late 1950s and early 1960s, the movement that most influenced white antiracist consciousness was the civil rights struggle, which, though it began in the South, eventually spread to include activity throughout the country. The story of how whites positioned themselves within the first decade of the Civil Rights Movement—and the political identities they forged—centers on the South. Even those activists who did not live in the South during that period took on identities that were shaped by southern civil rights organizations. The people I interviewed were spread out all over the country during the 1960s, yet all of them referred to the South as the window through which they saw and evaluated their own activism. Detroit native David Wellman's first participation in a civil rights event was a 1960 sit-in at a Woolworth's, organized by students at Wayne State University in support of the Black student sit-ins in Greensboro, North Carolina. As he says, "The idea was to put pressure on the store in Detroit and that would put pressure on the South to desegregate the lunch counter. At that point, people weren't going south yet," so people did what they could locally.

As the Civil Rights Movement grew, several of the people I interviewed either moved south or were already there and involved with the Student Nonviolent Coordinating Committee (SNCC), the Highlander Folk School, or the Southern Conference Educational Fund (SCEF). Several people moved to or already lived in northern cities that had active civil rights organizations—SNCC, Friends of SNCC, and the Northern Student Movement. Some of the younger people I interviewed were not yet activists but have vivid memories of key moments in the early Civil Rights Movement in southern states.

For whites and Blacks during the first half of the Civil Rights Movement—whose beginnings are often traced to the Montgomery, Alabama, bus boycott of 1955–56—to actively oppose racism meant that one was "in the struggle" or "in the Movement" or part of the "beloved community." David Wellman says that in those days, "I would have called myself a Movement person. The issue was, 'Is she in the Movement?' 'Is he a Movement person?' 'Is she a Movement person?' It was not white or Black. It was 'movement person.'" The shared terminology certainly did not mean that racism did not exist among white activists or that Blacks' and whites' relations to the struggle were the same. But the language used to identify white civil rights workers reflected an ideology of a shared community, a belief in integration as a necessary ingredient of civil rights organizing. Being "in the Movement" meant believing that racial integration was the desired outcome of freedom rides, sit-ins, civil disobedience, and civil rights legislation.

The two organizations that most shaped the terms of the political struggle in the first half of the Civil Rights Movement were the Southern Christian Leadership Conference (SCLC) and SNCC. Born of the Montgomery bus boycott, SCLC, led by Martin Luther King Jr., considered the church the foundation of the Movement and the philosophy of integration and nonviolence its two core tenets (a position it has never amended). It considered Black-led interracialism the key to organizing a national Civil Rights Movement. Interracialism during the process of struggling for civil rights was also considered the necessary template for integration in the long run.

The origins of SNCC and SCLC were rooted in a pacifist, interracial ethic. SNCC was begun by student activists first drawn together in 1960 by Ella Baker, former field secretary for the National Association for the Advancement of Colored People (NAACP) and the first executive secretary of SCLC.[3] SNCC sought to be a voice for young people who drew on an ethic of love and nonviolence. Although many early SNCC activists had roots in the Black church, they did not want to be beholden to it or to more-established Black activists, including Martin Luther King Jr. From the start, SNCC activists were clear that the organization had to be led by young Black people, most of whom needed to be from the South, since indigenous, grassroots organizing was the centerpiece of SNCC's strategy.

Within this framework, there was room for white people as long as they accepted and were respectful of Black leadership and believed in nonviolence and racial equality. The integrationist ethic was predicated upon Black control and Black leadership. The ethic within the organization—that activism was as much a goal as it was a process—meant that white and Black people worked, ate, lived, and relaxed together. Organizing in rural areas often meant living with Black families and attending Black churches. As progressive historian William Chafe writes, "SNCC workers were revolutionaries for whom the word revolution meant the creation of a beloved community where people would care for each other."[4]

In the organization's early days, the few white people involved tended to be from or to have ties to the South. They were college students and other young white people who entered the Movement through their churches, schools, or activist relatives. The first white person to be appointed as a field worker was Bob Zellner, who was raised in southern Alabama.⁵ Jane Stembridge, who was from Virginia, was asked by Ella Baker to become the first executive secretary in 1960. Casey Hayden, a woman from a populist background in Texas, was the YWCA's first liaison to SNCC in Atlanta before Mary King, a white woman whose father was a minister, took Hayden's place in 1962.

In the early 1960s the white establishment treated overt opposition to racism by these and other young white people in the South as deliberate rebellion. SNCC workers traveling in interracial teams to colleges or churches were often harassed or arrested. Whites who directly associated with Blacks inevitably put themselves at risk of being seen as traitors to their race. So although the number of whites in early civil rights organizations was small (never more than 20 percent of those in SNCC), their presence did give the lie to the notion of a singularly united white community.

Of the arrest of white southern activist Bob Zellner, historian Howard Zinn writes, "The presence of Bob Zellner and other white workers affected Danville [Virginia] that summer [1963] as Zellner and others like him have affected so many towns in the Deep South since the sit-ins began in the 1960s. The point was made vividly to Negroes that compassion as much as cruelty crossed racial lines. And the point was made to southern whites that, try as they might to obliterate the image, someone like them, someone with white skin and from the South, had a different view of the way people should live together on earth. Those points, reiterated again and again these past few years every time whites and Negroes have gone together on sit-ins, on Freedom Rides, on picket lines, on Freedom walks, constitute one of the truly splendid achievements of the current civil rights revolt."⁶

For SNCC workers the politics of integration and cross-race collaboration of the early 1960s partly reflected an idealism that was a product of a historical moment before the assassinations of John Kennedy (1963), Malcolm X (1965), Martin Luther King Jr. (1968), Robert Kennedy (1968), Fred Hampton (1969), and others. Although there were many ideological differences between SNCC and SCLC, both organizations portrayed white activists as working for civil rights out of a moral commitment to create a society where people, in the oft-quoted words of Martin Luther King Jr., "will not be judged by the color of their skin but by the content of their character."[7] Sociologist and former SNCC worker Joyce Ladner wrote of this time, "Our enemy was always an external one. It was not internal, at least not through those early years, and I think we do have to make a division between pre-1964 and post-1964. There were very, very different kinds of ideas and ideologies and values that operated then."[8]

Reebee Garofalo, who grew up in an Italian, Catholic, middle-class home in the North, was one of the Yale University students recruited by SNCC to go south for Freedom Summer. In retrospect, he believes he was initially drawn to the South by a fairly idealistic sense of just wanting to do the right thing—in keeping with ethics he had learned from his parents about treating people fairly. During Freedom Summer Reebee came to understand that he might die for his beliefs, and he felt sure he was willing to do that. The man who was staying across the hall from him in the dorm in Oxford, Mississippi, was Andy Goodman, who, with James Chaney and Mickey Schwerner, was killed during the first few days of Freedom Summer by a gang of white men.[9] Reebee remembers being completely awestruck by the leadership of Bob Moses, a former graduate student at Harvard University who had joined SNCC in 1960 and who became known for his big vision, humility, and wisdom.[10] After learning that Goodman, Chaney, and Schwerner were missing, Moses spent hours talking with a small group of people, including Reebee, about the many dangers of registering voters. Moses and other SNCC leaders wanted to be sure the northern recruits knew what they were getting themselves into. Reebee understood and stayed, with a sense of community and a shared sense of justice forever emblazoned on his consciousness.

The integrationist politics of the Highlander Folk School, a training center for labor organizers and civil rights activists, also reflected a long-standing belief that the product of social change would inevitably reflect the seeds from which it grew.[11] Of the race strategy employed at Highlander and in demonstrations, Bonnie Kerness says, "There were very few distinctions made [between Blacks and whites]. . . . I can remember in marches, the biggest distinction was, two white people couldn't stay together. Spread the whites out, is what they used to say because there weren't a whole lot of us, at least not at that time. It was just very mixed. And of course I was young so mostly I listened. I was told what to do and I did it."

As the number of white people in SNCC began to increase, its members began to discuss what roles were most effective for white activists to assume in a southern, Black-led movement. From early on, Black workers encouraged whites to work within their own communities. Mary King describes Ella Baker's encouraging her to live in a white community when Mary first moved to Atlanta to lead workshops on interracial alliances on college campuses, remembering that Ella Baker had "some notion that I might influence someone or penetrate somebody's thinking," which, according to King, "was wholly unrealistic."[12] She writes that she was "bored and unhappy" living at Agnes Scott College, a white women's college, and that, "none of my black friends could visit me, and I spent all my spare time away from there" (57). Eventually convincing Baker that she could be "more productive" if she lived near her friends from SNCC, King moved to a Black community in Atlanta and lived in Black communities during the next four years. Baker's encouragement reflected her knowledge that white-to-white education about racism is invaluable, particularly when done through everyday interactions. King's perspective paralleled that of many white activists, who were far more comfortable with other activists and working in Black communities than they were working and living with whites.

Beginning in 1961, the organization attempted to support and guide specific white community organizing. Much of the initial impetus came from Anne Braden, who was an adviser to SNCC and worked with SCEF. According to historian Clayborne Carson, Anne and Carl Braden "had gained the trust of SNCC workers because they understood better than most white leftists the militant mood of Black activists and they respected the desire of those in SNCC to remain independent of all outside control."[13] The Bradens were labor and antisegregation activists of the 1950s who had faced one of the most grueling sedition trials of the century; they well knew how important it was to remain free from outside influences. They also knew—after having watched white people in Louisville attempt to destroy the lives of a Black family who had moved into a white neighborhood—why standing against racism required militancy.[14]

Anne Braden had also learned early in the 1950s that white support for the liberation of Blacks started with white respect for Black leadership. Of the relationship between Black and white antisegregationists in Louisville in the 1950s, she says, "The African American groups in Louisville were glad to have white support. There simply wasn't any question about white leadership. Blacks were clearly leading it. You were there to be supportive. So that didn't become an issue like it did later when whites were dominating things. The NAACP was the main activist organization then. It was clearly Black. I joined it, and a number of whites were part of it. But we were not there to run it. That was just understood."

In the early 1950s the importance of Anne's work as a white woman was confirmed again, this time through the sage advice of an African American Communist activist, William Patterson.[15] Anne and many others had been working to stop the execution of Willie McGee, a Black man wrongfully accused of raping a white woman. The Militant Church movement, a coalition of Black churches in Kentucky, contributed some money to Anne for her traveling and organizing to stop the execution. On her return, Anne reported at one of the Militant Church movement meetings about the execution and racism. After writing about her work to William Patterson, she received a reply that "included two things that have stuck with me. One, I didn't need to be going to the Black churches. Black people know they are oppressed. They don't need you to tell them. You should be going to white churches. From then on, there was never any doubt that is what I should be doing. That is what white people should be doing. Getting with white people. . . . The other thing he said in the letter that shaped my life, and I have never understood why he took the time to write, he had never met me but once. From his point of view, I was probably this little white racist from Alabama not quite dry behind the ears. But he did. He said, you don't have to be part of the world of the lynchers. You do have a choice. You can join the other America. The other America has always been here. From the time the first slave ship arrived. It is the people who fought against slavery. Against injustice. The people who fought for humanity. It was Black and it was white. It just hit me at the right time and that is what I joined. And it has felt like I have been a part of it ever since."

With these lessons in mind, Anne, on behalf of SCEF, encouraged SNCC to accept seed money to pay a white activist to work directly with white communities. Bob Zellner, who had been involved in non-violent protests against segregation and workshops at the Highlander Folk School, was hired for the first position.[16] Zellner had gained the respect of activists over the years because he hung in there, protest after protest, enduring terrible beatings. He also believed his activism needed to include working with other whites. According to Anne, Zellner "had a great talent. He liked people. He didn't have the sense of rejecting his own people. Even though he identified more with the Black movement and I guess he got arrested more than most whites."

This commitment to whites was not easy for Bob to uphold, particularly when whites were the ones beating him and fellow Black activists. The challenge, as Carson explains it, was to "relate to the white Southern moderate or liberal and at the same time relate to a group of people who are as militant and as activist as students in [SNCC]."[17] Sam Shirah, who in 1963 became the SCEF-sponsored field secretary after Bob Zellner, also believed white people had to be shown how the southern movement for racial equality was in their interest. He maintained that "something had to be done to reach the great number of white people in the South who have felt that this movement is their enemy. It's not their enemy. It might be their salvation."[18]

In addition to supporting staff members who were working with white people, SNCC sponsored two projects aimed at getting white communities involved in the civil rights struggle. The White Folks Project was intended to establish a movement among whites beginning in Biloxi, Mississippi. SNCC workers first trained in Oxford, Mississippi, and then at the Highlander Folk School in Tennessee. However, according to Carson, "most of the group were newcomers to the southern movement, none had previously organized in white communities."[19] Ultimately, the white organizers were kicked out of the community. According to Anne Braden, "except for the White Folks Project nobody was talking to white Mississippians. Maybe you couldn't have talked with them. It was such a police state."

The Southern Student Organizing Committee (SSOC) was another white project created by several white SNCC activists in 1964. There was much discussion among civil rights workers about the relationship SSOC should have to SNCC. When consulted on the issue, Anne argued forcefully that a white project should never be autonomous from SNCC. Anne remembers a SNCC meeting when "Robb Burlage stood up and said he didn't see any use in having a white organization. He said white people never get together as white people except for a bad purpose. You might get together as women or as workers but not as white people unless it was for a bad reason. That just struck me."

The night before the white activists voted to set up SSOC, Jim Forman called Anne to talk about it. As she remembers, "The white activists had called some of the SNCC people to come to Nashville to talk about the new organization. I know John Lewis was there. People had driven from all over the South. They never did get much money together. You know people just found money and got in the car and went places. You didn't wait for someone to subsidize a conference like people do now. I remember Jim called me and I said, 'Jim what do you think they ought to do?' He said, 'I don't think they ought to leave SNCC but I'll tell you Anne, I am not going to beg them to stay.' He said, 'It is power. They want a power base of their own.' I think some of that is true."

According to Anne, one of the white activists' rationales for a separate organization was that they believed "they could reach more white students if they weren't too closely associated with SNCC, which had a very radical reputation. This was before the Black Power days. SNCC's original reputation was radical on white campuses. I thought, that is just not so. How did you all get involved? You were inspired by SNCC. You were just like any other white student. So you think other people don't have as much sense as you? But that is what they said. Jim may have been right. They wanted their own thing."

Positions within SNCC varied from seeing the development of a white project as a drain on SNCC energies to asserting that any such project should have autonomy. Eventually, SNCC decided to support a conference of white students and to continue to discuss a possible future relationship between SNCC and SSOC.[20] Ray Luc Levasseur, who was raised in a working-class French Canadian family in Maine, worked with SSOC after returning from the Vietnam War in 1967. He and others started a community-based alternative paper, supported Black and white workers on strike against a large meatpacking corporation, and pressed the local university to desegregate the student newspaper. He writes, "I felt as a white working-class person having seen some of the racism in the United States that I saw, that it was my responsibility not to go to Black people and tell them what their agenda is. They were making it clear what they wanted. They wanted freedom. They made it clear in Watts. They made it clear in Detroit. Malcolm X was making it clear. My task was to organize white people to support that struggle. And the union struggle was a multinational struggle of Black and white workers together, so that was part of our agenda."[21] With SSOC, Ray Luc marched as part of a contingent in Atlanta to honor the first anniversary of the assassination of Martin Luther King Jr., and he conducted demonstrations at the Atlanta jail and state house. Soon after that, Ray Luc and his wife were evicted from their apartment and run out of town.

Although SSOC attempted to organize white people in multiple arenas, its relationship to SNCC was tenuous. According to Carson, SSOC projects generally were independent, and it moved closer to Students for a Democratic Society (SDS) than to SNCC.[22] According to Anne Braden, part of the reason the contact between SSNC and SSOC lessened over time had to do with quick turnover in political generations: "What happened is you have two or three generations in SSOC because generations happen really quickly when history is moving fast. The people who originally formed it got a little overwhelmed. There was some overlap, and then you had another layer coming in and a third layer before it broke up. . . . The second generation and the third generation, a wave of them, had totally different ideas about race. Racism and race did not impinge upon them as it had on the kids who came out of SNCC. . . . So if you are white, and you have all sorts of great ideas about changing the world, but you are not somewhat in touch with the Black community where this oppression is, that is going to go off your radar screen and other things become more important."

Through the mid-1960s, SNCC's strategies regarding the role of whites in the Movement also reflected an attempt by Black leaders, including Bob Moses and Ella Baker, to turn white racial privilege into something of benefit to the civil rights struggle. Inviting whites to the South, first as a trial run in 1963 and then officially in 1964, was the result of SNCC leaders' political savvy: They knew that where whites went, the media would follow. Bob Moses knew as well as or better than anyone that segregation and racist violence in the South would not be significantly undermined until white people believed that white people were at risk.[23] In discussions about the purpose of recruiting northerners (99 percent of whom were white) to the South for Mississippi

Freedom Summer, Ella Baker had said, "Young people will make the Justice Department move. If we can simply let the concept that the rest of the nation bears responsibility for what happens in Mississippi sink in, then we will have accomplished something."[24]

It was widely understood that white students, particularly from the North, would bring national attention to civil rights work. Whereas door-to-door conversations between civil rights workers and southern Blacks accomplished a great deal on a grassroots level, the television coverage of the white opposition to voter-registration drives and civil disobedience began to shame the country into taking the Civil Rights Movement seriously. During this period, SNCC leaders understood well the power of portraying white and Black activists as united.

In this way, Black leaders created strategies that defined what white people were supposed to do to be part of the struggle. Initially, Bob Moses argued that white involvement remained important. For Moses, the crucial distinction was between rational and irrational people. The rational people supported civil rights, and the irrational people opposed them.[25] To separate Blacks from whites would effectively eliminate that political distinction. As Reebee Garofalo says of that period, "I came to Mississippi at the tail end of what I would describe as the early Civil Rights Movement. The Movement was essentially integrationist, a movement that was essentially nonviolent and a movement that followed the slogan, 'Black and white together.'" Clayborne Carson writes, "The antiwhite feelings that later confronted white organizers in Black communities were as yet hardly visible during the summer's [1964] unprecedented experiment in race relations."[26]

The integrationist philosophy emanating from the southern-based civil rights organizations was also the dominant philosophy in the North through the mid-1960s. Of his early years as an activist in Detroit, David Wellman says, "There was this little group of people who organized the pickets. It was an interracial group. There was a wonderful Black minister who was the dean of students at Wayne State. . . . Then there was a rather radical Episcopalian priest by the name of Malcolm Boyd—who wrote a book called *Are You Running with Me, Jesus?*— who happened to be a Freedom Rider. . . . So, you have a Black minister and a white priest who were kind of advisers to us."

The leadership of these two men meant the world to David, partly because he wanted to travel south to work with SNCC, but for reasons of politics and class, he could not: "One of the reasons I didn't go south is that a number of us in an incipient Civil Rights Movement in Detroit thought that if I went south, either as a Freedom Rider or to participate in sit-ins, that I would immediately be identified as the son of a Communist. That would taint—I think the word that we actually used was 'taint'—the Civil Rights Movement." The other reason David did not go south was because he needed to earn money to pay for college: "There was something else which at the time I didn't feel good about. I kind of viewed it as a cover for cowardice. I worked while I went to college. I was a waiter in country clubs in Detroit. . . . It was a part-time job but it was thirty hours a week and it was a regular union job and I needed that money and I couldn't see how I could keep that job and go south. I do recall worrying about to what extent that was really about money and to what extent the question of money was an excuse for cowardice." David's story is not unlike those of many other working-class northern students who supported southern civil rights work. His decision not to go south reveals why most white people who did go south were from middle-class backgrounds.

Once David moved to California to attend graduate school, he became involved with a multiracial group of union organizers that was part of the "wonderful Civil Rights Movement that was exploding in San Francisco at the time." These activists, in concert with people from the NAACP and Congress of Racial Equality (CORE), organized demonstrations against racism at hotels and restaurants, in automobile dealerships, and in movie theaters. David recalls, "This was in 1963. It was in incredible experience, because at one point we had demonstrations where we were able to surround an entire block around the Sheraton Hotel. We moved into lobbies and sat down. There were thousands of us. It was heady stuff because we were successful. We got the hotel to sign an agreement to hire Black people. We got the automobile dealers to sign an agreement to hire Black people."

For white people involved in civil rights organizations in the North, the challenge was to take part in direct action that both supported activism in the South and was tailored to issues specific to the North. For Maggie Nolan Donovan, who first got involved with SNCC under the guidance of Jim Forman and Bob and Dottie Zellner, working in a chapter in Boston essentially meant recruiting and raising funds. For Maggie, who was raised by devout, Irish Catholic, pro-union parents and who had spent much of her life bearing the elitist classism of wealthy Protestant Bostonians, this work included reckoning with complicated class issues. From Maggie's perspective, the fund-raising base in Boston had a patronizing attitude toward civil rights workers. "They were Cambridge, Newton, Brookline intellectuals. I would become affronted very easily, and sometimes my Black comrades would tell me to cool it because 'We were trying to make some money here.' I remember going to a meeting in West Haven, which is a pretty wealthy suburb of New Haven, with Stokely [Carmichael]. . . . All the guests at the party were white and very affluent, and there were Black women maids passing and serving hors d'oeuvres. I remember walking into this house and stiffening up and saying, 'Oh, wait a minute,' and Stokely saying, 'Come on now, we've got a job here. Don't start that stuff. We can talk about it later.' He did what he was there to do, talking to the people, and I followed his lead. I had a real hard time with that. But to him, it was 'What do you expect?' I was just always expecting something different. For him, that was just the way the world was." Maggie learned that from Stokely's perspective, a critique of class was a privilege that had a time and place. Organizing across race inevitably meant crossing several divides.

The SNCC chapter in Boston also organized around access to housing and employment and led a boycott of the Levi Strauss Company that had begun in the South. When Dottie and Bob Zellner left Boston in 1964, Dottie encouraged Maggie to continue to run the SNCC office. Maggie could not do that full time because she had promised her mother she would not leave college. A white woman from Detroit came to Boston to work with Maggie, which meant there were two white people in the office. SNCC recruited a Black woman from Roxbury so that the three could run the office together. In this and many other instances, two principles were operating simultaneously: a we-are-all-in-this-together ideology that reflected Bob Moses' distinction between the rational and irrational people, alongside very explicit attention to Black involvement at every level of decision making. In both the North and the South, these two principles went to the core of SNCC's integrationist philosophy.

Go Forward, with a Vision in Hand

By the mid-1960s, however, an increasing number of Black activists were beginning to rethink the propositions that civil rights could be peacefully attained, that an integrationist strategy would be successful, and that education itself could bring the government to support racial equality. A plethora of national events began to blow apart previous notions of a "beloved community." Among them were the federal government's refusal to stop assaults on Black voters; President Lyndon Johnson's refusal to seat the members of the Mississippi Freedom Democrats at the Democratic National Convention in Atlantic City, New Jersey, in 1964; and the killing of Sammy Younge, a war veteran and SNCC volunteer, within months of the signing of the Voting Rights Act of 1965.[27] SNCC's consistent refusal to back down on its open door policy—an acceptance of any organization that supported their goals, even a group that might have Communist ties—led many liberals to back away from supporting SNCC.[28] This reality reaffirmed the organization's understanding that it could not rely upon the establishment for its longevity as it continued to broaden its critique of U.S. society.

Dynamics within SNCC also contributed to a rethinking of an interracial organization. Many Black activists were understandably ambivalent about working with white volunteers, especially those from the North, who were often thought to be (and who often were) wealthy, inexperienced, and naive. It was part of the organization's success as an integrated activist organization that Black people were clearly in charge. They decided which white people could work with them as field secretaries and as representatives of the organization. Black people interviewed and then selected the young white people who were asked to come south for Freedom Summer, and Black people, in effect, chose the white people who would be asked to stay on. White people were constantly held accountable to Black people in the way they handled themselves, in the policy they carried out, and in how they framed events, publicity, and the vision of the organization. Although some Black and white activists were worried that the influx of white northerners might change power dynamics, other white staff were concerned for different reasons. Mary King writes, "It meant that their specialness would be gone."[29] Although the organization's integrationist strategy remained dominant through Freedom Summer, once the summer was over the often-dramatic differences in life experiences of northern students and Black southerners cast doubt on the notion of a community of activists undivided by race and class.

In his analysis of the integrationist ethic of the late 1950s and early 1960s, Reebee Garofalo explains, "There was a notion that there was no difference between us that you can attribute to color. There was a sense in which that was very comfortable. It was really warm and fuzzy, you know, during that brief period. I think some of the older SNCC people really saw that as a moment when they transcended race. That Black and white really were together. In retrospect, I don't see it that way. In retrospect I see the notion of Black and white together, the notion that we were just color-blind, as a movement in denial, a movement based on a denial of real differences." As Reebee remembers it, people did not talk about the "fact that I wasn't the same as the sharecroppers that I was registering to vote in Mississippi and that I had infinitely more options than they had. . . . As warm and fuzzy as it was, in retrospect, it was pretty clear that was going to get undone." In effect, the integrationist philosophy that initially made room for whites within the Movement masked distinctions between whites and Blacks and class differences that posed obstinate questions for the organization in the long run.

By the mid-1960s the Black Power Movement, whose naming is often traced to Stokely Carmichael's use of the phrase "Black power" in speeches in 1966, reflected a transformation in Black consciousness from interracialism and civil rights to a politics based on Black political and economic autonomy. As the turn toward Black Power developed, white activists needed to develop strategies for keeping at the center of their agenda an antiracism that did not depend upon being in Black-led organizations. Some white people who had been working with SNCC began working with SCEF. According to its director, Anne Braden, "Everybody knew that SCEF's focus was to organize white people. By that time, we were trying to break out of middle-class intellectual circles and get some working-class whites. Along about then, we set up a grassroots rural project, Bob Zellner's project, working with white workers, ex-Klansmen. We set up the Southern Mountain Project because we thought we had less racism in the mountains." SCEF had done work among poor whites that "had gotten kind of stymied because we all got indicted for sedition again. But we were trying to reach out more. So we needed people. Some of them were very good but some of them were crazy as hoot owls. I remember I called Jim Forman one day, he was still at SNCC, and I said, 'Jim, for God's sake, quit sending up all these crazy white people.'"

According to Anne, there were many "good white people" in the

Movement in that period who had a hard time. "A lot of them tried to work on our mountain project but it just destroyed one person after another. They had what I call a reentry problem. This is understandable and I am not being critical of anybody for this. These are whites who had worked in the Black community in Mississippi and Alabama for so long, a few years is enough, where every white face is an enemy. Maybe out to kill you. So then you get them out and they are supposed to be organizing white people and they really don't like white people. You can't organize people if you don't like them."

When SCEF incorporated many more white activists into its organization, the racial balance in the organization was lost. According to Anne, "The Blacks didn't leave mad, it is just that it wasn't relevant to them anymore." The organization was then faced with volunteer staff meetings attended by fifty people, many of whom began to seek out theory as a way of figuring out their next steps. Anne remembers, "So they all started reading Marx and so you had all these different interpretations of what he said. Parties and pre-parties and all that. The people who got the most excited about this were people who just a few years ago were antitheory." From Anne and Carl Braden's perspective, leftists had backed away from theory in the 1960s in reaction to the Old Left, which had been bogged down by theory. But by the late 1960s Anne and Carl saw the young people "all into theory. Knee-deep in theory." As a consequence, "SCEF became a battleground of white leftists fighting over these theories."

Anne now believes the government played a major role in the fights as well. "We have never gotten the files and so will never be able to prove it. The only thing I don't know is who it was and I don't really care. . . . All these battles over how many angels could stand on a needle. Medieval Christians. But I think the government took advantage of that." Anne remembers many weekend meetings where people would fight endlessly about theory. During the sessions, Anne saw and emphasized agreement between the positions. She remembers that in the process "they were very patronizing toward me sometimes. Little Anne. She just doesn't understand how important these issues are."

In 1973 SCEF split bitterly, a break that Anne believes affected many people across the country. SCEF had been a stable civil rights organization that had weathered the 1950s witch hunts and stood strong through the 1960s. According to Anne, the organization "was well known and had a lot of support. The thing that attracted people to SCEF was unity. For many years, we had the unity. Things didn't divide us." Then and now, Anne was convinced that "what made SCEF so vulnerable to the government is that it had become so white. I honestly think that if it had had a significant Black presence, they just wouldn't have put up with all the bickering that went on among these different leftist groups. It was ridiculous. I made up my mind because that was a terrible trauma for me, I had spent sixteen years of my life building that organization and I saw it destroyed in six months. I made up my mind then, that never again would I be part of building something that was all white, and I haven't."

SCEF was not alone in struggling to make the transition from civil rights to Black Power. Ironically, despite SNCC's significant attention to whites' positions in the organization, many whites at the time had not fully understood how their race and class affected their work. In her memoir about the years she worked with SNCC, Mary King explains that a fundamental issue she did not deal with at the time was the "diversity of race, class, background and experience of the staff members."[30] She writes, "I have written of the shared perspective held by SNCC workers and of the ethos of the organization. Yet there is an important aspect of the group with which I worked and lived that has only over time become clear to me. This element was so fundamental and played so central a part in the eventual disintegration of our group that it must appear extraordinarily naïve of me not to have been aware of it at the time. The failure to see, respond and address this reality, however, was not simply naïveté on my part, but was interwoven with the attitudes and hopes of the young people of SNCC. Furthermore, if it was a key weakness that ultimately helped to destroy the group, it was also, ironically our greatest strength" (297).

The great strength that King refers to was embodied in the tremendous sense of community born of accomplishment shared by SNCC people, Black and white. Many former SNCC activists have written about their willingness to die for each other if need be, and some did. A key weakness of the shared project among whites and Blacks, however, was the lack of a fully articulated plan for how and why white and Black people needed different agendas to be effective. King concludes: "What this fierce, all-embracing vital force of loyalty disguised was the real and ultimately unassimilable differences in class, race, gender and experiential backgrounds in our circle" (297).

In the transition from integration to Black Power, a fair number of white people who had been involved in early civil rights work got lost in the shuffle, at least temporarily. When SNCC began to fall apart, what took its place for many Black people (in terms of political effectiveness and national prominence) was the Black Power Movement, most notably in the form of the Black Panther Party. The Panthers' racial politics, vis-à-vis white organizers, was dramatically different from the politics within SNCC. Many white activists who wanted to keep antiracism central now needed to do it on their own, without on-going Black feedback and without the guidance, encouragement, or accountability they found in a Black-led organization.

Some SNCC-trained white activists had a hard time figuring out what to do next. To Maggie Nolan Donovan, the prospect of working within the white community seemed simply untenable. Maggie's work with the organization had transformed her life forever. She remembers, "I lived in such a small world—such an incredibly small world—up to that point that the ideas and the people who talked and acted and thought differently were so intoxicating to me." From the moment Maggie first borrowed her father's car to attend a SNCC meeting, she had felt a deep affinity with the other activists. "I went to a meeting just outside of Harvard Square and walked into a room of an interracial gathering of people my age and had an enormous sense of homecoming. An absolute epiphany before one person said a single word to me." The organization became Maggie's life, the location of her political coming-of-age, and a place that meant family when becoming politically conscious meant moving away from the friends and family with whom she grew up.

When SNCC started to unravel, Maggie (and many other activists) was devastated. At that point in her life, Maggie found herself having to choose one of three equally complicated options. Jim Forman, who had been her mentor, suggested that Maggie move to South Boston—the heart of the working-class Irish Catholic community—and organize against racism there. As Maggie recalls, "Forman always wanted to use my Irish Catholicism as an organizing vehicle, to put me in place in certain places, to get access to certain people." For Maggie, such a plan meant "getting eaten alive." She thought that if she tried to organize in South Boston by herself, especially during the busing crisis, she would not last a week. Although she believed in Forman's model in theory,

Maggie could not conceive of doing the work alone, and there were no other activists willing to do it with her.

The Zellners had hoped that Maggie would continue to raise funds in Boston for Grass Roots Organizing Work (GROW), a program first supported by SNCC and then by SCEF which organized poor white southerners around local economic issues. From the Zellners' point of view, Maggie's connections to white-based funders in Boston were crucial. From Maggie's perspective, hobnobbing with wealthy white people in Boston sounded like a nightmare. "The more SNCC became a nationalist organization, the more valuable I was in a sense because I was a connection to the white fund-raising base. So my work was only enhanced by nationalism because my role became more pivotal in keeping the white fund-raising base interested in supporting an increasingly antiwhite posture. But I couldn't really see myself working with that affluent white community." The classism Maggie experienced in Boston while growing up and as an activist left her with little interest in working primarily with wealthy white donors.

Meanwhile, the man with whom Maggie was in love told her in no uncertain terms that if she continued to be an activist, their relationship was over. He proposed marriage and a move to Cape Cod to start a family. At that moment in her life, when she felt she had lost the family she cherished with SNCC, Maggie chose what she thought was stability: starting her own family.

Maggie's paradox was that she both agreed politically with Black Power and the concept of white people working with white people *and* found this transition personally devastating. Even then, she knew to separate the two issues, partly because the African American leaders who had mentored her—Ella Baker and Jim Forman—never saw the existence of white allies as antithetical to Black Power. When Jim Forman encouraged Maggie to work with white people in South Boston, "He was still continuing to mentor me. He was trying to make sense of white people's role in the Movement and how we could work with Black people. He cared deeply about that question and about me, and he was trying to work out his questions with me. Similarly, in the spring of 1967, when the decision about the future of white people in SNCC was being made, Ella Baker came to Boston and requested that she be the house guest at Edward's and my house. While staying with us, she didn't discuss the future of SNCC. She did give me exquisite cooking lessons and held me in her arms. She was also clearly there to check Edward out. Her opinion was that he was a good man and that I should marry him."

After Maggie married and moved to Cape Cod, she did not stop being political. Raising children to be race-conscious, bringing issues of racial and gender equity to the table in the districts where she taught grammar school, and continuing her education were all political acts during that era. But Maggie found no political organization or affiliation that considered race central in the way that SNCC had.

Some white activists were less disrupted by changing racial politics. For those who had never come to know SNCC as family, its breakup did not result in the same level of discontinuity. David Gilbert, for example, an activist in New York City in the middle to late 1960s, "was not as jostled by the Black Power Movement as some other white people were—for example, many white people who had gone South—because I was already working in white organizations and organizing against racism in the white community. Although there were some people of color in CORE at Columbia, most of its members were white. Because of CORE's makeup, I didn't feel as if I was being asked to leave an organization."

People who became involved in the East Harlem Block Schools in the early 1960s also remained there as teachers and administrators long after the split in SNCC. The East Harlem Block Schools were based on a model in which the Black and Latino parents and the school board had direct control over the hiring and firing of teachers and administrators. Dorothy Stoneman, who worked with the East Harlem Block Schools for twenty years, explains that for white people "there was a power relationship that made it clear that they were subordinate. I was always subordinate and that was fine. That became a really central piece of theory that I have used as I have gone forward. If any white person is going to be useful, or any person who is not part of an oppressed group is going to be useful, they have to be subordinate. From that position they can be as useful as their resources and skills will allow them to be."

Of the impact of the turn toward Black Power on her own position in the East Harlem Block Schools, Dorothy says, "The Black community is not, itself, antiwhite. It is not racist. Racism is a white thing. It is a very narrow piece of the politicized Black community that expresses antiwhite sentiment. You get targeted by that, but it doesn't have very deep roots. Most whites don't know that. It is a very important thing for whites to know." As Dorothy sees it, "My being a lone white person in the North, I was always able to just be myself in any organization. And I made sure I was accountable to the community. Even though I had to deal at various times with antiwhite feelings, and antiwhite theory and Black nationalism, with people saying I shouldn't be in a position of influence, it was always manageable because I was alone." At no point in Dorothy's work in Harlem was there a threat that white people would take charge of an agenda that clearly belonged to Blacks and Latinos. This was in contrast to the post-1964 concern within SNCC that white people would attempt to dominate what was clearly not theirs to control.

Other white activists of this period took the shift from integrationism to Black Power in stride, in part because of their understanding of power and institutionalized oppression. As David Wellman observes, "When SNCC went though a transformation to Black Power, I know that a lot of my white friends were very disturbed and thought the organization was making a mistake. I was part of a group of white people that didn't think it was a mistake." Many Black activists at that time were arguing that integrated activist organizations were reproducing some of the old relationships of domination and subordination. David says, "It was important for Black people to organize Black people so that Black people wouldn't go and register to vote because a white person had asked them to do it."

David understood the Black nationalist commitment to Black leadership and autonomy. That politic "made sense to me, coming from Detroit where Black people were always in positions of leadership, where white people didn't lead Black people. Black people were always leading Black people in Detroit." David had long been skeptical of an integrationist philosophy as well. "I was always sympathetic to Black nationalism, although I would never call myself a Black nationalist. . . . I saw integrationism as a kind of liberal, reformist approach."

Integrationism was, for David, a pie-in-the-sky philosophy that had little basis in reality in U.S. history. "Part of my feeling is that I could never see white people going along with integration. I could never see America reforming itself, which is what integration is all about. So I was much more sympathetic to what Black nationalism was about, even though I am not a nationalist and I am not Black. When people started talking about Black Power, for the first time they were talking about power instead of a beloved community. I saw Black Power as a critique of pluralism. For the first time I could begin to see how the theory of pluralism was a theory of continued white domination. I was much closer in some sense to Stokely Carmichael and Rap Brown than I was to John Lewis and Bob Moses."[31] John Lewis and Bob Moses represented the spiritual side of the beloved community, within the Gunnar Myrdal tradition of trying to make America live up to its ideals. Stokely Carmichael talked more about race and racism as a system of power and exclusion, a framework that departed from the notion of a beloved community. David understood the Black Power politics captured in words he recalls from Malcolm X: "We don't want to integrate into a burning house. We don't want a place at your table. We want the whole fucking table." After reading a great deal of Malcolm X's work, David heard him speak in 1964. He was taken with Malcolm X's talent as a brilliant orator and agreed with Malcolm's argument about the need for bullets rather than ballots.

Because of David's analysis of power, he was not among those white people who felt pushed out by Black Power. As he says, "I never saw it as a personal thing but as a political movement." David criticized SNCC for making voting its central priority when the Democratic Party "stabbed the Black activists in the back" in 1964 by refusing to seat the delegation of the Mississippi Freedom Democratic Party (MFDP), including Fannie Lou Hamer, a revered civil rights activist and one of the MFDP's national representatives. But he was quickly called on the carpet by Black activists for the white privilege at the root of his position. He remembers, "One of the wonderful things about that period is that Black and white people could talk about it. And we did talk about that. People told me, 'You've got a good critique, but look where you're coming from. There are people in the South who don't have the same benefits you have.'" The constant dialogues and debates offered David a way to simultaneously understand how being a white northerner influenced his critique of integration and why being a son of Communists helped him understand Black Power.

David's understanding of power relations was, no doubt, first nurtured by seeing his father arrested and by living, with his family, under constant government surveillance. "I have always felt very passionate and angry about these issues, so that when somebody would be jailed or somebody would be killed I felt it personally. When people got beaten and clubbed and hosed, it wasn't those people. It was my brothers and sisters." Explaining the connection between this reaction to his childhood, David says, "I imagine it had a lot to do with the way my parents were treated by this government. My parents were, in fact, enemies of the state. My mother was publicly and legally defined as an 'undesirable alien.' That is a quote. And my father was defined as an 'enemy of the state.' So I guess in some sense I saw the same state that was going after Black people was going after my family. I wouldn't have put it in such personal terms at that time . . . but what Black people were doing to transform this government was part of a process that I was part of by virtue of what my parents were involved in and the hits that we had taken."

David's commitment to the Black neighborhood he grew up in and his parents' racial politics is lifelong. Of his passion for militant struggle against racism, David says, "It was the Black women who looked out for me in Detroit. The Black women who ran interference for me when the cops would hassle me as a kid. Who would invite me and my sister to stay at their place if we got locked out of the house or if there was a problem. This whole movement was about issues that affected people who were very much a part of my life." In the early 1950s David's father was arrested for violating the Smith Act.[32] His mother was arrested for violating the Walter-McCarran Act (an immigrant act). Amid these assaults on David's family, the Black children at his school refused to treat David and his sister as pariahs, as did some of the white children. David was accepted by Black people in his neighborhood, and he knew he belonged there. "What was happening to Black people wasn't an abstraction for me. It was a part of an experience I had had based on my family and community."

Like David Wellman's, Anne Braden's support for the Black Power Movement was informed by activist experiences prior to the Civil Rights Movement. SCEF supported the Black Power Movement. "We saw it as a healthy development, a thrust forward for our region and the country, one that would ultimately increase rather than decrease the possibility of building strong, honest, and viable coalitions across the color line. I think history has proven us right in that analysis."[33] For Anne personally, who had been persecuted by the government and most people in her community throughout most of the 1950s, "being a part-pariah, even among people on my side of the social struggle" prepared her for changing race politics during the Black Power Movement. In Anne's view, some white people in the southern Civil Rights Movement were made into heroes and heroines. "I was never accorded that status; my subversive label precluded it. I think that saved me from some problems that some whites in the Movement had later when the Black Power Movement of the mid-1960s suggested to them they weren't needed or wanted in organizations of African Americans, and that, although they had important roles to play in the struggle against racism, those roles were elsewhere. Lots of hurt feelings resulted as people felt rejected. It didn't bother me; I had been rejected too many times before. Thus I, and others in somewhat similar positions, were able to look more objectively at the significance of the Black Power Movement."[34]

Beyond the "White People Kicked Out" Reading of History

The popular assumption is that the whites who left SNCC in 1967 went unwillingly and that the racial split in SNCC was the primary cause of the organization's demise. However, a more careful reading of this history—which includes accounting for the range of experiences of white activists—suggests otherwise. First, as Clayborne Carson is careful to point out, the split between whites and blacks in 1967 was only one piece of the story of the organization's fragmentation. Debates about the efficacy of nonviolent direct action and decentralized leadership also led to significant changes within the organization during that period.[35]

Second, many experienced white activists within SNCC also saw compelling reasons for change. What really happened during the meeting in 1967, when the vote was taken about continued white involvement, is still open to debate. Maggie Nolan Donovan said that as far as she knows, Bob Zellner and other white people in SNCC argued in favor of remaining in the organization. By contrast, former SDS activist Tom Hayden writes, "In December 1967 the inevitable happened with odd formality: Whites were expelled from SNCC by a vote of nineteen to eighteen with twenty-four abstaining. Though the decision was by secret ballot, it is clear that whites themselves provided the critical votes to guarantee their own departure."[36] Regardless of who exactly voted in which direction, it remains important to counter the popular notion that white activists were "done to"—kicked out by ungrateful Black activists. The change in SNCC relations was not about individual white people per se; instead, it reflected realities of the times: that the work against racism needed to be done in the South as well as in the North and that white people's work included being agitators in white communities.

It is also revealing that more attention has been generated in the public imagination to the portrayal of Black activists kicking out white activists in 1967 than to the decision by several white activists in 1964 to set up the SSOC, a white organization that voluntarily set itself apart from and ultimately lost close contact with SNCC. At least from Anne Braden's perspective, attempts by SSOC to maintain autonomy from SNCC have much to do with white unwillingness to accept Black leadership over the long run. Knowing both of these stories certainly dispels any notion that white people were victims in the process.

Third, not all white activists were disoriented, disgruntled, or disappointed by the shift in politics. As Anne describes, "Those of us involved in social struggle in the South during the second half of the twentieth century learned many things. In the 1940s and 1950s, I, like many others, both African American and white, thought the problem was mainly one of our region. We learned that this was an illusion and that the same problem, although in different form, permeated the entire country. In those days, we talked about 'segregation' as the problem. But our movement killed Jim Crow; that is, we did indeed destroy segregation enforced by law. Doing so was no small accomplishment, one achieved by the blood and sacrifice of many people. But we found that, even after that, the evil still existed. We learned to call it 'racism,' and later, more accurately, 'white supremacy.' We learned that the real problem was (and is) the assumption that everything should be run by white people for the benefit of whites, which is actually how I define racism. And we came to realize that the process of integration, even desegregation, often failed because African Americans, on the one hand, and whites, on the other, had very different concepts of the struggle against segregation. To African Americans, this struggle sought freedom, dignity, liberation; for many whites, it meant people of color being absorbed into 'their' white world, which whites would still run."[37] Ultimately, the move toward autonomous Black organizations had far less to do with white activists and more to do with a movement unwilling to stop fighting for genuine access to education, health care, and jobs for African Americans.

A final danger in focusing on the racial split in SNCC is that that story often overshadows the tremendous impact the organization had on the education of white antiracist activists. White involvement had the power to explode whole childhoods' worth of racist socialization. In the place of this socialization SNCC encouraged the growth of political consciousness that has accompanied many, many white people for the rest of their lives.

Many white activists developed sophisticated analyses of race and class. They also came to understand the power and promise of a Black-led movement and that such a movement made room for whites willing to take racism seriously. Within this context SNCC supported important projects that started many people working in white communities while maintaining accountability to Black leadership. The organization confronted the real limitations of whites organizing in Black communities. It also fostered intense sessions during which white and Black people told truths about their fears about working with each other and the tendency of whites to try to take over what was not theirs to take. White people learned of the intransigence of racism and its impact in little and big ways on everyday life. They saw that racism needed to be dealt with institutionally as well as in activist organizations. They also learned that racism could not be considered solely a southern issue, that the president of the country as well as northern businessmen stalled in making significant changes as much as or more than did southern leaders.

The egalitarian approach in SNCC and the formidable leadership of African American women also gave white women a chance to develop their leadership skills. Historian Paula Giddings writes that "white women could perform just about any task in SNCC that they had heart enough to do. . . . Thus many of the white women gained a respect for their own abilities that might not have been possible in other organizations."[38] Maggie Nolan Donovan's experience staffing SNCC's Boston office with an African American woman and a white woman is a powerful example of this opportunity. Maggie recalls that a field secretary had told the three women that a "SNCC guy was coming into town, you know, striding into the office in a kind of cowboy fashion. We

would put them in their place so fast. We just had these codes and sig-
nals we would do and you know, 'You're in the Boston office now so
don't mess with us.' Very strong feminists, for then, such a strong feminist presence. I mean we were so efficient and so good at what we did,
and so aware that we were good at what we did, that there was nobody telling us how to run that office." Dottie Zellner had run the office the same way before Maggie and the others took over. "We certainly had a sense that we were putting these guys in their place in
terms of work, in terms of sex. . . . My experience with SNCC was
these enormously powerful women working all the time with these
enormously powerful women. I have a very feminist analysis of SNCC.
The people who influenced me in a transforming way were overwhelmingly female. They had such a sense of themselves as such strong voices
and were so smart."

In her important critique of characterizations of SNCC as male dominated, Joyce Ladner writes, "They say that feminism emerged because
of dissension within the ranks. Rather, feminism is an outgrowth, it
emerged because SNCC served as a model, a prototype of what could
become a better kind of society."[39] In part, Ladner is responding to
Sara Evans's often-cited *Personal Politics,* a book about women in
SNCC and the New Left.[40] Many SNCC activists disagree with Evans,
believing that she underestimates the way in which women's opposition to sexism was taken seriously in SNCC and that she marginalizes
Black women's feminism in the process.[41] Many SNCC women have
stressed that the critique of sexism that did emerge in SNCC was a sign
women had the power and respect needed to make such a critique.
According to African Americanist and former field secretary, Michael
Thelwell, respect for SNCC women was one of many consequences of
the organization's having been started by Ella Baker, who "had struggled with chauvinism all her life and particularly in SCLC, and she
mourned it. . . . She wasn't going to create no organization that would
recapitulate that."[42]

Many other Black women followed in the footsteps of Ella Baker in
exacting a nonsexist standard. The critique of sexism that white women
offered in SNCC was the product of a space created by women, most of
whom were Black. In response to the notion that this critique largely
came from white women, former SNCC Freedom Singer and historian
Bernice Johnson Reagon writes, "We really have to watch racism, be-

cause if the group is integrated and an energy is created by some White people in the group, often when it is transmitted to the larger culture, and other people start to read into it, they will separate it out as if it was not created by the structure that made it possible for it to occur. And you can just look at the struggle in the women's movement around how White it is. I mean people really try to make stuff White, even if it ain't."[43]

In addition to offering women across races enormous opportunity to develop leadership skills, the life-and-death atmosphere that SNCC workers survived also made room for long-lasting and powerful ties across race, ties that have lasted over generations. Historian Cheryl Lynn Greenberg writes that almost all the speakers at the 1998 SNCC reunion conference emphasized the revolutionary structure of its early days: "its radical egalitarianism, its transformative and empowering potential, its crucial support system of love and trust. The bitterest of fights seemed to most of them, in retrospect, only another indication of their depth of commitment to the Movement and to one another."[44]

3

. . . Be Unbroken

As the Student Nonviolent Coordinating Committee (SNCC) emerged in the 1960s as the premier organization in the country for training white antiracists in the South, its influence in the North could also be seen in Students for a Democratic Society (SDS), the free speech movement, and the antiwar movement. As the Civil Rights Movement began to change, white activists could be found working in several locations: in the free speech movement in colleges and universities, in anti-poverty and community-change programs, in the antiwar movement, in the early second-wave women's movement, and in white militant organizations. Some whites stayed in the South, especially those who grew up there. Some dropped out of activism entirely. From the late 1960s on, being a white activist typically meant being involved in white-led organizations, which had trouble keeping antiracism at the center of their agendas. Although retrospective accounts of the 1960s have identified multiple forces that eventually undermined activism in general, little has been written about what whittled away at the white antiracist consciousness that SNCC had so carefully nurtured.

White-Led New Left Activism

By the time Black Power was supplanting integrationist politics, SDS had become the most prominent New Left organization among white activists in the North.[1] First formed in 1960 as a youth caucus of the League for Industrial Democracy, SDS became an organization in its own right in 1962 with the writing of its manifesto, the Port Huron Statement (named after a meeting held in Port Huron, Michigan). The statement decried hierarchical and authoritarian structures, rallied for egalitarianism, and upheld the rights of students to participate in their own education. SDS's organizational structure was loose and decentralized, in keeping with its belief in participatory democracy (although the notion of participatory democracy is misleading, given that the SDS leadership was overwhelmingly white, middle-class, and male dominated).

In the early years there were multiple links between SDS and SNCC. Clayborne Carson writes, "The black-dominated southern movement had a significant effect on the white student Left. Without the non-violent tactics and organizing techniques developed by SNCC in the South, white student activism would probably not have expanded as quickly as it did. Not only did [Tom] Hayden and other SDS leaders learn from their experiences in the South, but SDS, the Northern Student Movement and other predominantly white student organizations attracted students whose initial political activities involved civil rights issues."[2] An early SDS conference in Ann Arbor, Michigan, included several civil rights leaders. Many early SDS leaders considered it the northern arm of SNCC and explicitly named racism and poverty as evils SDS was committed to fight. Early SDS and SNCC connections also included a 1962 workshop in North Carolina, which brought activists from both organizations together for the first time.

Although much of SDS's initial work was intellectual rather than organizational, early efforts included sitting in at Woolworth's stores in northern cities to show support for sit-ins in the South and sending money and people south to work with SNCC.[3] Both organizations supported nonviolence and believed participatory democracy was in keeping with the ideals of U.S. society. Both groups also refused to assume an anticommunist stance, not because Communists were in high numbers in either group but because both organizations were unwilling to have outside influences (including the government or Old Left Communist activists) dictate their organizations' politics. As sociologist Todd Gitlin writes, "What haunted [the SDS] generation was not the specter of Communism but the force and mood of McCarthyism."[4]

The first campus-based movement inspired by SDS, which eventually achieved national attention, was the free speech movement. It first erupted in 1964 at the University of California at Berkeley after university officials banned the recruitment and support of SNCC workers on the campus. Eventually the free speech movement spread across the country, fueled by student anger at university policy that rarely took their voices into account with regard to curriculum, policy, hiring and firing, or educational philosophy.

Several of the leaders of the free speech movement got their initial training as activists in SNCC, some through Freedom Summer in particular. This experience buoyed their abilities to confront higher education, one of the most powerful bureaucracies in the country. Free speech movement activists asserted that students had the right to speak and organize against war research, to press for activist-based curriculum, and to be represented in key university decisions (including where universities invest their money and university-community relationships). According to Mario Savio, who worked with SNCC and became a spokesperson for the free speech movement, "The university is the place where people begin seriously to question the conditions of their existence and raise the issue of whether they can be committed to the society they were born into."[5] For students who came to recognize universities as businesses more dedicated to managing students than to nurturing critical thought, the free speech movement was a way to claim an education that linked learning and social activism. The early work done by free speech movement activists became the foundation for articulating the rights of students to protest the Vietnam War on college campuses, at a period when many college officials were saying that such activity was irrelevant and therefore had no place on university premises.

Although the free speech movement incited great numbers of students to demand quality education inside and outside of the classroom, its central thrust was to ensure that everyone at universities had the right to speak openly. The movement did not ask about those unable to make it to the university in the first place. As Mary King writes in her account of why "free speech" was not at the top of SNCC's agenda, "The issue for us [SNCC activists] was not free speech as in the late Free Speech Movement in Berkeley, led by one of our 1964 volunteers, Mario Savio, but admission of Blacks to good colleges and universities."[6] The difference in priorities that Mary King describes—fighting for the right to speak freely on campus versus fighting for the opportunity to be a college student at all—would reverberate again in debates about affirmative action and First Amendment rights in the 1980s and 1990s. Liberals have opposed hate speech codes on the grounds that they deny First Amendment rights to free speech. By contrast, progressive Asian and African American activists have argued that the assault on affirmative action limits the right to speech of any kind for students of color. Without access for students of color to academic tables, the point of free speech is moot.[7]

Although some free speech movement leaders had ties to SNCC (or referred to supporting civil rights), the comparisons made between civil rights activism in the South and activism on college campuses in the North revealed problematic assumptions about power and privilege. In a speech at the Berkeley demonstration in 1964 that ignited the free speech movement, Mario Savio said, "Last summer I went to Mississippi to join the struggle there for civil rights. This fall I am engaged in another phase of the same struggle, this time in Berkeley. The two battlefields may seem quite different to some observers, but this is not the case. The same rights are at stake in both places—the right to participate as citizens in democratic society and the right to due process of law."[8]

Actually, the same rights were not at stake. In the South people were fighting for the right to vote; the right to a quality precollege education, let alone a college education; and the right to walk down the street without fear of being indiscriminately shot by a white person (police or private citizen). The rights white college students were fighting for assumed access to rights not yet secured for most Blacks and Latinos. Berkeley students were seeking to make relevant an education made accessible to those who had already benefited from a primary and secondary education system that had not been undermined by racism. When Mexican American students organized themselves at the University of California at Berkeley, San Jose State College, and other college campuses, their demands began with the creation of a Third World college, open admission for all Third World people and poor and working-class whites, and the recruitment of Third World staff and faculty. For Mexican Americans the right to speak and organize freely on campus depended first on being admitted and seeing their culture, race, and ethnicity reflected in those who taught them.[9]

Another problem with Savio's analogy stems from a commonly held assumption in the free speech movement that students had little or no power against the bureaucracies they were working to change. Sociologist Wini Breines explains that SDS's "counter-institutional experiments often developed directly out of a sense of powerlessness, with little illusion they could replace the powers that be."[10] The notion of college students as powerless is dubious, particularly since many activists came from first-tier or elite schools. In fact, by 1967 there were written accounts by New Left activists that openly questioned the idea that college students were a subordinate group. Breines traces a reversal in the New Left from treating students as part of the new working class (a theoretical thread maintained through the mid-1960s) to identifying students as a group that was being trained to be the world's next leaders or lackeys to the leaders.[11] In 1967 SDS member Carl Davidson writes, "students are oppressed. Bullshit. We are being trained to be oppressors and the underlings of oppressors. Only the moral among us are being hurt. Even then, the damage is only done to our sensitivities. Most of us don't know the meaning of a hard day's work."[12]

Although the ideological connections between SNCC and the free speech movement were tenuous, there were other early links between SNCC and SDS. In 1963 SDS developed the Economic Research and Action Program (ERAP), which aimed to support community organizing among poor people in northern cities. Todd Gitlin writes that the idea for ERAP initially came from a 1963 conversation between Stokely Carmichael, of SNCC, and Tom Hayden, of SDS: Carmichael proposed that "SDS organize poor whites to ally with SNCC's poor blacks in a class-based alliance."[13] Another impetus behind ERAP was the SDS leaders' belief that student activism could not afford to remain isolated on campuses. The bureaucratic hierarchies and inequalities of universities were reproduced in other institutions as well, including government-sponsored social service programs. In 1964, as hundreds of whites traveled south for Freedom Summer, SDS recruited students to move to northern cities and help organize a cross-race movement of poor people. With its intention to facilitate alliances between poor whites and Blacks, ERAP was philosophically similar to the White Folks Project sponsored by the Southern Conference Educational Fund (SCEF) and SNCC in the South. In fact, SDS consulted Sam Shirah, one of the directors of a SCEF-sponsored white community organizing project, for help with ERAP.[14]

There were some in SDS who opposed ERAP, referring to it as "ghetto jumping" and insisting that SDS focus on campus and electoral politics instead. These critiques identified grave contradictions as a group of overwhelmingly middle-class, college-educated, white students attempted to organize poor people. Wini Breines notes that ERAP's hope to encourage grassroots leadership and support while not dictating community change reflected the New Left belief in participatory democracy and antiauthoritarianism.[15] ERAP's organizers "evaluated themselves on the basis of how successfully they *gave away* their power" (139).

Embedded in this approach was a notion that race and class privilege (and the cultural assumptions that accompany it) can be individually "given away." In fact, the idea of power as something that white (primarily middle-class) people can "give away" supported a belief in individualism that many New Left activists claimed to oppose. Jim Forman's term for the dynamics that often resulted from these class and race differences was "local-people-itis," a tendency to romanticize poor people and see them as pillars of moral fortitude by virtue of their struggles with poverty, racism, or both.[16] Many white SNCC workers attempting to organize in white communities came from working-class backgrounds or had significant, long-term contact with other working-class activists. SDS activists had little of that experience, exposure, or accountability, a problem that substantially limited the success of ERAP over the long run.

Although there were numerous contradictions embedded in ERAP, many SDS activists believed that ERAP's autonomy (from the government and other activist organizations) helped it avoid pitfalls associated with government-sponsored antipoverty programs.[17] By the mid-1960s years of activist agitation by civil rights workers had forced the U.S. government to create programs to address poverty and racism in urban areas across the country. These programs provided essential resources for individuals and families in the form of Head Start programs, free lunch programs, and financial help for mothers and their children. At the same time, the projects also contained and co-opted activist strategies. Civil rights activists—both white and Black—who had received little or no money for their activism in the 1950s and 1960s were often, by the mid-1960s, seeking paying jobs that in one way or another seemed to carry on work done within civil rights organizations. Not surprisingly, activists who took paid positions frequently found themselves within hierarchies that reinforced the very class and race dynamics that the Movement sought to undermine. The class and race contradictions white activists faced within bureaucracies often severely compromised an antiracist agenda.

Reebee Garofalo found a position as a director of an urban youth program serving several cities, in large part because of his experience working with SNCC. Although those who hired him never said so explicitly, Reebee was among many white activists who obtained leadership positions in the social service sector because they were *white* and had experience working with SNCC—sometimes supervising Black activists who had as much or more experience. Reebee's race and class privilege helped get him to Yale University, where he was recruited by SNCC workers for Freedom Summer. That same race and class privilege—along with invaluable experience gained by working with SNCC activists—helped him get the position of director in an urban program ostensibly set up to empower young people of color.

Although Reebee believes that the work he did with inner-city youth programs was important and that he brought skills to the work, he found it increasingly impossible to live with the contradiction of being a white guy going into cities to train people of color to work with other people of color. He says, "The notion of me, this white kid, going into places like Flint, Michigan, and Detroit and Cleveland to train all-Black staffs how to work with Black inner-city kids just seemed totally nuts to me." Eventually he resolved this political contradiction by going to graduate school, a path taken by other civil rights activists unsure about what step to take in the late 1960s.

Dottye Burt-Markowitz also spoke of painful contradictions she faced as a working-class white woman holding a position as a social worker in New York City. Although she wanted a job that would enable her to work for justice, she came to see multiple ways in which the very structure of this job worked against that vision. After growing up in East St. Louis, Illinois, in the 1940s and 1950s, Dottye moved to New York City in 1967 and began working for the Department of Social Services. She quickly saw that one policy after another discriminated against the Black, Puerto Rican, and Haitian families with whom she was working. She came to know the families quite well, since she made it her business to spend time with them in their homes and neighborhoods. As Dottye recalls, "This was the heyday of the welfare rights movement, so a lot of very positive changes in terms of the welfare movement were being made. It was as good as it was ever going to get. But it was still hideous."

During the years Dottye worked in New York, she quickly developed her own code of ethics to make the system work for the families instead of against them. At that time in welfare history there was enough play in the system that she could find ways to do that. For example, the department had a rule against granting moving expenses if the father of the family got a job in another area of the country. This policy meant the family could continue to receive welfare benefits only if it split up. Dottye found a way to get moving expenses for families: by calling them something different. She wrote a grant to pay for a mother to fly to Puerto Rico to be with her sick child, even though she couldn't be candid about how that grant was being used. Dottye had to work independently most of the time because other caseworkers were more interested in complying with the existing rules than Dottye felt comfortable with ethically. She got much support from the families with whom she worked; they clearly saw that she cared about them and was interested in getting them what they needed for their children.

A pivotal experience for Dottye occurred during a protest by families against welfare policies, a protest that included the takeover of the Department of Social Services building. When Dottye heard people had taken over the building and were not letting the caseworkers go home, she thought she would have no problem; the families she worked with respected her. They would understand she was not part of the problem, and they would let her out. But when she proceeded to the first floor to leave, Coke bottles flew by her head; the protesters clearly had no intention of letting her out. She did not see any of the families she knew, but she quickly realized that even if she did, they would be just a handful among hundreds who had never met her and who saw her first and foremost as a white social worker and therefore part of the problem. This is when Dottye realized that to be an effective ally, she could not afford to ignore the fact that she is white and that being known and trusted by one group of Black, Latino, or Haitian people did not mean that all people of color knew and trusted her. In this instance and many others, she was by definition part of the problem. She came to understand that trust was a quality she needed to earn. It was not something to be assumed or taken for granted. The scene in the Department of Social Services building showed her that programs that are supposed to help poor people and people of color often function in ways that undermine them. Furthermore, her whiteness was not something she could check at the door or dismiss.

The contradiction Dottye was up against—wanting to support poor families and yet being part of a structure that undermines them—is a conundrum white activists faced continually. White workers in SNCC were not immune to it. ERAP workers were not immune to it. Of the pervasiveness of this contradiction, former SDS activist Marilyn Buck says, "White people might go into communities in the South, for good reasons, voter registration and things, but by not really understanding, step on toes. The toes not only of the white opposition but also in the name of the Black people you say you are helping. Are you helping someone or are you in solidarity? I think there is a big difference. What I call the social worker mentality. A social worker mentality can co-opt a culture. United States society is a master at co-optation."

For white people in SDS and other New Left organizations, understanding their position as white people meant grappling with the distinction between "helping" and "standing in solidarity." Marilyn Buck learned this distinction through mistakes. In the late 1960s Marilyn was the coeditor of *New Left Notes*—SDS's newspaper—and worked in the SDS national office in Chicago (what she calls her "tendency toward being a bureaucratic hack"). Marilyn had "heard about the Freedom Wall on the south side of Chicago that had been painted by the SNCC office and where the old SDS office had been. We [she and another SDS activist] wanted to write an article about it and put it in *New Left Notes*. So we were going down to take a picture of it. This other young woman was even less conscious of things than me, much more from a petit bourgeois background than me. We got there around four on a winter afternoon, so it is getting dark and I get out of the car to take the picture. I am getting ready to get back in the car and this young Black woman comes and says, 'What the fuck are you doing?' I said, 'We are from SDS and are taking pictures of the wall because we are writing an article.' She said, 'Who the hell gave you permission to take pictures of our wall?' Well, we said that we support the Black liberation struggle. My consciousness wasn't there. I am a very white girl. She said that I couldn't have the pictures. We had this pushing and shoving. She tore my purse. A crowd started gathering. A young man came over from the SNCC office. He interceded. I gave the film back and we left and the situation was diffused. But I was frightened. I was mind-boggled. I had to really think about it. It didn't come to me at the time. I was incensed. I mean I support the Black movement. We are just trying to build solidarity."

This was the first time that Marilyn came "face to face with self-determination. Who gets to set the terms of how to help somebody or how to be supportive of someone? On the one hand, it became liberating. On the other hand, it became an inhibitory thing, because it meant I had to be conscious all of the time. On the most personal, experiential level, it made me think about what self-determination was and that white people can't set the terms. We can't just say we are antiracist and do what we think is right in a given situation. Sometimes you go into a situation and it is hard to know what is right. There are contending forces in the Black community as well. There is always a multiplicity of contending forces. Where do you line up? Where is your heart? Your mind? Your body? That is the difficult part of practically anything we do in life. In the world of social change and the possibility of human liberation, all those abstractions are actually very real. Hard to put names to them unless you write a poem and write about something specific."

Anti–Vietnam War Protests

The first national protest against the Vietnam War, in 1965, attracted 25,000 people, in large part because of student organizing. Perhaps the most successful of SDS's many efforts, antiwar organizing grew in power and intensity as the 1960s progressed. Students held teach-ins across the country, at small liberal arts schools and Big Ten universities. Students protested university involvement in war research and rallied against universities that provided class rankings to the Selective Service for use in the draft. In 1967 SDS and other antiwar groups organized "Stop the Draft" weeks on college campuses, whose activities included the burning of draft cards. By the end of 1969, 34,000 men had refused to be inducted, and between 50,000 and 100,000 "deserters" had fled to western Europe and Canada.[18] Draft card burning was soon coupled with massive antidraft counseling that publicized ways to avoid going to war and the political importance of resistance. Draft resisters included conscientious objectors who opposed the war as pacifists as well as those Marilyn Buck calls the "Hell no, I won't fight a U.S. imperialist war" resisters.

As the war escalated—in spite of a parallel escalation of protests nationwide and the increasing number of people opposing it—students often led the way in adopting creative methods of protesting. They performed guerilla theater on the streets, organized rallies that included civil disobedience, and reached out to people who were not familiar with antiwar activism (including the annual influx of new students). Vietnam veterans also provided some of the most powerful opposition to the war. Ray Luc Levasseur, a state organizer in Maine for Vietnam Vets against the War, came back from Vietnam enraged by the U.S.-sponsored war. Ray explains, "I enlisted in the Army in 1967. I went to Vietnam and I served a full tour of duty, twelve months. And what I saw there was another side of war. Not some Hollywood production, not some Rambo type of thing that they feed young guys so they can manipulate them into the military and use them. I saw another side of United States foreign policy. Bombings, killings, search and destroy, devastation, poverty, hunger. I was part of a foreign occupation army. I saw human rights violations when I was there, and I saw violations of international law. . . . I was trained to kill. And I was fully armed and sent to Vietnam. You know, there's a lot of vets who came back with post-Vietnam stress disorder. I've worked with those veterans. I didn't suffer any mental illness or syndromes when I came back. I came back enraged by what I saw. To see open and blatant racism by white American soldiers towards Vietnamese people because of the colour of their skin, or their religion, or their culture, their language, was shocking to me. I had never seen anything that devastating."[19]

It was largely because of the Vietnam War that many activists first began using the term "anti-imperialist" to describe their politics. The anti-imperialist agenda recognized that people in the United States were, by virtue of paying taxes, financing what was becoming a permanent war economy. Militarism was big money for the defense industry, and taxpayers were footing the bill. By calling themselves "anti-imperialists," activists were asserting that global capitalism—in which First World nations controlled the economies of Third World countries—was held together in part by the threat or use of military power by colonizing nations.

Some antiwar protesters coupled their critique of capitalism and militarism with a political analysis that treated the war in Vietnam as a race issue: A First World white nation was bombing (and attempting to destroy) a Third World nation. The term "anti-imperialism" included opposition to the government that was applying anti-Asian racism to justify the war. U.S. officials consistently claimed that the Vietnamese placed less value on human life than did U.S. citizens. Meanwhile, members of the U.S. armed forces were taught to decimate the Vietnamese countryside. On the side of one U.S. plane was emblazoned the motto "Only you can prevent forests."[20] When a reporter asked a U.S. doctor about the Hippocratic oath—after the doctor had boasted that he had refused to treat wounded Vietnamese—the doctor replied, "Yeah, I took it in America."[21] Soldiers learned the U.S. military policy: The only way to protect a village is to destroy it. This and a plethora of other policies treated the Vietnamese as subhuman.

Like the early boycotts of segregated businesses, opposition to the Vietnam War was an issue that linked SDS and SNCC. Both groups were among the earliest activist organizations to oppose the war. Both groups refused to buy into the notion that U.S. involvement in Vietnam was intended to stop communism. Both groups had long since rejected anticommunist rhetoric in general, including that which the government used to justify the war. Early on, SNCC also stood against the war (before the Southern Christian Leadership Conference [SCLC] and other more moderate civil rights groups) both because of the disproportionate number of African Americans who were being drafted and sent to the front lines and because of the many political connections SNCC saw between people of color in the United States and people in Third World countries. SNCC's position statement against the Vietnam War stated, "We take note of the fact that 16% of the draftees from this country are Negroes called on to stifle the liberation of Vietnam, to preserve a 'democracy' which does not exist at home."[22]

Some SDS leaders highlighted that connection as well, able to show the hypocrisy of a government willing to spend millions of dollars to send men to Vietnam while dragging its feet in providing money and other resources to support the civil rights struggle. At an antiwar rally in 1965, Carl Oglesby, president of SDS, asked, "This country, with its thirty-some years of liberalism, can send 200,000 young men to Vietnam to kill and die in the most dubious of wars, but it cannot get 100 voter registrars to go into Mississippi. What do you make of it?"[23] Media footage of the carnage in Vietnam was on a par with footage of police using fire hoses on school children in the South: Both galvanized hundreds of thousands of people to rally for dramatic social change. For a growing number of activists, the two assaults went hand in hand.

We All Fall Down

Despite the white New Left's many accomplishments in rallying against the war nationally, its emphasis on the war also signaled a retreat from a domestic antiracist agenda. Although the anti-imperialist framework recognized U.S. racism directed at the Vietnamese, typically it did not include significant attention to how race shaped the strategies and direction of antiwar protest in the United States. David Gilbert was a founding member of the Columbia University SDS and wrote the first SDS pamphlet on "U.S. imperialism." Retrospectively, he sees many contradictions embedded in white activism that conceived of itself as "anti-imperialist": "As the Vietnam war escalated and we became aware of international struggles, we started to call ourselves 'anti-imperialists,' but this was a struggle within SDS. In 1965, SDS leadership defined the system as 'corporate liberalism.'. . . From the late 1960s on the overall term we used to call ourselves was 'anti-imperialist' because that seemed to best summarize the system. However, as it turned out, the anti-racism was too shallow. There was a lot of support engendered for anti-imperialism in the sense of foreign wars only because of fear of the draft. But it was harder to get people to deal with the structures of white supremacy much closer to home."[24] The anti-imperialist language presented the victimized people of color as living "over there" in a foreign country. The people of color that white antiwar protesters held themselves accountable to were far more distant than were the Black people that white SNCC activists interacted with on a daily basis.

The white student–led protests against the war also did little to reach out to people of color and working-class white people—those who made up a disproportionate percentage of the draft. Stan Markowitz, who grew up in a working-class home, had an ambivalent relationship with SDS because of the class bias in the organization. He says, "A whole lot of working-class people were going into the military. There was all this self-righteousness about how someone who did that was a baby killer. I don't think that [accusation] played in the same way in the African American community or communities of color as it did in the white, middle-class community. That term 'baby killer' didn't play well in the white, working-class community either. To oppose the war was one thing. To trash the people fighting was quite another—to not recognize the circumstances that would lead a working-class kid to go into the military." Although several studies have shown that working-class people were even more likely to oppose the war than were middle- and upper-class people, working-class opposition did not typically mean working-class people could avoid the draft.[25]

Antiwar protesters typically presented U.S. soldiers as the agents of the U.S. government's war—the enemy. Those working-class young people—both white and of color—who could not get a student deferment to avoid the draft or who saw the army as a viable ticket to eventually getting a college education were then on the opposite side of the picket line from the white middle-class students protesting the war. This divide was the opposite of a progressive political alliance across race. Anne Braden sees the organizing against the Vietnam War as one of many times when African Americans went off the radar screen of white New Left activists: "There was work against the Vietnam War in the Black community, but these white peace activists often didn't know how to relate to it. They didn't know how to relate to Black people." This lack of knowledge often extended to Chicano antiwar activism as well. Most white antiwar activists, for example, had little or no real connection with the Brown Berets, a Mexican American activist group. They organized the Chicano Moratorium Rally against the Vietnam War in 1969, which was attended by at least 20,000 people, and a march in East Los Angeles in 1970, during which police assaulted the protesters and killed Ruben Salazar, who was a member of the Brown Berets and a well-known Chicano journalist.[26]

Race and class assumptions in antiwar protesting are also echoed in Suzanne Ross's critique of the Indochinese peace campaign of the early 1970s. During this period Suzanne was involved in several activist projects: protesting university firings of radical faculty (including herself), organizing against the war, and advocating for Black youth in health care and in public schools. She was also working with Tom Hayden and many others on the Indochinese peace campaign. By the early 1970s, she recalls, "The all-white formations of many antiwar organizations were beginning to drive me crazy. There is always this breaking point where something happens and you cross that line. That breaking point for me was the Indochinese peace campaign, which I was involved in from 1972 to 1974. Tom Hayden and Jane Fonda were both involved, and they had a fair amount of experience with Black people from what I could gather. Tom had been in Newark, where he had been denounced for coming in as a white person. Amiri Baraka had criticized him for 'flying in as a white person.' The Indochinese peace campaign was all white except, of course, for some Chinese and Cambodians. The whiteness of the peace campaign began to drive me really crazy. It wasn't just their whiteness. It was also their politics. It was not rooted in the oppression of this country and in understanding that ultimately our job, which the Cubans and Vietnamese had always told us, was to build a revolutionary movement in this country. You don't just support the Vietnamese without being conscious of who you are bringing together and how. It was aimed completely at white congressmen."

In 1974 Suzanne went to an Indochina peace conference in Pittsburgh, just after attending a huge rally for the independence of Puerto Rico at Madison Square Garden in New York City. Suzanne moved that the conference endorse the Puerto Rican rally, a position that was quickly voted down. Suzanne remembers, "One of the arguments was that Puerto Rico was a New York issue. That was the whiteness. Anti-imperialists supposedly fighting the war in Vietnam and not understanding that Puerto Rico should have its independence." Suzanne was troubled by a campaign that saw the enemy as "out there"—in this instance, the U.S. government—but had not developed a multiracial antiwar movement in the United States. Most SDS activists had little or no contact with the Young Lords Party in New York and Chicago, which in the late 1960s established clinics and schools, stood up against police brutality, opposed the Vietnam War, and were widely respected within Puerto Rican communities. Most white antiwar activists had little or no real connection with the Puerto Rican independence struggle that, in various forms, had been organizing against U.S. control of the island since the United States invaded it and made it a U.S. territory in 1898.[27] Like Anne Braden, Suzanne Ross believed an anti-imperialist stance was only as strong as its domestic antiracist stance. This was a dual focus that SDS and most other New Left organizations of the 1960s found very hard to achieve.

Another reason why SDS (and other antiwar activism groups) was not able to keep antiracism on its radar screen relates to male dominance within the organization. This hierarchy cramped the capacities of many white women, whose antiracist skills originally came from working with SNCC. Maggie Nolan Donovan explains, "There was a certain white male arrogance about some SDS people that I think precluded them from not being at the top of the power position. You know, certain men that came out of SDS to this day have an incredible white privilege arrogance. . . . A political landscape that doesn't have them at the center is very hard for them to accept. . . . I think it was very hard for them to get out of their own way in that sense. Whereas women in both organizations were much more prepared to work collaboratively. They did not have this investment in heroics and their individual identities as movers and shakers." In Maggie's experience, male ego precluded some white men from working with white antiracist women as well as with men and women of color, a reality that greatly hampered cross-race alliances.

Based on her years working with SDS, Marilyn Buck believes that men's sexism often hindered their recognition of women's intellectual and political contributions. To this day, Marilyn believes there are "issues of hierarchy that men can't see." Recently, for example, Marilyn has had particular difficulties with a "comrade man in prison." As she describes it, "The man talks well to all the women. Is polite to all the women. But I think any time you want to go head-to-head politically or intellectually, or challenge or criticize, he just reminds me of the guys in SDS."

By the time SNCC, SDS, and other groups came out against the Vietnam War, the number of political connections between SDS and SNCC was impressive. Many early SDS leaders also worked with SNCC. Both groups shared hopes for community organizing among poor white people, believed in young people as the driving force behind radical political change, refused to bow down to anticommunist rhetoric, and were committed to nonviolence and democracy.

Ironically, these shared commitments, noteworthy in themselves, render even more troubling the number of ways that antiracism went off the radar screen of white New Left organizing. Although there were early alliances between SDS and SNCC activists, the New Left had a hard time establishing and maintaining an antiracist agenda. Each of the SDS projects involved contradictions that undermined antiracism. Eric Mann, who was in SDS, explains, "There were some chapters that were just white, white, white. Places like Smith and Amherst were just totally white. But at Columbia University and in Harlem there was a real antiracist component. There were wings of SDS that were very aligned with the Panthers, the Young Lords, which came out of New York City, and the Puerto Rican revolutionary movement. So there were some places where there was more vibrancy to the antiracist politics. . . . Then there were places where Black Power, which had its strengths and its weaknesses, left white kids trying to figure out what it means to be antiracist in an all-white context. And that is, historically, as they would say, problematic."

David Wellman, who was a member of SDS in the mid-1960s, recalls, "There were very few white people in SDS who were arguing with SDS about race issues from the left. There were very few who were arguing that SDS had to be involved in antiracism—that they couldn't just be involved in student stuff." SDS was an overwhelmingly white organization that never developed a sustained analysis of how its racial makeup—and its often weak or nonexistent connection with Black and Latino organizations—might stand in the way of keeping antiracism central.

The fact that there is more retrospective analysis of white privilege in SNCC than in SDS and other northern activism is telling, particularly since the New Left was overwhelmingly white while SNCC was primarily Black. What might, in the abstract, be reasonable to assume— that a critique of whiteness in SDS would be possible because of the sheer number of white members—seemed to have worked against any such analysis. For example, in his memoir, *Reunion,* Tom Hayden is much more facile in criticizing his sexism and homophobia (and that of many SDS members) than he is about racism. Even though the first half of his book is about his involvement in the civil rights struggle, there is almost no critical analysis about how whiteness—white ways of doing things, white assumptions, white privilege—shaped organizing. And yet Hayden strives to evaluate the sexism within SDS. The northern understanding of racism through the mid-1960s as a largely southern problem may have also contributed to a dearth of attention to the way the white makeup of the northern groups influenced their agenda. The whiteness of SDS appears to have played a major role in rendering whiteness invisible.

1968 and Onward: Got to Be Willing to Give Up Everything

By 1968 debates about strategy and philosophy raged within and around SDS. Activists tried to respond to widespread violence, often government sponsored, including the military assault during the Newark rebellion in 1967 and the police assault on protesters at the Democratic National Convention in Chicago in 1968. The United States continued to profess that it was winning the war in Vietnam despite the Tet Offensive in 1968.[28] COINTELPRO, the FBI program that led an extensive program to destroy Black, Latino, and Native American organizing from 1956 through the 1970s, continued to harass and kill movement leaders while infiltrating their organizations.[29]

Splits in SDS partly developed in response to differing perspectives on what whites needed to do to fully participate in revolutionary change as confrontations between the U.S. government and activist organizations continued to escalate. Radical organizations were gaining ground within communities of color across the country, especially in urban areas, and the government knew it. The Black Panther Party, which was founded by Bobby Seale and Huey P. Newton in Oakland, California, in 1966, set up an expansive, community-based ten-point plan to organize for land, food, jobs, education, and peace. Their projects included setting up breakfast programs for schoolchildren, supporting independent Black schools and health care clinics, providing legal and material aid to prisoners, and organizing against police harassment and brutality. Their militancy was rooted in a belief that Black people needed economic and political power and that they could not wait for the white government to decide when and if they would grant it.[30]

While the media was showing images of Black Panthers carrying guns and verbally standing up to the police (and the government was exploiting these images to justify repression of the group), what was really destabilizing to white authorities was the Panthers' growing appeal and influence among urban working-class Black youth across the country, its willingness to work with white radicals, and its synergistic relationship to Native American and Latino (Chicano and Puerto Rican) activists. The 1967 founding of the Brown Berets in Los Angeles signaled increasing radicalism among Chicanos. Black Power made sense to Chicano activists who were facing constant police surveillance in their communities, substandard education, and inadequate health care. The 1968 founding by Dennis Banks, George Mitchell, and Mary Jane Wilson of the American Indian Movement (AIM), with its emphasis on self-defense and education and its struggle to end the Bureau of Indian Affairs occupation of Indian land, paralleled many aspects of the Panthers. For Native American activists the Black Power emphasis on self-determination and autonomy dovetailed with the centuries of struggle for sovereignty and the recognition of treaties with the U.S. government.[31]

The Black Panthers, the American Indian Movement (AIM), the Brown Berets, the Young Lords, and other militant groups inspired and influenced each other. The Panther position was that they were willing to work with anybody and everybody, of any race, who supported their goals. Although many of the ties among and between groups were informal, there were activists who traveled between the movements with a willingness to seek out shared agendas.[32]

The increasingly multiracial tone and tenor of the activism threatened the white power structure that had long tried to separate activism among communities of color. The government responded to this multiracial organizing with a devastating crackdown on Black, Latino, and Native American activists as well as white allies. Within this context, although some activists continued to maintain a nonviolent orientation, many began to believe that a new level of risk taking was required.[33] By 1969 what had long been thought of as the Student Nonviolent Coordinating Committee was painfully referred to by SNCC leader Rap Brown as the Nonstudent Violent Coordinating Committee. The nonviolence SNCC had considered as its bedrock was now seen as sand as SNCC's strength was eroded.[34] By 1968 increasing debates in SDS about militancy reflected a rise in militancy among college students in general. By 1970 "a Gallop Poll of college students indicated that 44 percent felt violence was justified to bring about social change in the United States while 37 percent described themselves politically as 'far left' or 'left.'"[35] Wini Breines writes, "The guilt, horror, and frustration compelled the leadership of SDS, and of the New Left, to become more militant, angry, and revolutionary in ideology."[36]

Within SDS one sector of activists argued that the group's priority must be on building a majority-based movement of working-class people through nonviolent, grassroots organizing. Another group based their analysis on the developing notion of white-skin privilege. David Wellman observes, "There was a group of people within SDS with whom I was aligned who were analyzing American politics in terms of white-skin privilege. We made the argument that white-skin privilege is the central contradiction in American society." The logic of this perspective was that white-skin privilege had historically divided working-class whites and Blacks. Therefore, the white working class could not be the foundation of a revolutionary party. If activists were going to be effective, they had to be willing to use militant tactics. This sector, as David Gilbert explains it, "supported the perspective that the struggle against racism was a life-and-death struggle that mandated militancy." White people needed to work in parallel organizations alongside Black militant organizations domestically and with liberation movements in Third World countries to bring down white supremacy.

Key to this position was an awareness that white privilege continued to protect white activists from much of the violence leveled at Black Panthers and American Indian Movement members. As COINTELPRO continued to step up its assault on activist leaders, a faction of people within SDS began to argue that they could no longer back a revolution theoretically and yet be unwilling to take physical risks to support it. By 1968 SDS activist David Gilbert "had come to believe that I couldn't be the one to say, it is necessary for Third World people to fight and die for their very survival and future and then not take those risks myself."

David had grown up in a white, middle-class suburb of Boston where "health care, good education, and economic security were pretty much guaranteed." David was a "believer in democracy and the myth that there was equal opportunity for all. That myth was exploded for me at the age of fifteen, with the 1960 Greensboro North Carolina sit-in. Not only did the growing Civil Rights Movement expose the disgusting racism and inequality, but it also served as an inspiring example because of its humane sense of purpose, its strong sense of community, and the hopefulness that it generated."[37]

While a student at Columbia University, David began working in Harlem, "a huge politicizing moment in my life. In Harlem, I saw many of the community's strengths—the vitality of extended families and sense of community, the dynamic music, and a liveliness that stood in direct contrast to the individualism and alienation I experienced in the suburb where I grew up. My recognition of the community's strength is not intended to romanticize Harlem, because there were certainly troubles, but the vitality I saw contrasted dramatically with the public imagery I had seen before working there."

By 1969 David had come to realize that he was willing to risk his life for justice. He deeply respected the Black Panthers' comprehensive mission and was outraged by the state murders of Panthers and other Black activists. He was also devastated by the photographs of Vietnamese children running from napalm and the enormous human loss resulting from the war in Indochina. The greatest violence David saw "was the violence done by the social system." And yet it was traumatic for him to wrestle with "how it is possible for people to keep their moral bearings if they let go of pacifism." He remembers asking himself if letting go of pacifism would "lead down the path of Stalin." Would embracing armed struggle lead to abuse of power and brutality? Over time, he and others in SDS began to answer that question with fellow activists as they made distinctions between revolutionary and reactionary violence and then tried to make their actions reflect these distinctions. Revolutionary violence had to clearly focus on the top sources of power and take the greatest care to minimize violence and avoid harm to innocent and random civilians. Revolutionaries should also avoid actions that established the power and prestige of their organization without fighting oppression.

The rhetoric of the more militant faction of SDS signaled an attempt by young people to stop falling back on the race and class privileges that had so far protected them in ways Black activists had not been insulated. David was among those who helped organize the 1968 student protest at Columbia, the largest student rebellion of the 1960s, lasting three days and resulting in seven hundred arrests. Yet David was critical of the safety he found, even in that role, as a white, middle-class man. He says, "In a way, being a campus radical was comfortable. One could benefit from the prestige of taking a high moral ground without the costs and challenges of direct confrontation with the power structure." David saw himself needing to be more willing to fight against the system, even if that meant making sacrifices. For him, this required being willing to be part of an armed struggle that was international in scope. "This was a historical period in which there were multiple, powerful, Third World struggles and hundreds of thousands of people participating in resisting arrest and opposing the war. One of the most striking things about this period was that history was moving very quickly. People were winning revolutionary change, and the change felt palpable."

The Weather Underground

By 1969 SDS had split in two over which tactics most closely reflected the political realities of the time. Of the several small, white-led organizations that saw armed struggle as a necessary component of activism, the most visible was the Weather Underground.[38] The Weather Underground (whose name came from the saying, "You don't need a weatherman to tell you which way the wind blows") was founded in 1969 by SDS members who no longer saw legislative change, nonviolent collective protest, or reform policies as politically effective. The Weather Underground drew upon many sources to help guide their strategies: the speeches and politics of Ho Chi Minh, Fidel Castro, Black Panther leaders, and Frantz Fanon. Their analysis of the futility of reformist strategy relied in part on the work of Herbert Marcuse and his concept of "repressive tolerance": by "allowing certain non-confrontational forms of dissent, the state could continue its policies while providing a safety valve for those who disagreed with them. This safety valve placated the opposition without challenging the power of the state."[39] The militants' tactics, some of which were illegal, forced the Weather Underground to become clandestine. Their purpose, according to David Gilbert, was to create another "front" of militancy so that the military and police could not concentrate all their forces against the Black Liberation Army (BLA); Fuerza Amanda Liberacion Nacional (Armed Forces of National Liberation, FALN), a Puerto Rican independence organization; and AIM.[40] By creating a clear and visible pole of white revolutionaries that fought militantly in support of people of color, the Weather Underground intended to show that there were many ways to continue to fight against government repression.

White activists of the late 1960s and early 1970s who took the path of militancy have been criticized from several directions: by former members of the white New Left; by the media, which has largely treated this group as a bunch of idealistic, self-destructive crazies; and by historical accounts, which have typically reduced these groups to footnotes.[41] The fact that many in this group were imprisoned has also contributed to the lack of information about it.[42]

I began my research on this sector of white activism with a troubling combination of naïveté, untethered misinformation about the groups, and fear that a serious consideration of militancy might shake my previous nonviolent stance. I mistakenly assumed that those who were the political prisoners in this country were Black, Puerto Rican, or Native American—Mumia Abu-Jamal, Elizam Escobar, Leonard Peltier, and others.[43] I had not thought of white people as political prisoners—embarrassing but true. After interviewing people who were members of or supported the Weather Underground and other militant organizations, I learned that some of the most principled and committed antiracists in the country are now in prison because of their activism. I also began to discover that there has been little attempt to offer an even and in-depth analysis of the Weather Underground's philosophy vis-à-vis antiracist activism and white privilege.

Part of what is compelling about the Weather Underground is what their tactics reveal about the conundrums white people faced in their attempts to organize against racism. David Gilbert says, "As a white organization, we did actions that took advantage of our invisibility: in the seats of power—i.e., bombings of government and corporate buildings and obtaining large sums of money through robbery. Even going underground to fight, we had many advantages. We had a much larger population to blend into. There was much less likelihood of routine police stops and checks." According to David, "It is a powerful lesson about racism that, even when taking on the high level of commitment of building an underground, there was such a big relative cushion of white privilege. We had access to more sources of funds, including middle-class friends—which means we didn't require high-risk bank robberies (which is the way many Black Liberation Army comrades fell)." The Weather Underground sought to help fund a movement that had essentially been defunded. Liberal support of SNCC and other radical Black organizations declined significantly when SNCC refused to give up its autonomy in decision making. White funding for the Black Panthers never even came close to the financial support afforded to SNCC and SCLC. The Weather Underground recognized this discrepancy and saw countering it as one of its core responsibilities.

David believes the Weather Underground's most important accomplishment was piercing the myth of government invisibility. From 1969 to 1976, the Weather Underground carried out multiple acts of sabotage on government and corporate buildings. It also raised funds for BLA and Black political prisoners and funded Black-controlled community projects. David believes the group's other main achievement was the political example they made about fighting in solidarity with Third World struggles. "Our practice in this area was inconsistent and inadequate, but we did succeed at times in making it a visible priority. The logic was that the willingness of the Weather Underground to put their lives on the line would push other white radicals to make a similar commitment, to the point where the government would have to really sit up and take notice."

According to Suzanne Ross, who worked closely with the Weather Underground for many years, the organization "made a tremendous contribution in what the Vietnamese called 'armed propaganda.' I didn't think of it as armed struggle. I think the whole idea of calling it that was exaggerated. Armed struggle is when you are involved in an open military battle. These were very targeted attacks against the enemies, total symbols." From Suzanne's perspective, millions of people supported the bombings. "The relationship between the overground and the underground was phenomenal. When the United States bombed Vietnam, threatening to bomb its dikes and killing several million people in Southeast Asia, people were feeling so powerless. Some of the demonstrations at the time had a million people. With all that, the war didn't stop. You wanted to attack the enemy on a level that they couldn't fight back either. Those bombings signified that." According to Suzanne, the idea was that "if you could attack the enemy—the U.S. government—from all sides and have people demonstrate against them while some people were arrested and some people used armed propaganda, then the government would have to take the movement seriously." When Laos was invaded, for example, people led protests on multiple fronts with the lines understandably blurred about what was "legal" and "illegal" activity. From Suzanne's perspective, "All those kinds of actions strengthened the movement and were inspiring."[44]

Suzanne believes the Weather Underground should be recognized for the risks its members took at a time when little seemed to be deterring the government. "For that time and period, for the level of crime that the United States was committing and the kind of mass movement that could understand those actions," the armed propaganda was very important. "The problem with the Weather Underground was not that it was too militant or that it was prematurely involved in armed actions. . . . When you go into real revolutionary struggle, armed revolutionary struggle, then you can't say you are not going to kill anyone. That is ridiculous. If you are the Vietnamese fighting for independence, for example. I used to hate the Christian religious groups who would denounce the Vietnamese. They wanted the United States out of Vietnam, but they were against both sides because both sides were using guns. Come on. I was at many meetings when the revolutionaries of Vietnam were denounced for using armed struggle. That is insane to me. I am not saying that anybody should just kill anybody. It better be the right time and worth it and not some jive bullshit. But that is not what the Weather Underground was doing. It was engaged in armed propaganda to highlight who the enemy is and the nature of the enemy."

Suzanne's position about the realities of violence during revolutionary struggle illuminates a key question that militants struggled with during that period. Do white people have a moral obligation to take risks commensurate with those taken by Black, Native American, and Latino activists who are under assault? Of his position on the use of violence in the Brinks robbery in particular and by militants in general, David Gilbert writes, "During our trial, we were besieged by attacks on armed struggle—of course from the mainstream, but also, in various forms, from within the Left. We felt embattled, and we in turn were very dogmatic in treating armed struggle as the principle rather than as one of the necessary means to fight to stop oppression. On a personal level, I regret that we weren't capable of expressing publicly a feeling of loss and pain for the families of the two officers and the guard who were killed. Even in a battle for a just cause, we can't lose our feeling for the human element. It's not like these three men were picked as targets for being especially heinous or conscious enforcers of the system. Rather, they just happened to be the representatives of the state's and bank's armed forces who responded on that day. So it must have felt like a completely senseless and bitter loss to their families. On our side, Mtayari Shabaka Sundiata was gunned down by police two days later, an irreparable loss of a committed and courageous BLA warrior. . . . The cost of errors that are made in the course of armed struggle are very visible. It is a lot of responsibility."[45]

At the same time, David believes it is a "shame that the very grave errors of inaction, of not fighting hard enough, are rarely even noticed. What were the costs, in terms of violence, of the terrible passivity of most of the white Left during the FBI and police campaigns of the 1960s and 1970s, whose acts of annihilation against Black liberation resulted in the murder of dozens of Black activists and the decimation of the movement that has been the spearhead for social change in the U.S.? What was the toll from radicals' inaction while the FBI orchestrated the murders of sixty-nine AIM members and supporters around the Pine Ridge Reservation in the three years after the high tide of resistance there?" (39–40).

From David's perspective, the power of key U.S. institutions must be accounted for when discussing militancy. David writes that the corporate media is very effective in manipulating "the most humane of emotions. Whenever enforcers of the system, or its allies, are hurt, they are presented, most vividly, with the human reality of their lives and the grieving of their families. But there is a terrible media silence about the far, far greater number of innocent victims of imperialist violence. They are not considered human beings; they are relegated to limbo, considered nonentities, by a media that simply presses the erase button on the video equipment" (40).

Despite the position on accountability that the Weather Underground attempted to uphold, its approach was limited in multiple ways, each of which reflects difficulties that white people have always encountered when attempting to do antiracist work. One mistake, according to David, is that the militants abdicated their responsibility to organize a large number of white people to work with Third World struggles. Retrospectively, he believes that no organization can afford to "abandon our responsibility for organizing whites in an antiracist and revolutionary way."

In addition, the Weather Underground had difficulties defining the most politically effective relationship with Third World organizations. Its difficulties in this regard signaled two forms of racism. David believes that "in some periods, we just built our own organization, enjoying the greater resources and protection of being white without offering significant support to Black or Latino or Native armed struggle. The opposite end of this difficulty emerged when some ex–Weather Underground people decided to work under the direct leadership of a revolutionary Third World organization. The problem with this model is that by throwing our resources to one group within the Black liberation movement, we were in effect making a choice as to who should lead the New Afrikan Independence Movement. In effect, we developed a more 'service' relationship to the New Afrikan Independence Movement, which meant there were fewer political exchanges and engagement." He adds, "There was an edge of 'corruption' in the sense of ego and power for us whites in that we used a relationship with a heavy Black group to validate ourselves as the most revolutionary whites." David has concluded that white people need to find ways to take responsibility for some level of solidarity without, in effect, picking Black leadership.

David's retrospective account of the Weather Underground also reveals problems with the hierarchical structure of the organization. He suggests there were big problems with ego: People put their own leadership and power above the burning needs of qualitative change for oppressed people. "Very decent people, once in leadership, would become highly manipulative; former iconoclasts, once they became cadre, would abandon their critical faculties in order to curry favor with leadership. These patterns recurred so often that I think recriminations over which individuals were better or worse miss the point—there's been a deep problem around the process for building a revolutionary movement. By 'process' I mean how we conduct political discussion, how we make and implement policy decisions, how we treat each other as individuals. The [Leninist] theory of democratic-centralism sounded beautiful, but in my experience, the result was always overly hierarchical organizations. So I can only conclude that the theory itself is seriously flawed."

David believes the women's movement and Christian communities in Latin America present two examples of movements that consider top-down, authoritarian structures to be impediments to antiracist work. From his perspective, "It is very difficult to achieve, simultaneously, a disciplined combat organization and a fully democratic and humane process—yet both are emphatically necessary. There is an important sense in which we have to try to implement 'the personal is political': the ideals we express in our politics must also be put into practice in our human relationships."

Suzanne Ross agrees with David that the downfalls of the Weather Underground were its "whiteness and its self-centeredness." The fact that the Weather Underground was created as an all-white organization meant the leadership "had a tremendously exaggerated sense of itself." Suzanne believes there were many opportunities for working more closely with people of color. She knows people who to this day argue in support of all-white formations. She disagrees.

Although the Weather Underground talked about racism directed at Third World people as well as racism in the United States, Suzanne says that "it never talked about its own racism." The essential problem was that the Weather Underground's understanding of racism came from an anti-imperialist analysis. It saw Black people as an internal nation in the United States. Just as the United States was trying to conquer Vietnam, it had always colonized Black people within its own borders. Suzanne did not first come to her understanding of racism from understanding imperialism. "I came to it from having seen and worked with Black kids in a city hospital. Seeing how differently the psychiatrists in particular dealt with the white kids than the Black kids. There was once a white, middle-upper-class kid who came into the hospital because he had tried to hang himself. I still remember him. He was a blond kid, young, maybe thirteen or fourteen at the most. They started running around trying to do what they could to get him out of the hospital as quickly as possible, to get him into a private place. Now, dozens and dozens of Black kids had been admitted in equally serious conditions and nobody ran around to do nothing. If you were Black, you usually ended up going to state hospitals if you needed further treatment. If you were white, you ended up going to a private hospital. In my own way, I began to do a one-woman campaign to get the Black kids into the elite white hospitals. Now God knows what these white hospitals did to or with them but it became, I used to say that it was like getting kids into Harvard. I used to write these passionate reports. They were like novels about who these kids were, to send them to the more elite hospitals. They would get psychotherapy, not just medication." From this and many other scenes of racial inequity, Suzanne came to understand racism from the inside out rather than from the outside in, as she believes was the case for many people involved with the Weather Underground.

Suzanne also wonders why, if the Weather Underground really saw itself as leading a revolution, so few of its members are still active today. She asks, "Here are people who thought they were leading the revolution, but where are they now? The Black Panthers thought they were leading the revolution too, but a lot of the ex-Panthers are completely active today: Geronimo Pratt; Safiya Bukhari, who leads the political prisoner work in New York; Kathleen Cleaver; Dhoruba Bin Wahad. There are dozens and dozens of Panthers who are active today in whatever formation. Where is the Weather Underground? There are people like Naomi Jaffe, who is completely active. There is David

Gilbert, who is so strong in his politics, and others who are still in prison. But the people who did not go into prison, there isn't a strong voice that carries over. There isn't a strong voice among those who were the leaders who could say, maybe we didn't do it perfectly but that was a stage and this is what we are doing today. To have that vanish takes away from the history."

The challenges embedded in the Weather Underground's activism paralleled many of those faced by other white militants of that period. In the late 1960s and throughout the 1970s, Marilyn Buck worked with the Black liberation movement, activism that gave her the opportunity to think through the position of white people in relation to the Black liberation struggle. Marilyn says, "This was a time when we were really trying to come to terms with what we should do as white people." After working in the national SDS office in Chicago, Marilyn moved to Berkeley. She lived with two women who were working on a Civil Rights Movement paper that had once been a SNCC paper, so it still had strong connections with Black people. Marilyn remembers, "That opened some doors to where I started being around more Black people and hearing what they thought. It was 1968. Shortly after I got there is when Martin Luther King was murdered. Shortly after that was this birthday party for Huey Newton. It was this major event where Stokely Carmichael spoke and Rap Brown and Bobby Seale and other people from the Black Panther Party. Some of these things started to come together on an ideological level. Not on a practical level. So, as a young white person, you hear that you have to work with Black people but the Black people are saying, go work with your own people. So what did all this mean? I think it is still a difficult thing to deal with, because I think it is very hard for white people to become serious antiracists if they don't engage with other people. It is hard to just be an antiracist theoretically. You have to be able to engage with Black and Latino people or people who come from former colonies. So there are a number of contradictions with that."

With these contradictions staring at her, Marilyn "sort of floated" into working with Newsreel, an activist, community-based film company that produced and distributed films about revolutionary struggle. At the time, Newsreel was making a film about the Black Panthers. She moved into a house owned by a relative of one of the Black Panthers. Marilyn remembers, "We had this 'Free Huey Newton' sign on the front door. One night we opened the door and there were all these Black Panthers. . . . We started having these joint political education meetings reading Chairman Mao and others, which started a more political relationship with the Black Panther Party. We showed films and went to events such as union meetings of Black bus drivers. *The Battle of Algiers* was always a big film, as well as movies about Mozambique and then the Panther film when it was done. I did some high school organizing. In the midst of making a high school film, several of us ended up participating in a rally at a high school. We got arrested." During that period, there was much organizing among African Americans, Chicanos, and Asian Americans. Several Chicanos had been arrested for killing a police officer in San Francisco. The Red Guard, a Chinese organization, was also active. Marilyn remembers that during that time "there were a lot more intersections and a lot more arenas for struggle. There was a carving out of what self-determination means and what it means to be an antiracist."

For Marilyn, developing an antiracist, anti-imperialist consciousness meant taking the "steps necessary to make a revolution." Marilyn saw anti-imperialism and antiracism as inextricably linked, a position that meant working closely with activists of color in the United States while learning from activists seeking liberation in other countries— Vietnam, the Middle East, Cuba, Zimbabwe. She explains, "I think a number of us—Blacks, Latinos, Asians, and whites—were really guided by the concept of the heroic guerrilla and making a revolution. We tried really hard to make the conditions be what we thought they needed to be to make a revolution. On an ideological level and a practical level we felt we had to become guerrillas." For Marilyn, the revolution required militancy, which she defines as "a spirit of resistance of taking on the power structure, of taking on the state," and recognizing that one cannot work entirely within the system to bring about dramatic change. At that time, several dominantly white organizations were working alongside the Black Panthers. "There was a Berkeley collective . . . with Tom Hayden and Anne Scheer and other leftists with whom we all had big problems. They were so middle-class. They had more money. In Los Angeles, Hollywood in particular, there was a Friends of the Panthers group. The Peace and Freedom Party was also there to support the Black Panther Party in a more traditional political mode."

When a split in the Black Panther Party—a split that was fueled by COINTELPRO—led to the formation of the BLA, Marilyn continued to work with both Black Panther Party members who were later targeted as the Black Liberation Army. In 1973 she was arrested for buying two boxes of ammunition with false identification and sentenced to ten years in prison. About the irony of this trumped-up sentence, Marilyn explains, "At the same time Dean Martin's son was arrested in Los Angeles with a whole cache of military arms—illegal automatic weapons—and he was given probation. The police had me pegged as a white woman associated with the Black Liberation Army. They tried to pressure me, in that first period of arrests, to try to see if I would talk with the state and give them information." Marilyn was in prison for four years and then did not return from a furlough. She went underground for eight years, until she was arrested and convicted of conspiracy charges, which the government was "using against a conglomeration of white antiracist imperialists and folks from the New Afrikan Independence Movement." She is currently serving an eighty-year sentence. Marilyn is one of several political prisoners now incarcerated because of antiracist activism in solidarity with BLA and the Black Panthers, the Puerto Rican Independistas, Palestinian activists, anti-apartheid organizers, anti-Klan activists, and other women political prisoners and prisoners of war.

Ray Luc Levasseur's radicalism, like Marilyn Buck's, developed as a consequence of his increasing understanding of racism. For Ray lessons about racism began in Vietnam and continued as his politics grew more radical. His first political activism after returning from Vietnam was as a member of the Southern Student Organizing Committee (SSOC) in Tennessee. In 1969 he was set up by a police undercover agent and convicted of selling seven dollars' worth of marijuana. He was sentenced to five years in prison, a sentence that he considers retaliation for his political activism in Tennessee. He was sent to a locked-down prison at Brushy Mountain in Tennessee, where he remained from 1969 to 1971. While in prison he studied political theory and was labeled an agitator for leading a food strike by Black and white prisoners and defying the Jim Crow rules enforced in the food line, in recreation, and in bunking. He writes, "I went to Vietnam as a working-class stiff and returned a radical. I entered prison a radical and exited a revolutionary. War and prison can have that kind of effect."[46]

In a retrospective account of the change in consciousness he experienced as an antiwar protester, Ray explains, "About three decades ago as an organizer with Vietnam Veterans Against the War I encountered a startling realization—most Americans didn't care about a million and a half Vietnamese people dead from a hailstorm of U.S. bombs and bullets. The overwhelming majority of these deaths—civilian. Americans didn't seriously perk up to U.S. military casualties until the draft was expanded. What then caught their attention was body bags and broken bodies finding their way to suburbia with alarming frequency" (7). Ray came back to the United States with an honorable discharge to ask what he considers "the most seditious question of all: Why? Why is this government committing crimes in our name? Why were so many Black and Latino GI's over there told to do the killing and the fighting while the kids who have the money are going to the good schools in the United States? I wasn't coming back to a university. I was going to come back and face the prospect of going back and making some more heels for those shoes" in factories in Maine, where relatives of Ray's had long worked.[47]

With this race and class consciousness in mind, Ray began working in Maine with a community-based group, the Statewide Correctional Alliance for Reform (SCAR). Its primary focus was on prison issues: supporting a prison union, a bail fund, literacy programs in county jails, and Attica prison in New York. SCAR was an "adoption of what the Black Panther Party were doing at the time. Our motto was: serve the people. And our programmes were always free to the people we served. . . . We were involved in getting jobs for people. We were involved in getting temporary housing for people. We were involved in day care of children. We put out our own paper. We did support work for political prisoners. We monitored cases of police brutality in the community in which we lived" (19).

Ray also began working with Red Star North Bookstore, which provided radical books and literature to prisoners. From 1974 to 1984 he went underground to "build a revolutionary movement," which included supporting the African National Congress, liberation struggles in Central America, and activism against the escalation of the prison industry in the United States. In 1986 he was convicted in New York of actions carried out by the United Freedom Front (a militant antiracist organization) and sentenced to forty-five years in prison.[48] He was confined to control units in a maximum security prison in Marion, Illinois, for five years and in Florence, Colorado, for four and a half years and was recently shipped to a federal maximum security prison in Atlanta, Georgia.

Retrospective analyses of militant organizing suggest that those activists best able to sustain an anti-imperialist focus that also opposed racism domestically were those who had direct and constant contact with people of color. Suzanne Ross's point—that an anti-imperialist perspective needs to come from the inside out rather than from the outside in—is instructive. Over and over again, white activists directly link that dual focus to lessons they learned from Black activists. In one of his recent essays from prison, Ray Luc Levasseur writes about living and learning from Black prisoners, including Ralph Canady, an African American activist who was lynched in his cell in 1986. Ray first met Canady when they were both in prison in Tennessee in 1970. Ray remembers, "The day I met Ralph he gave me a copy of Fanon's *Wretched of the Earth,* and we easily fell into discussion about the Panthers, Stokely, Coltrane, Mingus, Marx, and jim crow. We talked about jim crow because the color line was rigidly drawn in Nashville. Rigidly drawn. The cells were segregated, the mess hall was segregated, recreation was segregated, and the pauper's cemetery at the rear of the penitentiary was segregated."[49] Ray was eventually punished severely for refusing to uphold this segregation. "A goon squad picked me up in the yard one day and a classification board determined that because I was 'agitating the racial situation,' it would be necessary to isolate me from the general population. So, as a first time offender doing two to five, I was placed in a cell on death row. The ultimate irony was that during the one hour a day I was let out of my cell to exercise, I was in the company of those prisoners scheduled to be executed—most of whom were Black. It was largely from these brothers that I came to understand the role of Malcolm X, Islam, poverty, culture, and Black history in the process of Black people's struggle for human rights" (1).

The Circle Was So Broken

Interpreting civil rights history from the mid-1950s through the early 1970s from the point of view of white antiracism illuminates two substantial turning points in terms of strategy and consciousness. The first occurred in the mid-1960s, when white people needed to help carry the antiracist baton already carried by people in SNCC and other Black-led organizations. When Blacks and whites in SNCC split in 1967, the essential issue was the future of Black self-determination and leadership. It was then up to white people to decide how they, as white people, could help undermine racism within white contexts while maintaining strong ties to communities of color.

The accomplishments of SDS activists (and activists within other organizations) were substantial. They mounted a national campaign against the Vietnam War. They rallied for long-term democratic change in higher education. They affirmed the power of young people as agents of change. Much less impressive, however, was the extent to which SDS and other northern activist organizations were able to keep anti-racism on the table domestically. By the time SDS split over issues of militancy, people of color and white people were rarely working together in integrated, progressive organizations. The rise of Black Power and the intransigence of white supremacy had whittled away at that strategy. Instead, white activists faced decisions about how best to work alongside Black Power groups. White antiracist perspectives about that period suggest the baton was rarely passed with success: The antiwar and free speech movements did little to put issues of race at the center of the agenda.

The second crucial turning point pivots on questions of militancy, sabotage, and revolutionary change. It became impossible for me to dismiss the philosophy of the Weather Underground and other militant organizations once I understood how the support for militancy centered on recognizing the brutality of the state. I have also been moved and changed by the particular people whom I interviewed and have come to know—David Gilbert, Marilyn Buck, and Naomi Jaffe—who did go the way of militancy. They are among the most principled people I have ever met. They have also been able to sustain their activism across the decades, some in the most horrendous of circumstances. In the late 1960s these and other militant activists took seriously a challenge to be willing to put their lives on the line for justice.[50] They still do.

Perhaps one reason why the stories of white militants have been buried is that at the end of the 1960s no strategy seemed sufficient. For David Wellman, who was keenly involved in debates about the direction white activists needed to take in the late 1960s, no solution was satisfactory. He reasons, "What made it so difficult for me was that I subscribed to the analysis [of militancy]. I thought the analysis was correct. But I also thought that the politics (of terrorism) that followed from it were self-defeating, which to some extent rendered me incapable of doing anything. At the same time, some of my very dear and committed friends went in that direction and paid incredible prices for that. Some of them with their lives and some of them are still in jail and will never get out of jail. Unlike a lot of my friends who came through that period who just want to condemn them for being stupid or adventurous, I felt like there, but for the grace of God, would go I. I am not critical. . . . I am really caught in an awful situation where my analysis of the United States says to do one thing. But my political perspective says that ain't going to go any place."

David saw neither strategy—building a broad-based aboveground or a strong underground movement—as sufficient partly because of what he had learned, through personal experience, about history. His Communist parents were always interested in alliance building and popular front politics. In some sense, David does not consider their politics militant enough. "Their politics were majoritarian, even though they were part of an organization that was a cadre organization. On some level I understood that if you didn't have a majoritarian politic, you couldn't convince the majority. And if you had an unarmed minority, how could you change things? If you had an armed minority, I knew what they had done to the Communists in the 1950s. So I had no hesitation that they wouldn't do the same thing to Blacks. In fact, they had already begun to do that."

One of the most frightening realities about this turning point in the activism of the 1960s is that people stopped being able to talk with each other in a principled way about strategy and history. David explains, "This awful thing that happened inside the movement is that we stopped arguing about these things in a principled, sensitive, idealistic way and began to guilt-trip each other. And gut check each other. It became a very macho approach to politics about how militant are you ready to be." At this point in the struggle, white women who supported militancy were as or even more susceptible to this macho approach. Marilyn Buck says that to be taken seriously by the men with whom she worked—white men involved in solidarity organizations and Black men working within BLA and the Black Panthers alike—she had to be willing to take serious risks time and time again. David Wellman says, "This was a time when white women in the New Left were beginning to assert themselves as a silent segment of the movement. So that some of our bravest, most articulate, most persuasive people arguing this military position were women—Bernadine Dorhn, Kathy Boudin, Judy Clark, Jennifer Dorhn, and Marilyn Buck. So while it was macho, it wasn't just for guys, and that is important to point out because, in some sense, what this movement was trying to do was overcome a sense of powerlessness. Instead of having these kinds of principled arguments and being able to say, 'We can agree to disagree,' it was, 'Look, there is only one way to do it,' and if you didn't do it you were either a coward or a traitor."

Although the dynamics behind the split in SNCC and the split in SDS were quite different (one occurring in a Black-led integrated organization, one in a white-led group), both splits demanded that whites ask themselves similar questions: What is required for white people to be allies to people of color? By the time white activists were working within white organizations, another question had been added to the mix: How closely should white antiracist organizations work with organizations led by people of color? The Weather Underground saw itself as an organization that followed the lead of militant groups of color—Black, Latino, and Native American—by raising funds, serving as decoys, and putting their lives on the line alongside activists of color. In the end, though, the mechanisms for close communication across race were shaky at best, in part due to the difficulty of developing and maintaining coherent and long-term strategy for people working underground. The questions raised by militancy continue: Are there privileges that white people can tap into that can further a movement without co-opting it? Are there limits to a pacifist stance when the state is killing activists in cold blood? Why has there seemed to be more popular support in the United States for the African National Congress (which explicitly advocated sabotage and other forms of militancy) than there has been for the U.S. militants of the 1960s and 1970s who are still activists in prison?

The fact that one of the most deliberate attempts at cross-race affiliation took place underground from 1969 to 1976 is a telling sign of a movement in trouble: a movement that had seen many of its leaders killed or imprisoned; a movement whose white leaders had articulated an international vision and yet had an easier time taking guidance from the writings of Third World leaders than from the words of people of color in their own cities; a movement that had yet to come to terms with the great damage done by hierarchical, male-run organizations; a movement that sometimes ended up rating people's commitment to the struggle by their willingness to take up arms, even when that meant isolating themselves from the larger activist community in the process.

Conclusion

Although the reasons for the songlessness at the 1997 conference Race and Racism in the 1990s may not all be identified through retrospective analysis, it did feel as if history was in pieces during the event. It was not that there was no energy, no energy for activism, no organizing in the present. The conference had been filled with stories of what people across generation and race and class were doing. But a movement there was not. In my mind, this yearning—this songlessness—was not, as some writers have recently suggested, the result of identity politics.[51] The young people's insistence during the conference that they be seen as raced and classed and gendered did not cause the songlessness.[52] To me, the searching for the not-yet-found songs signaled progressive communities in transition.[53] The activists were regrouping in the 1990s, at a time when "We Shall Overcome" could no longer be the anthem but when there were many people still seeking progressive songs of protest and change.

My overwhelming feeling is that a piece of the songlessness also came from ruptures in community in the 1960s that have yet to be healed: ruptures from disagreements about strategy that remain unresolved; ruptures from the pervasiveness of racism, both as it is upheld by the government and as it shaped antiracist politics; ruptures related to questions of accountability and militancy that are signs of the toll exacted when activists stood up against the most powerful government in the world.

Harkening back to the Movement through the mid-1960s, David Wellman says, "In 1963–1964, my closest friends were all . . . we were like a family and . . . we shared food, we partied, some people shared lovers, we ate, slept, drank politics. We were part of a national movement, part of an international movement. It was a group of people in the Bay Area who were in regular association and contact. We all identified ourselves as Movement people in various parts of the Movement. It wasn't organized in any old fashioned way, that is with a hierarchy." It is within this family, this large, extended family, that David experienced the rupture that occurred as one group went the way of militancy while the other did not.

In the late 1960s David got a call from his partner, who told him to come home immediately. Several Movement people were telling him that militancy was the way the Movement needed to go and that he needed to be on board with them. He explains that, at that moment, "It wasn't even a political decision we were making. It was almost like a decision about family, about being part of a family. . . . It was at that moment that I said, 'I can't go along with bombing right now.'. . . Those people never spoke to us again. Well, they spoke to us years later. But what I am trying to illustrate is how much of a community thing it was. It wasn't a spiritual thing or even a political thing. You know, my father's and mother's politics were decided to some extent through a process called democratic centralism. They were expected to follow the leadership of the Party. Well, we didn't have that kind of politics. So it wasn't like we were going to resign from the Movement. . . . It really was this community. But even then, at a certain point, I guess, that is when it ran out of gas for me." When I asked David if he has since felt part of a political community, he said, "It has never happened since and I can't say that I have tried to re-create it. . . . I don't feel like I am part of a movement. I don't feel like there is a vision. There was a vision then. There was a movement then."

The accomplishments and the work left undone in the 1960s and early 1970s leave me with many questions: What steps do white people need to take to genuinely use their white privilege to undermine the system that has created it? What steps do white people need to be willing to take for the sake of racial justice? What would it take to build a multiracial movement in which white people are truly accountable for creating antiracist alliances while not co-opting people of color? What might have been done to maintain a sense of a "beloved community" that remained Black-led? What contradictions were not faced, leaving many circles so broken?

part ii

Multiracial Feminism and the 1970s

Multiracial Feminism and the 1970s

The story that is typically told about the history of second-wave feminism reaches back to the publication of Betty Friedan's *The Feminine Mystique* in 1963 and the founding of the National Organization for Women in 1966. Both signaled a rising number of white, middle-class women unwilling to be treated like second-class citizens in the boardroom, in education, or in the bed. Many of the early protests waged by this sector of the feminist movement picked up on the courage and forthrightness of the struggles of the 1960s; they demonstrated a willingness to stop traffic, break existing laws to provide safe and accessible abortions, and contradict an older generation tied in many ways to sex roles that younger women found completely out of touch with the leadership women had demonstrated in the activism of the 1960s. This version of second-wave history is not, however, where the story of early white antiracist feminism can be found—a reality that speaks volumes to competing visions of what constitutes liberation and early schisms in feminist consciousness that are still with us today.

In chapter 4 I examine the lives of white women activists who, in the late 1960s and early 1970s, chose to work in anti-imperialist, anti-racist organizations connected with Black Power groups rather than in overwhelmingly white feminist contexts. I argue that although they were often hesitant to call themselves feminists, their trajectories need to be considered integral to early second-wave feminist history. Such a history accounts not only for the impact of civil rights organizing on the burgeoning feminist movement but also recognizes the impact of the Black Power Movement on white activist sensibilities.

The fact that these women's stories are rarely considered part of early second-wave feminism speaks to a number of ideological assumptions made during the late 1960s and early 1970s: that "real" feminists were those who worked primarily or exclusively with other women; that "women's ways of knowing" were more collaborative, less hierarchical, and more peace loving than men's; and that women's liberation would come from women's deepening understanding that "sisterhood is powerful." These politics were upheld by both liberal feminists (who saw institutional change in politics and education as key to women's equality) and radical feminists (who supported the elimination of patriarchy in the paid labor market and at home).

These politics did not, however, sit well with many women of color and militant white women, who refused to consider sexism the biggest or most destructive oppression and recognized the limits of gaining equality in a system that, as Malcolm X had explained, was already on fire. The women of color and white militant women who supported a race, class, and gender analysis in the late 1960s and 1970s often found themselves trying to explain their politics in mixed-gender settings (at home, at work, and in their activism), sometimes alienated from the men (and some women) who didn't get it while simultaneously alienated from white feminists, whose politics they considered narrow at best and frivolous at worst.

By the mid-1970s this political logjam began to break apart for a number of reasons, not the least of which was the government's continued attack on the Black Panthers and the American Indian Movement (AIM), and the country's general turn to the right. Both factors, while weakening militant organizing, paradoxically also opened a space for women of color and white antiracist women to begin to work together in women-led, multiracial spaces. Women who had been raised on the politics of the Civil Rights and Black Power Movements reached out for each other, in hopes of building organizations that could sustain them as women and as people of color, as lesbians and straight women, and as women with an international perspective who also knew, often from experience to the contrary, that justice begins in the bedroom.

What was lost with the government's assault on progressive activism and the country's increasingly conservative shift was a sense that the revolution was imminent, a hope that had been fueled by the Student Nonviolent Coordinating Committee's (SNCC's)direct action and carried forward by the courage and determination of Black Power leaders. What also was put to rest with the end of the Black Power Movement was the sense that women's rights could be achieved without an autonomous feminist base. By the mid-1970s, what emerged among women of color was the energy to build a multiracial feminist movement created and sustained by women who had grown up on the Civil

Rights and Black Power Movements and by a younger generation who were benefiting from the gains won by these struggles.

In chapter 5 I chronicle the emergence of the multiracial feminist movement, founded upon the creation of autonomous women-of-color organizations. These groups provided the foundation for the expansive and transformative organizing and fueled a veritable explosion of writing by women of color, including the works collected in the foundational *This Bridge Called My Back: Writings by Radical Women of Color* and *Home Girls: A Black Feminist Anthology* in 1981 and 1983, respectively. While chronicling the dynamism and complexity of a multidimensional vision for women of color, these books also traced for white women what is required to be allies to women of color.

By the late 1970s the militant women who had wanted little to do with white feminism in the late 1960s and 1970s became deeply involved in multiracial feminism. Meanwhile, a younger cohort of white women, who were first politicized in the 1970s, saw feminism from a wholly different vantage point than did the older white antiracist women. For the younger group, exposure to multiracial feminism led by women of color meant an early lesson that race, class, and gender were inextricably linked: By that time there were also multiple organizations where women were, with much struggle, attempting to uphold this politic. From this politic came the emergence of a small but important group of white women determined to understand how white privilege had historically blocked cross-race alliances and what they needed to do to work closely with women of color.

Not surprisingly, as I document in chapter 6, Jewish women and lesbians led the way among white women in articulating a politic that accounted for white women's position as both oppressed and oppressors—as both women and white. Both groups knew what it meant to be marginalized from a women's movement that was, nevertheless, still homophobic and Christian biased. Both groups knew "There is no place like home"—among other Jews or lesbians. And they knew the limits of that home if the Jewish home was male dominated or if the lesbian home was exclusively white. The paradoxes of "home" for these groups paralleled many of the paradoxes experienced by women of color, who, over and over again, found themselves to be the bridges that everyone assumed would be built on their backs. As the straight Black women dialogued with the Black lesbians, the first-generation Chinese women talked with the Native American activists, the Latina women talked with the Black and white women about the walls that go up when people cannot speak Spanish, white women attempting to understand race knew they had a lot of listening to do, a lot of truth telling to reckon with, and a lot of networking to do, among other white women and across race as well.

Many of the conversations and disputes were amplified through festivals, conferences, feminist bookstores, women's studies and Black studies departments, and scholarship created through feminist activism of the 1970s and 1980s. All of these institutions in one way or another required women to ask, of themselves and others, a pivotal question Audre Lorde had posed: Are you doing your work? The tremendous strength of these cultural and political institutions included the artistic, political, and social contributions they helped generate. And yet by the mid-1980s the resurgence of the radical right in the United States, which fueled a monumental backlash against gays and lesbians, people of color, and women across race, led multiracial feminists to ask again, Where and with whom are you doing your work? Many white antiracist feminists who had helped build the largely women-led cultural institutions that left a paper trail of multiracial feminism moved on, into mixed-gender multiracial grassroots organizations, working against the Klan, in support of affirmative action and immigrant rights, and against police brutality and the prison industry.

4

Black Power and White Accountability:
Women Choosing Sides

As a woman who was introduced to antiracist work through the feminist movement in the late 1970s—a movement shaped in large part by women of color who called themselves "womanists," "feminists," and "radical women of color"—I came to this project especially interested in how white antiracist women across the generations positioned themselves vis-à-vis second-wave feminism. I wanted to learn how sexism played itself out in the 1960s and how antiracist white women responded to second-wave feminism. And I wanted to find out whether the antiracist baton carried in the 1960s was passed on or dropped by feminist activists.

One of the most compelling lessons I learned from women who came of age politically before or during the Civil Rights and Black Power Movements was how difficult it was for many of them to relate to or embrace feminism of the late 1960s and early 1970s. Their critique of early feminism parallels (and was informed by) an analysis made by many women of color, who had historically stood up against sexism in their families and in organizations but did not see white feminism as a movement equipped to further that work. Women I interviewed told of ways in which they had resisted sexism in Students for a Democratic Society (SDS) and in militant organizations. As they talked about the exclusions they faced in 1960s organizations and criticized early feminist organizing that considered gender oppression its main target, I realized how much different the feminist movement they saw in the early 1970s was from the feminist movement I was introduced to in the late 1970s. By then there was a critical mass of seasoned feminist activists—mostly women of color and a few white antiracist women— who were keeping race at the center of the agenda. They were teaching younger feminists that race and gender are inextricably connected, that it is not possible to call oneself a feminist without dealing with race.

Accounting for the antiracist women who initially rejected white feminism as part of the history of second-wave feminism exposes the limits of what historian Sherna Berger Gluck has dubbed the "master historical narrative" of the feminist movement.[1] This telling of the history of second-wave feminism resorts to an "old litany" of the women's movement: three or four branches of feminism—liberal, socialist, radical, and sometimes cultural feminism—all of which privilege gender and keep white women at the center of focus.[2] None of the women I interviewed who came up politically through the Civil Rights and Black Power Movements had an interest in organizations that did not have antiracism at the top of their agendas or that had a single focus on gender. The women I interviewed excluded themselves from this "master historical narrative," as they have been written out of the story by historians who also rely upon those categories.[3] Historian Nancy MacLean writes, "Recent accounts of the rise of modern feminism depart little from the story line first advanced two decades ago and since enshrined as orthodoxy. That story stars white middle-class women triangulated between the pulls of liberal, radical/cultural, and socialist feminism. Working-class women and women of color assume walk-on parts late in the plot, after tendencies and allegiances are already in place. The problem with this script is not simply that it has grown stale from repeated re-telling. It is not accurate."[4]

The most egregious consequence of this script is its failure to take seriously the Black, Latina, Asian, and Native American women whose activism made possible the most multiracial feminist movement in U.S. history. This organizing provides crucial examples of their simultaneous resistance to sexism, racism, and classism. Narrow interpretations of second-wave feminism also make it difficult to find a history of white women who did not, in the words of Barbara Smith, "enter feminism through a white door."[5] Recognizing these white women is not only important because their stories count. Grappling with their stories moves us forward in developing a complex understanding of feminist history.

In this chapter, I analyze why some white women, whose initial race consciousness came from the Civil Rights and Black Power Movements, did not see the early feminist movement (1966 to the mid-1970s) as a location to continue antiracist work. I also analyze why their stories—in particular the impact of the Black Power Movement on their politics—should not continue to be left out of the history of second-wave feminism.

"We Do Not Support Attica. We Are Attica."

For Naomi Jaffe attempts to be part of both early second-wave feminism and the anti-imperialist struggle were untenable. After attending Brandeis University and beginning graduate work at the New School for Social Research in the mid 1960s, Naomi founded a chapter of SDS in 1967 and joined the New York chapter of Women's International Terrorist Conspiracy from Hell (WITCH), a radical women's liberation group. Through her involvement with SDS, Naomi continued to develop a Marxist analysis first introduced to her by Communist relatives, along with an understanding of imperialism as she protested, with thousands of others, against the Vietnam War. During this period she attempted to work with white feminist organizations and with the Weather Underground, a dual commitment that revealed the limitations of both. In the Weather Underground she faced sexism. Among white feminists she missed an anti-imperialist, antiracist analysis.

The 1971 rebellion at Attica Prison in New York pushed Naomi to decide between the two. Prisoners organized the protest in response to inhumane conditions. New York's governor, Nelson Rockefeller, responded to the uprising with orders to attack, which resulted in the massacre by national guardsmen, prison guards, and local police of thirty-one prisoners and nine guards. The Attica uprising was one of many prison protests across the country during that period (at San Quentin and Folsom Prisons, among others); they were staged in response to cruel treatment, race and class biases in sentencing, the murder of African American leader George Jackson, and other injustices.[6]

Naomi vividly remembers white feminist women arguing that there was no room for remorse for the "male chauvinists" who had died at Attica. Naomi disagreed vehemently, arguing that if the white feminists could not understand Attica as a feminist issue, then she was not a feminist. Naomi remembers that at the time, Black lesbian activist and lawyer Florynce Kennedy said, "We do not support Attica. We ARE Attica. We are Attica or we are nothing." Naomi says, "That about summed up my feelings on the subject."[7] With this consciousness and with her increasing awareness of the violence of the state against the Black Panthers, antiwar protesters, and in liberation struggles around the world, Naomi continued to work with the Weather Underground. She went underground from 1970 to 1978.

Going underground was Naomi's way of committing herself to the principle that justice was what she most valued in life. This vision required a total transformation of society, including a dramatic redistribution of resources. Naomi's transition from SDS to the Weather Underground was "based on the feeling that this was a revolutionary period and that the only way to be part of that was to make some really decisive break with ordinary life. If I wanted to be part of this, I was going to have to give up everything." She adds, "There was a lot about the Weather Underground I didn't like. I was an emerging feminist and the organization was patriarchal. But I decided to go with it anyway. I didn't want to miss the opportunity to be part of the revolution. In the course of that I suppressed a lot of feminism."

Naomi decided to go underground largely because white feminism did not offer the radical analysis of imperialism and racism she was seeking. The consequences of that decision included never being treated as a first-class citizen or as a leader within the Weather Underground and devoting herself to a movement, a politic, and a way of life that asked her to work against herself as a woman. Naomi says that through the years she was a "bit of a thorn in their side and they never trusted me because I was a feminist."

Once Naomi went underground she had almost no contact with feminists of color. "One of the reasons I went with the Weather Underground was that I knew I needed to understand that racism was the center of the problem. I was hearing that from white leadership." But, she adds, "it took me years to figure out that the key was women of color. That wasn't until I had been through the Weather Underground and out the other side. It takes a long time to learn that. Women of color were so invisible."

For Marilyn Buck attempts to develop an antiracist politic in the 1960s and 1970s also meant choosing to work in organizations that did not actively support a feminist politic.[8] After working with SDS, where she "tried to find a little niche inside a male-dominated place," she began working with the Black Panthers, which demanded she develop an internationalist perspective and believe in both men's and women's rights to self-determination. Like many young women activists of the late 1960s, Marilyn was moved by the courage of the Vietnamese women "who were not feeding the troops. They were the troops." She explains, "The Vietnamese women elevated all of us as women. . . . With the Vietnamese you did see a political base with women in leadership. Women doing the work . . . We wanted to be like that and we wanted to do that here. I think that was a product of our youth and a true spirit of internationalism."

To Marilyn, separate organizations for men and women did not make sense. "Separate organizations didn't exist with the Panthers or Third World organizations. . . . I didn't believe in separatism." In describing the historical context in which Black men and women worked together—not separately—in the late 1960s and early 1970s, activist lawyer and former Black Panther Kathleen Cleaver writes, "Leaders with progressive views—from the Democratic President Kennedy to the NAACP leader Medgar Evers to Malcolm X to Black Panther Fred Hampton—were all assassinated because their eloquent pleas for change inspired a generation. . . . Such conditions made it obvious to women within the Black Panther Party that liberation was not something we could obtain separately, nor would consciousness-raising groups serve as an appropriate channel for our rage."[9] During that period, Marilyn and many others believed "they had to win the war first [against U.S. imperialism] before women's issues could come to the forefront." When activists around Marilyn became militant—which included multiple methods of undermining white domination and capitalism—she believed both men and women should be involved.

Marilyn believed that if men carried guns, then women should be able to as well. This was a position she had also taken as a child. "When I was growing up, I was just about the only girl in the neighborhood. I had no one to play with but the boys. I had to prove that I could be badder than the boys. Not that I had to prove it, but they told me that if I wanted to play with them, I had to do x, y, and z. I am the one who had to ride my bicycle down the ravine. I am the one who had to drive down the canyon into the ravine. Climb the highest trees. Do all the stupidest stuff just so I wouldn't be by myself all the time. So I liked playing with dolls, but I also wanted to shoot the BB gun. But I have felt driven to do these kinds of things—to take the plunge into the ice water. I hated it and lost my breath every time I did it. But I have done it and I am here." By "here" Marilyn is referring to being in prison in large part related to her unwillingness to stay in her place as a woman or as a white person during her years of work with the Black liberation struggle.

For Marilyn, taking the plunge in the context of revolutionary politics in the late 1960s and '70s had meant earning the trust of members of the Black liberation struggle. What was most important to her was to be "a person of honor, a person to be respected and who followed through. It is much easier as a white person, when the shit hits the fan or the going gets rough, to be able to stop at a certain point and say, 'I am not doing that.'" Being a white person of honor required working alongside Black and Latino revolutionaries and forming political relationships with them. At the time that meant primarily relationships with men "because mostly men were in charge of everything."

Marilyn's dedication to militancy came from her belief, shared by many others at the time, that revolution was imminent and required total commitment. In that historical context, her long-held belief that girls and women should be able to do whatever boys and men do, coupled with knowledge of her white privilege, reinforced her militancy. As a white woman, she knew she could do certain things that the Black men and women she worked with could not. There were some Black women in leadership positions in Black organizations. However, sexism on the part of some Black and white men complicated dynamics within organizations. Marilyn remembers that some Black men were more willing to accept white women on the front lines than they were to support Black women. Some Black men did not want to put their wives and the mothers of their children at risk. During that period, rhetoric among some Black male nationalists included a pronatalist position, in which the birth control pill was considered a form of genocide. Some men argued that Black women's primary contribution to the struggle involved giving birth and raising children. Black women's activism in this context included rallying against these sexist attitudes. For Marilyn, taking risks as a militant activist was a necessary consequence of not hiding behind her white privilege and of showing her willingness to take risks on a par with those that men took.

Although Marilyn has no regrets about her principles and activism, she believes the path she took divided her from other women. Once she was a fugitive, her options for working closely with women—opportunities for dialogue about ideological differences among women—

diminished further. "If I could live my life over, I would make some different choices so I wouldn't have been so male dominated. By being so isolated I suffered more from male domination. I think at particular points we make particular choices. I look at other people's lives in certain situations, and wish I was walking more in their shoes. Not because it is easier but because they have done some things I think are important and they are respected people. They have done good work. Maybe work I would have liked to have done. I think some of the work in the women's community, some of the struggle among white women and Latinas and Asian women. In looking back, in some ways I would have really rather been there because I would feel more sisterhood and connections. Those struggles are some of the fundamental struggles that will inform our ability to have a different world."

In the 1960s and early 1970s Marilyn kept her distance from feminism. "I didn't like the term 'feminist' because I associated it with bourgeois white women who didn't have to deal with the harsh realities of women and men fighting all over the world." Today Marilyn would use the term "feminist," but only with a small *f*. "There is nothing else to use. I want to be identified as a woman and I do not regret not having a better political analysis way back when. I may regret some political decisions I made but I don't regret one iota of supporting national liberation with all my breath. . . . Until there is equality of nations I don't think we are going to change the world very much. But I no longer believe that everything will come to women when the revolution is over."

Like many of her comrades, Marilyn was a major supporter of the Zimbabwe women's military detachment of the Zimbabwe African National Union (ZANU), which ultimately emerged victorious from the 1966–79 war against a white supremacist government. But Marilyn adds, "Women are in terrible shape in Zimbabwe. It is what happened afterwards that has led me to change my analysis." A similar pattern took place for Palestinian women, which demonstrated to Marilyn that women's liberation cannot be ranked behind other struggles. She believes that "the most exciting and most important tendency in the whole world today is among women. I don't believe there will be serious political change in this country that is not led by Black and Latina women and women from oppressed nations. I think that the movements that are male dominated—which are most of them except for

Black, Latina, and Asian radical feminist women-led groups—are doomed on a certain level."

Although women who went underground offer the starkest examples of the consequences of choosing between white feminism and solidarity with Black struggles, women who worked aboveground in solidarity organizations also encountered dilemmas involving race and gender. Jeanine Cohen, whose early understanding of race and racism came from growing up with antiapartheid parents in South Africa, was involved in the squatters' movement and battered women's movement in England in the mid-1970s before moving to the Bay Area in northern California. There she began working with a white group organizing in solidarity with a Black liberation organization. She was drawn to the group because of its explicitly antiracist platform and African American leadership. Over time, however, "things started happening that made me wary of the politics. I felt that even though I have my fair share of guilt and shame as a white person, I really had a problem with the system that was sort of feeding off of that. Motivating people from that place." Jeanine felt that having grown up around the politics of the African National Congress and its desire to create a nonracialized society had given her an intuitive sense that there "was something divisive and hierarchical about the Black liberation organization. First, they were ranking racism over other oppressions. The Black male leaders of the solidarity group stepped in and subverted the women when they wanted to deal with issues of class and gender as well as race."

Only after she came out as a lesbian and became involved with an Afro-British woman, who was appalled by the organization's politics, did Jeanine find a way to extricate herself from the group. With her partner's help, she started to see the cult-like characteristics of the group's tactics, its history of excommunicating people who disagreed with the leadership, and the limitations of an organization that prohibited interracial relationships. Of all the people I interviewed, only Jeanine and one other woman, who was also involved in this white solidarity group, used a pseudonym for this book. Both women feared they might be sought out and targeted by this organization if their critique of the group were publicized. This in itself speaks to the organization's coercive and manipulative techniques. Their involvement in these organizations—and the difficulty they had in leaving—also reflects the reality that during the early 1970s, organizations in which white women could do antiracist, feminist work alongside feminists of color were scarce.

Naomi Jaffe, Marilyn Buck, Jeanine Cohen, and others often found that attempts to keep antiracism at the center of focus and to work with Black-led organizations left them in precarious positions in their attempt to uphold a feminist analysis that was also antiracist and class conscious. Dawn Gomes explains that when she got involved in Black Power, it "represented liberation" for her as a working-class woman. "You know, on some level I didn't see the women's movement as having that for me because of my class. I had more of a class alignment with Black Power." Although Dawn resonated deeply with Black Power's analysis of class and race, the sexism of the particular nationalist group she worked with meant she was both alienated from the male leadership and from white feminism.

Not surprisingly, one of the most passionate and compelling calls for white women to deal with race, class, and gender simultaneously came from Anne Braden, who had already been on the fringes of several social movements, only the latest of which was second-wave feminism.[10] In her two open letters to southern white women, she urges white women to build a women's movement that is not at odds with the Black liberation struggle.[11] Anne wrote the first letter in 1972 after a young Black man, Thomas Wansley, had been wrongly charged and convicted of raping a white woman. "I called on white women, for their own liberation, to refuse any longer to be used, to act in the tradition of Jessie Daniel Ames and the white women who fought in an earlier period to end lynching, and to join our Black sisters in a fight to free Wansley."[12] Braden argued that while women fight against rape they must not forget "the racist way the charge of rape can be used" (50).

In 1977 Anne Braden wrote her second letter, this time critiquing Susan Brownmiller's book *Against Our Will: Men, Women, and Rape*.[13] Although Anne commends Brownmiller for documenting the unwritten history of rape, she is troubled by white feminists' unwillingness to take seriously the history of falsely accusing Black men of rape. She writes, "It might be comfortable for those of us who are white to dismiss the racial implications of the rape issue; but they will not go away. We only need to listen, as I did, to the Black woman who asked Brownmiller, 'What you are saying may help me protect myself but how can I

protect my son?' A movement that has no answer to that question ignores the fact that in a society anchored by racism, there can be no liberation for anyone until the race issue is met head on."[14]

In her second letter Anne also recognizes the import of the women's
movement in confronting "atrocious" male attitudes of the 1960s:
"Women were right to rebel; and I feel now that some of us who continued to concentrate on fighting racism were not sensitive enough to
the issues they were raising" (52). Although Anne was willing to honor
the utility of feminism in principle, her pronouns in that sentence speak
volumes of her position vis-à-vis early second-wave feminism: "Some
of *us* who continued to concentrate on fighting racism were not sensitive enough to the issues *they* were raising" (my emphasis). Anne continues, "They were wrong to turn away from other problems and to
focus only on sexism. I believe that all issues are 'women's issues,' including war and peace, economics, and racism" (52).

Anne's writing gives painful evidence of a white woman who, like
other white antiracists, recognized the value of feminist organizing and
yet feared that "white women might find themselves objectively on the
side of the most reactionary social forces, used once again" (50). She
stood on one side, white feminists on the other, and as her 1958 book
had foretold, there was "a wall between."[15]

Beyond "Old Litanies": Black Power's Influence on Antiracist Feminism

Perhaps the most important reason for including white antiracist
women in tellings of the origins of second-wave feminism is because
their involvement in the Black Power Movement dramatically shaped
their ability to respond to multiracial feminism as it developed through
the 1970s. As I chronicle in detail in chapters 5, 6, and 7, I use the term
"multiracial feminism" to identify the liberation movement spearheaded by women of color in the 1970s and '80s, a movement that included
the emergence of a small but important group of antiracist white
women. Among multiracial feminism's most significant characteristics
were (1) its international perspective, which recognized the role of colonialism and imperialism and drew links between women in Third World
countries and Black, Latina, Asian, and Native American women in
the United States; (2) a political analysis that treated race, class, and
gender as interconnected and refused to consider sexism the ultimate

oppression; (3) a wariness about single-issue organizations that did not account for women's multiple identities; and (4) a recognition of the need for racially autonomous caucus groups through which various identity groups could come together to form coalitions.

For white antiracist women, being involved in the Black Power Movement (in solidarity organizations or in mixed-race groups that supported Black Power) introduced them to many of these principles and the debates surrounding them. Although their exposure to Black Power ideology left them alienated from white liberal and radical feminists, it gave them the training necessary to become allies to women of color in multiracial feminist coalitions.

Among the lessons white women learned from their associations with Black Power organizations was their understanding of liberation as both a domestic and an international struggle, involving both externally and internally colonized people. By the late 1960s and early 1970s Black Power initiatives were increasingly coupled with the liberation struggles of Native Americans and Latinos.[16] Many nationalist groups also saw connections between their liberation in the United States and the liberation of colonized countries (both from old-fashioned colonialism and from the neocolonialism of corporate capitalism). The Puerto Rican activists who struggled for community control of education in the New York City school system in the 1960s and 1970s linked race and class inequities in education and U.S. control of the Puerto Rican economy, which forced so many Puerto Ricans to leave the island in search of education and jobs. From the perspective of Chicano activists, the exploitation of Chicanos in the United States was rooted in the U.S. invasion of Mexico and U.S. annexation of much of Mexico's land in the Mexican-American War of 1846–48.

White antiracist women's exposure to internationalist, anti-imperialist ideology helped them understand why, in the 1970s, many women of color in the United States began claiming the term "Third World women/feminists."[17] The term "Third World women" connected them linguistically and politically to the African, Latin, and Asian diaspora and drew parallels between external and internal colonialism by First World countries. Theorist Chandra Mohanty writes that Third World women in the United States have "insisted on the complex interrelationship between feminist, antiracist and nationalist struggles. In fact, the challenge of Third World feminisms to white, Western feminisms has been precisely this inescapable link between feminist and political liberation movements."[18]

Marilyn Buck and Naomi Jaffe both knew that a strong antiracist movement in the United States depended upon sustaining links with Third World activists outside the United States. This internationalist, anti-imperialist perspective was assumed by Black Panther and other liberation organizations in the late 1960s and was honed in the multiracial feminist movement. As Marilyn explains, "You can't take African slaves and depopulate Latin America except in the name of saying that your culture is better. You can justify that kind of barbarity and say that you are superior." When I asked Marilyn to explain to me the difference between anti-imperialist and antiracist, she said, "To be a serious anti-imperialist, one has to be an antiracist. You can be an antiracist but not be an anti-imperialist. Anti-imperialist means trying to be an internationalist and believe in the right to self determination. To be an antiracist doesn't necessarily mean you believe in the right to one's own nation and the legal steps you might take to establish sovereignty. This is different than people who think that everybody has the right to be equal in society but that doesn't necessarily require major social change. I don't think you can be a very good antiracist and stay there because it is limited. It doesn't take on capitalist society."

The Black Power Movement also discouraged white antiracist women from accepting the essentialist notions many white feminists were making about women's nature. A preponderance of early white feminist writing professed that women are, by nature and nurture, more nonviolent, less aggressive, and more peace-loving than men. Much early white feminist writing treated nonviolence as a bedrock of feminist consciousness. Radical and liberal feminists disagreed vehemently with militant activists who refused to consider armed struggle antithetical to liberation. Although white radical feminists were willing to disrupt the Miss America beauty pageant and to break laws in order to provide women with reproductive choices, ideologically they saw the militancy of the Black Power Movement as a male invention. Within this framework, white feminists considered militant women either duped or brainwashed into accepting male models of confrontation.

For those involved in the Black Power Movement, the white feminist pairing of men with violence and women with nonviolence seemed both facile and unhelpful.[19] For one thing, women in the Black Panther

Party and white militant groups knew that both men and women had carried guns in reaction to the government's assault on communities of color in general and leaders of color in particular. The Black Power Movement also consistently reframed mainstream debates about what constitutes violence in order to account for the power of a white supremacist state. The Black Panthers saw poverty that left children with hungry bellies as a form of race violence perpetrated by white people in power—both men and women. Police brutality aimed mainly at African Americans and Latinos affected the entire Black and Latino community—both men and women. An analysis of state violence (perpetrated by the courts, legislation, and the media), an analysis developed in militant organizations, helped prepare white militant women for nuanced analyses of violence that emerged through multiracial feminism. Although the government was overwhelmingly run by white men, antiracist women of the late 1960s and early 1970s knew that white women were also implicated in violence done to communities of color. Similarly, when women organized against the Ku Klux Klan, they had to come to terms with the reality that the Klan and other radical right organizations include both male and female members.[20] Anti-Klan organizing could not afford to see the Klan's racist violence as solely the domain of white men.

Given the ideological divides between radical feminists and white women in solidarity organizations, it is no surprise that white militant women often found it difficult to straddle the two movements. Vicki Gabriner, who was involved in the Civil Rights Movement in the mid-1960s, in the Boston Weatherman Collective in the 1970s, and in the Atlanta lesbian community in the late 1970s, writes about a devastating pull she felt as she tried to hold onto her experience in all three movements. Gabriner was tried and convicted in 1977 and was later, in 1978, retried and acquitted of charges dating to her work with the Weather Underground. During her case, she felt alienated from the lesbian/feminist women with whom she had worked but who could not understand the conditions that led her to turn to militancy. Gabriner was furious with the Weather Underground for their "excesses," respectful of the enormous frustration about the Vietnam War and the struggle to end it, and angered by narrow thinking in white lesbian/feminist circles.[21] She writes, "I found myself alienated from the Atlanta lesbian community in a way I hadn't anticipated. Womyn I had been best friends with, lovers with, played softball with, camped with, sat through the Atlanta Lesbian/Feminist Alliance meetings with, didn't connect to my hystory in the way I needed. My experience had been pre-lesbian, pre-Atlanta" (116).

Alienation from white feminism reflects the sentiments of a small group of white women unwilling to cast aside the race-conscious, anti-imperialist perspective they had gained from the Black Power Movement. When Susan Saxe, a white militant lesbian, was arrested in 1975, few in the white lesbian community claimed her as their own. In her reflection about lesbian/feminist responses to the arrest of Susan Saxe, Vicki Gabriner expresses her concern about lesbians who shared no sympathy with her: "My heart had immediately leaped out to her that first night in 1975 when I saw her on the 6 o'clock news, clenched fist, body stating she was a lesbian, an amazon. I felt a gut connection that has stayed all these years, feeling that there but for the grace of the goddess go I. We were all caught in a pressure-cooker moment of hystory and responded with great intensity. Susan, for me, is someone who has been selected out of hystory to 'take the rap' for a lot of us" (116). Ambivalence may be the kindest word to describe the response of many white feminists to militant women activists in the 1970s and 1980s.[22] Vicki Gabriner was calling for an understanding of feminism and lesbian politics that was big enough to include the feminism being developed in lesbian communities as well as the lesbians in militant organizations. In the early 1970s such an expansive understanding was rare.

While white women in mixed-gender antiracist organizations were often alienated from liberal or radical feminism, white women in women's liberation groups who were attempting to develop a feminist and antiracist perspective often felt misunderstood by white militants as well. White leftist men often exploited that divide, accusing white women who were attempting to create an autonomous women's movement of being by definition racist. Although the majority of white women in feminist groups rarely seriously considered race, there were some who sought an autonomous women's movement that was also antiracist. Of the binds that this group of women experienced Adrienne Rich writes, "The charge of 'racism' flung at white women in the earliest groupings of the independent feminist movement was a charge made in the most obscene bad faith by white 'radical' men (and by some Leftist women) against the daring leap of self-definition needed to create an autonomous feminist analysis. That leap, as group after group, woman after woman, has discovered, often involves feelings of extreme dislocation, 'craziness,' and terror. . . . It corresponded, for us [white women], to charges black feminists have had to withstand, of 'fragmenting' the black struggle or 'castrating' the black man. In other words, and ironically, the more deeply a woman might recognize and hate the fact of racist oppression (and many of the first white independent feminists had learned its realities in the Civil Rights Movement in the South), the more vulnerable she felt in her struggle to define a politics which would, for once, take the position of women as central."[23] With tensions and accusations coming from all sides, the locations where antiracist feminist alliances could be found in the early 1970s were far and few between.

Who Gets to Be Radical

Understanding second-wave feminism from the vantage point of the Black Power Movement also enables a reassessment of historians' frequent assignment of the term "radical" only to the white, antipatriarchal feminists of the late 1960s and early 1970s. Many early chronicles of second-wave feminism begin with the founding in 1966 of the National Organization for Women (NOW), which came to represent liberal feminism, and the explosion in the late 1960s of consciousness-raising groups, which became a foundation for what was soon referred to as radical feminism. Many feminist historians link the development of radical feminism to the creation of several antipatriarchy organizations: the Redstockings, Radicalesbians, WITCH, and other consciousness-raising groups. When feminist scholars use the term "radical" exclusively to describe these women, whole other categories of women are left out of the equation. In fact, there were three groups of women who used the term "radical": radical women of color, radical feminists, and radical/militant white antiracists. If white radical women who emphasize patriarchy over all other oppressions are the only ones considered "radical," what, then, is to be done with *Writings by Radical Women of Color,* the subtitle of *This Bridge Called My Back*?[24] The book's editors write, "[This book] intends to reflect an uncompromised definition of feminism by women of color in the U.S. We named this anthology 'radical' for we were interested in the writing of women of color who want nothing short of a revolution. . . . We use the term in its original form—

stemming from the word 'root'—for our feminist politic emerges from the roots of both our cultural oppression and heritage."[25]

The white, antipatriarchy version of "radical" feminism that focuses on the period 1968 to 1975 also makes no mention of other self-identified "radical women" who were, as women, supporting an internationalist, race-conscious perspective. What does it mean when white feminist history applies the term "radical" to white, antipatriarchy women but not to white women of the same era whose "radicalism" included attention to race and imperialism and a belief that revolution might require literally laying their lives on the line? The term "radical" was used in markedly different ways by three groups of women: white antipatriarchy women; lesbian and heterosexual women of color, and white anti-imperialist women. To my mind, a nuanced and accurate telling of second-wave feminism is one that shows why and how the term "radical" was itself contested. Such a history emphasizes that second-wave feminism drew on the Civil Rights Movement, the New Left, and the Black Power Movement, which together helped produce three groups of "radical" women.

Marilyn Buck's poem "Autobiograph" (1999) clarifies why white antiracist women of the late 1960s and the early 1970s need to be considered part of the story of the women's liberation movement:

> Post-war 1947
> born on the white
> side of the tracks
> Texas segregation
> civil rights preacher's child
> fled Texas with honor's diploma
> for UC Berkeley and free speech
> though I did not know then
> that's why I left
>
> Vietnam war 1965
> what war
> are you fighting for
> make love not war
> college books tossed into a trunk in some room
> I've never seen since
> fires of internationalism called me

a girl
to enlist
in the anti-war
war against Amerikka
my own women's liberation on the line

war in Amerikka
war against the warmakers
> *white-skinned haters*
> *capitalist consumers of human lives*
following the tradition
> *Nat Turner John Brown*
> *Wobblies* subversives
resistance in the belly of the beast

clandestine war 1973
captured by the killers
spirit killers nationkillers
a political prisoner
enemy of the state
terrorist and traitor
white women dangerous
to white Amerikka
condemned to years
and years of absence
a lifetime

warmakers
waiting for its prisoners to die
or go crazy
or simply wither away into insignificance

I rest, a grain of sand
significant on the beach head that meets the sea
to face the storm
I wage resistance
to stay alive
I learn to search out freedom in the breath
my cells send out dendrites
to absorb the world and its offerings

> *I offer back*
> *poems*
> *and occasional grains of sand*
> *mixed into clay and fired*
> *into sturdiness.*[26]

Marilyn's own conception of "women's liberation" was internationalist, anti-imperialist, and antiracist, which means she both thought globally and yet did not fall into the trap of making racism an issue primarily happening outside the United States. As "a girl," she was called to "to enlist / in the anti-war / war against Amerikka"—against America's own people. The price she paid was needing to resist "in *the belly of the beast*" after having been "condemned to years / and years of absence / a lifetime." If any one deserves the term "radical," it is Marilyn and other antiracist militants of that period. To write them out of the rise of second-wave feminism reduces feminism to a caricature that is both narrow and reductionist.

The Nation: In Whose Name?

Another reason it is important to include women who worked with solidarity organizations in second-wave feminist history is that their stories illuminate parallel dilemmas faced by these white women and by Black women during this period. Black women in Black Power organizations and white women in white solidarity groups were often caught between a "personal rock and a political hard place."[27] The egalitarian, nonhierarchical structure of SNCC in the early 1960s was a far cry from many male-dominated Black nationalist and white solidarity groups of the late 1960s and early 1970s. According to historian Deborah Gray White, Black women in the late 1960s and early 1970s in many organizations, including the Southern Christian Leadership Conference (SCLC), the Student Nonviolent Coordinating Committee (SNCC), and the Congress of Racial Equality (CORE), and later in the Black Panthers, were "bombarded with demands that they stop competing with Black men for jobs, and that they stay at home and have babies 'for the revolution.' Although compliance would have left them proverbially barefoot and pregnant, Black women could not aggressively object without reinforcing the image of the emasculating matriarch they sought to challenge."[28]

Angela Davis, Assata Shakur, Kathleen Cleaver, and others did assume leadership positions in Black Power organizations in the 1960s and 1970s, but not without a paying a price. Opposing sexism within these organizations was sometimes seen as going against one's race. Black women activists of this period, Deborah Gray White writes, "were at odds with both Black men and white women. . . . It seemed that Black women could not work on both fronts [race and gender issues] at the same time, could not embrace one part of their identity without denying the other. They needed new organizations to represent the parts of their identities that had gone unrepresented."[29]

Chicana feminists document a similarly untenable position during the same period.[30] Chicanas ran the risk of being accused of undermining Chicano culture and undercutting Chicano families, which had always been seen as the strength of Chicano culture.[31] A Chicana who questioned a nationalist political position ran the risk of being labeled a *vendida* (sellout), *agabachadas* (white-identified), or a feminist—a tag that was used to silence active women in the community.[32] Cherríe Moraga writes, "The potential accusation of 'traitor' or 'vendida' is what hangs about the heads and beats in the hearts of most Chicanas seeking to develop an autonomous sense of ourselves, particularly through sexuality."[33]

If Black women and Latinas rallied against sexism, they risked being seen as unrevolutionary. Although this accusation blunted women's ability to put sexism on the front burner, it also reflected realities of state repression facing both men and women activists during that period. Psychologist Aída Hurtado writes, "Women in the Chicano and Black Civil Rights Movements were not silent about the restrictions that the men imposed upon them. Simultaneously, however, they came from a long line of political resisters who understood well the consequences of breaking ranks when they were so severely under attack by powerful institutions and repressive organizations such as the FBI and the local police."[34]

For white women in antiracist organizations, rallying against sexism meant breaking rank and going the way of white feminism, an option they believed would drastically compromise their politics, including their hope of standing in solidarity with people of color. Latinas, Black women, and white antiracist women were vulnerable to accusations that they were sellouts if they professed an analysis of race, class, and gender.

At the same time, women also found ways to support a multidimensional analysis, despite the potential costs. In her retrospective account of the Black Panther Party, Tracye Matthews argues against a tendency to lump the Black Power Movement into one monolithic sexist category. The cultural nationalism of Maulana Karenga's Los Angeles–based organization Us was deeply and unabashedly patriarchal, whereas the Black Panther Party made significant attempts to confront sexism both theoretically and practically within the organization. Matthews writes, "Black women in Black (mixed gender) organizations did not necessarily relate to the label *feminist* as defined by the theories and activities of the predominantly White Liberation Movement organizations. However, this lack of identification with the terms 'feminist' or 'women's lib' should not preclude the recognition that Black women who organized on issues, such as police brutality, racism, poverty, imperialism, and Black women's liberation, had a significant impact on the development of gender consciousness during this time."[35] It is not surprising that these same issues were central to the expansive platform developed by Black feminist organizations, including the National Black Feminist Organization and the Combahee River Collective, in the mid-1970s and to the alliances formed between women of color and white women during that period.[36]

Black Power ideology also exposed white women to complicated issues about identity, issues that were taken up and elaborated upon by feminists across race during the next two decades. Psychologist Aída Hurtado writes that the Chicano and Black Civil Rights Movements "did a magnificent job of fully creating the generic 'progressive person' completely enculturated with the symbols of each group's history, language and culture. For activists in the Black Civil Rights Movement, it was finding the Black within the Negro, as illustrated by Malcolm X."[37] For Chicanos, it was the concept of Aztlán, an imagined geographical region that went to the heart and soul of Chicanos (108). For the white political movement, this imagined ideal was embodied in the work of C. W. Mills and Simone de Beauvoir (109). Chicano and Black images drew on a nationalist rhetoric that, according to Hurtado, was "full of passion, love and idealism" and deeply embedded in liberatory religious traditions (109–10). From Hurtado's perspective, the power of these imagined identities was crucial to the movements' longevity.

And yet, with the exception of Beauvoir, all of these ideals are male, a reality that speaks to why women-of-color set about re-creating themselves in their own image through autonomous women-of-color feminist organizing in the 1970s and 1980s. Although antiracist white women I interviewed had read Simone de Beauvoir, more germane to their interests and identification were the writings of Assata Shakur, Angela Davis, and Frantz Fanon. For them, finding ways to be antiracists and feminists inevitably required grappling with the complexity of nationalism for women of color. Since the early 1970s women of color have identified how and why "nationalism" was a mixed blessing. Nationalism affirmed roots to communities of descent and to communities with long histories of resisting colonialism, slavery, and genocide, but it also imposed patriarchal standards in the name of the nation. For Native American women, male-centered nationalism was especially problematic, since it flew in the face of the gynecentric culture of previous generations. Paradoxically, Native American women activists faced the challenge of supporting tribal sovereignty while identifying that what has been done by men in the name of tribal sovereignty was often accomplished at the expense of Native American women's equality.[38] For African American women, the nationalism embodied in the slogan "Black is beautiful" is one reason why Angela Davis's Afro became one of many symbols of Black pride in the Black Power Movement. And yet in the 1980s and 1990s Davis watched as the political message associated with her hair was consistently reduced to a fashion statement, a reduction tinged with sexism.[39]

Recognizing that principles of nationalism, internationalism, and self-determination informed multiracial feminism brings us closer to understanding challenges for white antiracist women since the 1960s. Whereas an imagined community of descent/dissent born out of nationalism was crucial for liberation struggles for people of color, antiracism for white women necessarily meant assuming an antinationalist position (since nationalism for white people is in effect white supremacy). White antiracists needed to generate a consciousness that respected Black and Chicano nationalism and Native American sovereignty (and its attendant symbols) while rejecting white nationalism. These are among the many issues white antiracist women dealt with in solidarity organizations in the late 1960s and early 1970s, issues that were then elaborated upon in multiracial feminist contexts later in the 1970s and 1980s.

Why the Missing Stories

There are several interconnected reasons why the influence of the Black Power Movement has largely been missing in tellings of second-wave feminism. First, many books about 1960s activism—whether they are about the early Civil Rights Movement or Black Power—have marginalized the contributions of women across race and class.[40] Second, there is tremendous ambivalence about that period (1966–1973) in progressive white history in general. When accounts of early civil rights organizing pivot on the racial split in SNCC, the myriad forces that complicated and severely taxed the civil rights agenda are overshadowed by a story of a separation between white and Black activists. With such a reduction, it is hard to recognize those who did carry on, who did go forward, who were not taken down by that schism.

New Left historical accounts by white men have also typically ignored the positive impact of the Black Power Movement on subsequent organizing. These histories tend to stop around 1968, just as Black Power was reaching full swing. Wini Breines writes, "Because new-left accounts focus on the period before 1968, the influence of nonviolent resistance and especially SNCC are acknowledged and honored but the influence of the Black Power Movement on white activists is not."[41] Meanwhile, some white men and women were learning a great deal about race, gender, organizing, and state repression through their work with Black militant groups. Naomi Jaffe knew that repression of prisoners at Attica Prison had to be a feminist issue. The forces that ordered and carried out the assault on the prisoners were white *and* male and had state power behind them. This is the same state power that has funded the construction of an overwhelming number of new prisons for both men and women in the 1980s and 1990s and against which Naomi has been organizing for two decades. Marilyn Buck knew that Black and white women were positioned differently in early civil rights and late civil rights work. The work they needed to do and the risks they took had to be calibrated with an awareness of white privilege.

There are also reasons why the influence of the Black Power Movement is rarely addressed in white accounts of second-wave feminism. Part of the problem is that social movement history is typically one step behind the making of that history. The feminist movement is not over. It is not dead. Many of those who might write about it are still busy being in it. But the problem is not only a matter of time and energy. The lack of attention to the Black Power Movement in the histories that do exist reflect enduring ideological conflicts among feminists about what counts and what does not. Some radical white feminists take exception to the notion that the feminist movement had its roots in the Civil Rights Movement, never mind the Black Power Movement.[42] From their perspective, such an interpretation belittles the ingenuity and uniqueness of the feminist movement.[43] When feminist writers do make connections between the feminist movement, the Civil Rights Movement, and the New Left, they typically see the rise of feminism as a defensive reaction against the sexism women faced in these movements.[44] The logic of this version of feminist history is that women came to see themselves as autonomous subjects as a consequence of their subjugation by men in SNCC, SDS, and other New Left organizations. This perspective understates the positive lessons about organizing learned within mixed-gender groups.

Although some feminist writers do draw positive links between the early Civil Rights Movement and feminism, few name the Black Power Movement as a positive influence. And yet the skills and leadership abilities women developed in that context gave them many tools for working in multiracial feminist contexts over the next decades. When women of color began creating autonomous feminist caucuses and organizations in the 1970s and 1980s, those white women who had worked with the Black Panther Party or other Black liberation organizations already knew that political work done in racially distinct groups was useful and that white groups need to have specific ways of remaining accountable to Black groups.

White solidarity organizations had a distinct, albeit uneven and imperfect, relation to Black groups. By contrast, white feminist consciousness-raising groups rarely had any real connections to Black groups. Feminist writers have often rationalized exclusively white consciousness-raising groups and other feminist organizations by claiming that Black, Asian, and Latina women were too busy, uninterested, or unwilling do feminist organizing during that period (that is, they were busy doing work with men and therefore did not have the time or consciousness necessary to do "feminist" work.) In her critique of the historiography of early second-wave feminism, Barbara Smith writes, "Appallingly, Black activists' demands for autonomous organizations in order to determine Black political agendas during this period are cited as a legitimate excuse for not altering the all-white composition of early women's organizations. White women's comfort level with de facto segregation, which they had experienced since childhood, and their lack of significant connections to women of color in their daily lives, were much more likely causes."[45] That Black women did feminist work within mixed-gender Black organizations and that white militant women sought mixed-gender groups in hopes of keeping antiracism and anti-imperialism central both show the limits of seeing feminism's whiteness as either inevitable or somehow the fault of Black women.

For white women who wanted to keep anti-imperialism and racial justice a central focus, working with white groups in solidarity with Black groups was a necessary solution. Although women's liberation groups that remained all white partly reflected their familiarity with "de facto segregation," the experience of white women who worked alongside Black nationalist organizations suggests a different dynamic. White accountability to Black organizations required at that time a form of "parallel play"—what sociologist Guida West termed a "twin-track approach to organizing."[46] This approach reflected a transition from early-1960s integrationist politics to Black Power politics. In the late 1960s and the early 1970s the twin-track antiracist organizations were mixed gender. They served as a stepping-stone to the coalition politics at the foundation of multiracial feminism.

5

Multiracial Feminism

Whereas militant white women of the late 1960s and early 1970s found little workable space in the white feminist movement, the situation for the next cohort of white women—those who came to feminism in the mid-1970s and the 1980s—was quite different. By the late 1970s a decade of self-conscious organizing among lesbians and gay men meant that issues of sexuality could not be sidelined as they had often been in the Civil Rights Movement, the Black Power Movement, and the early second-wave liberal feminist movement. Black, Latina, Asian, and Native American women's efforts to create autonomous organizations led by women of color in the 1970s—organizations that did not include men or white women—created a foundation for coalition politics between women of color and white antiracist women in the 1980s. With these organizations and the concurrent explosion of writing by women of color as their base, women of color confronted what history of consciousness theorist Chela Sandoval identifies as "the ideological differences [that] divided and helped to dissipate the movement from within between the years 1972 and 1980."[1]

Organizations of women of color became bridges between the nationalism of the 1960s and the multiracial feminist activism of the 1980s. By the early 1980s there were multiple venues for collaboration. It was in this context and in response to the limitations of mainstream feminist organizing that a small but growing group of white women began to articulate an explicitly antiracist feminist politic.

From the beginning, the story of the emergence of white antiracist activism has been intertwined with and dependent upon the development of feminism among women of color. For the most part, the story of antiracist white activism simply is not told in the recent histories of radical, liberal, or cultural feminism, since much of antiracist white feminist work has been in reaction to what Chela Sandoval refers to as "hegemonic feminism."[2] As is true of the story of white antiracist activism in the Civil Rights and Black Power Movements, the story of white antiracism in feminism cannot be separated from the work of women of color at the level of culture, strategy, or ideology.

That there is no single source history of contemporary African American, Latina, Asian American, and Native American feminisms complicates a tracing of white antiracism, since it was through feminism developed by women of color that white antiracist feminism emerged. The tendency in much white feminist history to marginalize the activism of women of color is a key reason for this absence. Differences in the histories of these groups is another reason why the stories have largely been told separately. Although separate tellings do justice to the different histories of women of color, white antiracism did not form solely alongside Asian American and African American feminism, for example; rather, it developed through the interaction among and between feminists across race. I open this chapter, then, with a brief sketch of the development of feminism among women of color, even though I am cognizant that an abbreviated rendering runs the risk of flattening significant differences among African American, Latina, Native American, and Asian American women.

Organizing by Women of Color in the United States

During the early period of the feminist movement (the late 1960s and early 1970s), women of color in the United States were working on three fronts: forming women's caucuses in existing mixed-gender organizations, developing autonomous feminist organizations, and working in white-dominated feminist groups.[3] This three-pronged approach contrasts sharply with the common notion that feminism among women of color emerged in reaction to (and therefore later than) white feminism.

Among the earliest women-of-color organizations were women's caucuses formed within existing Third World and nationalist organizations. These caucuses either remained within such organizations or became autonomous. The Third World Women's Alliance, for example, grew out of Student Nonviolent Coordinating Committee (SNCC) chapters on the East Coast and focused on racism, sexism, and imperialism.[4] One of the earliest feminist activist organizations of the second wave was a Chicana group, Hijas de Cuauhtemoc, founded in 1971 and named after a Mexican women's underground newspaper that was published during the 1910 Mexican revolution. The feminist consciousness-raising group that led to the founding of Hijas de Cuauhtemoc was initially convened by women in the United Mexican American Student Organization, which was part of the Chicano student movement of the late 1960s.[5] Many of the founders of Hijas de Cuauhtemoc were later involved in launching the first national Chicana studies journal, *Encuentro Feminil*.

An early Asian American women's group, Asian Sisters, focused on drug abuse intervention for young women in Los Angeles. It emerged out of the Asian American Political Alliance, a broad-based, grassroots organization largely fueled by the consciousness of first-generation Asian American college students.[6] Networking between Asian American and other women during this period included participation by a contingent of 150 Third World and white women from North America at the historic Vancouver Indochinese Women's Conference (1971) to work with Indochinese women against U.S. imperialism.[7] Asian American women also provided services for battered women, worked as advocates for refugees and recent immigrants, produced events spotlighting Asian women's cultural and political diversity, and organized with other women of color.[8]

In her history of the early Asian women's movement (1966–1974), Miya Iwataki writes that by the early 1970s Asian American women were building organizations directed to, for, and by women while "remaining integrated with the movement as a whole."[9] About these dual commitments Iwataki writes, "The roots of the woman's question are centuries deep, and like the roots of centuries-old trees, cannot be suddenly ripped out of the soil without leaving huge gaps and fissures that would be destructive to the rest of the ecology (or the communities). A separatist woman's movement would fall right into the divide and conquer tactics of the government" (41).

The best-known Native American women's organization of the 1970s was Women of All Red Nations (WARN), initiated in 1974 by women, many of whom were also members of AIM, founded in 1968 by Dennis Banks, George Mitchell, and Mary Jane Wilson.[10] WARN's activism included fighting sterilization in public health-service hospitals, suing the U.S. government for attempts to sell Pine Ridge water in

South Dakota to corporations, and networking with indigenous people in Guatemala and Nicaragua.[11] WARN reflected a whole generation of Native American women activists who had been leaders in the takeover at Wounded Knee, South Dakota, in 1973; on the Pine Ridge Reservation, and elsewhere. WARN, like Asian Sisters and Hijas de Cuauhtemoc, grew out of and often worked with mixed-gender nationalist organizations.

The autonomous feminist organizations that women of color were forming during the early 1970s drew on nationalist traditions through their recognition of the need for independent organizations led by people of color.[12] At the same time, unlike earlier nationalist organizations that included men and women, these were organizations specifically for women. Among Black women, the foremost autonomous feminist organization of the early 1970s was the National Black Feminist Organization (NBFO). Founded in 1973 by Florynce Kennedy, Margaret Sloan, and Doris Wright, it included many other well-known Black women, including Faith Ringgold, Michelle Wallace, Alice Walker, and Barbara Smith. According to Deborah Gray White, "more than any organization in the century [NBFO] launched a frontal assault on sexism and racism."[13] Its first conference in New York was attended by four hundred women from a range of class backgrounds.

Although NBFO was short-lived nationally (1973–1975), chapters in major cities remained together for years, including one in Chicago that survived until 1981. Although its members employed the tool of consciousness-raising also used in white feminist groups, the content of these sessions was decidedly Black women's issues: stereotypes of Black women in the media, discrimination in the workplace, myths about Black women as matriarchs, and Black women's beauty and self esteem.[14] NBFO also helped inspire the founding, in 1974, of the Combahee River Collective, an organization named after a river in South Carolina where Harriet Tubman led an insurgent action that freed 750 slaves. The Combahee River Collective not only led the way for crucial antiracist activism in Boston through the decade but also provided a blueprint for Black feminism that still stands a quarter of a century later.

A foundational principle of the Combahee River Collective statement was the concept of identity politics. In 1977 members of the collective wrote, "We believe that the most profound and potentially most radical politics come directly out of our own identity, as opposed to working to end somebody else's oppression. In the case of Black women this is a particularly repugnant, dangerous, threatening, and therefore revolutionary concept because it is obvious from looking at all the political movements that have preceded us that anyone is more worthy of liberation than ourselves. We reject pedestals, queenhood, and walking ten paces behind. To be recognized as human, levelly human is enough."[15] Identity politics did not mean there were any natural, inevitable, or necessarily long-lasting alliances among Black women simply on the basis of a shared identity. In fact, the Combahee River Collective knew better than that even in 1977; class and educational differences between women in the collective threatened to destroy it on more than one occasion, and eventually did. Identity politics underscored the reason why separate caucus groups were a necessary component of coalition work. Just as Black women needed time to look each other in the eye, white women needed to confront the ways they failed to take racism seriously. Identity politics was the strategic basis for Combahee's protests against the Boston Police Department and the media in 1979, when those two institutions attempted to dismiss the murders of twelve black women (based on the notion that they were alleged to be prostitutes and therefore not worthy of protection or investigation).

For Combahee, taking identity politics seriously as a strategy meant recognizing it as a two-step process. Identity politics was more than naming an identity based on group affiliation: It was the naming of that identity for the purpose of subversive action. Because Black women had been murdered, Black women needed to be the ones to name the strategies for organizing on behalf of Black women's safety.[16] In her journal entry about the organizing in 1979, Barbara Smith wrote, "That winter and spring were a time of great demoralization, anger, sadness and fear for many Black women in Boston, including myself. It was also for me a time of some of the most intensive and meaningful political organizing I have ever done. The Black feminist political analysis and practice the Combahee River Collective had developed since 1974 enabled us to grasp both the sexual-political and racial-political implications of the murders and positioned us to be the link between the various communities that were outraged: Black people, especially Black women; other women of color; and white feminists, many of whom were also Lesbians."[17]

Of the coalition between Black and white women that developed during that time, Smith wrote, "This is *new*. Black and white, feminists and non-feminists, women have never come together and worked on a woman's issue, an issue of racial-sexual politics, at least not in this era. I am thinking about the anti-lynching movement at the beginning of the century as the nearest parallel—and that of course was different. So this has never been tried before. It could work. I think about sitting up at Harriet Tubman House three or four years ago in CESA [the Committee to End Sterilization Abuse] trying to figure out how to involve Third World women in our work. And now it is the other way around. White women taking leadership from Black women around one of those 'universal' issues we as Black feminists have always said would pull in everyone" (318–19).

The Combahee River Collective saw race, class, and gender as interlocking and refused to rank one oppression over another. In recognizing a "simultaneity of oppressions," the members of Combahee were following in the footsteps of their foremothers who had argued for a multidimensional analysis in previous decades.[18] Combahee also offered an anticapitalist, anti-imperialist critique that drew on Black Marxism and nationalism of the 1960s and earlier.[19] A dramatic departure from the past, however, was Combahee's explicit attention to sexuality in addition to race, class, and gender.

Combahee was critical of a narrow Black nationalism that was male dominated. At the same time, Combahee rejected the separatism of some white lesbians as untenable, given Black women's commitment to working with Black men. In the space between Black male nationalists and white lesbian separatists were Black lesbians who, though representing one of the smallest subsets of people in liberation struggles, fashioned a stunningly inclusive definition of feminism. Barbara Smith writes, "Feminism is the political theory and practice that struggles to free *all* women: women of color, working-class women, poor women, disabled women, lesbians, old women—as well as white economically privileged, heterosexual women. Anything less than this vision of total freedom is not feminism but merely female self-aggrandizement."[20]

This definition of feminism went far beyond white feminist definitions in its refusal to sideline any woman—most particularly women of color—in the process. This expansiveness, along with Combahee's commitment to socialism and their international perspective, resulted in a Black feminist politic that, as sociologist Patricia Hill Collins has noted, was about "fairness, equality, and justice for all human beings, not just African American women. Black feminism's fundamental goal of creating a humanistic vision of community is more comprehensive than that of other social action movements."[21]

Alice Walker's 1983 term "womanism," like Smith's definition of feminism, also offered an understanding of women's liberation that went far beyond white feminist versions of the time.[22] The politic emerging among many Chicanas in the 1970s had similar breadth and scope. One term used, "Chicana womanism," bridged antiracist and antisexist struggle. Like Walker's "womanism," this term distinguished Chicana liberation from liberal or radical white feminism while holding Chicanos accountable for challenging patriarchy within Latino struggles.[23] According to Chela Sandoval, each of these terms—and others: Gloria Anzaldúa's "new mestiza," Audre Lorde's "sister outsider," Maxine Hong Kingston's "woman warrior"—and all the political and cultural work they represented made the emergence of U.S. Third World feminism impossible to ignore.[24]

A third location in which women of color worked in the 1970s was white-dominated, early second-wave feminist organizations. Just a few of many examples: Margaret Sloan and Pauli Murray helped found the National Organization for Women in 1966 and continued to try to push for a multidimensional feminist politic in that organization for many years. Doris Wright, who helped found NBFO, was also a founding member of *Ms. Magazine* in 1972. Elizabeth Martínez was one of the initial members of New York Radical Women, along with Chude Pam Allen, Kathie Amatniek Sarachild, Shulamith Firestone, and Anne Koedt.[25] Celestine Ware, author of *Woman Power,* one of the earliest radical feminist books, was a founder of the New York Radical Women.[26]

I note these examples (and many more are to be found) in part to counter the tendency in white feminist historiography to consider the feminism of women of color and white feminism as completely separate in the early years. This tendency not only renders invisible women of color's early contributions to and interventions in white-dominated feminism, but it also fails to account for the skills required to negotiate in multiple communities simultaneously. Chicana studies scholars Beatriz Pesquera and Denise Segura write, "It is theoretically possible and likely that Chicanas' multiple sources of group identification con-flict at times with one another, rendering the development of a group consciousness based on the privileging of one social location over the others ahistorical and untenable."27 This part of the story—the bal-ancing acts—is especially relevant for white antiracist women who since the 1970s have often found themselves straddling multiple com-munities as well.

Each of these arenas of activism had their own struggles, a reality compounded for women of color, who had commitments in more than one location. Members of women's caucuses in mixed-gender national-ist groups faced the challenge of keeping the attention on women: as leaders, in the organization's priorities, and in networks with other groups. As Angela Davis writes, "Even though we may have considered the feminism of that period white, middle-class, and utterly irrelevant, we also found compulsory male leadership utterly unacceptable."28 The struggles of members of autonomous groups led by women of color included finding common ground when class, color, and sexual differ-ences came to the fore. Women of color involved in white-dominated organizations struggled to be heard when outnumbered and to be respected rather than tokenized. Not surprisingly, a great deal of the most-successful and longest-lasting organizing took place in autono-mous organizations—organizing that within a decade enabled a vibrant women-of-color movement to emerge.

Through the 1970s and 1980s, grassroots activism by women of color focused on multiple issues: organizing for reproductive rights, es-pecially against sterilization abuse; building battered-women's shelters and rape crisis centers; advocating for welfare rights; sponsoring Black, Latina, and Asian American women's conferences; developing Black and Latina women's studies in higher education; supporting work-place organizing; and opposing police brutality.29

This activism, in concert with an explosion of writing by women of color, made a much wider space for feminism among women of color. The literary, political, and artistic writing of the 1970s—Toni Cade's *The Black Woman;* Ntozake Shange's *For Colored Girls Who Have Considered Suicide / When the Rainbow Is Enuf;* Maxine Hong King-ston's *The Woman Warrior; Conditions: Five, the Black Women's Issue;* Audre Lorde's *The Cancer Journals*—reflected an extraordinary range of artistic and political contributions.30 The writing included a dizzying array of genres—theory, poetry, plays, songs, novels, essays, auto-biography—all of which pushed beyond existing intellectual and cultural boundaries.

By the early 1980s "the development of women of color as a new political subject" had clearly taken place due to substantial work done in multiple arenas.[31] According to Angela Davis, "Most people date this new political subject from 1981, when *This Bridge Called My Back: Writings by Radical Women of Color*, was first published."[32] Originally conceived of by Chicana lesbians Cherríe Moraga and Gloria Anzaldúa in 1979, *This Bridge Called My Back* reflected the tremendous cultural work and activism of women of color in the years before its publication.[33] It was published at a time when the editors and many contributors saw a real possibility for a unified Third World women's movement, a movement made possible by women of color putting themselves and each other at the top of the agenda.

In the foreword to the second edition of *This Bridge Called My Back,* Moraga writes, "In response to a proliferation of writing by women of color up until 1980 which in the name of feminism focused almost exclusively on heterosexual relations—either by apologizing for or condemning the sexism of Third World men—*Bridge* intended to make a clean break from that phenomenon. Instead, we created a book which concentrated on relationships *between women*."[34] About the title of the book, Moraga explains, "[It] was a way to make physical our experience of having to bridge. . . . it acknowledges the fact that Third World women *do* lay their bodies down to make a connection. But at the same time, being able to say it in a way where it's not a submission, it's a self-declaration: I am a bridge. I lay myself down; I'm the one doing it, no one's pushing me down."[35] It is this paradoxical message, in part, that gave the book its power. In her review of *This Bridge Called My Back,* Paula Gunn Allen, a Laguna Pueblo/Sioux-Lebanese woman, writes that the book "provided me ways to view myself and my history/experiences that gave me order, coherence and meaning. I was by turns delighted, enraged, grieved and stunned. I was deeply conscious of how wounded I have been."[36]

The vision for the contributors to *Bridge* was to find ways for women of color to communicate and activate together—mother to daughter, sister to sister, lover to lover, friend to friend; in small and large groups; through artistic connection and activist organizations;

locally, regionally, and internationally; across multiple divides. Merle Woo, the daughter of a Korean mother and Chinese father, writes "A Letter to Ma," about how her radicalism is informed by her heritage, what it took for her parents to send her to college, why her mother's stories and her grandmother's stories have been so hidden, and why she came to identify herself as an Asian American feminist.[37] Mitsuye Yamada's "Asian American Women and Feminism" sees women of color in the United States as a link to Third World women throughout the world.[38]

In her letter to Third World women writers, "Speaking in Tongues" Gloria Anzaldúa urges herself and other women writers to "forget the room of one's own—write in the kitchen, lock yourself up in the bathroom. Write on the bus or the welfare line, on the job or during meals, between sleeping or waking."[39] For Anzaldúa, writing by women of color is a lifeline between them. She writes, "In the San Francisco area, where I now live, none can stir the audience with their craft and truth saying as do Cherríe Moraga (Chicana), Gennie Lim (Asian American), and Luisah Teish (Black). With women like these, the loneliness of writing and the sense of powerlessness can be dispelled. We can walk among each other talking of our writing, reading to each other. And more and more when I'm alone, though still in communion with each other, the writing possesses me and propels me to leap into a timeless spaceless no-place where I forget myself and feel I am the universe. *This* is power" (172).

Although *Bridge* was written by and for women of color, it and other writing of the period exposed growing numbers of white women to the politics articulated by women of color. Political scientist Jane Mansbridge writes, "Despite the efforts of individual Black and Latina and Asian women to influence their mostly White organizations and their standing up at conferences to present their points of view, it was not until a significant literature by women of color appeared that the larger feminist movement began to learn significantly from those differences and be transformed. It was too painful for each Black woman individually to have to teach the White feminists in her organizations about their experiences. But through the written word, which can teach many at once, and through the controversies and understanding generated when people talk about what they have read, the movement as a discursive entity is now beginning to absorb, confront and be transformed by these new insights."[40]

White readers of *This Bridge Called My Back* and other writing by women of color of that period had much to learn about racism. Sherna Berger Gluck writes, "By 1982, on the heels of difficult political struggles waged by activist scholars of color, ground breaking essays and anthologies by and about women of color opened a new chapter in U.S. feminism. The future of the women's movement in the U.S. was reshaped irrevocably by the introduction of the expansive notion of feminismS."[41]

This Bridge Called My Back; *Home Girls: A Black Feminist Anthology*; and Beth Brant's edited volume, *A Gathering of Spirit: Writing and Art by North American Indian Women,* were all wake-up calls for white women, alerting them to the fact that dealing with racism was an absolute must.[42] In the preface to *This Bridge Called My Back,* Cherríe Moraga writes, "What drew me to politics was my love of women, the agony I felt in observing the straight-jackets of poverty and repression I saw people in my own family in. But the deepest political tragedy I have experienced is how with such grace, such blind faith, this commitment to women in the feminist movement grew to be exclusive and reactionary. *I call my white sisters on this.*"[43] In "—But I Know You, American Woman," Judith Moschkovich explains that as a Latina, Jewish, immigrant woman, she knows much more about white Anglo culture than white Anglos know about her culture. In response to the many women who have assumed that it is her responsibility to educate them, she says, "Anyone that was raised and educated in this country has a very good chance of being ignorant about other cultures. . . . It's a sort of cultural isolationism, a way of life enforced on the people in this country so as to let them have a free conscience with respect to how they deal with the rest of the world."[44] To that ignorance Moschkovich replies, Educate yourself: "I say: *read and listen.* We may, then, have something to share" (80).

The works in *This Bridge Called My Back* and other writings of the time provided a sturdy and clear template for white antiracist activism for the 1980s and beyond. Among its directives were the following: Do not expect women of color to be your educators, to do all the bridge work. White women need to be the bridge a lot of the time. Do not lump African American, Latina, Asian American, and Native American into one category. History, culture, imperialism, language, class, region, and sexuality often make a monolithic concept of a "woman of color" indefensible. Listen to the anger of women of color. It is informed by centuries of struggle, erasure, and experience. White women, look to your own history for signs of heresy and rebellion. Do not take on the histories of Black, Latina, or American Indian women as your own. They are not and never were yours.

Many white women came to see antiracism racism as a centerpiece of feminism through the activism and writing of women of color. Equally important, the identity politics first articulated by the Combahee River Collective opened a way for white women to explore how their own multiple identities—class, religion, family, sexuality—might inform their strategies for opposing racism.

Turned Away, Stepped Back In

Along with this "new political subject" among women of color came the creation of a space, a testing ground, and the possibility for an increasing number of white women to develop antiracist feminist politics. Among them were white women activists of the 1960s who had steered clear of feminism in the early 1970s. The presence of prominent women of color who were embracing class- and race-conscious feminist politics forced them to reexamine their belief that feminism was by definition white and bourgeois.

Naomi Jaffe, who had turned away from white radical feminism in the early days (late 1960s and early 1970s), came back to it later, mainly through her work with Black and Latina women, particularly lesbians. When I interviewed her in 1997, she was working at Holding Our Own, a multiracial feminist funding organization in Albany, New York, where she has been on the staff since 1991. The Women's Building in which Holding Our Own has an office is sandwiched between Lawau's Braids and Beauty Salon; the Tattoo Shop; AAA Used Furniture; a leftist, independently owned bookstore; the Last Straw Cafe; and Alewaba African Braids. Unlike many women's centers, which are housed in white sections of town, this one is in a central location within a working- and middle-class Black community. Not that maintaining this location has not been a struggle, Naomi tells me: Getting the Women's Building to value and nurture a thoroughgoing commitment to diversity has not been an easy task. But the struggle has been worth it.

One question, of course, is how and why a woman who initially left the women's movement—a former member of the radical feminist organization Women's International Terrorist Conspiracy from Hell

(WITCH) in New York—came to consider feminist organizing key to her activism. As was the case for other women I interviewed, not until the early 1980s did Naomi begin to see that feminism and an anti-imperialist perspective need not contradict each other. After she came up from the underground (in 1978), Naomi moved to Minnesota with her partner, who was going to chiropractic school. Naomi tried to get involved with activism but had trouble "rejoining" the movement. Eventually she began doing antiapartheid work in the Twin Cities. Although there were some South Africans in the movement, Naomi had almost no contact with Black or Native American women in the area, an absence she had also experienced in the late 1960s. The anti-apartheid movement was largely white women and Black men. She remembers, "I was working full time and I was pregnant and very tired when I read *This Bridge Called My Back,* just when I needed it most. I read *This Bridge* and I realized, oh, that is what has been missing all my life—women of color."

Although it was a number of years before Naomi began working primarily with women of color, her basic insight remained. Once she moved to Albany, she worked with the Central America solidarity organization there, which included some Latinos, most of whom were Central Americans. But it was a predominantly white organization, and there were very few Latinas. Naomi and a few others worked to change the racial consciousness of the organization by sponsoring multiracial events. But Naomi continued to feel isolated: "There was still this pull to be in organizations that were all white, and I decided that I wasn't going to do that any more. I couldn't do it as a white person in a predominantly white organization. I needed to be situated differently. I needed to be in rooms that were predominantly filled with people of color in order to figure out what work I had to do. I had never done that. I had been an activist for twenty-five years, and I had never worked in predominantly people-of-color organizations."

During this period Naomi was also asked by women in her community to account for the ways heterosexism had shaped her life, resources, and assumptions—to figure out how being a straight woman affected her activism. For Naomi, confronting issues of homophobia and sexuality finally guided her to work directly with women of color. In a Nicaraguan women's solidarity group the two lesbian members said it was not a comfortable place for them. Naomi remembers them saying, "This is a married women's club and that does not work for us." The married women said, "Oh God, we can't deal with this. We have so little time. We have our kids and our families and our jobs and we are trying to do this one thing. We can't do ten things. We can only do one thing." That, Naomi says, "is when I remembered where I came from in my feminist life." She said to the other straight women, all of whom were younger than she, "You guys don't understand. You guys wouldn't be here if it weren't for lesbians. There were no women's organizations in solidarity with anything when I started doing political work. The way we got to a point where we can have feminist organizations is a struggle led by lesbians. We wouldn't be here. Homophobia is not just another issue. It is the work we are doing. If we can't do this right, we can't do anything. We won't have any women's organizations. So I remembered where I came from, just in the nick of time. I had come from a feminist background, but I hadn't done feminist work for many years. . . . When it came to arguing issues around homophobia, I found myself arguing a position that I didn't know I understood."

Soon after taking that position, Naomi went to a gay and lesbian rights march in Washington in 1983. "At that point, I was trying to figure out ways to be an ally of lesbians. So I went to this march with a couple of lesbian women I had known from the Nicaraguan affinity group. It was really affirming. They were just so welcoming of me. They made this big beautiful banner that said, 'Commies, Dykes, and Friends for Liberation.' I saw it and felt like allies were welcome. I started making connections with lesbians in the community, including lesbians of color. The lesbian feminist community, with all its deep contradictions, was a little more multiracial than the other parts of our movement." Through these connections Naomi got involved with Feminist Action Network (FAN), a predominantly lesbian and woman-of-color activist organization. Naomi remembers, "I thought it was one of the most wonderful things that ever happened to me, when I got invited to join this group. I was so thrilled. It was just where I needed to be working, in a place where issues of race and gender and sexuality are predominant. A place led by women of color, led by lesbians."

Suzanne Ross's entry into feminist organizing was also a direct consequence of working and developing friendships with Black feminists. Her long-term political work with women across race has taught her much about her complex and sometimes contradictory position within multiracial feminism. She was raised in the late 1930s and early 1940s in a Jewish family that lived in Europe and Palestine to escape the Holocaust. In the 1960s and early 1970s Suzanne became an activist against the Vietnam War and U.S. imperialism. While earning her Ph.D. in psychology, she also became a lifelong advocate for young people through her work with African American adolescents. By the early 1970s, Suzanne was teaching at Lehman College and began working closely with Audre Lorde, J. D. Franklin, and other Black women scholars. Although she was aware of the feminist movement in the 1970s, "I didn't like it even though I always had an inclination and identified with the politics." Suzanne was asked to speak at the first feminist conference at Barnard College in 1970, but she turned the opportunity down: "I didn't like the fact that it wasn't as militant at that time. I lumped all of them as racists. I had a very undialectical understanding of it. I saw it as too white, too lacking in militancy, too elitist. The stereotype of the white women's movement is what I bought into and missed a lot of opportunities to either raise it to a different level or relate to it differently. I always posed it against the antiracist movement."

Suzanne saw the class makeup and whiteness of the movement as a tragedy but did not, at that point, try to intervene. Until the mid-1970s she kept her distance from feminist activism. Once she began teaching and organizing alongside Black women, she began to examine her initial reaction to feminism. Meeting and working with Black feminists is "what turned me around. A lot of them gave me a hard time for not taking the feminist movement seriously enough. With someone like Audre Lorde, her mere presence, you couldn't say that feminism was white. Barbara Smith and hattie gossett became friends of mine. I met hattie on a trip to Cuba along with Toni Cade Bambara. She is an amazing thinker and a wonderful human being who taught me a lot. These women taught me a lot." By the late 1970s Suzanne had added the term "feminist" to the term "revolutionary" to describe her politics. Since the mid-1970s her feminist activism has largely taken place in multiracial organizations composed largely of women of color, including her annual work with a multiracial collective for International Women's Day.

It was precisely the emergence of a multiracial movement that was attempting to come to terms with race, sexuality, and gender that made room for Suzanne, Naomi, and other militant women of the 1960s to apply the skills they had developed in the Civil Rights and Black Power Movements. Because of their involvement with and commitment to women of color, they could no longer reject feminism as inherently racist. Moreover, identity politics first articulated by Black women gave them tools to understand how what Adrienne Rich termed the "politics of location" informed their perspectives.[45] For Naomi, that meant dealing with the ways heterosexism kept women of color and white women from connecting with each other. The lessons Suzanne learned working with African American adolescents and feminists of color required her to reconsider feminism as key to revolutionary politics. Multiracial feminism allowed Suzanne and Naomi to see that women of color had been invisible to them in the 1960s. For both women, multiracial feminism provided a community they had missed in the 1960s.

White Antiracist Feminism: Stumbling Blocks, Turning Points

Whereas some white women came to antiracist feminism after having been involved in the Civil Rights and Black Power Movements, a younger cohort of white women—most of whom were in their twenties at the time—were first exposed to race consciousness through multiracial lesbian feminist contexts. Unlike white militant women of the 1960s, they came to political consciousness through feminism at a time when women of color had made it clear that to call oneself a "feminist" and not deal with race is not to be a feminist. As one woman said at the National Women's Studies Association (NWSA) conference in 1981, "Shall we, as Third World women, decide to 'join' the 'movement'? We can't join the movement . . . because we are the movement."[46]

One women I interviewed, Laurie Holmes, describes her entry into activism as having been filtered from the beginning through her work in a multiracial workforce and multiracial feminism. Laurie was raised in a Protestant family in working- and middle-class bedroom communities in New England. As a child she was involved in a local United Church of Christ community, where lessons of race revolved around Martin Luther King Jr.'s "I Have a Dream" speech and the idea that all people are equal. As a teenager she began to believe that the world she was living in was not "the real world," so she set her sights on moving to a multiracial city. She moved to Boston at the age of seventeen, in 1976, and she soon came out as a lesbian. She began living with "other women who were discovering women's music, and got very psyched about feminism." In the gathering places she frequented—Saints, a women's bar; the Cambridge Women's Center; and women's concerts and conferences—she soon heard Black, Latina, and Asian American women saying that white women needed to do a serious examination of their racism. "The scene I have in my mind is of women of color standing up at concerts and conferences, talking about the work white women needed to do, immediately. I agreed with them and believed them. The message I heard was that white women had a lot of fucking work to do on ourselves. Go do it. Simple as that. I said, yeah. That is true for me. I have a lot of work to do. I had no idea where to start, but I am going to do it. I felt like I needed to start schooling myself."

Laurie's education about race began when she started driving a public school bus soon after Boston began school desegregation. In 1972 the National Association for the Advancement of Colored People (NAACP) and Black parents had sued the Boston School Committee to challenge school segregation.[47] The school bus drivers supported desegregation while, as an organization, modeling an integrated group that many hoped would exist in the school as well. The drivers drove children to and from school through angry crowds and barrages of rocks and other violence from whites opposed to integration. Laurie believes that the seven years she drove a bus "ended up being the best schooling I could have ever had. I joined what I think was one of the very few integrated workforces in Boston, along with the Gillette Company and maybe the post office. We were really mixed. Folks from all over the city. There was just so much in it for me. I got to know every single neighborhood in the city. I got to become friends with the kids on an ally level rather than from a position of authority." Had Laurie been a teacher, there would have been a formalized process for interacting with the parents. As a bus driver, relationships could develop more naturally.

At the same time, Laurie began "hitting up against my own racism." She believed a lot of stereotypes about neighborhoods and city life. But "going into neighborhoods and listening to the way people talk, I noticed my own fears as I developed relationships with people of color. . . . The most classic stuff is thinking some place is a bad neighborhood, but then, going in and seeing how people live busts all of that." Laurie had big fears that people of color were going to reject her. "My racism told me that I want to be friends with everybody, but no people of color would want to know anything about me. So let me not push myself onto them." This too was a fear she began to confront. Laurie sought information everywhere. "I was trying to read. I didn't read. I am probably the least well read antiracist activist in the world. You could probably name any number of theorists and I probably haven't read them. But I started reading novels written by women of color."

Laurie was also part of a bus drivers' union that was predominantly Black both in the rank and file and in the leadership and 25–35 percent women.[48] The union, which was well known for its organization and cohesion, staged several successful strikes to secure a decent wage, benefits, and accountability in hiring. In the process, according to Laurie, the bus drivers "did the kind of struggling with each other that people do in developing relationships." For example, as one of the only out lesbians in the union, Laurie "was hanging out with a lot of Black men who I think hated the idea of lesbianism. And yet we were all developing relationships across lines of difference that I believe challenged all of us." One year Laurie tried to play on a softball team with a group of Black women bus drivers. "They didn't have any white players on the team and no lesbians. They let me play, but it didn't work out as a positive experience. . . . It didn't get comfortable enough. They had social gatherings after games, but I never knew where those were. I somehow didn't get myself there. I wanted to challenge myself to do that and I wanted to build relationships with those women but it was really hard. And we didn't find a way to articulate together what was in the way."

Despite difficulties, people in the union kept working together. Laurie remembers Mel King (a progressive Black leader who ran for mayor of Boston under the Rainbow Coalition in 1983) coming to their union meetings. "He would rally us together. I remember this one meeting where he had us all hugging each other. It was wonderful. I remember those as really great times. Probably greater than they were, but I felt like we were walking the talk. We weren't talking that we were doing antiracism work, ever. That is true of my whole story. We were just doing it. We were trying to get the kids to school on buses. We were trying to get a better contract. We were aware that we were a diverse group of folks. We spoke of an appreciation of that which worked in our favor." At that time Laurie and many others across race believed that busing was the "only way that communities of color were going to get equal resources. . . . We would line up with police escorts and go into South Boston and have rocks thrown at us. That kind of stuff. It kind of felt that all of us were united—the drivers and the parents and the kids on the buses. Trying to keep the kids safe and get everybody where they needed to go."

Through a combination of lessons she learned as a bus driver and from multiracial lesbian feminism, Laurie was coming to believe that fighting racism centered on being part of people's real-life struggles. Of her work at that time, Laurie says, "I would have called it activism. I just wouldn't have called it antiracism. I am here because this is my job. Antiracism has always been a subtitle for other work I am doing." Laurie continued to develop organizing skills she associated with feminism: consensus making, building activist organizations through individual relationships, and "giving everyone a voice that wants to be involved." There were times, however, in the early 1980s where the life she was leading and her work with lesbian feminist organizing felt separate to her. She would drive a bus in multiracial communities as part of a multiracial union during the day and then go to the Cambridge Women's Center, which was mostly a white feminist center, at night. For example, the affinity group she was involved with in the early 1980s, Lesbians United in Nonnuclear Action (LUNA), did a great job of confronting the larger, male-dominated, antinuclear organization Clamshell Alliance, "pushing their way into the decision-making process if they had to." But the lesbian affinity group itself was mostly white. Laurie pushed to get the alliance to think beyond white women, working, for example, to make sure the story she wrote about Karen Silkwood was translated into Spanish.

Over time Laurie's community was becoming more and more mixed racially. In 1981 she fell in love with a Puerto Rican woman who had three children. That relationship and her parenting pulled her away from white feminists and toward daily life in a Puerto Rican family. "In those days," she explains, "it was not cool to be a lesbian and have boys. . . . My focus was really at home. Little boys were not accepted. I had four brothers and no sisters and always loved boys. I didn't move away from feminism. I moved away from feminists."

Not until the 1990s—when Laurie began working at the Elizabeth

Stone House, a grassroots mental health alternative founded in 1974 by a group of radical social workers and women who had formerly been incarcerated on psychiatric wards—did Laurie find a place where her feminism and antiracism need not be separated. She recalls, "As soon as I walked through the doors at the Stone House, I felt like I had come home. . . . It was a place that consciously thought through its policies to reflect the experiences of the people it serves and to walk that politic and honor the experience of everyone walking through the door. . . . Through a process of plenty of struggle, the organization is explicit about reflecting the communities it serves—women of color, lesbians, bilingual, bicultural women—and operates based on a non-hierarchical model."

Laurie's story illustrates the tensions felt by a group of white women in the late 1970s and early 1980s who, in their attempts to understand race, class, gender, and sexuality, ended up straddling several worlds simultaneously. She, like many lesbian feminists of her generation, first began dealing with racism because of what they were learning from women of color. Laurie was working in a multiracial, highly politicized setting at a time when many white people were openly hostile toward school bus drivers and their young charges. Laurie came out as a lesbian into an increasingly vocal and politicized gay and lesbian community at a time when, as she remembers it, "gay and lesbian pride marches were political rather than a picnic." For Laurie, the personal was political, and the political was personal in every aspect of her life.

Ruth Frankenberg also links her consciousness about racism directly to lessons learned from women of color during the rise of Third World feminism. Ruth grew up in England and moved to northern California in 1979. As a child she saw the world as both an insider, being white and English-speaking, and an outsider, being the daughter of a Jewish father and Protestant mother, a child of leftist parents, and from a single-parent household in a period when divorce was not yet common. As a young adult, Ruth was involved in challenging the National Front, a neo-Nazi organization that was gaining political power in England in the mid-1960s. During that period, she identified herself as a socialist feminist. When she moved to Santa Cruz in 1979, she quickly learned that the feminist movement in Britain lagged behind the movement in California, which meant she still considered antiracism and feminism as completely separate. Like many white women who came to see the two as intertwined, Ruth learned much from women of color who considered themselves feminists or were intensely involved in women's rights issues. A Puerto Rican woman who had come of age in the National Welfare Rights Organization (NWRO) became Ruth's particular mentor and friend.[49] Ruth began to recognize racism in the feminist movement, in graduate classes and scholarship, and in American culture and daily life.

Like many white women, Ruth initially responded to these lessons with disbelief. In graduate school, where women of color and white women students were openly confronting issues of race, Ruth remembers stages of her own reactions. At first she thought the women of color were kidding or wrong when they identified limits of socialist feminism. She went though a "whole process of trying to prove them wrong on everything and thinking that they must be thinking about liberal feminism, not Marxist feminism." She then went through a lengthy period of feeling great "shame about being part of this big category of people called white people, or this subcategory called white women, or even smaller category called white feminists, who were not on the right side but on the wrong side." Until then Ruth had felt like "one of the good guys. . . . So it was an about face. . . . Being very conscious that everything I thought I knew I didn't know. Because everything I thought I knew was inadequate." During that period Ruth went from thinking everything she had learned and thought was right to thinking nothing was. She assumed everything a person of color said was correct, which became a real bind for her when two people of color disagreed.

A turning point came when she became close friends with an Indian woman who, like Ruth, was an immigrant. "She had experienced a lot of misrecognition and misunderstanding and nonrecognition as an Indian who had been a feminist activist and a leftist in India who then came here and encountered a lot of the same kinds of incomprehension from women of color that you might get from white people—the presumption of How could there be a feminist movement in India?" Ruth's relationship with her friend taught Ruth to "think for myself": to question her own limited knowledge as a white woman but not glorify women of color in the process.

As Ruth continued to engage with African American, Puerto Rican,

Chicana, and South Asian women—through both friendships and activism—she began to uncover part of what makes confronting racism so scary. In an open letter to Gloria Watkins (bell hooks), who was also enrolled in a graduate course Ruth was taking, Ruth included an analysis of another white woman in the class who Ruth believed did not want to confront her own racism because the woman thought it would mean questioning her own self-worth, her Ph.D., and her credibility. Ruth's appraisal was accurate, but with time she began to see that her analysis of the other white woman applied to herself as well. She was projecting onto another white woman her own fears. "Everything I knew to be true was really dubious, so in other words, for me, my political work, my academic work were very connected. I mean, you have your line, your act. So if Gloria was right, then everything I knew was wrong, therefore my entire epistemology was up shit creek. So in that sense, I feared for my Ph.D., my intellectual credibility, my competency, and therefore my self-worth. My self-worth was very tied to . . . my political consciousness."

Ruth was aware of the problems with white women's identities, but at that period in her life she had trouble claiming those problems as her own. Instead, she made it another white woman's problem, setting herself up as separate from other white women. "I ended up in a very polarized situation where my whole first-year cohort [in graduate school] hated me, because it was a very strong cohort of white feminists. I thought they hated me because of the line I was taking about racism, and in fact that was true. But the other thing that was true is that, had I been ten years down the road with my practice of antiracism, I could have addressed all of this in a different way. One thing that is changed about me is my improved ability to talk with other white people about racism in a way that doesn't freak them out. So I was going like a herd of elephants, blundering through with my new shock, horror, discoveries." Ten years down the line, Ruth might have "had the honesty to take it on myself, to take on my issues, and then say, 'I wonder if that issue is true for this other person as well.'"

About two years into the process of developing race-consciousness, Ruth "hit the wall." She explains, "I got to this place where I had no place to sit or fit. . . . I was in this body that was entirely filled with white privilege; that was the totality of myself." Although Ruth had white friends, she had no white allies. A lot of her "white friends literally didn't want to deal with me because they felt I was too closely identified with my friends of color. . . . But, to be really frank, I don't think those white friends were interested in a thoroughgoing engagement with racism." During this same period, Ruth also could not figure out if she were a lesbian or not, which only added to her confusion and tentativeness.

Amid this cognitive dissonance Ruth became very sick. She returned to England to take care of her grandmother, who was recuperating from surgery. In the process she learned much about the health care system, the social welfare system, and her own mother's struggle to care for her mother. At the same time she was doing graduate work on the difference race makes in how feminists talk about female consciousness. "All of that helped me to remember that there is no binary path. . . . Women's lives are shaped not just by race but by a range of other issues as well."

In the ten years between Ruth's "going like a herd of elephants" and finding a way to walk with other white people, she did a lot of learning. She came out as a lesbian, continued to sustain long-term relationships with women of color, and began finding ways to develop close friendships with white antiracist women. She came to trust that her partner "would equally well call me on my racism and support me on my antiracism." From Ricky Marcuse and Terry Berman, both white antiracist consultants and teachers, Ruth learned that antiracist work for white people requires "doing the work from a place of self-love."

All these influences led her to see antiracist work as a political as well as a spiritual process. Coming from a left background, she had grown up with a narrow understanding of what constitutes "activism." She now has a larger understanding. She has also come to believe that her biggest challenge is "working with other white people around racism. . . . My work is really about waking white people up to who they are in terms of racial formation."

By the time Ruth and Laurie came to feminism (in the late 1970s and early 1980s), there were multiple arenas in which white women learned that dealing with race and women's multiple identities was essential. They did not come of age as feminists thinking feminism started and ended with white women. It was a time when race was an openly contested issue in multiple places: in conferences, speak-outs, and political forums; in neighborhood organizing; in women-founded organizations; and in intimate interracial relationships and friendship circles.

At the same time, there are important differences in their stories, differences that speak to the range of ways in which white women contended with race through feminism in the late 1970s and 1980s. Much of Ruth's early exposure to and many of her conversations with women of color took place in a university setting, in writing, and through multiracial feminist theory. Laurie, by contrast, went to college "for a quick minute" but dropped out after coming to believe that that Hampshire College (a small alternative liberal arts school in a predominantly white community) was as unreal an environment as the bedroom communities in which she had grown up. Her early understanding about racism took shape in the working world, among and with working-class people. For her, antiracism was always work she did through other work—driving a bus, raising a family, resisting separatist politics—straddling many worlds simultaneously.

Alongside this key difference are important parallels in Ruth's and Laurie's stories that are indicative of the dilemmas many white women faced during this period. Their stories of coming to consciousness about antiracism cannot be told without attending to their private as well as their public lives. The lessons they learned in intimate relationships were as compelling as those they learned in the work world. Both women attributed early lessons about race to women of color—lessons they learned in conferences, conversations, organizing, and intimate relationships. Both went through a period of isolation from other white women. Ruth's isolation is captured in her story about projecting onto another white woman her own fears and confusion; Laurie's is expressed in her skepticism about separatist politics and limits she experienced in white-dominated feminist circles. To me, it is telling that neither of them saw other white women as their potential allies in taking on issues of race in the late 1970s or early 1980s. In fact, both women's coming to consciousness as white antiracist women slightly predated what was, by the mid-1980s, the emergence of a more visible group of white antiracist feminists.

Conclusion

The striking differences in the views held by militant white women about early second-wave feminism, as compared to the experiences of women who came to feminism by the late 1970s and early 1980s, led me to ask two questions about feminist movement history: What pushed the Naomi Jaffes and Marilyn Bucks of the world (left, militant, and anti-imperialist women) away from feminism in the 1960s and early 1970s and then pulled them toward it in the 1980s? What opened a space for some white women to see antiracism—from the outset—as a quintessential feminist principle? In both cases, the emergence of feminism spearheaded by women of color created a context for making issues of race and racism central feminist priorities.

In *White Women, Race Matters* Ruth Frankenberg raises a key question about why the women's movement came to be known as white: "Class- and nation-based movements [of the 1960s and early 1970s] were themselves the inspiration and in some ways provided the moment of origin for second-wave feminism or 'women's liberation.' Not only did they provide models for the women's movement, but many women activists either moved from antiracist movements into the feminist movement or participated simultaneously in both. The obvious question here is why, given these origins, by the mid-1970s, the most clearly audible feminist discourses were those that failed to address racism?"[50] The most obvious answer to this question involves the gaze of the mass media, which was directed almost entirely at radical white feminist actions. But the mass media is certainly not the sole culprit. White women who conceived of feminism as finally getting to "their issue," as if racism was not also a white feminist question, also played into the image of feminism as a white woman's issue. Nationalist politics of the time—which recognized the value of autonomous political organizations—also contributed to separate spheres for women of color and white women. These and other factors contributed to an image of feminism that excluded both Black, Latina, and Asian American feminist work and white women who refused to let go of an antiracist analysis.

Incorporating their experiences into the story of early second-wave feminism requires consideration of a number of key realities. First, the growth of organizations of feminists of color in the 1970s and 1980s contributed to the willingness of anti-imperialist women to treat feminism as central to their politics. Second, the stories of these antiracist white women also counter the notion that the "best days of the movement were over by the mid or even early 1970s."[51] What feminist

Ellen Willis identifies as the height of the radical feminist movement (1968–1974) was a period in which many antiracist women absented themselves from white feminism.[52] Considering 1968 to 1974 the height of the radical feminist movement really only considers white women who saw sexism as the ultimate oppression.[53] In fact, from the perspective of white antiracism, the early 1970s were a low point of feminism, a time when many women who were committed to an antiracist analysis had to put their feminism on the back burner in order to work with men and women of color and against racism. For antiracist white women, the best days of feminism were yet to come. As Barbara Smith explains, the early 1980s was "the period when those issues that had divided many of the movement's constituencies—such as racism, anti-Semitism, ableism, ageism and classism—were put out on the table."[54]

From a multiracial perspective, a high in the feminist movement took place in the early to middle 1980s with the rise of feminism and coalition building among women of color and with the emergence of a small but important white antiracist voice.[55] Barbara Smith writes that "the most progressive sectors of the movement responded to the challenge to transform their analysis and practice in order to build a stronger movement that encompassed a variety of feminisms."[56] What white feminist scholars typically consider the period of abeyance of the feminist movement in the 1980s was actually the height of multiracial feminism.[57]

Viewing feminist history from the point of view of multiracial feminism does not invalidate the import of dates often assigned to a time line of second-wave feminism: the founding of the National Organization for Women (NOW) in 1966; the formation of the first radical feminist group, New York Radical Women, in 1967; the *Roe v. Wade* Supreme Court decision legalizing abortion in 1973; the founding of the Coalition of Labor Union Women (CLUW) in 1973; and the struggle to ratify the equal rights amendment from 1970 to 1982. It does, however, add a whole new set of dates to that time line, including the rebellion at Attica Prison in 1971; Angela Davis's acquittal of all charges in 1972; the founding of WARN in 1974; the work of the Combahee River Collective from 1974 to 1979; the conference on racism and sexism cosponsored by NBFO and the Sagaris Collective in 1976; the murders of antiracist activists in Greensboro, North Carolina, in 1979; and the publication of *This Bridge Called My Back* and *Home Girls* in the early 1980s. Adding these dates to the story of second-wave feminism provides a necessary introduction to understanding the development of antiracist consciousness within multiracial feminism of the late-1970s and beyond.

When the various political generations of white antiracist women are included in the telling of second-wave feminist history, commonly accepted ideas about the origins of feminism must be reconsidered. The most problematic is the notion that white women brought feminism to women of color. From the perspective of many white antiracist women, it was largely the other way around. White women, whose early political training was in the Civil Rights Movement, saw modeled all around them Black women leaders who not only were the backbone of the movement but also provided much of its vision. White women involved in the antiwar movement who developed an international, anti-imperialist analysis considered militant women in Vietnam, Cuba, and Puerto Rico as their role models—women who, as Marilyn Buck says, not only fed the troops but "were the troops." White women who avoided early second-wave feminism because of its white biases struggled against sexism in male-dominated nationalist and solidarity organizations. At the same time, work to free Angela Davis and then Assata Shakur were among their highest priorities.

At the Liberation Day March in 1970, the Third World Women's Alliance, a Black feminist group led by Frances Beal that emerged out of SNCC, took part in the demonstration with signs in support of Angela Davis. Frances Beal recalls, "We had signs reading 'Hands Off Angela Davis' and one of the leaders of NOW ran up to us and said angrily, 'Angela Davis has nothing to do with Women's Liberation.' It has nothing to do with the kind of liberation you're talking about, retorted Beal, but it has everything to do with the kind of liberation we're talking about."[58]

Both this scene and the white feminists' dismissal of the rebellion at Attica speak to an expansive consciousness on the part of Black women and a few white antiracist women in the early 1970s. Even within male-dominated organizations, where rank-and-file women did not work closely together across race, white women identified Black women as leaders and those to whom they held themselves accountable. By the time white women of the next generation—those coming of age politically in the late 1970s and early 1980s—were introduced to feminism, the explosion of art, activism, and scholarship of women of color provided multiple arenas for white women to learn about race and racism.

6

Seeking a Critical Mass, Ample Work to Be Done

The number of white feminists doing antiracist work has never been substantial, a reality that is troubling given women's tremendous potential to be change agents. And yet by the early to mid-1980s white feminists who did consider race central to their politics had become more visible. The publication of several books by self-defined antiracist feminist activists, a rise in coalition work between and among women across race, and increasing debate and action about what it means to do antiracist work put white antiracist activism on the feminist map.

In this chapter I trace several developments of the 1970s and 1980s that nurtured this activism. Coalitions among women across race, made possible by feminism of women of color, and the emergence and development of key ideological components of multiracial feminism— its attention to sexuality and critique of heterosexism, and the rise of Jewish feminist activism—helped spawn a small but growing group of white activists and writers who continued to push an antiracist agenda forward. The emergence of a feminist publishing industry and of feminist conferences and festivals also provided cultural locations where much cross-race dialogue and struggle occurred.

Jewish Feminism

A key reason for the increasing presence of white women in coalition politics in the early to middle 1980s relates to the power of identity politics as a principle of consciousness-raising and activism. Although first introduced by the Combahee River Collective with regard to Black women, identity politics also paved the way for women who were not Black to explore how their own multiple identities—class, religion, sexuality—might inform their strategies for opposing racism. Just as there is no monolithic Black or Latina woman, there is no monolithic white woman, a reality that became increasingly apparent in the middle to late 1970s as working-class white women, Jewish women, and lesbians realized and articulated the fact that what was said in the name of "woman" often did not include them. Given that one's personal knowledge of oppression is so often the catalyst for seeking to understand the oppression of others, it is no surprise that Jews or lesbians then led the way for other white women in doing bridge work with women of color.

Some of the most important dialogues and alliances of the early 1980s were among Latinas, Black women, and Jewish feminists. For example, beginning in the early 1980s, the National Women's Studies Association (NWSA) conferences included several sessions on anti-Semitism, racism, Jewish feminism, and coalition politics. *Conditions,* a feminist journal that reconstituted its editorial staff so that women of color were a majority, was founded by four women, three of whom are Jewish. The founder of the Lesbian Herstory Archives, Joan Nestle, is Jewish. One of the first and most highly contested articles to analyze racism in white feminist writing was written by Jewish lesbian Elly Bulkin,[1] who also cofounded *Conditions,* Dykes against Racism Everywhere (DARE), and the later Jewish feminist journal *Bridges: A Journal for Jewish Feminists and Our Friends.* Adrienne Rich, perhaps the best-known white lesbian poet to treat antiracism as central to her political and literary work, traces her perspective in part to having been "split at the root" as the daughter of a Jewish father and a Christian mother.[2]

The majority of women I interviewed who identify with the feminist movement are Jewish, a number that is disproportionate to their representation in the U.S. population but consistent with the significant Jewish presence in antiracist movements historically.[3] Many of the Jewish women made connections among their commitment to antiracism, their understanding of anti-Semitism, and their feminist identities as Jewish women. One woman, elana levy, tied her "revolutionary feminism" (which for her includes opposition to racism, imperialism, patriarchy, anti-Semitism, and heterosexism) directly to being Jewish. She was born in the United States two years after her parents escaped Nazi Germany. Her mother's entire immediate family had been tortured and murdered in the Holocaust. As a child of newly arrived immigrants, elana always felt like an outsider, although she had few words to describe that feeling. Once her family escaped, they did not talk about anti-Semitism or the racial contradictions elana witnessed. One contradiction elana remembers in particular took place when she was a teenager. After her father had begun earning enough money so that her mother could return to college, elana's family hired a Black woman to clean the house. She remembers, "My mother called her by her first name, but she called my mother by the last name." This discrepancy between the women's titles stuck with elana, as did others.

Once in college, she became a socialist (partly in response to her parent's support of capitalism and the competition it bred), and she joined the Congress of Racial Equality (CORE) in New York City. Once her daughter was born, elana also became involved in feminist activism. She remembers, "For a long time, I just assumed that feminists were antiracists. Just like when I entered lesbian circles, I assumed that lesbians had a certain consciousness." Over time, she realized the connections did not necessarily hold true.

For elana, being a Jewish feminist has meant working in multiple directions simultaneously. Her feminist work has included participating in and leading ten delegations of women to Cuba, making a video on women in Nicaragua and a video on Palestinian women, supporting Native American sovereignty, advocating for prisoners, and founding a women's coffee house in Syracuse, where she lives. In grassroots feminist organizing she finds herself insisting the work and the community be multiracial. For example, when white women began to organize a woman's coffee house in Syracuse, she and others worked to be sure that the initial committee was multiracial and that the commitment was to sponsor a diverse group of performers. In some feminist organizing, elana has worked in organizations that are white dominant—in hopes of pushing them to consider issues of race—but she has also withdrawn if the composition and priorities have not changed over time.

In Jewish circles, feminist and not, she finds herself raising questions about racism (against Palestinians) and sexism. In 1982 ten Jews in Syracuse, including elana, wrote a letter to Syracuse newspapers criticizing the bombing of Palestinian refugee camps in Lebanon and Beirut. The group was heavily criticized by many established Jews, including rabbis. In 1984 this group founded a chapter of the New Jewish Agenda, and elana became involved on a national level. Her work mainly focuses on the national and human rights of Palestinians and on coalition work with Jews and African Americans. From elana's perspective, "Part of what was important is that just because you were Jewish doesn't mean you couldn't see the sovereignty rights of the Palestinians." During that period elana traveled to Israel and made a video, *The Intifada: A Jewish Eyewitness,* based on the Palestinian women's struggle. Over time, however, elana backed away from further work on this issue even though she still defends the national rights of Palestinians and opposes the settlements. "I just can't imagine doing that work anymore because it is so male. If women are going to be kept at home, behind veils, like they are in Gaza, that is not my goal. It is not what I am working for. I am not working for half of Gaza."

Although elana sees valuable connections between her family's persecution as Jews and her lifelong opposition to racism, she is also careful to note that the outsider consciousness she was afforded is not without cost. One of the lessons she learned from the Holocaust is that "there is no one who will protect you. Your neighbors won't protect you, even though you live next to them." That basic lesson and the message she was taught early on—that women's lives need to be centered around men—have chipped away at her confidence most of her life. This is one reason the politic is so important to her: The personal is political. Antiracism requires staring down contradictions and trying to resolve them in everyday life. From elana's perspective, for example, men can say they believe in women's rights, but it is how they treat women in their lives that really matters. White women can say they support Third World feminism, but if their lives are racially exclusive, that is an untenable contradiction.

Feminism, for elana, is less about the political positions she has taken that have received national attention than it is about what her daily life looks like. "I think the most important thing about antiracist work is about the life you create. It is not so much about being a leader of a group or the leaflets you produce or the articles you write. It is about the choices you make—every single choice. If you are going to study philosophy. Where you live. The kind of school where you teach. Every single thing you do. People so often don't take responsibility for the whiteness of their lives," including what it means to be living in all-white suburbs. In this country, "the way you really learn about racism is by living in a world that includes people of color. Once in a while a Mumia or Geronimo Pratt event will deal with the structural issue. But

I don't think that is how it becomes part of your insides." When elana asked her now-adult daughter what she thought was most important to emphasize in an interview about elana's antiracism, her daughter said, "Talk about your mothering." In response, elana says, "The fact that my daughter grew up where the people coming through the door were from all different worlds. Lots of different worlds and they were all part of our world. Like at Seder, sometimes we will be the only Jews. Twelve people there. Sharing what I think is really beautiful."

Anne Litwin, another Jewish feminist woman, links her commitment to antiracism and sexism directly to her experience with anti-Semitism. Anne grew up in the only Jewish family in a small town in Kansas, where she was denied membership in youth and community organizations because she was Jewish. Many members of her family had been killed in the Holocaust, a reality that meant the Holocaust was a huge presence during her childhood. Her parents taught her that as a Jew she had a moral obligation to stand up against any form of injustice. That message was fairly confusing, since Anne's parents were blatantly prejudiced against Black people. Nevertheless, Anne grew up being taught that the reason Jews must stand up against injustice is that if they do not, then there will not be anyone to stop injustice aimed at them.

After attending college, Anne moved to a back-to-the-earth community in upstate New York, where she worked with other feminists to ensure women had access to abortion in what was an overwhelmingly Catholic region. In 1976 Anne moved to New York City, primarily so that she could live and work in mixed-race communities. By 1976 there was much conversation about race in the women's movement, much of it initiated by women of color. Anne helped found a multiracial organization—West Side Action for Peace and Social Justice— which worked closely with Black and white churches. In the 1980s she began working with the NTL Institute, an organization founded by white men in 1945 to confront discrimination in the workplace. In 1975, just before Anne joined it, the organization "blew itself up." It reconstituted itself after Black men and women and two white women in the organization demanded the leadership reflect its mission to confront racism and sexism. Since then it has been a multiracial organization with a commitment to feminism and racial parity at every level.

In the 1980s Anne also teamed up with a Black feminist colleague to start a long-standing support group for Black and white women.

She also helped found a women's leadership collaborative of Asian American, Latina, Black, and white women (one-third of whom are lesbian) who make a commitment to work together for at least five years on issues of race, community building, and leadership.

Over the years, what has consistently driven her commitment has been "deeply and firmly connected to my being Jewish." Anne knows that there are many reasons why some Black people distrust Jews and that there is a long history of white Jews who have been racists. She is aware that some African Americans only see her as part of an oppressor group. Although she knows that some people believe "it is ridiculous for Jews in this country to continue to feel afraid," Anne's fear remains real. Of her motivation to do antiracist work, Anne says, "My experience as a Jew is what I tap into every day. I never stop being afraid about being Jewish. I live feeling that at any time, I could be hauled away. I never lose that sensation. So I live with that fear about my personal safety all of the time. I continue, it continues to be a source of energy for me about doing antiracist work."

Certainly not all of the Jewish women I interviewed tie their feminist activism to being Jewish. Bonnie Kerness makes almost no connection between being Jewish and her activism. Nor does being raised Jewish mean that people organize as Jews or against anti-Semitism automatically. One woman I interviewed, Laurie Schecter, grew up in a left-of-liberal reform Jewish family in Florida. In a letter following our interview Laurie wrote, "Feminism is like Judaism for me. They are part of who I am, but I don't think I can articulate generally what that means. It's part of the way I think and act. I don't know that I can separate it from the rest of my thinking." Recognizing diversity among Jewish feminists—in terms of the degree to which they draw links between antiracism and racism—is important, partly because it interrupts a tendency to automatically equate outsider status with consciousness. At the same time, the proportion of feminists I interviewed who see deep connections among their feminism, antiracism, and Jewish identities parallels the rich presence of Jews among antiracist feminists in second-wave feminism.

The reasons for this presence and its contribution are many. Jewish women often led the way (among white women) in the late 1970s and early 1980s in forging alliances with women of color, partly because they had some practice in coalition work among themselves. By the late 1970s an increasing number of women had come to define themselves as Jewish and feminist, a growth partly spurred by a rise in anti-Semitism in the United States in that decade. When Jewish feminists and/or lesbians began meeting as feminists and/or lesbians and Jews, much conversation was required about how little common ground really existed once significant differences among them were taken into account: class differences, ethnic differences, differences between religious and secular Jews, differences in histories of Sephardic and Ashkenazic Jews, and differences in perspectives on Israel and Palestine.

Conversations among Jewish feminists often had to deal with divisive assumptions about who is a real Jew and who is not. (Who speaks Hebrew, who attended temple, who is a Zionist, whose last name was changed, who had Communist parents—all are loaded qualifiers that have been created out of a context of anti-Semitism.) In her account of the first decade of Jewish lesbian feminism, Faith Rogow writes that differences among Jews sometimes "produced more tension than groups could bear, especially because women often depended on the groups as a place of safety, as a place that would be comfortably familiar and supportive rather than a source of further conflict."[4]

This dilemma—facing conflict in a group that was supposed to be a safe haven—is one that Black, Latina, and Asian American women were also experiencing during this time. In the second edition of *This Bridge Called My Back,* Cherríe Moraga writes, "In the last three years I have learned that Third World feminism does not provide the kind of easy political framework that women of color are running to in droves. The *idea* of Third World feminism has proved to be much easier between the covers of a book than between real live women."[5] For Latinas (who include Chicanas, Puerto Ricans, and Dominicans, to name just a few ethnic groups) and Jews (who include Ashkenazic, Sephardic, and Adot Ha-Mizrach, among many other ethnic or regional groups), coalition politics exist *within* each group. Feminist activist Elly Bulkin writes, "While we often think of coalitions as *crossing* lines of identity—women of color and white women working together, Jews and non-Jews, lesbians and non-lesbians—the interactions [Bernice Johnson] Reagon describes as typifying 'coalition politics' do, in fact, exist within each identity group."[6] Since coalition politics, as Bernice Johnson Reagon explains, involves some of the most dangerous, energy-draining, and necessary work people do, Jewish feminists' commitment to coalition politics among themselves gave them vital experience for doing this work with non-Jewish women of color and white Christian-raised women as well.[7]

A second place of convergence between women of color and white Jewish women concerns the history of anti-Semitism and Jewish ethnic identity. In many early alliances between white women and women of color in the late 1970s and early 1980s, white women spoke of feeling guilty about their privilege and of being confused by the anger of Black women and Latinas. These emotions often left white women mute and fearful of taking risks, afraid that if they spoke, "frogs would come out of their mouths."[8] This withdrawal was often coupled with many white women's fears that examining their families of origin or ethnic backgrounds would elicit further problems by illuminating examples of racism among family members and white women's continued complicity in racism and classism. Mab Segrest writes, "For white women doing anti-racist work, one of our chief challenges is to find ways of overcoming our feelings of self-hatred and despair brought about by an increased knowledge of our white heritage."[9] Some white women attempted to divorce their present from their past: to see feminism or lesbianism as their legacy, to see political life as their legacy, to see anything but their own ethnic background or biological family as their heritage.

This defensive reaction made for many problems across race. White women often attempted to make the cultures of women of color their own. This reaction is particularly problematic given the long history of white attempts to appropriate, co-opt, and in the process destroy Native American, Black, and Latino culture. There are many reasons why the editors of *This Bridge Called My Back* titled one of the book sections "And When You Leave, Take Your Pictures with You: Racism in the Women's Movement."[10] Lorraine Bethel's poem "What Chou Mean, 'We,' White Girl? Or, the Cullud Lesbian Feminist Declaration of Independence (Dedicated to the proposition that all women are not equal, i.e. identical/ly oppressed)," clarifies that a "we" between white and Black is provisional, at best.[11] Anthropologist Wendy Rose's critique of "white shamanism"—white people's attempt to become Native in order to grow spiritually—also applies as well to white feminists who treat Native American women as automatically spiritual, as automatically their spiritual mothers.[12]

In Eleanor Johnson's discussion of the barriers she felt to intimacy, friendships, and alliances with white (Jewish and Christian raised) women in the 1970s and early 1980s, she explains, "I felt a lot of the time, for me to share who I am as a Black woman would somehow legitimize these other women because they felt so awful about who they were and where they came from. So, when you talked about holding part of you back, I felt that a lot. I couldn't totally share 'cause I felt like I would be ripped off. As though my identity would somehow legitimize these other women. It's almost like a leech, sort of hooking on to someone else's identity, to make you feel better about who you are. I felt that a lot. So I think I also held back and I feel a lot of these women hooked up with ethnic cultures other than their own."[13] When white women attempted to dissociate themselves from their pasts and from the white privilege afforded them, one consequence was that they tried to attach themselves to, borrow from, and co-opt Black, Latina, or Native American culture.

For Jewish women, "hooking onto someone else's identity" is riskier than for Christian-raised women, partly because Jewish women need to remain at least partially connected to their ethnic and religious backgrounds, which is a key location for resistance against anti-Semitism. Although some Jewish feminists in the 1970s did try to understate their Jewish heritage as a way to cope with anti-Semitism inside and outside the feminist movement, this was a costly step. The domination of white Christian-raised women in feminism made many Jewish feminists increasingly hesitant, if not loathe, to blend in, to assimilate, and to dissociate from their Jewish heritage.

The multiple dilemmas that Jewish women faced in attempting to not separate their feminism from their Judaism or their lesbian identity from their Judaism put some of them on better footing than Christian-raised white middle-class women in dialogues with women of color. Although the processes of exclusion and discrimination faced by Black women and Jewish women are not the same, there are enough parallels to allow some important initial conceptual leaps. Both groups understand what it means to be persecuted. And both groups can ill afford to separate themselves entirely from their ethnic backgrounds.

In 1982 Cherríe Moraga spoke to this connection: "White women don't always realize that Third World women are not just anti-racists but pro our cultures. That's an important distinction. The ways that

Third World feminism can be different is that it's coming from a real belief and commitment to the integrity of our own race and culture, and keeping that. The white women's movement tried to create a new form of women's culture that on some level had denied where people came from. . . . You don't need to cut off an arm for a movement. Actually, it gives white women a lot of latitude now. It's no accident that Jewish women are beginning to talk about their own identities and anti-Semitism right around the time that Third World feminism is surfacing as a movement. We're talking about a cultural revolution which is not making up something new, but critiquing what is oppressive and retaining and cultivating what is rich, which is our culture."[14]

What some Jewish feminists brought to the table in working with women of color was a sense of having come from a people—in their family or their community—who had fought to survive. Many also came from families who stood up against racism. Following in the footsteps of their forebears was a possibility. As poet Irena Klepfisz explains, "It was Jews that first instilled in me the meaning of what oppression and its consequences are. It was Jews who first taught me about socialism, classism, racism . . . and injustice. . . . It was from Jews that I learned about the necessity for resistance."[15] Other Jewish women uncovered ambivalent, contradictory, and sometimes blatantly false messages about race that they were first taught as children: that all Jews are antiracists; that Jews cannot be racist because they also suffer discrimination; that persecution of Palestinians by Jews is not a form of racism. In Jewish women's consciousness-raising groups, in workshops on anti-Semitism and racism, and in writing, Jewish women grappled with these complex messages and their impact on cross-race alliances. In this space, Jewish women of color also spoke about being excluded from discussions by white Jews as well as by Christian-raised women of color.

The experience that some Jewish feminists had with coalition politics among themselves through the 1970s, their experience of being outsiders as a consequence of anti-Semitism in the Christian- and white-dominated feminist movement, and their knowledge of progressive Jewish history opened a place for alliances between women of color and Jewish white women. This background did not mean that the alliances were easy. That they happened is itself important.

The publication of *Yours in Struggle* in 1984 serves as a quintessential example of this bridge building. The book included three essays: one by Black Christian lesbian activist and writer Barbara Smith; one by Southern-born and Christian-raised lesbian writer Minnie Bruce Pratt; and one by lesbian Elly Bulkin, an Ashkenazi Jewish feminist writer and editor from New York. The idea for the book followed a NWSA conference in 1983 at which Barbara Smith and Minnie Bruce Pratt were both on a panel on racism and anti-Semitism. Smith, Bulkin, and Pratt had worked together for years as friends and fellow activists.[16]

In her essay "Identity: Skin Blood Heart," Minnie Bruce Pratt explains how her emerging consciousness about race coincided with facing oppression as a woman who had been raised to be a "proper" southern lady.[17] When she refused to follow that path—as she came out as a feminist and a lesbian—all hell broke loose around her. When her children were taken from her, she began to see that "I gain truth when I expand my constricted eye, an eye that has only let in what I have been taught to see."[18]

Once the bankruptcy of southern female socialization was uncovered, Pratt could then begin to unravel lies she had learned about southern history, Jewish history, women's history, and the connections among them. In this essay, she joined a long line of southern white women—including Anne Braden, Adrienne Rich, Lillian Smith, and Jessie Daniel Ames—who questioned the patriarchal white Christian doctrine upon which slavery and racial apartheid had been based; she saw "the *need* to look differently because I've learned that what is presented to me as an accurate view of the world is frequently a lie" (17).

Barbara Smith's essay in *Yours in Struggle* is written in two parts, the first a letter to Black women, the second, a letter to Jewish women. This methodology speaks volumes to the bridge work Smith was attempting. To Jewish women, Smith writes: One, although there is indeed anti-Semitism among Black women, Jewish women must not single out Black women as somehow more anti-Semitic than other women. Two, although there can be no room for argument about whether or not anti-Semitism exists, it does not take away the white-skin privilege afforded to Ashkenazic Jews. Three, attempts to consider anti-Semitism on a par with racism make little sense historically or currently; it is better to avoid battles of "oppression privilege" and figure out ways to stand against both. To Black women, Smith writes that even though it may be hard for Blacks to accept that white people can be oppressed, the

Holocaust, hate crimes against Jews in the United States, and anti-Semitism in U.S. society, including in the feminist movement, are real. Therefore Black women need to take anti-Semitism seriously.

Smith also writes that a principled Black feminist politic requires seeing that the Christian right wing has a hit list that includes Blacks as well as Jews. One point of coalition politics is to build bridges between communities to create a stronger opposition against oppression. In the case of opposing the Right, alliances between progressive Jews and Blacks are vital.

The last essay in *Yours in Struggle,* by Elly Bulkin, celebrates alliances between the Barbara Smiths and Minnie Bruce Pratts of the world and in so doing offers what has become a key text for the emerging Jewish feminist movement of the 1980s and since. Although there is a history of antiracism among progressive Jews in U.S. history, it was not until the late 1970s, after women of color had made racism an "open and critical issue" in the feminist movement, that Jewish women began to address connections between anti-Semitism and Jewish identity.[19] For many Jewish women, identifying openly among feminists as Jewish had been risky early in the movement, partly because of the anti-Semitic characterizations of Jews as domineering and controlling. An Old Left tendency to encourage people to choose between opposing anti-Semitism and opposing racism also slowed the development of a Jewish feminist movement. From Bulkin's perspective, Jewish feminists are indebted to Third World feminists, especially lesbians, who insisted that it is possible to stand against multiple oppressions simultaneously. Third World feminists also recognized the importance of differences among women and the positive aspects of cultures and identities.

For Bulkin, identity politics opens the way for self-affirmation, including the affirmation needed to spur Jewish feminists to build on their considerable history of opposing racism. Bulkin warns, however, that romanticizing that history will do little to create current alliances. It is better, she suggests, to be up-front about the contradictions, to admit the good as well as the problematic work that Jewish people have done in cross-race organizing historically.

Bulkin also lays out principles for organizing against racism. Although these principles draw on lessons she learned as a Jewish lesbian, they offer a template for non-Jewish white women as well. Included in this politic is a critique of feminist or lesbian separatism that, from Bulkin's perspective, blocks coalition politics. As a lesbian feminist and a Jew, Bulkin is careful to clarify that she in no way wants men to feel they can hold her down. But, she explains, "I will support a politics that mourns all of the Jews locked in Soviet prisons, all of the Palestinians massacred at Sabra and Shatila—regardless of sex—even though such politics are shared by men whose sexism and homophobia I have also to confront" (130).

Through this politic, Bulkin writes against the tendency of some white feminists to disregard the Left as inherently oppressive because it was male dominated. She refutes the politic of white radical feminists who considered any alliance with men a waste of time. With this critique, Bulkin reaches out to Latina, Asian American, Black, Native American, and Arab American feminists who while opposing sexism in any community also oppose racism aimed at men of color. By implication, Bulkin's politic also reaches out to the white militant women of the 1960s and 1970s who considered the repression of male prisoners and the prison system to be one of their issues.

Bulkin also asks women across race to create a feminist theory that "fully incorporates anti-Semitism and racism into its analysis of woman hating" (124). She asks Christian-raised women of color *and* white women to not attribute solely to Jews what is in reality an issue of white privilege shared by Christian-raised people and Ashkenazic Jews. For Bulkin, incorporating anti-Semitism as a key aspect of feminist organizing does not have to add to people's work. Rather, it adds the nuance needed for a multidimensional progressive politic.

By the time *Yours in Struggle* was published in 1984, the work that Jewish feminists did among themselves and with women of color helped to usher in a small but important Jewish feminist movement that has its own paper trail. Evelyn Torton Beck's *Nice Jewish Girls: A Lesbian Anthology;* Melanie Kaye/Kantrowitz's and Irena Klepfisz's edited volume *The Tribe of Dina: A Jewish Women's Anthology;* and Kaye/Kantrowitz's *The Issue Is Power: Essays on Women, Jews, Violence, and Resistance;* the poetry and essays of Irena Klepfisz; and the continuing writing of Adrienne Rich put on the page words about how to take racism and anti-Semitism seriously in feminist activism.[20]

By the mid-1980s an increasing number of feminists recognized why multiracial organizations needed to include a Jewish presence and why dealing with issues of anti-Semitism was crucial for communication among white women as well as across race. Naomi Jaffe, for example, was recruited into the multiracial organization Feminist Action Network (FAN) in Albany, New York, in the late 1980s in part because she was a Jewish woman who had a history of confronting anti-Semitism and racism. FAN's commitment to ensure the group was 60 percent lesbian and 60 percent women of color meant it thought long and hard about new members. Naomi was asked to join as a white antiracist *and* as a Jewish feminist, given that Elly Bulkin was the only Jewish woman in the organization at the time.

Lesbian Antiracist Feminism

It is no coincidence that Jewish feminism emerged on the heels of Third World feminism and that a visible presence of white antiracist activism coincided with the emergence of Jewish feminism. A second and inter-related influence in the growth of white antiracist activism has to do with lesbian sexuality and a critique of heterosexism. Among the feminists I interviewed, about equal numbers of heterosexual and lesbian women, almost all drew connections between their antiracist feminism and their work on issues of sexuality. Although heterosexual feminists have contributed to the discussion of heterosexism and racism, the lion's share of the work has been done by lesbians, particularly lesbians of color. There are many reasons this is true, but perhaps Paula Gunn Allen explains it most succinctly: "The fact that we [radical women of color] don't fit any context comfortably makes us a threat and this is true; it also makes us the focal point for any true revolution."[21] Adrienne Rich writes, "As a lesbian/feminist, my nerves and my flesh, as well as my intellect, tell me that the connections between and among women are the most feared, the most problematic and the most potentially transforming force on the planet."[22]

Among the most visible feminists involved in multiracial coalition building in the late 1970s and early 1980s, an overwhelming proportion are lesbians: Beth Brant, Adrienne Rich, Elly Bulkin, Cherríe Moraga, Minnie Bruce Pratt, Gloria Anzaldúa, Paula Gunn Allen, Mab Segrest, Barbara Smith, and many others. The Combahee River Collective was a largely lesbian organization. *Home Girls, This Bridge Called My Back, A Gathering of Spirit, Yours in Struggle, My Mama's Dead Squirrel,* and *All the Women Are White* are all key texts in articulating cross-race feminist coalition politics, and they include a substantial number of lesbian writers. Nine out of ten of the planning committee members for the 1982 conference of Jewish feminism were lesbians.[23] Lesbians were the backbone of much multiracial institution building in the 1970s and 1980s: in battered-women's shelters and the rape crisis movement, feminist conferences, labor union organizing, and prisoner's rights groups, and the list goes on.

There are many reasons for the substantial lesbian presence in antiracist coalition work. One is that for many women, crossing the boundary from safety to danger, from what is expected in the name of heterosexuality to naming oneself as a lesbian, can be a huge step in questioning other destructive boundaries, including those between races. Many lesbians across race believe their lesbian identity is what first pushed them to deal openly with racism. Southern lesbian feminist anti-Klan organizer and author Mab Segrest writes, "I am almost thirty. I grew up in a small Alabama town, where my family on both sides has lived for four generations. I felt from an early age that something was dreadfully wrong. I knew in my guts that my strongest feelings for women and girls put me somehow on the outside. Set me apart. Although I did not know what a *lesbian* was, I felt myself a closet freak. As racial conflict increased in Alabama in the 1960s, I also knew in my gut that what I heard people saying about Black people had somehow also to do with me. This knowledge crystalizes around one image: I am thirteen, lying on my stomach beneath some bushes across from the public high school. It is ringed with two hundred Alabama Highway Patrol troopers at two-yard intervals, their hips slung with pistols. Inside that terrible circle are twelve Black children, the only students allowed in. . . . I have a tremendous flash of empathy, of identification, with their vulnerability and their aloneness inside that circle of force. Their separation is mine. And I know from now on that everything people have told me is 'right' has to be reexamined. I am on my own. Lillian Smith's experiences parallels mine: 'I realized there were deep chasms between me and what I wanted to know: the real things I longed to understand.'"[24]

In a different place and cultural context but with similar awareness of connections between lesbian consciousness and race consciousness, Cherríe Moraga writes, "When I finally lifted the lid to my lesbianism, a profound connection with my mother reawakened in me. It wasn't until I acknowledged and confronted by own lesbianism in the flesh, that my heartfelt identification with and empathy for my mother's oppression—due to being a poor, uneducated Chicana—was realized. My lesbianism is the avenue through which I have learned the most about silence and oppression, and it continues to be the most tactile reminder to me that we are not free human beings."[25]

Several feminists I interviewed see their early consciousness about race and lesbian identity as intertwined. For example, Sarah Stearns, who grew up in a Protestant middle-class family in Connecticut, directly linked coming out as a lesbian to her early consciousness about racism. When Sarah was in graduate school studying clinical psychology, and just beginning to come out as a lesbian, a straight woman faculty member in Sarah's department made a sexual advance. When Sarah did not respond, the woman told her husband (who was also on the faculty) and several other faculty members that Sarah had approached her. The rumor devastated Sarah, who felt that she had been prejudged by those in a positions of authority all around her. Later in her graduate training Sarah was questioned by her superior after a client had "eroticized her connection" with Sarah. Although Sarah had maintained professional boundaries, the supervisor and the ethics review board in the Psychology Department ruled that Sarah had acted unethically. In both instances, Sarah felt tremendous pain and isolation from being accused by individuals for acts she did not commit, accusations that were institutionally upheld.

At the time, Sarah confided in a Black woman friend and fellow graduate student. Although Sarah's friend knew little about lesbian culture and life, she knew much about institutional racism: She was facing it as the first Black woman to earn a Ph.D. in clinical psychology from that institution. As Sarah and her friend spoke, they saw links between racism and heterosexism as systems that depend upon institutionally enforced prejudgments. The many conversations on sexuality and race between Sarah and her friend turned out to be a stepping-stone to a lifelong friendship and political collaboration.

Other women I interviewed spoke about interracial lesbian relationships as a location for tremendous learning about race and racism. For example, Jeanine Cohen calls her involvement with a Black woman from Britain a crucial homecoming process for her. As immigrants to this country (Jeanine from South Africa and her partner from England), the two fell into each other's arms, both "freaked out" by the dislocation they felt living in the United States. Jeanine remembers, "I was totally in love with her. I adored her and the love and connection we shared." The two of them did political work together, made music together, and lived together as partners for six years. Even though they are not still lovers, Jeanine is the half-time coparent of her former partner's daughter, and they still consider each other family.

The deep connection they formed as lovers and in cultural work did not mean the relationship was racially uncomplicated. For example, with her partner, Jeanine began drumming and joined a multiracial group that performed in the San Francisco area. Jeanine explained, "Those things fed me because it was a way to get access to Africa again, having that cultural stuff I had growing up that I could reclaim. Maybe being with her made it more accessible, less contradictory." Jeanine faced many complications as a white woman in the United States who had been profoundly influenced by Black cultural life as a child and who had spent much time in black townships in South Africa. Somehow it was easier for her to begin "African" drumming with a Black partner than on her own, even though Jeanine's familiarity with and closeness to African drumming had been closer (regionally) than was her Black partner's association to drumming. Rarely, though, did she and her partner have the language they needed to sort out the racial dynamics in their relationship.

Over time, Jeanine realized that what they had in common was so important to them that it was very scary to deal with their differences. Neither of them knew other interracial lesbian couples, a fact that led to isolation and an inability to talk about how race came between them. Jeanine found herself constantly considering her partner's needs more important than her own, constantly thinking that "the oppression she experienced as a Black woman was more intense than anything I might experience. In a way, I didn't have rights in this picture."

Jeanine also did not know exactly where to put her body in some public settings with her partner. For example, Jeanine knew that there were certain things she, as a white woman, could not give her partner, that her partner needed time and space to make friendships and political connections with other Black women. Although Jeanine tried to be supportive, she remembers attending certain multiracial parties where she felt her partner ignored her—"that she didn't want to be associated with me"—which Jeanine interpreted as her partner's ambivalence about being part of an interracial couple. In those instances Jeanine's feelings would be hurt, but neither she nor her partner had the language or community support to sort the problem out. Jeanine had a political community through her work with Lesbians against Police Violence (a group that organized in opposition to police violence against gays, lesbians, and Latino youth). Yet "no one in my life was talking about what it meant to be in an interracial relationship. The two of us were just bumping along together." Later in her life, when Jeanine became involved with another Black woman, both of them decided that they would try from the outset to deal explicitly and deliberately with how race played itself out in their relationship. By then Jeanine also knew other interracial lesbian couples and had begun working on what became the first video in the United States to profile interracial lesbian couples.

The number of lesbian relationships that are interracial has never been high, even since the Stonewall rebellion in New York City in 1969, which helped ignite the lesbian and gay movement in the United States.[26] Deep-seated strictures against such bonding still exist among many heterosexuals, gay men, and lesbians. However, many lesbian communities tend to be more ethnically and racially mixed than heterosexual communities. As Aída Hurtado notes, "The distance white lesbians have from white men and the distance from their ethnic/racial communities that many lesbians of Color are forced into creates a bond across ethnic/racial lines.[27] "Furthermore," Hurtado continues, "lesbian communities are more likely to transgress the usual rules of coupling with a greater number of cross-ethnic/racial relationships, more cross-generational relationships, and more cross-class relationships than in society generally. . . . This intimate contact among lesbians of different ethnic/racial groups, although not unproblematic, lends itself to developing common political goals that go beyond issues of sexuality because of the intimate knowledge that daily interaction brings about class and ethnic/racial differences" (24).

This intimate contact is a key reason why some of the most important antiracist coalition work of the early 1980s was done by lesbians and why many of the most visible lesbians (those whose lives have been written about or who are writers themselves) did this work while in partnership with other race-conscious lesbians. The erotic energy among lesbians in general, in combination with the energy that comes from political activism, was synergistic.

This is not to say that coalition politics would not have happened in the 1980s were it not for lesbian relationships. However, many partnerships of that period occurred among women whose contributions to multiracial feminism remain with us today. Adrienne Rich, for example, wrote "Disloyal to Civilization: Feminism, Racism, and Gynophobia," and presented the highly influential keynote address at the NWSA conference at Storrs, Connecticut, in 1981, during and around the period when she was coediting *Sinister Wisdom* with Michelle Cliff, her partner at the time and since.[28] Kitchen Table Women of Color Press—which published both *This Bridge Called My Back* and *Home Girls*—was founded in 1981, around the time when Cherríe Moraga and Barbara Smith were lovers. In her preface to the first edition of *This Bridge Called My Back*, Moraga writes, "Arriving in Roxbury, arriving at Barbara's. . . . By the end of the evening of our first visit together, Barbara comes into the front room where she has made a bed for me. She kisses me. Then, grabbing my shoulders she says, very solid-like, 'we're sisters.' I nod, put myself into bed, and roll around with this word, *sisters,* for two hours before sleep takes on. I earned this with Barbara. It is not a given between us—Chicana and Black—to come to see each other as sisters. This is not a given. I keep wanting to repeat over and over and over again, the pain and shock of difference, the joy of commonness, the exhilaration of meeting through incredible odds against it."[29]

Joan Gibbs and Sara Bennett, an interracial lesbian couple, were the editors of *Top Ranking: A Collection of Articles on Racism and Classism in the Lesbian Community,* the first book-length anthology on racism and classism in the lesbian community.[30] Ruth Frankenberg, author of *White Women, Race Matters: The Social Construction of Whiteness,* first met Lata Mani, author of several key works on Third World feminism, when they were graduate students at the University of California at Santa Cruz in the early 1980s. They wrote many articles on racism and colonialism together, and to this day they are life partners.[31]

Deep friendships and familial relationships among lesbian feminists during that period coincided with their political activism and, my guess is, also fueled it. Adrienne Rich and Audre Lorde worked closely together for years, reading each other's work, speaking on panels together, pushing each other politically. Joan Nestle and Mabel Hampton have been friends and comrades for decades, including their long-term work to sustain the Lesbian Herstory Archives.[32]

I give these examples not with the intention of invading people's privacy but, rather, because they are representative of many lesbian relationships and families of the last three decades that have provided tremendous energy for coalition work. There are many reasons why the connection between erotic energy in lesbian relationships and coalition work has rarely been documented. First, lesbians, like many Jewish women of the 1970s (and with significant overlap), have often taken precautions against openly identifying themselves as disproportionately represented in the feminist movement. Lesbian baiting has a long history, as does the tendency for women just coming to feminism to fear that claiming the term "feminist" will automatically mean that they are lesbian (or that they will be assumed by others to be gay). Lesbians have been sensitive to that equation and have sometimes understated themselves as a consequence.

Second, the vulnerabilities, discrimination, and isolation many lesbians face undermine the longevity of many lesbian partnerships, a reality that makes it hard to track who has been with whom and for how long. Racism within and outside the feminist movement makes interracial lesbian relationships even more precarious.

Third, lesbians in interracial relationships who do coalition work may be hesitant to call attention to their interracial partnerships. White women run the risk of appearing to use that relationship as a credential: "Look, I am an antiracist. My partner is Black." Being in a lover relationship across race is certainly no assurance that the couple is dealing with race and racism within the relationship. In fact, in Jeanine's case, the similarities between her and her Afro-British partner were so precious to them that dealing with differences—including how Jeanine's racism may have influenced the relationship—was too risky for either of them to bear.

All these issues and more are among the reasons the synergism between the erotic energy of lesbian partnerships and coalition politics is rarely celebrated. What get lost with the invisibility of this story, however, are powerful lessons that women learn across race when in intimate, everyday partnerships. These lessons include how white women come to understand race experientially (not just abstractly), how they learn not to distance themselves from the realities of racism, and what they may learn about bicultural living as a consequence. Cherríe Moraga writes in her review of *Top Ranking,* "At the risk of setting up a racial split in this review, I cannot ignore the basic difference in approach between the white and Black contributors. When discussing racism—how it shows its face in our lives—the white contributors tend to write more theoretically and less personally. Conversely, over and over again, the Black women use their *experiences* in order to extrapolate a theory. The difference showed. I emphasize this because it is this phenomenon, using theory in the name of feelings, that permeates most 'antiracist' discussion by white women. And until these women start dealing from the heart, the racial split holds (and plenty of muddy water at that)."[33]

For white women, long-term intimate relationships across race require that they be willing to "start dealing from the heart." In intimate lesbian partnerships there are many day-to-day cross-race discussions: about which channel to watch on TV, what it means when a pizza parlor will not make a delivery into a Black neighborhood, why finding a cab is iffy for a mixed-race group of women late at night, why pronouncing *"pakoras"* and *"raita"* correctly is essential everyday knowledge for a white lesbian in a partnership with an Indian woman. These and other topics reveal subtleties and nuances of race and racism that need to be understood for close, trusting relationships and political alliances.

For white women, one challenge in interracial relationships is to always keep race in focus while avoiding reducing every interaction to race. Pat Parker succinctly writes, "The first thing you do is forget that i'm Black / Second, you must never forget that i'm Black."[34] The erotic and love can push people beyond the violence of racist boundaries. There are crucial connections between love and everyday acts of resistance.

Love across race cannot, by itself, make a revolution. But it is an essential part of the process. Adrienne Rich writes, "Taught to deny my longings for another female body, taught that dark skin was stigma, shame, I look at you and see your flesh is beautiful; different from my own, but taboo to me no longer. Whether we choose to act on this or not (and whatever pain we may explore in touching one another) if we both have this knowledge, if my flesh is beautiful to you and yours to me, because it belongs to us, in affirmation of our similar and different powers, in affirmation of scars, stretch-marks, life-lines, the mind that burns in each body, we lay claim to ourselves and each other beyond the most extreme patriarchal taboo. We take each other up in our strong arms. We do not infantilize each other; we refuse to be infantilized. We drink at each other's difference. We begin to fuse our powers."[35]

Although the lesbian movement contributed to interracial lesbian alliances, it also opened up new ways of dealing with sexuality, period. The energy made possible through intimacies among women was one of the most powerful forces underlying coalition politics of the 1970s and 1980s. Consciousness-raising groups among women—which included Black, Latina, Asian American, and white groups—were among the many ways women came to see each other as central. Autonomous feminist groups—the National Black Feminist Organization (NBFO), Combahee River Collective, Asian Sisters, NWSA, feminist journals and bookstores, battered-women's shelters—provided space for women to recognize and marvel at themselves as being those "holding up half the sky," and then some.

Autonomous women's organizations also gave women a context for grappling with what keeps them apart. Although women have always had close friendships with other women, the lesbian and feminist movement asked women—heterosexual, bisexual, and lesbian—to examine the ways that heterosexism stands in the way of friendships and political collaborations. Compulsory heterosexuality, as Adrienne Rich defines it, not only enforces tight strictures on erotic connections between women. It also sets narrow standards on what is appropriate between straight women as well.[36]

A few heterosexual women I interviewed, for example, spoke of the ways heterosexism in the 1960s and 1970s kept them from working closely with women, especially women of color. One woman, elana levy, whose antiracist activism extends back to work she did in CORE in the early 1960s in New York City, learned early on that antiracist activism for white people depended upon developing close working relationships with people of color. In retrospect, however, she is critical of herself because she "didn't develop relationships with women of color. I was pretty male-centered at the time, unfortunately." Some of her most significant lover relationships have been with men of color, including partnerships during the Civil Rights Movement. But she believes she also "acted out" feelings of guilt about being white in the ways she conducted herself in lover relationships across race. And there were times when men would manipulate her insecurities in the process. She explains, "It is a gendered script. Not feeling good. Not feeling confident about yourself. Thinking that your primary worth is your sexuality or your looks. Not thinking that your mind is worth shit. Being a leader by sleeping with a leader. That is about as close as you could get to leadership. A lot of that lack of confidence comes from early trauma and abuse."

For elana, heterosexism meant learning she should define herself though sexual relationships with men. Sexism meant being unable to envision herself as a leader in her own right. These two restrictions, combined with psychological consequences of childhood trauma, whittled away at elana's self-confidence. The imbalance of veering toward men, not women, in the 1960s and 1970s hindered her close work with women of color. It was not until her involvement in multiracial feminism—through her work with women in Cuba and in Nicaragua, with Palestinian women, and with multiracial groups of lesbians and straight women in the United States—that elana began to develop deep relationships with women across race.

Other heterosexual women I interviewed also spoke of the ways in which feminist attention to sexuality encouraged them to deal with how they had allowed men of color to get in the way of working relationships with women of color. Naomi Jaffe said that in the 1960s, "I started to try to figure [myself out racially] by having affairs with Black men. I was trying to figure this race thing the best way I knew how. I was trying to figure out how you connect. I had grown up in a very white setting. . . . When I did connect with people of color at Brandeis University, it was by ignoring their color. Then there were a lot of foreign students, and I wanted to know how to connect. Again, I don't remember women of color. There weren't many of them. I connected with them by exoticizing them. There was no critique around that at Brandeis. . . . I thought it was the defiant thing to do. I think that people of color were kind of disgusted by it. I think they saw me as experimenting with something I had no clue about." One of the men with whom Naomi had an affair was married to a woman of color: "It was a mess. I was exoticizing. It took me a lot of years to figure out that the key was women of color."

Racialized dynamics of sexuality had been a huge issue long before the feminist movement. Sexuality was a complicated issue in the Students for a Democratic Society (SDS), the Student Nonviolent Coordinating Committee (SNCC), CORE, the Black Panthers, Southern Christian Leadership Conference (SCLC), and many other organizations. When white women got involved with Black men during the 1960s, it often, for many historically sound reasons, hindered white and Black women from seeing each other as allies. In her account of her work in SNCC, Cynthia Washington explained that Black and white women "started from different ends of the spectrum."[37] Although Black women and men in SNCC often held equally powerful and central positions within the organization, some Black men desexualized the Black women. When Black men and white women dated, it reinforced a notion of white women as sexually attractive and Black women as "other."[38] This dynamic did little to keep open lines of communication between women across race.

The multiracial women's movement opened this topic for scrutiny. When Black and Latina women placed issues of sexuality at the center of the agenda—along with race, class, and gender—all kinds of discussions and conflicts between women across race could be had on subjects that, although real in the 1960s, had rarely been discussed. For example, when writer and activist Joan Nestle went south from the Lower East Side in New York City in 1965 to be part of freedom marches, she was "out" as a Jew but not as a lesbian. While in Selma she had a passionate affair with a Black man, but she had no words to explain why and how she was going back to her life as a lesbian in New York.[39] The multiracial lesbian feminist movement—and in no small part the sense of community made possible with Joan Nestle's founding of the Lesbian Herstory Archives—created the space necessary to talk about the complexity of her reality in 1965.[40] It was not an expansive space, but it was enough to get things going. These conversations have been and continue to be crucial for creating and maintaining working relationships across race.

Making Activist Culture: Words, Festivals, Conferences

Alongside the antiracism nurtured by Jewish feminism and multiracial lesbian feminism in the 1970s and 1980s was the emergence of a feminist publishing industry, conferences, and festivals, which made room for an extraordinary range of debates about feminist activism.[41] At the heart of progressive political movements, including multiracial feminism, is its activist writing. The feminist publishing industry that began in the 1970s included independent journals, newspapers, magazines, presses, and dozens of bookstores that published and distributed a stunning array of women's writing. By the mid-1970s there were more than five hundred feminist magazines, periodicals, and newsletters in the United States. By 1980 there were more than seventy women's bookstores.[42]

Journals founded by Latinas in the 1970s and 1980s that explicitly focused on Latina politics and culture included *Regeneracion, Encuentro Feminil, Imagines de la Chicana,* and others.[43] Audre Lorde and others founded *Azalea: Third World Lesbians* in 1977. The founding by white women of *Feminary: A Feminist Journal for the South Emphasizing Lesbian Visions, Quest: A Feminist Quarterly, Chrysalis: A Magazine of Women's Culture, Sinister Wisdom, Conditions, Lilith, Big Mama Rag, off our backs, Sojourner: The Women's Forum,* and other journals and newspapers provided freedom of expression—in editorial decision making, distribution, and production—not available at male-dominated heterosexual presses. These journals and newspapers published many authors who, by the 1980s and 1990s, were considered among the most visionary and prophetic of feminist voices: Audre Lorde, June Jordan, Cherríe Moraga, Mitsuye Yamada, Paula Gunn Allen, Adrienne Rich, Minnie Bruce Pratt, hattie gossett, Michelle Cliff, Elly Bulkin, Dorothy Allison, and many others.

Creating and sustaining this feminist publishing industry made room for—in fact, demanded—dialogues among women across race about access, voice, and control.[44] Of her experience as one of the editors of *Feminary,* Mab Segrest says, "The first people who taught me my antiracist politics were lesbians of color in the lesbian movement of the late 1970s. In the lesbian feminist community, there were heated discussions on antiracism, critiquing capitalism. There was still a lot of the revolutionary impetus of the '60s there. And those politics totally engaged me. When I started doing cultural work with *Feminary,* we started coming to the attention—because we were dealing with racism—of lesbians of color around the country and started having cross-race and cross-class relationships and relationships with Jewish lesbians. That opened me up to a pretty complex analysis of racism and white supremacy."[45] In her reflections about working with the *Feminary* collective in the 1970s, Segrest explains, "With *Feminary*, I was very blessed to be with women who went for the gut of these things and really didn't tolerate less in ourselves, who really helped each other work on ways we had internalized oppressor roles."[46] It is through these exchanges—among white women and women of color and among white women themselves—that many white women cut their teeth as they wrote about race and racism.

About the import of these journals and the debates they nurtured, Adrienne Rich writes, "Those publications in the '70s and early '80s provided not just the space for new voices in poetry and fiction, exploring themes that had not been pursued before, but space for intra-movement arguments and debates."[47] In many instances, women of color joined the editorial staff of white feminist journals, helping change the tone and tenor of the publications. Audre Lorde, for example, was the poetry editor for several issues of *Chrysalis: A Magazine of Women's Culture,* and June Jordan and Michelle Wallace were contributing editors.[48] Nearly-all-white editorial boards, however, meant that women of color typically did not come to the table on an equal footing.

Many journal issues during this period included passionate letters to the editor protesting race and class biases in the articles, as well as much internal dialogue about how to take race and class seriously.[49] The inordinate energy women of color spent educating others about white bias and encouraging journals and presses controlled by men or white women to rethink their biases is a key reason Barbara Smith, Audre Lorde and others eventually decided to create Kitchen Table Women of Color Press, the first press in the country to be owned and operated by women of color.

In a number of instances, dialogues between white women and women of color also resulted in special issues edited by women of color and, in a few instances, significant changes in the editorial boards of the journals so that women of color had real access to decision-making processes over the long term. Among the feminist journals controlled by white women that published "special issues" by women of color or that focused on race and racism were *Quest: A Feminist Quarterly,* which published an issue on race, class, and culture in 1977, and *Heresies,* which published a special issue on Third World women that included a remarkable collection of poems, essays, and art by Asian

American, Black, Latina, and Native American women.[50] *Sinister Wisdom,* which was founded by white feminists, was eventually coedited by a biracial team, Adrienne Rich and Michelle Cliff.

Of the white feminist journals of this period, *Conditions* consistently and from the outset published writing by lesbians of color.[51] In 1983 *Conditions* became the first journal to have a majority women of color on its expanded editorial board.[52] The journal's fifth volume was coedited by Barbara Smith and Lorraine Bethel. Many of the essays, poems, and articles first published in *Conditions: Five* were subsequently included in Barbara Smith's edited volume *Home Girls: A Black Feminist Anthology.*

The paper trail of white antiracist feminist writing begins in these journals in the mid-1970s in occasional letters, articles, and essays in feminist journals and newspapers. Bev Fisher's "Race and Class: Beyond Personal Politics," Dorothy Allison's interview "Confrontation: Black/White," and Anne Braden's "A Second Open Letter to Southern Women," all 1977, are among the earliest articles by white women confronting racism in the women's movement.[53] Soon after these articles came Adrienne Rich's "Disloyal to Civilization," which was first published in *Chrysalis.* Rich's introduction to this piece gives a prime example of the extraordinary cross-race communication taking place at that time, communication that, she acknowledges, made her essay possible. She wrote this piece over a year's time with much dialogue from other women writers and activists: Audre Lorde, June Jordan, Barbara Smith, Michelle Cliff, Mary Daly, and Judith McDaniel. Earlier versions of the essay had been given in support of an advocacy project for women in prison and as a talk at the Modern Language Association's 1977 conference.[54] Rich cites Barbara Smith's "Toward a Black Feminist Criticism" and "The Combahee River Collective Statement" as two contemporary impulses for her speech, as well as Toni Cade's *The Black Woman,* which is what she calls "a generative piece of feminist thinking."[55]

Soon after the publication of "Disloyal to Civilization" came the publication of Rich's *On Lies, Secrets, and Silence* (1979), followed by Bulkin, Pratt, and Smith's *Yours in Struggle* (1984) and Mab Segrest's *My Mama's Dead Squirrel* (1985). All these books were written by lesbians; two included Jewish lesbian authors. All attributed their consciousness about race to close work with women of color, and all laid out parameters for white women seeking to work in coalition with women of color. This writing featured essays and poetry by southern women on the history of racism in the United States and of disobedience to racism's stricture. It included writing by Jewish feminists, who were documenting the emergence of a Jewish feminist movement and a history of alliances being forged and faltering between Jewish people and people of color in the United States. The literature included poetry, essays, and speeches by white women seeking a politic that took class, gender, religion, sexuality, and race seriously. Most of the key books included articles or authors first published in independent feminist journals in the late 1970s and early 1980s.[56] All reflected a period during which there was much animated and heated discussion among editors during the process of publication and by readers once the articles were published.

Only a few of the activist journals and newspapers survived into the 1990s—a telling example of the reduction of independent, nonacademic, community-based spaces available for sustained multiracial feminist debates. In the place of the journals of the 1970s were the academic women's studies journals of the 1980s and 1990s, which, though publishing key debates in feminist theory, also included the writing of a smaller cross-section of women (in terms of education and class) and were not nearly as accessible to a wide feminist audience.[57] This constriction added to many other challenges for antiracist feminist organizing in the 1990s.

Additional hot spots for interracial dialogue in the 1970s were feminist conferences and workshops. The earliest conference to consider racism and sexism as its central agenda took place in 1976.[58] This conference, cosponsored by the Sagaris Collective (a white feminist organization) and NBFO, included a workshop coled by Ginny Appuzo, a white lesbian and director of the National Gay Task Force, and Betty Powell, a Black lesbian, director of the National Gay Task Force, and former NBFO member.[59] The conference structure required racial parity among the facilitators (50 percent Black, 50 percent white). The workshop on racism included time for separate caucus groups for white and Black women and intense cross-race conversation about what limits and facilitates cross-race work. In an interview with Appuzo and Powell, two of the facilitators, strategies for cross-race power sharing were discussed. Appuzo argued that a mandatory presence—an empowered presence of women of color and lesbians—was always necessary in order to ensure that issues of race and sexuality would be adequately addressed. Powell argued that a woman of color or lesbian should not have to be present in order for racism and homophobia to be taken seriously.[60]

The conference itself was emblematic of the state of the art of antiracist feminism at that time: It upheld racial parity in leadership, was cosponsored by Black and white feminist organizations, and focused on group process and interpersonal dynamics as building blocks for activism. The debate about a mandatory presence and the politic of accountability (the responsibility of straight women or white women to raise issues of sexuality and race) foreshadowed many debates in years to come. A mandatory presence and a politic of accountability needed to be upheld simultaneously. Racial parity protected against politics of exclusion and tokenism, and yet even with racial parity, women of color were often still expected to educate white women—hence the need for whites to be accountable for their own educations, on their own time.

Another important event in identifying an antiracist agenda for white women was the 1981 NWSA conference in Storrs, Connecticut. Like the Sagaris-NBFO conference of 1976, the NWSA conference was specifically intended to focus on racism: Its theme and title were Women Respond to Racism. Unlike the Sagaris-NBFO conference, however, NWSA was not co-sponsored by Black and white women's organizations. Although the NWSA conference planning committee included women of color, it was, in the assessment of Chela Sandoval, born of the white women's movement.[61]

From the outset the conference was based on a problematic structure. All conference members were expected to attend daily two-hour consciousness-raising groups that lumped all women of color into one group but allowed white women to choose from a differentiated list of groups: working-class women, Jewish women, immigrant women, educated women, and so on. This racialized structure assumed automatic commonalities among a dizzying array of more than three hundred women of color—Puerto Ricans, Chicanas, Black women, Asian American women, and other women of color—who certainly had no monolithic understanding of the term "women of color" or "feminism."[62] Unlike the biracial Sagaris-NBFO conference of 1976, the NWSA conference was clearly multiracial. The five years between 1976 and 1981 were huge in terms of work among women of color, work that was vital to counter the tendency to see racism in dualistic terms (Black/white) and in the process to make Latina, Asian American, and Native American women invisible. Although women of color conveyed to the NWSA organizers the deep problems in the consciousness-raising structure, they continued to meet, eventually turning the ghettoizing structure around to one in which they could, as Chela Sandoval noted, collectively see differences among women of color as the "source of a new kind of political movement."[63]

Many accomplishments were made possible by the many meetings among women of color. First, there was a brand-new recognition of, in the words of Chela Sandoval, "a major turning point" and a "coalescing" of a movement of U.S. Third World feminism (70). Through the meetings, women specified that the terms "women of color" and "Third World women" were simultaneously necessary organizational tools and hopelessly simplistic given the enormous differences among women of color when generation, ethnicity, language, and sexuality are accounted for. Along with this analysis, women of color also called for a coalition meeting between Third World women and "all interested white women." This meeting, which was attended by two hundred women (approximately half were women of color and half were white women), became an "energetic and committed gathering which provided its participants an opportunity to heal blistering divisions" (69). The outcome of this meeting was a collectively approved set of resolutions, including a demand that the NWSA conference organizing committee include the leadership of Third World women from the outset in the planning of subsequent conferences and to convene the next one in a location—California—more convenient to Third World women.

The Third World Women's Alliance was a milestone for women of color, but the coalition between white women and women of color also signaled the work ahead for white women. Much of this work was articulated by Adrienne Rich in "Disobedience and Women's Studies," her keynote address at the conference.[64] In this talk, Rich expressed her outrage at the coverage of the convention by a regional newspaper, whose reportage focused on housing arrangements for lesbians and alleged tensions between lesbians and heterosexual women at the preceding year's conference. For Rich, the fact that the newspaper focused on issues of sexuality when reporting on a conference that was explicitly structured to focus on racism was part of a long history of attempting to "erase the issue of racism, in a state where the Ku Klux Klan openly marches" (77). In her speech Rich encouraged women to resist such erasures, and white feminists to "understand both our obedience and complicity *and* our rebellions" (81). Rich warned against the immobility of guilt, calling guilt more "a form of defensive resentment or self-protection than an authentic response to the past and its warts" (82). Rich also reminded the audience that no white woman "has any competitive monopoly on understanding racism" (82).

The 1981 West Coast Women's Music Festival in Yosemite National Park was another key event at which a multiracial group of women came together to protest race and class inequities. The festival, which was attended by about four thousand women, included a protest and walkout by a multiracial group of about four hundred festival attendees in response to festival organizers' racist and classist policies toward women-of-color vendors, cooking staff, musicians, and cultural workers.

Race and class tensions began before the festival opened when conference organizers failed to give kitchen staff and other festival workers written contracts for their work. The tensions escalated during the festival when Latin America Solidarity Day events were positioned near an area where women were swimming and playing volleyball and tennis. Activists had to compete with a recreational atmosphere as they spoke about the forced relocation of Navajos in Arizona, the current work of women in Nicaragua and El Salvador, and the anniversary of Augusto Pinochet's 1973 coup in Chile. After separate caucuses of women—women of color and white women—drafted protest statements, they decided there was substantial agreement between the groups. They formed one caucus and hoped to present their statement to the festival at large. When a multiracial group of women representing the caucuses was finally allowed to present their concerns on stage, some in the audience booed their messages (with a can't-we-just-have-fun? attitude), and the conference producer, Robin Tyler, reacted defensively to the caucus representatives. With these rebuffs, the multiracial coalition walked out of the concert and held its own makeshift but incredibly powerful cultural event, which lasted many hours into the night.

During the festival and for several months thereafter, five different groups—women of color, white women, Jewish women, Latinas, and disabled women—met and fashioned statements about how to make the festival more democratic. Key to the separate "white women's" and "Jewish women's" groups was Jewish women's concern about the connection between racism and anti-Semitism at the festival. The Jewish women's statement opposed racism and classism at the festival while reminding people that "Robin Tyler is a Jewish sister, which should not be ignored. Because she is Jewish, issues of money, power and aggression have been discussed without careful consideration."[65] Common to all the statements was a demand for democratic representation at all levels of planning for future festivals.[66]

Among the white women who attended the organizing meetings at the festival was Holly Near. Although Near was represented as an "icon" of white lesbian music at the time because of her album *Imagine My Surprise* (which celebrated her coming out as a lesbian), her participation at the festival included her speaking openly about her own process of coming to terms with racism and what was required for her to attempt to be accountable to women of color nationally and internationally. At the caucus meetings during the festival, she supported the protests and encouraged white women to take steps in their own lives to come to terms with the legacy of racism.[67]

Bernice Johnson Reagon's "Coalition Politics: Turning the Century" is the best-known document to emerge from that festival. It is based on the speech she gave Sunday morning following the protests of the night before.[68] In the speech she responded to the hostility, defensiveness, and anger expressed by some white organizers and participants when the multiracial group of women questioned whether the festival was really meant for *all* women. Reagon explained that the whole notion of "women-only" festivals is erroneous since, in effect, it is a code for white lesbians.

Reagon warned that white lesbian politics and culture had become a "barred room" that left everybody but white lesbians out. Reagon maintained that a festival, concert, or conference is not a "woman's space" if it is really only for white women. Based on her thirty-plus years as an activist and cultural worker, Reagon explained that barred rooms had to be replaced by an understanding of coalition politics. In a barred room everyone might look, act, and be the same. "Coalition work, by contrast, is not done in your home. Coalition work has to be done in the streets. And it is some of the most dangerous work you can do."[69]

Reagon's wisdom about the danger and risk taking involved in doing coalition work partly reflected her own experiences going into what she labeled "alien" territory to do justice work. In 1977 the a cappella group Sweet Honey in the Rock had consented to do a tour in northern California at the request of tour organizers Holly Near and Amy Horowitz. Reagon recalls, "It was a shock to go from Washington D.C. where we sang for Black people, churches, schools, theaters, folk festivals, and political rallies to the radical, separatist, white women–dominated, lesbian cultural network in California. There were immediate and constant conflicts. Most of the time we felt as if we were in alien territory and had to protect our identity and the integrity of who we were."[70] From her negotiations with white lesbians working on the tour, Reagon understood that "a lot of conflicts came from racism. A lot of conflicts came from their radicalism—the community wanting to be sure that they protected themselves and that they were dealing with women-identified-women" (178).

By the time the West Coast Women's Music Festival took place in 1981, Reagon had also seen that "despite the tensions, the community took an extraordinary risk to present us to the public events they sponsored. There was clearly a Movement energy I understood. People turned over their houses and cars and lugged around sound equipment. In two cases, that I will never forget, all-women establishments that had never allowed men—Artemis in San Francisco and a bar in Albany, California—changed their policy when we sang. We were fierce about our need to be accessible to men and women, as well as to women-only spaces, but I was very aware of the trauma some of our early sponsors went through to organize a platform we would accept; a platform that was life-threatening to them in many ways. It was a coalition of the riskiest kind" (178).

From Reagon's perspective, white women's ability to do coalition work depended on their understanding that there would be no women's or lesbian movement had there not been the Civil Rights Movement. She told the women who attended her speech at the festival, "Black folks started it, Black folks did it, so everything you've done politically rests on the efforts of my people—that's my arrogance! Yes and it's the truth: it's my truth."[71] Reagon asserted that although nationalism—including that which led white lesbians to coalesce—had its time and place, by the 1980s it had become "reactionary" and "totally inadequate for surviving in the world with many peoples" (358). Given the multiracial roots of the lesbian movement, white-only lesbian space (whether called that or not) made no sense—strategically, politically, or culturally. From Reagon's speech and the multiracial protest at the festival came a recognition that white women could not dominate the organizing of a festival and then profess it was for all women. Coalition politics had to be implemented from the start, a reality partially but not fully realized in subsequent festivals.

Another key conference of this period, Common Differences: Third World Women and Feminist Perspectives (1983), was organized by a multiracial international group of women (mostly academics) including Ann Russo, Lourdes Torres, and Chandra Talpade Mohanty.[72] The 850 women attending represented thirty-five countries, and according to its conveners, it "was one of the very first occasions for women of color and white women in the United States and women from Third World countries to come together around their/our common differences."[73] Like the NWSA conference and the West Coast Women's Music Festival, Common Differences stressed the danger of thinking in terms of a monolithic "woman." The conference was unprecedented in its attention to imperialism, its critique of much First World feminist theory (beginning with its overwhelming reliance upon English), and the significant representation of women from Third World countries among conference participants.

The conference also inspired an edited anthology, *Third World Women and the Politics of Feminism*, which chronicles Third World women's negotiations with feminism. The anthology also includes Ann Russo's "'We Cannot Live without Our Lives': White Women, Antiracism, and Feminism," which specified the synergistic potential of multiracial alliances. Russo also clarifies that white women's attempts to challenge racism are really acts of self-interest: acts against the impoverishment that comes from leading monoracial lives.[74]

Another pivotal conference of this period was sponsored in 1984 by New York Women against Rape (NYWAR); its special focus was combating sexual violence from a multiracial perspective. The antirape movement that had begun in the 1970s was overwhelmingly white. A survey of rape crisis centers had indicated that the vast majority of members, staff, and clients were white. In the eight-five centers studied, there were more male staff members of rape crisis centers in 1976 than there were Black and Hispanic women combined.[75] NYWAR, which was coordinated by Cherríe Moraga and Stephanie Roth, recognized that a "predominantly white women's anti-violence movement cannot adequately meet the needs of women of color until it begins to reflect a multiracial perspective."[76] The conference offered consciousness-raising sessions on racism for white women and dialogues among women of color on racism (including on anti-Semitism and on color and ethnic differences), as well as sessions for caucusing between women of color and white women. Of the sixty-five workshop leaders, forty-five were women of color. Workshops included a discussion on homophobia in Third World communities; Jewish women and women of color; Third World women working within white and multiracial organizations; lesbian incest survivors; and violence against women in prison.[77]

The conference provided space for women to talk about how race and class bias manifested themselves in organizing against violence against women. In the 1970s and 1980s, in education, health care, and work to end violence against women, women of color confronted the subtle and transparent practices that sidelined them. Several women I interviewed told stories of organizations that went through transformations as women of color (sometimes joined by a few white women) confronted these exclusions. Dawn Gomes worked for several years with a nonprofit women's organization that canvased and educated about child sexual abuse, rape, and domestic violence. Eventually women of color pushed to make the organization more inclusive. The director was a Swedish woman who supervised the Black, Latina, and white canvasers. When the Black women canvased, they faced everything from outright hostility and difficulty in raising money at the door to sometimes being assaulted in the neighborhoods. Dawn remembers that the "director basically had no consciousness about it and kept trying to sweep it under the rug."

The women of color met and decided they wanted their own canvasing crews and control over education and training. Some of the white women supported them, but the director and other white women got together and "tried to thwart it." Dawn was among the white women who supported the women of color. At one point, the director called Dawn in and told her that "the whole organization would go to hell in a hand basket if any of these Black women got any power. It was actually the most scary thing. I was incredulous."[78] Ultimately, the white director was ousted and a new board was established. Dawn became codirector with a woman of color. The organization got out of debt and prospered. For Dawn, it was amazing to come through a situation "where racism is right in your face" to another, stronger time in the organization.

As obvious as it was that women of color needed to have input and leadership within the organization, their struggle for this basic right was common in feminist organizations across the country. The NYWAR conference provided a meeting place for women to hear about and learn from racial dynamics within organizations, to see patterns in how white domination manifests itself in groups, and to learn what enables power shifts to occur while keeping organizations afloat.

The conferences and festivals I have chronicled—the Sagaris-NBFO conference, the 1981 NWSA conference, Common Differences, the West Coast Women's Music Festival, and the NYWAR conference— reflect a few of many settings in the early 1980s that attracted a range of women across race, region, age, religion, and occupation.[79] This diversity was, in fact, why they were successful locations for antiracist dialogue.

There was a limit, however, to these conferences and festivals as locations where women hammered out the complexity of antiracism: Many feminists did not attend these events. Treating the conflicts in these locations as emblematic of debates in general reinforces a class bias in the story of antiracism. With the exception of the NYWAR conference, these settings were dominated by middle-class women. Furthermore, conflicts in conferences and festivals are not dealt with in the same way as they are in permanent organizations. There is an intensity and artificiality about conferences and festivals that amplifies conflicts and pushes people to deal quickly with controversies. Their short life span, however, works against long-term organizing.

Yet the story of race and racism in these locations remains important for several reasons. Women took the lessons learned from these conferences and festivals back to the organizations where they worked (and vice versa)—in education, labor organizing, feminist presses, battered-women's shelters, and nursing homes—where many similar conflicts were occurring. Within these organizations were many animated, often contentious discussions about restructuring organizations to gain racial parity, changing the culture of organizations so that they are not white centered, and confronting the way class issues affect group priorities.

I also highlight conflicts in conferences and festivals because there is at least some paper trail or collective history about race and racism. Many organizations in which important antiracist actions took place in this period have left no paper trail. For example, Lesbians against Police Violence conducted multiple trainings for white women about antiracism and worked to create successful coalitions with heterosexual Latinos to confront police harassment in the mission. This organization has no paper trial. Dykes against Racism Everywhere (DARE) was an early 1980s, New York–based multiracial group that opposed right-wing racism as well as racism within the gay and lesbian movement. It organized against the Klan, the passage of the Family Protection Act, apartheid in South Africa, nuclear testing in Micronesia, and uranium mining on Navajo land. The paper trail for DARE includes a handful of informational flyers—period. I include attention to conferences and festivals wary of the limits of this story, humbled by the extent to which the history of grassroots antiracism has yet to be recovered, and grateful for the feminist independent newspapers that did consistently chronicle conferences and festivals of the 1970s and 1980s.

Finally, I highlight these conferences and festivals as locations for serious dialogue about race knowing that many of them no longer exist. Although women's music festivals continue, they, like gay pride marches, have come to be more like celebrations than political forums. And although some conferences continue to provide a platform for open debates about racism, there are far fewer activist-based feminist conferences now than in the past. One of the many side effects of the institutionalization of women's, ethnic, and African American studies has been the emergence of academic-based conferences that for the most part have replaced activist-based feminist forums. In this way, the story of changes in feminist conferences parallels that of independent journals of the 1970s and 1980s. A polished professionalism has replaced the in-your-face conversations about race and class characteristic of 1970s and 1980s multiracial feminism.

7

Fight the Power, Hold On to Community

A jurisprudence of antisubordination is an attempt to bring home the lost ones, to make them part of the center, to end the soul-killing tyranny of inside/outside thinking. Accountability revisited. I want to bring home the women who hate their own bodies so much that they would let a surgeon's hand cut fat from it, or a man's hand batter and bruise it. I want to bring home the hungry ones eating from the trashbins; the angry ones who call me names; the little ones in foster care.

Mari Matsuda, "Voices of America"

Accountability Revisited

The emergence of a white feminist antiracist politic in the early 1980s was dependent on feminism among women of color, on Jewish and multiracial lesbian feminism, and on the building of multiracial cultural institutions. Although these influences provided a foundation, by the mid-1980s what might best be said to characterize antiracism for white feminists was the flexibility to continually broaden their focus in the face of complex political alliances. The rise in racism throughout the country required feminist activism that defied a formulaic recipe. In Chela Sandoval's breathtaking philosophy of U.S. Third World feminism, she compares the oppositional consciousness that developed among women of color feminists to "the clutch of an automobile: the mechanism that permits the driver to select, engage, and disengage gears in a system for the transmission of power."[1] Oppositional consciousness requires a capacity to switch political gears, size up and understand changes in state power, and use multiple tactics to undermine oppression.

Gear shifting through changing political challenges is powerfully exemplified in the activism of southern lesbian antiracist activist Mab Segrest. Her first book, *My Mama's Dead Squirrel* (1985), and her second, *Memoir of a Race Traitor* (1994), trace the trajectory of a woman whose antiracism was born out of the lesbian feminism of the 1970s but who by the 1980s had moved into organizing against Klan violence.[2] Segrest did not leave lesbian feminism or her respect for building lesbian cultural institutions behind in the process, but she did see the limits of this work in developing a comprehensive antiracist politic.

In *My Mama's Dead Squirrel,* a book of nine essays written in the 1970s and early 1980s, Segrest argues for a southern canon in literature that begins with slave narratives and includes the work of Carson McCullers and Lillian Smith alongside William Faulkner and Flannery O'Connor. She dialogues with antiracist pacifist Barbara Deming about her work in the Civil Rights, antinuclear, and lesbian movements.[3] Segrest struggles with the racial contradictions involved for her, as a white woman, in teaching English to migrant farm workers, given that their landlessness is deeply rooted in a history of slavery and colonialism from which her family benefited directly.[4]

At the center of the book is an essay about Segrest's mother and grandmother, in particular about their vexed relationships with two African American women, Belle and Carrie, a former servant to the Segrest family and her niece, respectively. Reflecting upon her relatives' complicity in racism throughout their lives, Segrest writes, "That my mother could make passionate statements and actions about her love for Belle and Carrie in one breath and then in the next explain how these same women were born to clean her house is a kind of cultural/personal schizophrenia bound to take its toll."[5] Segrest knows that for whites, the legacy of slavery is one of a people who did not do the right thing, so "they could not afford to listen to their consciences, and consequently cut themselves from the better part of themselves" (26).

Despite her commitment to write about her family and racism, Segrest was afraid that she would lose those who were dear to her. She writes, "I was afraid that I would lose everybody: white middle class friends who might want to distance themselves from my confessions; women of color and working class women for naming my own tradition of race and class privilege from which they have suffered and which will always be some part of me, no matter how hard I might work; white Christian women like my sister who gets much of her identity from her religion; Jewish and Arab women who have found the church's history lethal; and finally my mother and the ghost of my grandmother for naming what I see as their failures as I try to find the part of their heritage I can build on" (147).

The heritage Segrest can build on requires reaching back into history, inside as well as outside of her biological family: to southern antiracists Lillian Smith and Angelina Grimke; to her mother, who did not untangle herself from racism but whispered to Mab in the kitchen that Mab was right when she countered racist assumptions at the dinner table; and to a southern heritage of recognizing the power of humor as a tool of repression as well as a tool of liberation.

My Mama's Dead Squirrel offers a quintessential example of antiracist lesbian feminist politics in the early to middle 1980s.[6] The book is grounded in autobiography, an approach made possible by the supposition in identity politics that the most profound and radical perspectives come from one's own experience. The core of Segrest's radical perspectives was born out of her experiences as a southern lesbian middle-class Christian-raised woman and out of all the contradictions embodied in that identity. Segrest writes, "In sorting through the various strata of my identity over the past several years, I have come to view differently its different components: white and middle class, raised to expect the world at my feet; lesbian and female, expecting the kick of that same booted foot."[7] *My Mama's Dead Squirrel* also takes seriously the plea and mandate put forward by many second-wave feminists of color that white women must seek out their own histories of heresy and resistance rather than attempt to attach themselves to others' cultures. Segrest writes, "If the South is the cradle of the Confederacy and of many subsequent right-wing movements it is also the mother of all resistance."[8]

And yet, as is true of the writings of many antiracists who are dedicated to the work for the long haul, Segrest's *My Mama's Dead Squirrel* contained within it the seeds of its own transformation. Its essays, written over an eight-year period, show important changes in Segrest's thinking. In the preface to the book Segrest writes, "In the first [essay] I wrote 'I believe that the oppression of women is the first oppression.' Now I am not so sure. Later I wrote, 'Relationships between women matter to me more than anything else in my life.' Now what matters most is more abstract or totally specific: the closest word to it, justice. . . . During the early years the writing comes primarily out of work with other lesbians; later on, from work where I am the only lesbian."[9] The book opens with autobiographical essays about her family and women's writing and ends with essays chronicling the beginning of her organizing against the Klan—essays that became the backdrop to *Memoir of a Race Traitor.*

In Segrest's view, by 1983 her work in building lesbian culture—through editing *Feminary* and through her own writing—"no longer seemed to be enough; it seemed too literary."[10] Segrest found herself both "inspired by and frustrated with the lesbian feminist movement."[11] She had heard Barbara Smith say many times, "I don't live in the women's movement. I live on the streets of North America." Segrest writes that she "had sat in many rooms and participated in many conversations between lesbians about painful differences in race and class, about anti-Semitism and ageism and able-bodiedism. They had been hard discussions, but they had given me some glimpse of the possibility of spinning a wider lesbian movement, a women's movement that truly incorporates diversity as strength. But in all those discussions, difficult as they were, we had never been out to kill each other. In the faces of Klan and Nazi men—and women—in North Carolina I saw people who would kill us all. I felt I needed to shift from perfecting consciousness to putting consciousness to the continual test of action. I wanted to answer a question that had resonated through the lesbian writing I had taken most to heart: 'What will you undertake?'"[12]

In *Memoir of a Race Traitor* Segrest explores what it means to be organizing (as staff with North Carolinians against Racist and Religious Violence) against the Klan, which has lesbians, Jews, and African Americans on its immediate hit list. In her organizing she asks African American fundamentalist churchgoers to treat homophobia as a serious threat to humanity, and she asks members of the gay and lesbian movement to find ways to be a "bridge, not a wedge" to antiracist, anticapitalist organizing.[13] In the process of stepping beyond what had become familiar ground to organizing against the Klan, Segrest found communities ready and willing to work with her. In comparing lesbian feminist organizing to work against the Klan, Segrest comments, "One of the lines in lesbian-feminist organizing (which had to do more with organizing consciousness than with organizing communities) was that white women have to learn from each other. Women of color couldn't be expected or obligated to teach us anything. But I found when I was putting my life on the line—totally, seriously intent on what I was doing—I got an incredible range of help and mentoring from people of color. I learned from that that many people of color see the evolution of antiracist white people as important and are willing to put some time into that, if they see you are serious and already engaged."[14]

The continual opening of her world and politics were not without cost, a reality Segrest reveals along with the blessings that came with the work. In five years of organizing against the Klan, Segrest saw the repetition of violence over and over again—tortured bodies, trials of Klansmen that ended in acquittals, the stalking and terrorizing of whole communities. Segrest characterizes her writing before she began working against the Klan as "totally subjective, focusing on everything through this very autobiographical lens. I shifted for about five years to an objective voice but I suffered from it, having these intense experiences that I just didn't have the time to process. There didn't seem to be enough time to slow down and produce the kind of writing that comes when you can be more meditative and reflective and relaxed and have things float up" (1). What went underground at times with Mab's turn to organizing against the radical right was humorous attention to the macabre and outrageous that sprinkled *My Mama's Dead Squirrel*. There is a cautious quality to sections of *Memoir* that speaks volumes about the toll organizing against hate groups exacts. Along with the costs are the gifts. What *Memoir of a Race Traitor* conveys is the incredible, rich community of comrades and friends Segrest made through her organizing. As she explains, "It took organizing against the Klan and Nazis to show me that lesbian space is, ultimately, the world."[15]

Like Segrest, Suzanne Ross also speaks of feminist organizing in the 1980s and '90s as a commitment requiring the ability to hold multiple worldviews in one frame of reference and to consider oneself accountable to multiple communities simultaneously. Suzanne's activism in response to the rape of a white woman in Central Park in 1989 is perhaps the most telling example of the complexity of her politics. In the Central Park case, a white woman who worked on Wall Street was raped and beaten, allegedly by a group of young African American men. The dominant media ran headlines such as "Wilding" and "Wolf Gang" in describing the alleged rapists. Suzanne explains, "All the media presented them as horrible wild animals that were predators of innocent white people. The lines got drawn very quickly. In support of the woman, feminists, including NOW, said these kids were guilty. A certain number of Black people came out saying these kids were being railroaded. The fact is, both were true, if you ask me."

Women of color with whom Suzanne worked in the International Working Women's Day Committee (IWWDC) knew the mothers of the adolescents accused of the rape. "The mothers came to us for help. They said, 'These kids are going to be killed. We need help.' The debate was intense and furious. Some of the Black men and some of the Black women were saying that these kids were innocent victims and the woman was probably not raped or maybe it was her boyfriend who raped her. There was other semen found. All kinds of things went on. On the other hand, the white people who were speaking out were not saying anything about the history of railroading Black kids, especially for rape. It was intense."

The multiracial group of feminists with whom Suzanne worked believed it was important to have a white woman speak out in defense of the Black youth. Suzanne said she did not want to defend them without saying she also defended the woman. Suzanne was selected to give the presentation for her group at the upcoming Malcolm X conference. "We worked out a collective position. There was no question that this woman was raped and that she is the victim. We don't say alleged [rape]. We know she is a rape victim. Rape is something we oppose across the board. On the other hand, we did not know if these kids did it and they certainly did not have their rights recognized. They had been railroaded very quickly. The police got confessions out of them. The police spoke to them without their parents being around. The usual stuff. They didn't have money. Some of them didn't have parents. All of the weaknesses of young Black men in this society."

The IWWDC recognized that the history in the United States of Black men being charged with the rape of white women was a heavy one that could not be ignored. Suzanne and the other women knew the media presentation would have been different had the rape victim been a woman of color or had the rapist been white. In fact, a case in New York (in 1990) in which a Puerto Rican woman was thrown from a roof down a seven-story building had been largely ignored. And there had recently been an incident in New Jersey in which a group of white adolescents had brutally molested and raped a retarded white teenager.

But, as Suzanne remembers, the defendants' attorneys argued that "Boys will be boys."

Suzanne gave the talk, which had been written collectively by women in the multiracial feminist group, to a mostly Black audience. "I was picked to give it, consciously. I was very careful. I read every word from my text, what I said. Ironically, because I was surrounded by people of color, most of the criticism I got was from Black feminists. This is one of those amazing interesting stories. . . . It is like the Black Jewish thing. There are a few things you get a lot of shit from everybody about. Well, this is like the Black Jewish thing where everyone ended up hating me. Everyone was mad at me."

The Black feminists who were angry at Suzanne thought the kids were guilty. After Suzanne delivered the speech she drove home with three African American women, including her friend hattie gossett, all of whom were very angry about her speech. From their perspective, "People like me were sitting back from the struggle because these kids needed to be stopped. Their sexism and outrageous behavior had to be stopped. These weren't just feminists in the feminist scene. Two of them had long histories in the anti-imperialist, Communist movement. I was surprised how harsh they were." They thought Suzanne should not have included anything in the talk about the Scottsboro case. The Black women thought that reference implied that the teens in the Central Park incident were innocent. The Black women argued with Suzanne that "the Scottsboro Boys were completely framed. They had nothing to do with the crime. These kids were in Central Park. They were running around. Whether they raped this woman or not, they were nearby." In retrospect, Suzanne has wondered if some of the Black women's anger toward the Black youth had to do with their knowledge of domestic violence against Black women, violence that, so often, has not been taken seriously.

Suzanne says that if she had it to do over, she might not have delivered the speech. "All these issues that are complex on all sides are very debilitating." Several years after the controversial talk and the ensuing debates, Suzanne met one of the young men who had been convicted of crimes related to the incident. According to this young man, there had been two groups of teenagers involved. One of the groups had beaten a white man who was with the woman after he had made a racist comment. The young man said the group he was with did not rape the woman. Although this might be true, Suzanne also respected the complexity of the incident from the perspective of her Black feminist friends.

Looking back on it, Suzanne now believes that "the last thing in the world you need is a white woman coming in supporting the boys." With regard to the Central Park case, Suzanne was simultaneously part of a multiracial collective that was determined to recognize the reality of rape and the history of scapegoating Black men and part of a friendship network of Black feminists who did not want to let Black men off the hook for violating women, regardless of race.

From this experience and others, Suzanne has come to believe that "the whole phrase, 'Follow the leadership of people of color' is very complex. It is not simple to figure out how to follow without being a blind follower. How to lead without being the center. How to be responsible about choices without being an interventionist. All of those choices are very complicated and take a lot of experience. There is no simple formula for how to do it. You struggle with it and have to have that consciousness. That is one of the challenges of white activists."

For Suzanne, as a white woman committed to an analysis of racism, accountability is inevitably a complicated issue. In her political analysis of the Central Park case, Joy James explains that the binds people were in if they spoke out in support of a fair trial were "often customized to fit the ethnicity of the woman. If the fair-trial activist was Black or Latina, she was accused of being antiwhite and sympathetic to rapists. . . . If she was white, she was accused of being a race traitor, bleeding heart, and sympathetic to rapists because of her racial guilt. Any woman, regardless of her ethnicity, who criticized the state's procedures was susceptible to the charge that she had subordinated sexual politics to racial politics."[16]

Suzanne was caught between a rock and a hard place in her attempt to hold seemingly contradictory politics within a single frame. When the multiracial feminist organization decided a white woman should present the collectively written position paper, it did so to counter a white feminist response that had refused to account for the history of state-supported persecution of Black men. As the organization saw it, this position did not preclude also recognizing the epidemic of rape in the United States perpetrated by men across race. At the same time, Suzanne respected the position of some of her Black feminist friends, who knew well the racism involved in failing to hold Black men accountable for their actions, particularly when that lack of accountability by white women meant that Black women must come in and "be the heavies" with Black men. For Suzanne, identity politics—the recognition of herself as Jewish, white, and from a militant background—left her in a precarious position in relation to several different communities to which she tried to hold herself accountable. Suzanne's bind was not ultimately about an individual white woman; rather, it was about the complexity of an antiracist and antisexist position in a society that consistently attempts to pull those two analyses in opposite directions.

Like Suzanne Ross, Naomi Jaffe has struggled in the 1980s and 1990s to find a feminism big enough to take on racism in its myriad forms. The contrasts she has experienced between the civil rights activism of the 1960s and the feminist activism of the 1980s and 1990s speak volumes to the nature of her struggle. When Naomi spoke of her years working with the Students for a Democratic Society (SDS) and the Weather Underground, she did so with wisdom and depth, as a woman who had put in her time both aboveground and underground. Her face as she spoke of this period was not closed or tense, but the lines on her face were drawn, and the cadence of her voice was deliberate, measured, almost tired. When she spoke about the 1980s and 1990s, however, her voice and face lifted. This surprised me. What I have usually experienced with people who have been activists since the 1960s is a sense of "Those were the years," a feeling that often brings a wistful and lively sparkle to people's eyes and voices.

When Naomi talked about the 1960s, she was detailed and passionate, but there was nothing wistful or nostalgic about her words. Perhaps the many losses she has lived with contribute to this realism. Her close friend and former lover, David Gilbert, for example, now lives just down the road from her, only an hour's drive away along Route 4 in upstate New York; but whereas she lives in a house in Troy, he is in a maximum-security prison, serving a life sentence stemming from his work in the underground in the 1970s.

When I asked Naomi to help me understand the changes in her expressiveness when talking about the different decades, she explained that the gift of the 1960s was a precise and accurate understanding of power and a sense that a revolution was possible. It was clear, partly from the language people used in the 1960s, that there were many definite distinctions made about power: who had the power and who used it. For antiwar protesters, the state and the military-industrial complex had the power, and it was up to the people to stop its abuse. The Black Panthers had a clear class-race analysis of power. They also believed that the ruling class, made up overwhelmingly of white people, held the power, often with the collaboration of other white people who, for the most part, did not have ruling-class status. The activists believed it was up to young people to be militant to make a revolution. For civil rights activists, power was located in the government, in education, in housing, and in finance. Power could be shifted in favor of racial equality through the courts, civil disobedience, and education. Although there was no unanimity about how this was to be done, almost everyone agreed that a power analysis was crucial.

What Naomi feels is missing from feminism in the 1990s and since is a willingness to adopt a power analysis, to clearly state that there is an enemy, that there is a right and a wrong, that there are people who have power because they are part of institutions and structures that create and perpetuate it. What Naomi did not have in the 1990s—nor did people around her—was a framework for directly confronting those in power. There was such a framework in the 1960s. In the 1990s she also did not have—and missed terribly—a sense that people were working toward a revolution.

What Naomi does have now, gained through multiracial feminism, is a community. She devoted eight years of her life to an organization— the Weather Underground—whose sexism kept it from ever being a complete community for her. Since the 1980s she has been connected to a loving, committed, and hardworking group of people, mostly women of color, on whom she can count for political work and deep friendship. The vibrancy in her voice now is nurtured by the love and connection she derives from her feminist political community. Her life is more whole than it was in the 1960s.

What Naomi has seen since the 1980s is an emphasis on confronting internalized racism and sexism—the manifestations of oppression in people's personal lives. She believes that one of the contributions of the feminist, gay, and lesbian movement of the 1970s and 1980s is a willingness to take people's personal lives seriously. But she is concerned that this emphasis has been at the expense of continuing to name the enemy. She knows it is indeed terrifying to do that. But she believes it is only possible to take responsibility for what is wrong if we are clear about the power we are up against.

The dichotomy Naomi sees between building multiracial communities and sustaining a political analysis of power is one that Mab Segrest has bridged in her work against the Klan. Organizing against the radical right provides a steady and definable enemy, a clear understanding of power, and a definite, albeit overwhelming, set of goals for attacking racism. The dilemma Naomi articulates is how to maintain a strong sense of an enemy and an analysis of power alongside the feminist value placed on community building. "The identity politics direction, to me, has not come to grips with confronting power." In Albany the groups she feels the closest to are lesbians and gays of color, with whom she has worked for many years. But she clarifies, "Our antiracism projects, which are people-of-color led, are not yet, to my immense frustration, directly taking on the institutions of power." The criminal justice system and the state's assault on welfare have been attacking the most vulnerable communities in the nation. "I see those two as parallel prongs of an attack on poor people of color communities. Both of them are literally, not just metaphorically, a re-creation of slavery. People have no control of their labor, their bodies, their destiny. Overwhelmingly, they are people of color, whose labor, bodies, and destiny are being appropriated."

What frustrates Naomi is that she does not find feminists organizing where the most damage is being done. She gives an example: "I was in a courtroom when prisoners, one of whom is a friend of mine, had brought a federal civil suit against the prison system for punitively transferring them out of Comstock [a maximum-security prison in upstate New York] as a result of a petition they had done and gotten to the outside about racist beatings. The lawsuit is that they were retaliated against by exercising their constitutionally protected rights. It was in the federal courtroom in downtown Albany. I walked into this courtroom with big high ceilings and wood paneling and upholstered chairs and a white judge in black robes and a bunch of white men in business suits standing around. These three guys were brought in in shackles and sweatshirts. There they are. There it is. A white courtroom. And three Black men who were the defendants. They weren't even the plaintiffs in this case, shuffling in shackles. This is really not any different than slavery. This is what slavery was. We are in it. This is the power of the criminal justice system and the only three Black people in this room are in shackles. It is like that when you are in prison all the time . . . Something we are doing has to make it harder for them to do that. Not sometime down the line, but right now. And I don't see it. It is not happening. I don't know exactly how to make it happen."

Naomi says that when she is "in the places where there is some resistance to the criminal justice system or even resistance to the attacks on women and social services, I am not finding myself in a feminist place. I am not finding myself in a feminist context. When I am in a feminist context, we are doing all of this community building, which, you know, I love it. It is important. I care about it. But it is not enough. We have to be a thorn in their side in some way and so far we aren't. Black community organizations are with great difficulty and few resources and not even a lot of support from the Black community challenging the criminal justice system." In New York State Naomi has worked for a long time with organizations run by ex-prisoners and Black legislators, "who are male, certainly not feminists. It is not my context, but they are saying things that no one else is saying. I don't see our feminist movement saying that."

Dilemmas articulated by white antiracist feminists in the late 1980s reverberate with those faced by antiracist women of the late 1960s. Both groups of women were seeking an expansive politic. Whether organizing against sexual abuse of women and scapegoating of Black men in the criminal justice system, against the Klan, or against the assault on poor women and children, antiracist women were attempting to hold themselves accountable to multiple communities. What made their perspective different in the late 1990s is that they could draw upon twenty years of feminist organizing, twenty years of dialogues and struggle among feminists about what is required to create an expansive analysis. By the mid-1980s the question was certainly not whether feminism was relevant to women of color and white antiracist women but, rather, what white women needed to do to be consistently responsive to women across race, class, and generation.

Feminist Historiography and Antiracist Consciousness

Finding the origins and signs of white antiracist activism within the feminist movement is in some ways a more formidable task than doing so within the Civil Rights Movement. The difficulty first relates to differences in the forms of the two movements. Although the Civil Rights Movement eventually spread throughout the country, its epicenter was the South. Antiracism among white people began there, and even those activists who never lived in the South considered it their source of inspiration and guidance. From the outset, the women's movement, by contrast, emerged throughout the country—North, South, East, and West. Although the "master historical narrative" of the feminist movement has tended to emphasize activism coming from the Northeast, any serious attention to Asian American and Chicana feminism shows the grave limits of a northeastern bias.[17] The fact that the feminist movement has multiregional roots is exciting, but it makes the movement harder to track than the Civil Rights Movement.

Second, there has never been an organization in the women's movement to have gained the national influence of the Student Nonviolent Coordinating Committee (SNCC). The closest parallel in terms of organizational visibility is the National Organization for Women (NOW). NOW was white dominated from the beginning and has remained so. SNCC, by contrast, was Black led from the start and remained so. Whereas SNCC was clearly a center for antiracist work, at no time has that been true for NOW.

A third difference in the two movements relates to structure. The most important antiracist feminist work has occurred in small, local, grassroots, and typically transitory organizations. Although some organizations have been around a long time—the National Black Women's Health Project is a leading example—many of the most influential and successful antiracist organizations have had fairly short shelf lives. The National Black Feminist Organization (NBFO), for example, made substantial contributions to feminism in the early 1970s, spawning the Combahee River Collective, consciousness-raising groups among Black women that lasted into the 1980s, and support for what became a renaissance of Black women's literary and cultural production. Yet as a national organization, NBFO only lasted two years. The journal *Conditions,* which published some of the most influential writing by women of this century, lasted ten years. For an independent journal that depended almost entirely on voluntary labor and was published out of people's homes, that was a phenomenal life span. To historians attempting to trace the trajectory and longevity of antiracist work, its life span was short—barely long enough to see patterns, barely long enough to analyze its work alongside and against a national movement.

The hard truth is that the most exciting feminist antiracist work has been transitory. There is almost no paper trail for many grassroots, fewer-than-twenty-member, antiracist affinity groups or organizations of the 1980s. Although "grassroots" is the word that best character-ized the Civil Rights Movement, its small, sometimes short-lived or-ganizations existed alongside larger nationally recognized antiracist organizations that, thankfully, have been documented.

A fourth difference has to do with leadership. From the start the leadership of the feminist movement has been contested. For those women who came up through multiracial feminism, the key activists and writers have been women of color: Audre Lorde, Byllye Avery, June Jordan, Shirley Chisholm, Toni Cade, Angela Davis, Paula Gunn Allen, Shirley Geok-lin Lim, Evelyn Hu DeHart, Johnnie Tillmon, Bar-bara Smith, Joy James, Wilma Mankiller, Gloria Anzaldúa, and others. In addition to these women, there has also been a much smaller group of antiracist white women, a few of whom have gained national recog-nition because of their writing. Although women who came up through white feminism will probably recognize the names of the women cited above, the master historical narrative has hardly placed them at the center. There is no parallel to Martin Luther King Jr. or Malcolm X in terms of name recognition among women, for whom antiracism has been central to their feminism. Although multiracial feminism has been led by women of color, it remains only one segment of the feminist movement—albeit the one that has nurtured and sustained white anti-racist women.

It has been humbling to come to terms with the difficulties in identi-fying how white antiracist feminism emerged. Of the movements I focus on, this is the one I know the best. It is where I learned about antiracism, and it is the focus of much of my teaching. Perhaps being so close to this material has made the writing tougher for me. General-ly, though, I consider insider knowledge more of a help than a hin-drance to scholarship. What may have made the excavation of anti-racist feminism the hardest has been facing the myriad reasons it has largely been beyond the frame of reference in feminist histories. Adrienne Rich asks of an earlier place and time, "What happened be-tween the several thousand Northern white women and Southern Black women who together taught in schools founded under Re-construction by the Freedman's Bureau, side by side braving KKK ha-rassment, terrorism and the hostility of white communities?"[18] The production and reproduction of the master historical narrative hides the formative influences of women of color in many white women's lives, *and* it hides the paper trail of white women who have, even though with flaws, attempted to take racism seriously.

The master historical narrative also smooths out debates and controversies that explain the complexity of racial politics. For example, the fact that there is no comprehensive history, to date, of race and class dynamics in feminist newspapers and journals (their origins, trajectories, contributions, and internal politics) speaks to the way activist-based writing of that period has been hidden from view. In this absence, one aspect of the history of interracial dialogue about racism has been hidden. We need this story because of the emphasis many feminists place on creating literary and artistic culture. The story is also one of many about the way racism manifests itself in the creation of this culture.

Missing pieces in the story of multiracial activism have plagued our understanding of 1960s radicalism as well as of radicalism in the feminist movement. In her retrospective account of Black nationalism, Angela Davis writes that broad-minded nationalism of the 1960s has "all but been eradicated in popular representations of the black movement of the late 1960s and early 1970s."[19] This nationalism included alliances between Black and Chicano studies, in which students in San Diego were demanding the creation of a college called Lumumba-Zapata and Huey Newton was "urging an end to verbal gay bashing, urging an examination of black male sexuality, and calling for an alliance with the developing gay liberation movement" (292). Davis writes, "I resent that the legacy I consider my own—one I also helped to construct—has been rendered invisible. Young people with 'nationalist' proclivities ought, at least, to have the opportunity to choose which tradition of nationalism they will embrace. How will they position themselves en masse in defense of women's rights, in defense of gay rights if they are not aware of the historical precedents for such positionings?" (292).

In a parallel way, I want young women to be able to choose which tradition of feminism they will embrace. I want them to know that Shirley Chisholm ran for president in 1972; that Celestine Ware wrote a radical feminist text in the 1970s that offered an inspiring conception of revolution with a deep sense of humanity; that before Mab Segrest went to work for an organization against the Klan she and others published an independent lesbian journal in the 1970s that included some of the most important and compelling race-conscious writing by white women and women of color to date.[20] I want people to know that Ruth Frankenberg, whose *White Women, Race Matters* has become a classic on white women's racial identity, went through her own trials and tribulations about race. These stories help show that the work against race is hardly linear, that the consolidation of white-biased feminism was clearly costly to second-wave feminism.

Contributions and Conundrums

Although there are many challenges in identifying the contributions of antiracist feminism of the 1970s and 1980s, attempting such an identification does move us closer to understanding how and when the antiracist baton was carried by white women during this period. One of the most important characteristics of the baton carrying, and one discussed by all the feminists I interviewed, is how profoundly their politics were affected by personal relationships and small-group interactions across race. These, in effect, often served as mini-consciousness-raising sessions that contributed significantly to their understanding of race: Suzanne Ross's reappraisal of feminism through her friendships and working partnerships with Audre Lorde, hattie gossett, and Toni Cade Bambara; Ruth Frankenberg's maneuvering away from essentializing women of color through her many conversations with individual women of color, including bell hooks, Lata Mani, and several other women in her community; Laurie Holmes's coming to consciousness about race and racism through close working relationships with a multiracial group of bus drivers and lesbians of color—friends, coworkers, and lovers.

The multiracial feminist politics of the late 1970s and early 1980s encouraged people to speak openly about their multiple identities. This required an intimate delving into topics previously considered private. These conversations, along with a heightened attention to sexuality (its power, its distortions, its dynamism), all contributed to a pervasive sense that the "revolution begins at home." Cherríe Moraga captures this sense in her preface to the first edition of *This Bridge Called My Back:* "[This book] is about physical and psychic struggle. It is about intimacy, a desire for life between all of us, not settling for less than freedom, even in the most private aspects of our lives. A total vision."[21]

In the foreword to the second edition, Moraga continues, "If we are in-terested in building a movement that will not constantly be subverted from the inside at every turn, then we build from the inside out, not the other way around. Coming to terms with the suffering of others has never meant looking away from our own."[22]

Although some 1960s memoirs and biographies recognize the profound impact individual cross-race relationships had on white people's consciousness about race, there was a tendency among white people of that era to consider racism essentially something "out there" and separate from themselves. In "Disobedience and Women's Studies," Adrienne Rich explains that during the Civil Rights Movement she did not see herself as a carrier of racism. Racism was something separate from her. Something other people supported. Something she, clearly, opposed. The white male left did nothing to counter her method of distancing herself from the problem. She writes, "The racists were all 'out there': the pigs, the rednecks, the reactionary bourgeois professors, Nelson Rockefeller, the generic 'Jewish landlord.' The racists were my parents, my southern family, not those whites who marched singing 'We Shall Overcome' and certainly not anyone white who had worked in the early days with SNCC or traveled to Mississippi. Credentials were important—particularly a Black lover, a Black child—as if they could solve, once and for all, the problem of how and when, if ever, the white person stopped thinking racist thoughts or seeing in racist patterns; became washed clean, as it were, became 'part of the solution instead of the problem.' There was a very 'born again' spirit among white anti-racist activists in the 1960s—as if they could discard their pasts, as if they must, having once seen the political light, have no fear or hatred of darkness anywhere in their souls."[23]

By 1981, against this ethic of the 1960s, Rich placed racism at the heart of people's daily lives: "I think we need to get rid of the useless baggage that says that by opposing racist violence, by doing anti-racist work, or by becoming feminists white women somehow cease to carry racism within them" (83). For Rich, "Feminism became a political and spiritual base from which I could move to examine rather than try to hide my own racism, recognize that I have anti-racist work to do continuously within myself" (84). She adds, "[The] writings of contemporary lesbians and feminist women of color have moved and challenged me to push my horizons further, examine with fresh eyes the world I thought I knew and took for granted" (84).

This emphasis on personal lives poses challenges for white women. Reliance upon the personal to define what is political can only be limited; many experiences specific to African American or Asian American women, for example, are not likely to have been experienced personally by white women. This is a key reason why white women need to have peer relationships *and* political ties with women of color: to enable white women to consider issues "political" that they may not have experienced personally. A task for white women is to create lives that are multiracial (in their workplaces, neighborhoods, and close relationships) while not looking to people of color to be their teachers, preachers, or midwives. Within feminist circles, "talking the talk and walking the walk" not only means standing up for antiracist principles; it means leading multiracial lives that are self-reflective on every level.

Another tricky aspect of the "Personal is political" ethic for white antiracist women is the tendency to reduce racism to the realm of individual interactions and small-group relations. The feminist movement places value on community building, but this emphasis often translates into focusing on individual cross-race dynamics—what economist Kimberly Christensen has named "a personalized approach to racism."[24] The turn toward antiracism consciousness-raising groups or caucus groups specifically for white women helped guard against seeing racism as a force that is "out there"—that is, not manifest in white progressives' daily lives, neighborhoods, and job choices. At the same time, many women of color voiced frustration with white women who left their analysis of racism at the level of soul-searching. A challenge that white antiracist feminists face is to see themselves as implicated in racism in their individual lives—including their cross-race relationships— while developing the tools for organizing against racism as an institutional power. It is within this context that Mab Segrest writes, "If I am serious about friendships with women of color, I will keep working to transform the conditions of our lives. I will assume my share of the danger of living in a racist world."[25]

Along with the assertion that antiracism begins at home, antiracist feminists also tend to treat racism and antiracism as a process rather than a completed product. Elly Bulkin opens her essay on racism in white feminist literature with a crucial distinction between an antiracist and a nonracist. Bulkin maintains that if she waits until she is nonracist, she will never be able to act and speak because there is always more to do and learn. She writes, "I/we do not have to be non-racist in order to be antiracist. For me, this has been a crucial realization. As a vocal critic of heterosexism, I have been able to raise my voice confident in the knowledge that my own actions, my own words do not reflect that very bias. In taking an antiracist position, I can make no such claim. Yet I can hardly wait to take these positions until the day when I will be free of all I have been taught about race and when I will no longer reap the benefits of having white skin privilege in this particular society. Increasingly I am aware that deferring in antiracist action effectively silences me."[26]

If white feminists are to recognize antiracism as a process, they must reevaluate their own work, not for the purpose of browbeating or self-flagellation but, rather, to move on to a bigger, more inclusive focus. When Elly Bulkin received a number of scathing critiques of her analysis of racism in Mary Daly's *Gyn/Ecology: The Metaethics of Radical Feminism*, Adrienne Rich responded in writing, not only to commend Bulkin for "ethical and political courage" but also to say that Bulkin might as well have been writing to Rich as well as to Daly.[27] "I want to point out also that I was one of the lesbian/feminist reviewers who (in *The New York Times Book Review*) praised the feminist daring of *Gyn/Ecology* without questioning its racist blinders" (104). Although Rich's self-reflection is not easy to come by, it emerges from a movement in which white antiracist women were learning there is no such thing as perfection. In fact, the enormity of racism requires letting go of believing it can be fixed or solved through constant processing. That is a beginning, but it is certainly not an end.

A community that allows for constant processing is not without its problems. Some of the biggest and most painful experiences of those I interviewed occurred in the context of feminist organizing. It is among those from whom one most expects acceptance and support that the deepest hurt is often felt. Despite tensions and only limited success in many attempts at coalition building, multiracial feminism is both a politic and a community. At the same time, by the mid-1980s antiracist white women were defining the limits of this community, again seeking models for an expansive politic that would require building bridges in multiple directions simultaneously.

Did white feminists help carry an antiracist baton in the 1970s, '80s, and '90s? They have certainly not carried it enough. At the same time, since the mid-1970s there have been many feminist organizations that have substantially changed the race and class makeup of their leadership. There are health care and rape crisis centers that have recognized racial parity as crucial; some women's studies departments have moved beyond the divide named in *All the Women Are White, All the Blacks Are Men, But Some of Us Are Brave;* and a few feminist presses and newspapers have a substantial number of women of color in key positions and a long-term commitment to antiracist training within their organizations. Antiracist feminists have been key in organizing against the Klan and the radical right.[28] Along the way there have been successful long-term cross-race partnerships that have sustained important cross-race coalitions. Meanwhile, it is clear that the work—and the need for it—continues.

part iii

Antiracist Activism in the 1980s and 1990s

Antiracist Activism in the 1980s and 1990s

Although the rise of multiracial feminism in the late 1970s and early 1980s reflected one of the most progressive and far-reaching movements in U.S. history, the rest of the country was continuing its move to the right, a move begun with the election of Richard Nixon in 1968 and then continued with the elections of Ronald Reagan in 1980 and George Bush in 1988. Jimmy Carter's presidency was but a brief gap in what has been an overwhelmingly conservative period. "Cry me a river" may well capture the sentiments of many activists working in the 1980s and '90s, a period in U.S. history on a par with what was considered the nadir of racial history: the last decade of the nineteenth century.

The 1980s were the decade in which Ronald Reagan called ketchup a vegetable to justify reducing food assistance to poor mothers on Aid to Families with Dependent Children (AFDC).[1] Poverty deepened through the decade, especially among people of color and single-parent families, as the Reagan and then the Bush administrations sponsored multibillion dollar defense spending while cutting billions of dollars from domestic health and food programs.[2] Assaults on affirmative action and a state and federal refusal to equalize financial resources for schoolchildren are among myriad issues that threatened to roll back even the most modest of gains hard won in the civil rights era. The Clinton administration gave little more than lip service to progressive change, and Democrats and Republicans came to look more and more alike.

The 1980s were the decade in which gay men and their allies set up one of the most impressive national health education agendas ever, while Reagan and other officials refused to acknowledge the significance of AIDS—a refusal that slowed research and education so drastically that the epidemic is now threatening the basic existence of millions of families around the globe. The decade also saw the resurgence of radical-right organizations across the United States, a dramatic increase in hate crimes, and the infusion of hate politics into mainstream media and policies. To this list of conservative shifts, the Bush administration (1988–1992) added an almost religious quest to expand the prison system in the United States. As of 1995, 32 percent of African American men and 12 percent of Latino men in their twenties were either in jail, in prison, on parole, or on probation.[3]

The conservative Nixon-Reagan-Bush-Clinton years took a toll on progressive work. For the most part, liberals and radicals were put on the defensive, unable to match the organizing strategies and funding of the Right.[4] It is a challenge, therefore, to see how organizing in this period may serve as a bridge between 1960s-initiated transformations and social movements on the horizon. In *Progressive Women in Conservative Times: Racial Justice, Peace, and Feminism, 1945 to the 1960s,* Susan Lynn traces the significant cross-race organizing by women through the YWCA and the American Friends Service Committee in the 1940s and 1950s, which helped pave the way for the social movements of the 1960s and beyond. Although the activism she documents does not qualify as a "movement," it still counts as race-conscious work.[5] Aldon Morris makes a parallel argument in *The Origins of the Civil Rights Movement:* that the movement whose beginnings are often linked with Rosa Parks's sit-down protest in 1955 could never have flourished had it not been for the low-profile, grassroots organizing across the South for decades preceding the Civil Rights Movement.[6]

As is true of the activism of the 1940s and '50s leading up to the Civil Rights Movement, progressive activism of the 1980s and '90s did not constitute a coherent movement. That reality made momentum hard to muster or sustain, links between hot spots fragile and often transitory, and the memory of an earlier, more active time hard to hold onto. Nostalgia about the 1960s also makes it hard to believe that any organizing could possibly be as impressive as that already past—a reading of history that buries the contradictions and conundrums of that period. Bernice Johnson Reagon has often said that real social change is not what one can see in one's own lifetime; it is for the children to experience and surpass. The need for a long vision is a hard lesson to learn. The hope, however, is that current organizing is a bridge to another huge period of activism in the future.

For activists in the 1980s and '90s, it was a daunting challenge to organize amid the state's repressive politics. David Wellman explains, "The world today is radically different than the world that I inherited and that I tried to change. What I do in my teaching, and in my association with undergraduates, is try to communicate the seriousness of race and racism in American culture and life. What I try to communicate to them, without sounding hysterical, is that you don't need a Hitler to have a holocaust. You don't need a Nazi Party to exterminate a group of people. And you don't need to be a German to be involved in genocide. What I try to say to them, and try to say persuasively, is that America today, four years away from the millennium, is very close to wiping out one, possibly two generations of young Black men. And I can demonstrate that sociologically, unfortunately, in terms of AIDS, jail, and homicide. When you wipe out that population, you make it very difficult for the Black community to reproduce as a community. You add to that the issue of no jobs, and a declining economy, in some sense we stand in relationship to Black people the way the Germans did to Jews in 1934–1935. And I honestly believe that. That is something most people don't see. So I feel a little bit like the little boy with the emperor with no clothes. . . . In some ways it is more serious than what we faced in the '60s. Partly, this is because there is not a movement. But also because the stakes have been ratcheted up a whole bunch more." According to David, "The issues of the '60s had to do with the implementation of citizenship rights. They weren't even talking about economic rights. It wasn't until the late '60s and early '70s that people started adding the question of economic rights. I think now we are looking at the possibility of genocide of a generation. We weren't looking at that in the '60s. Nobody was talking about exterminating Black people. So I think the stakes are much higher. I don't know what to do about that."

A plethora of social and political issues of concern to progressive activists—the struggle for bilingual education and against English-only laws, the antiapartheid movement, U.S. interventionism, resegregation in public schools, the rise in anti-immigrant policies, the buildup of prisons—provide fertile ground for analyzing the contributions and limitations of white antiracism within multiple contexts. It would be instructive to examine white people's positions within each of these struggles: I focus on three.

In chapter 8, I examine white activists' position within the Central America peace movement (from 1980 to 1990), the best-organized and most effective of all anti-imperialist efforts since the Vietnam War. Although this initiative did not stop Ronald Reagan's support for military regimes in the region and his attempt to overthrow a popularly supported revolution in Nicaragua, it did put a significant dent in the U.S. government's efforts.

In chapter 9 I look at organizing to stop the escalation of the prison industry in the United States, which currently locks up more of its citizens than any other country in the world. My interest is in prison activism inside and outside prison and in the ways white antiracists situate themselves in both contexts. It is both ironic and telling that prisons have become among the largest—if not the largest—multiracial arena for organizing in the country. Although antiracist prisoners continue to organize, despite enormous obstacles, inside prison, they lead the way for activists working on the outside as well—to stop the escalation of the punishment industry and the dehumanizing conditions that have been its hallmark.

In chapter 10 I grapple with challenges faced by white activists working in multiracial organizations, specifically the challenge of sharing power—or not—within groups that are explicitly designed to confront racism. Most of these organizations are nonprofits, providing crucial social services and primary care to communities the government has abandoned or ignored. And yet white activists' positions within these groups raise troubling and enduring questions about white leadership and the limits of social service organizations in a capitalist economy. The rise in antiracist trainings and workshops as a method of educating for change raises similar complications. Although these trainings may bring to the corporate table vital discussion about race that might otherwise remain underground, the extent to which these trainings can facilitate long-term, institutional change remains open to debate.

Though on the surface this combination of issues may seem unrelated, the range speaks to a key characteristic of antiracist organizing in the 1980s and 1990s: namely, the ideological differences in the frameworks antiracists use. For this reason, I end chapter 10 with a brief discussion of these ideological frameworks and of why, even among antiracist activists, there is no monolithic position.

8

Central America Peace Movement

When Ronald Reagan was inaugurated as president in 1981, the writing was soon on the wall that his foreign policy would rest on "proclaiming that America's 'Vietnam syndrome' was over."[1] Reagan's foreign policy hinged on making the United States the dominant force in nuclear weapons and asserting control over the political and economic structures of Panama, El Salvador, Nicaragua, Honduras, Guatemala, and Costa Rica—all countries that Reagan, and many presidents before him, considered the U.S. backyard. Since 1900 the United States had invaded Latin America thirty-six times.[2] According to historian William Chafe, although Reagan's foreign policy directives provided financial and military support to "freedom fighters" in Angola, Ethiopia, and Afghanistan, "dearest to Reagan's heart . . . was Central America. With single-minded purpose, Reagan insisted on committing military advisors and millions of dollars to bolster a reactionary regime in El Salvador, while making the overthrow of the Sandinistas by Nicaraguan 'contras' his top foreign policy objective."[3]

Beginning in the late 1970s, U.S. support for El Salvador's military regime helped fund death squads that assassinated thousands of civilians and routinely bombed civilian targets, after a popularly supported group challenged the military government to make land reforms and to support democratic change.[4] Reagan increased funding for the military dictatorship in Guatemala, which the United States had sustained since 1954 when the CIA overthrew the democratically elected government.[5] By mid-1984 the U.S. government had made Honduras an armed camp through which military moves in Guatemala, El Salvador, and Nicaragua could be launched.[6]

In 1981 Reagan began pumping millions of dollars into recruiting, training, and sustaining the contras, a counterrevolutionary group

attempting to overthrow the popularly supported Sandinista government in Nicaragua. (In 1979 the Sandinistas had successfully defeated
the Somoza family dictatorship that had ruled since 1937.) The U.S.
government's "low intensity war" in Nicaragua was the latest of multiple times, dating back to the 1800s, that the United States compromised Nicaragua's sovereignty.[7] The Sandinistas, who had taken power
through a popular insurrection, made impressive improvements in
health care and education. They also implemented substantial land reform to counteract the Somoza family's previous control of almost 90
percent of the country's land, industry, and production.[8]

During the U.S. blockade in Nicaragua and the United States–funded
contra war (from 1982–1989), the resources the Sandinista government were forced to devote to defense drained their economic programs in support of literacy, health care, jobs, and education. Over time,
this situation undermined some Nicaraguans' faith in the Sandinista
government. By 1990 the Sandinistas had been voted out of office
in favor of a United States–sponsored candidate, Violeta Chamorro.
Many in Nicaragua believed the vote was less a sign of support for
Chamorro (and against the Sandinistas) than a vote of hope that a
United States–sponsored candidate might mean an end to intervention
in Nicaragua.[9]

Anti-intervention activism among people in the United States took
several forms. What came to be called the "sanctuary movement" provided resources and safety for Guatemalan and Salvadoran refugees
forced to flee from their countries. A national group, Witness for
Peace, organized trips of more than four thousand people from the
United States to Nicaraguan war zones to witness the effects of U.S.
aggression and then spread the word in the United States about this violence. Other United States–based groups also organized trips and extended stays in Central America. United States–based organizing also
included the Committee in Solidarity with the People of El Salvador
(CISPES), which led protests and organized blockades, and the National Pledge for Resistance Campaign, which led more than 80,000 people
in the United States to protest, commit civil disobedience, or both.[10]
Through the late 1980s many sister-city bonds were formed promoting
exchange of knowledge and resources between the United States, El
Salvador, and Nicaragua.

Each of these campaigns reveals complicated political relationships among white activists, Central Americans in the United States, and Central Americans in their own countries. In this chapter, as is in others, my intent is not to provide an exhaustive history of the peace movement. Rather, by examining key historical events, I hope to illuminate white activists' positions within this struggle. My interest is also in how earlier social movements influenced Central America peace work and how debates in earlier decades—about accountability, multiracial alliances, anti-imperialism, and antiracism—reverberate in later contexts.

Sanctuary: A Big Term

What is typically identified as the sanctuary movement includes the regional and national network of churches, synagogues, and Quaker meeting houses that, beginning in 1981, defied federal immigration laws by providing housing and other resources to Central American refugees who otherwise risked deportation, death, or both. Through this effort 70,000 U.S. citizens provided support for between two thousand and three thousand Central American refugees over a several-year period.[11] Beginning in Tucson, Arizona, and then spreading to Chicago and through thirty-four states, the public sanctuary movement comprised more than three thousand churches, synagogues, and Quaker meeting houses by 1984. Although most of the sanctuary locations were white, African American and Latino churches were represented as well. Early sanctuaries included the Hispanic Church of Christo Rey in Racine, Wisconsin; the Cross Lutheran Church of Milwaukee, an African American church; Operation Push in Chicago; and Riverside Church in New York City; along with many white congregations. One branch of the Mohawk Nation in New York State also declared its sacred land a sanctuary. [12]

What is deceptive about the label "sanctuary movement," however, is that the lion's share of the work with refugees was done clandestinely by Mexicans in Mexico and Latino and multiethnic communities in the United States who took in and sustained hundreds of thousands of refugees.[13] Although it is hard to pinpoint the number of refugees who entered the United States, it is estimated that half a million entered each year.[14] As of 1986, 350,000 Salvadoran refugees were hiding in California alone. There are more Salvadorans living in Los Angeles than in any other city in the world outside San Salvador. The Seminoles in Florida have also harbored hundreds of Guatemalan Indians.[15]

The work done to make a home for refugees in these communities, however, is not typically included in research on the sanctuary movement, although clearly it formed the basis of the grassroots response to the U.S. war in Central America. Just as the African American community had been the "receiving network" that harbored slaves during slavery, Latinos living in the United States have largely provided the protective communities for Central American refugees. According to poet-activists Renny Golden and Michael McConnell, the historical invisibility of the Black community "is due to the bias of the Western interpretation that focuses on individual heroism and overlooks the social courage of a people. Such a perspective succumbs to the attraction of white, male, clerical heroism, losing sight of the anonymous black community. . . . The inspiration and infrastructure for the railroad—and, in fact, the abolitionist movement itself—was created by blacks."[16] The same can be said about the enormous effort of Latino communities in response to the influx of refugees to Mexico and the United States.

A key difference between the Latino-based sanctuary movement and what is typically called the sanctuary movement is that whereas the first was necessarily clandestine, the second initially saw the media as its best protection once the refugees had arrived safely.[17] The public movement depended upon the media to spread the stories of refugees in sanctuary and the word that a growing number of largely mainstream congregations were harboring refugees. In its early years, sanctuary work was chronicled extensively in *Time* and *Newsweek,* on *60 Minutes* and PBS's *Front Line,* and in other national media. Meanwhile, media attention was the last thing people wanted in the communities that absorbed the overwhelming majority of refugees. For example, a small Protestant church in a Hispanic neighborhood in Chicago decided not to declare itself a sanctuary, given that 60 percent of its congregation were undocumented refugees.[18] This difference further supported the invisibility of the unnamed sanctuary movement.[19]

Recognizing both responses to refugees avoids the common portrayal of white sanctuary workers as the sole architects and heroes in the story. Furthermore, characterizing the public sanctuary movement as "white" makes invisible the refugees whose lives and stories catapulted many North Americans into action. Were it not for the testimonies of the Central American refugees, media attention would have been far less effective.

From the point of view of Central American refugees, recognizing both movements is also important. Many refugees have been forced to stay in the United States far beyond the years the public sanctuary movement was in operation. In the process, El Salvadorans and Guatemalans in Los Angeles, Chicago, New Jersey, and elsewhere have continued to draw upon and connect with larger and longer-standing Latino and multiethnic communities. Many Salvadoran refugees in the United States have been in a long-term legal holding pattern due to 1990 legislation that granted them temporary protected status (TPS). Under this status, they run the risk of being denied reentry to the United States if they travel to El Salvador. At the same time, there are few legal mechanisms available for them to obtain permanent residency in the United States.[20]

Another common misapprehension about the sanctuary movement relates to its origins. Although the public sanctuary movement is typically considered an overwhelmingly white initiative, its origins were cross-national (between Mexico and the United States) and biracial (Latino and white). The story of its origins, as told by journalist Anne Crittenden, begins with Jim Corbett, a Quaker rancher living in Tucson, whose grandmother was a Blackfoot Indian. He first learned of the mass exodus of the Central American refugees almost by happenstance.[21] A friend of Corbett's had picked up a Salvadoran hitchhiker who then was picked up and taken away with no explanation by the border patrol. Disturbed by his friend's story, Corbett tried to find the Salvadoran. Eventually Corbett contacted Manzo, a private social service agency in Tucson that had long assisted undocumented Mexican immigrants and had recently begun working with Central Americans.

Manzo's staff in 1981 included two political organizers, Margo Cowan, who had been trained by César Chávez, and Lupe Castillo, an activist of Mexican descent.[22] Manzo staff members suggested to Corbett that he continue to track down the Salvadoran hitchhiker, a process that eventually put him in touch with hundreds of Salvadoran and Guatemalan refugees fleeing repression. Corbett then contacted and began working closely with John Fife, the minister of a church in a Tucson barrio whose congregation was African American, Latino, and white. Fife's first parish had been in a Black church in Ohio, and he had participated in the Selma to Montgomery march in 1965. He spoke Spanish and had long been involved in progressive issues: computer sales to Argentina and Chile, antiapartheid organizing, and the Nestlé boycott.

Corbett and Fife began working closely with Manzo, the newly formed Religious Taskforce on Central America, and an activist priest in Nogales, Mexico, Ramon Dagoberto Quiñones, who had been working with refugees. The first collective rescue of Central Americans from a horrendous detention center in the United States culminated in sending two busloads of refugees to "a black church in Watts that offered temporary shelter for about eighty people."[23] John Fife then approached his mixed-race congregation, which decided to become the first church to officially declare itself a sanctuary.

That these various people knew each other and worked together is what initially made sanctuary (as a concept) possible. Without the work of the activist Catholic church in Nogales there would have been no organized place for refugees to go before crossing the border. Without Manzo there would have been no organization to initially encourage Corbett to get involved. In other words, the two white men credited with initiating the sanctuary movement both drew extensively on their ties to Mexican religious activists and Chicano activists in order to begin setting up a pathway for refugees.

An understanding of the biracial, cross-national roots of the sanctuary movement makes it possible to identify how race and nationality played themselves out in the initial organizing. Soon after Corbett and Fife began setting up sanctuaries for Central Americans, Manzo decided to focus full-time on Mexican immigrants. Ann Crittenden reports, "As Margo Cowan and Lupe Castillo saw it, sanctuary was primarily a tactic to educate middle- and upper-class American churchgoers on the Central America issue. In their view, most refugees didn't need gringos helping them across the border. . . . They needed more help in the tedious and unglamorous work of fighting their cases through the courts."[24]

Another core conflict facing sanctuary workers involved the precarious situation of deciding which Central Americans would be taken into sanctuary. Fife, Corbett, and others were overwhelmed by the number of people seeking asylum and knew the small but growing chain of churches and synagogues could not sustain them all. Tucson workers also reasoned that the legitimacy of their movement in the eyes of the media and the U.S. public rested upon its portrayal as helping only those refugees whose lives would be threatened were they to return to Guatemala or El Salvador. Sanctuary's publicity rested on distinguishing between those needing asylum for political reasons and those immigrants seeking to cross the border for economic reasons.

Tucson workers began interviewing Central Americans in an attempt to identify those refugees who were at "highest risk": those whose stories clearly demonstrated they would be killed if they returned to their country. From the sanctuary perspective, clarifying that they were working with high-risk refugees also provided the rationale they needed to explain why they were not working with the government, since the Immigration and Naturalization Service (INS) was refusing to recognize asylum as a legitimate category for Central Americans. According to Darlene Nicgorski, one of the sanctuary workers in southern Arizona, the people chosen for sanctuary were those who wanted to and could speak publicly.[25] The two-tiered system (those fleeing for their lives versus those leaving for other reasons), however, meant that U.S. sanctuary workers had the power to decide, often based on an interview of only a few hours, whether a Central American individual or family would be taken into protection.[26]

Frequently, white privilege is what made it possible for early workers to help Central Americans across the border. Early on, for example, Corbett pulled together "housewives, students, professional men, and retirees" who carried binoculars for "bird watching" as they guided people across the border with no interference from the border patrol.[27] That same white privilege and U.S. citizenship was responsible for the central contradiction in U.S. sanctuary workers' power to decide who did and did not qualify as a refugee. Clearly, the urban communities in Los Angeles and Phoenix that initially absorbed the lion's share of the Central American refugees did not screen the candidates; nor did the Catholic churches, which many Salvadoran refugees attended as they got settled in these communities, call themselves "sanctuary churches."

Those refugees taken in by the public sanctuary movement were afforded resources and legal protection not available to those in the unofficial movement. And yet, as anthropologist Susan Coutin reports, based on interviews with Central Americans and Anglos involved in sanctuary, the political positions of refugees in sanctuary was precarious. From the beginning Central Americans considered sanctuary a North American movement. As a critical mass of refugees came together in San Francisco, Tucson, and Los Angeles, they formed their own organizations such as CRECE (Central American Refugee Center) in San Francisco and El Comite in Tucson. Susan Coutin asserts that, although the relationship among sanctuary workers and members of refugee organizations was often one of respect, "sanctuary itself . . . remained a movement about, rather than of, Central Americans."[28]

Despite significant differences in the public and the unofficial sanctuary movements, both recognized that defiance of U.S. immigration laws was necessary. In 1984 the United States granted only 0.4 percent of applications for political asylum from Guatemalans and 2.5 percent from Salvadorans.[29] From the U.S. government's perspective, recognizing Central Americans as political refugees would mean acknowledging the political conflict that was fueled by the U.S. government. Furthermore, although the Refugee Act of 1980 was supposed to bring U.S. policy in line with U.N. definitions of who qualified as a refugee, the act excluded people fleeing from military repression or natural disasters. Thus, as Crittenden explains, U.S. officials would argue that "most Salvadorans do not qualify for political asylum in the United States because they are fleeing a generalized climate of terror and violence, rather than specific threats to their lives."[30]

Although the U.S. government did little initially to stop the public sanctuary work, by 1984 it had begun to crack down, arresting refugees and North American activists, infiltrating organizations, and creating dissent among movement activists. Ironically, this crackdown had a silver lining in terms of antiracism; it led those involved in sanctuary to create a national organizational process for decision making. At the 1985 national convention of sanctuary workers, refugees from different regions met for the first time and were thus able to collectively urge the sanctuary movement not only to defy existing immigration laws and to support refugees individually, but also to oppose the government's intervention in Central America.[31]

With this assertion, refugees were challenging a tendency among sanctuary churches to see their work as done once "their" refugees were safe. For those seeking asylum, accountability meant not only harboring refugees but also recognizing that the United States was an imperialist nation. Refugees maintained that activists needed to both make the United States safe for refugees and ensure that Central America was safe for Central Americans. As Golden and McConnell report, one Salvadoran explained, "We want to go back home. We want El Salvador and Guatemala to be sanctuaries."[32]

For many people who became involved in the sanctuary movement, consciousness-raising began when they heard refugees' testimonials about the repression that forced them to leave El Salvador or Guatemala, typically after family or friends had already been threatened or killed. For many people, opening a church or a meeting house to a refugee family was an act of conscience that took into account the resources available to the community of faith (usually money and access to safe haven) not otherwise accessible to the refugees.

An honest account of the decision making in faith communities about sanctuary often reveals complicated attitudes about property rights and U.S. citizenship. Dorothy Stoneman became involved in Central America solidarity work after many years of activism for other causes. In the 1980s she moved back to her hometown near Boston after having worked and lived in Harlem for twenty years. Living in the overwhelmingly white town where she had grown up and beginning to organize in a white community were a shock for Dorothy. She began attending a local Unitarian church, where she proposed that it become a sanctuary for refugees from El Salvador. For a year she and her husband convened a group of twelve people to study whether the church should become a sanctuary—a process that involved intensive consciousness-raising among church members. She tried to bring together long-standing members of the church—church elders, the choirmaster, and the president of the parish committee—with "people like ourselves who had a history of activism." Dorothy remembers, "The choirmaster was horrified to discover that the FBI had broken into churches. She was in the same stage of innocence that I was at eighteen, having grown up in that town all her life."

Eventually the resistance Dorothy and others faced from wary church members led them to scale back their original proposal that the church itself would provide a sanctuary. That possibility had caused concern among many congregation members about possible reduced property values and the wear-and-tear on the church building. A compromise was reached: The church itself would not be a sanctuary but would instead raise money to pay for housing for refugees in a nearby town. Dorothy explains, "The church community decided to raise enough money so that the refugees could live in Cambridge. They didn't necessarily need a hideout. They needed money. That way we could take a political stance without scaring people that the church might be messed up. The church voted 85 percent to do this."

The implications of this Unitarian church's decision are complicated. On the one hand, providing resources for refugees to live in a neighboring town gave them autonomy not afforded to refugees in congregations that were "unwittingly overresponding to refugee needs, thus depriving them of a vital sense of independence and initiative."[33] The major differences in language, culture, and class between refugees and many people in sanctuary groups often led to communication problems that were exacerbated when refugees had few ties outside the congregation. On the other hand, the Unitarian church's worry about property taxes and the responsibility of tenants in the church building is a troubling reminder of two parties coming to the table with extraordinarily different resources. Dorothy's willingness to compromise came from accepting that the church's decision to do something was better than doing nothing. Clearly, one of the strengths of the sanctuary movement was its ability to involve people at varying stages of risk taking. Its inherent limitation, however, was that North Americans always maintained the upper hand in deciding the direction of the movement.

Although refugees recognized the risks sanctuary workers took to make safe journeys and resettlement possible, Central Americans also often wrestled with patronizing North American attitudes, huge gulfs in understanding because of cultural differences, and North American expectations that refugees be model citizens by North American standards. Golden and McConnell report that "at a Presbyterian-sponsored conference on sanctuary, a refugee in sanctuary in Minnesota said, 'We don't want you to treat us like we were your pets.' Two others from upper New York state wrote to sanctuary organizers that 'the great majority of the members of the church still maintained their racism.' In their case, the refugees were never consulted about upcoming plans and the congregation went so far as to tell them when they could take a shower."[34]

White people in the sanctuary movement worked toward antiracism, with varying degrees of success, by taking steps to equalize power relationships, making sure that refugees were included in decision making on issues that affected their lives, and learning Spanish to ensure that the refugees were not doing all the linguistic bridge work.

Not surprisingly, those sanctuary workers with a history of involvement in Central American communities were often the best prepared to practice these steps. For Darlene Nicgorski, who lived in Guatemala in 1980 before beginning sanctuary work at the border in 1982, a key challenge was identifying how best to use her resources and knowledge to support refugees.[35] In her twenties Darlene had become a member of an order of nuns who were committed to justice. She moved to Guatemala in 1980 and began to run a preschool in 1981. At that time the Guatemalan military were killing whole villages of people, sometimes including church leaders (nuns, priests, ministers), whom the military considered dangerous simply because they were working with poor people.

When Darlene's parish priest was killed in cold blood, Darlene and the other nuns knew they had to run for their lives. Darlene went to a refugee camp in Honduras, where she worked for a year with refugees before returning to the United States. After having to leave the village where she worked, Darlene came to realize that she had always believed the Guatemalan government would think twice about killing North Americans. "I always had a sense that compared to a Guatemalan peasant, there would be a different level of recognition and protection." The murder of her parish priest showed Darlene that her sense of entitlement as a North American was deeply ingrained but did little to actually protect her given the political repression at the time.

Back in the United States in 1982, with a passionate commitment to Guatemalan people's rights to safety and freedom, Darlene considered whether her energy would be better spent returning to a refugee camp or helping refugees escape to the United States. After meeting migrant farm workers from Guatemala, Darlene saw painful connections between the work she had had to flee in Central America and the work in front of her in the Southwest. Having lived in Guatemala, she felt a real urgency to explain to people in the United States why the refugees were there and why they needed political asylum.

Darlene soon became a key figure in the sanctuary movement in Arizona, working closely with Central Americans to help prepare them for what they might face once they arrived in a church in Rochester,

New York, or Portland, Maine, or other locations throughout the country. Through this work she also became more in touch with her own oppression in the church as a woman. She explains, "In trying to help people find their voices, to find ways to speak to church people in the United States, to tell their story, to tell the truth about their lives, I became more and more able to tell the truth about my own life—as a woman who was oppressed within the church and in society in general, and as a lesbian." At that point Darlene was also just starting to come out, a process she had to put on hold once she was indicted by the U.S. government for her work with refugees.

The trial in 1985–1986 of Darlene and ten other sanctuary workers, whom the media dubbed the Tucson Eleven, became one of the most important and publicized political trials of the1980s and '90s.[36] The eleven defendants were accused of various heavy charges related to their sanctuary work.[37] In preparing for the trial, there was much discussion among the attorneys, the defendants, and the larger political community about how it should be run. From the beginning Darlene saw it as a political trial that required people to speak truthfully about why they defied immigration laws and helped refugees. Darlene says, "I was the one who fought to tell the truth. The attorneys decided not to put on a defense. They thought they had done the job by discrediting the government witnesses. I fought to the end to speak the truth. But we didn't get to present it as a political case." Eight of the eleven defendants were found guilty. Darlene was convicted of conspiracy to violate immigration law and of aiding and abetting in the transportation of illegal aliens. Of those on trial, Darlene received the longest sentence, twenty-five years in prison, a sentence that was later suspended.

After the trial Darlene knew she needed to get out of the political spotlight for a while. An indictment she had thought would be resolved in three to six months had turned into a several-year process. Through it, she received much support from Catholic women and from many in the sanctuary movement. One of the characteristics of the sanctuary movement that Darlene most appreciated "was its ability to break down a lot of barriers between people of different faiths." During the trial, a different religious observance was held each Monday: a silent Quaker meeting, a service led by a rabbi, and a Catholic service.

Although she was bouyed by the spiritual component of the movement, Darlene found it harder and harder to reconcile the patriarchal

underpinnings of the church. "I had always been affirmed and supported by the leadership in everything I had done. Here I was alone in
Arizona, which was my choice but difficult nevertheless, and I was
bombarded with questions. It was ironic. My faith had led me from the
convent to Guatemala, and when I came back, I felt like I no longer belonged."[38] Darlene explained that during the trial, for example, the
bishop in Tucson, who worked in close proximity to the court building, never came to the trial or showed support. As a nun, she had seen
how often, once Catholic women were able to get a program or initiative in place, the Catholic hierarchy would "show them the door." In
the sanctuary movement she watched as women's perspectives were
often dismissed or sidelined. For example, from early on in her work in
Tucson, Darlene had been skeptical of a small group of sanctuary
workers who turned out to be informants for the government.[39] She
had spoken openly about her suspicions, but they had been dismissed
as paranoid. Among other things, that response was a manifestation of
sexism in the movement. Working with Central American refugees and
doing political work had taught her again and again the import of
speaking openly.

Increasingly disturbed by the church hierarchy and the sexism within the sanctuary movement, Darlene was also angered by some sanctuary churches' attitudes of entitlement. In her biography of Darlene,
Julia Lieblich writes, "Sometimes the problem lay with the sanctuary
churches, which amazed Darlene with their special requests. Some
specified the nationality of the refugee they wanted; others requested
children by age. One congregation asked her to send a nonsmoking
vegetarian. Refugees were people, not pets, she reminded them. The
point was to shelter people in need."[40]

After the trial Darlene felt torn between wanting to move on and
wanting to continue to speak as a woman about sanctuary work. From
the beginning of the sanctuary movement, women were doing most of
the work while men were doing the speaking. Darlene wanted the public to know of political women's work in both Central America and the
United States. In the year after the trial Darlene spoke publicly in nine-
ty cities in Canada, Ireland, and the United States, each time having to
get permission to travel from her probation officer. During this period
she had a "coming out of the convent party"—a ritual of sadness
about leaving a community of women concerned about justice, and a

ritual of celebration as a lesbian and a woman still committed to progressive social change. She currently works in an envelope company in Massachusetts, which has had a long history of employing immigrants. Employees include people who speak thirteen different languages from thirty different countries, many from Central America. About this current work Darlene says, "When I started working at the company I saw all kinds of needs no one else recognized. As it turns out, it is possible to do social justice work in many locations." From Darlene's perspective, the works continues.

Bearing Witness

In addition to building a sanctuary movement, many activists in the 1980s traveled—usually in groups—to El Salvador, Nicaragua, and Guatemala. Among the groups that organized witnessing tours of Central America, Witness for Peace was the largest. This organization believed that placing North Americans in Central America alongside the religious people, health care workers, and union workers who were being persecuted would limit government repression.

Among those who participated in Witness for Peace, many were feminists, lesbians, or both, as was true about Central America solidarity work in general.[41] This was partly made possible by multiracial feminism, which included significant attention to the United States as a colonizing country—a critique brought home in part by feminists of color from previously colonized countries (such as Trinidad, India, and Argentina) now living and active in the United States.[42] Multiracial feminism encouraged women to think about themselves as activists who were raced and classed and who had a national affiliation that, in Audre Lorde's terms, was on the wrong side of every liberation struggle.[43] Multiracial feminism led by women of color encouraged anticapitalist, anti-imperialist activism. This analysis, along with the anti–Vietnam War protests that many women had been involved in through the early 1970s, readied them to stand up against U.S. imperialism in Central America in the 1980s.

For anti-intervention activists with a feminist agenda, attempts by the United States in the 1980s to overthrow the Sandinista government were particularly egregious; there had been more feminist involvement in the Sandinista revolution than in any other in the history of the hemisphere.[44] One-third of the Sandinista army had been women.[45] One of the earliest decrees by the new government prohibited the use of images of the female body to advertise products. The government encouraged domestic servants to organize for job security, and women's offices were established to attend to women's legal problems.

In some ways, the Sandinista government of the 1980s was more feminist than the U.S. government. The 1987 constitution in Nicaragua assured equal rights for women, a parity yet to be achieved in the United States. The Sandinista government abolished wage differences based on gender, which made an enormous difference for families, since women have always been a large part of the workforce. The government set up dozens of rural infant centers where there had been none, supported the emergence of two thousand unions (up from fewer than two hundred), funded what became a flourishing arts and poetry movement, redistributed land to farmers, and lowered the illiteracy rate dramatically (which was substantially higher among women than men).[46]

From the perspective of many feminists in Nicaragua, as the 1980s progressed, the Sandinista government backed off from genuinely supporting women's rights on many levels. In response feminists created an autonomous movement that flourished in the 1990s and did not (and still does not) depend upon the Sandinistas or the 1990s National Opposition Union (UNO) government.[47] For feminists in the United States, contact with their Nicaraguan counterparts was invaluable, in terms of both Nicaraguan feminists' involvement in the Sandinista revolution and their increasing assertion of autonomy from the government in order to build a multidimensional movement.[48]

Dawn Gomes went to Nicaragua twice, in 1983 and 1984. She went with the first wave of solidarity workers and picked coffee along with "brigades of people from all over the world." In 1986 she went again, this time to build houses with the Nicaraguan Solidarity Committee. Dawn was enthusiastic about and felt affirmed by the Nicaraguan revolution, partly because of the emphasis among many of the Sandinistas upon building an egalitarian society and breaking down class barriers. She was also grateful to feel a sense of being "selfless and breaking away from white supremacy while really wanting to do something worthwhile for other people."

Dawn believed that much could be said for "looking horrors and inhumane acts against people in the face"—a witnessing that thousands of people from the United States did and then came back to publicize. She also saw limits to the activists' approaches. From Dawn's perspective, "some of the drive or impetus clouded our judgment and created this magical thinking—essentially idealizing the Nicaraguans and Salvadorans. We didn't have a sense of our own selves, so we would idealize them, which I think came out of our own low self-esteem. When you idealize, then you are sure to do the opposite, when the clay begins to crack. We will surely then assault them or attack them or put them down." In this reflection, Dawn identifies two sides of the same racist coin: either romanticizing or demonizing Nicaraguan leaders, while failing to account for the way many U.S. activists' limited experience with working across race and culture blunted their abilities to recognize Nicaraguans as equals and to anticipate and guard against ethnocentrism.

This tendency to romanticize Central Americans was widespread in the sanctuary movement as well. Susan Coutin writes, "Central American poor were seen as closer to God, as examples to emulate, as victims of 'our gluttony,' and as representatives of the authenticity 'we' once had. Such images of Central Americans were made possible—despite efforts to create personal relationships with Salvadorans and Guatemalans—by the *distance* between sanctuary workers and refugees."[49] Coutin asserts that the romanticized portrayal of Central Americans was yet another version of "what Edward Said has termed 'Orientalism'—the tendency of Western societies to produce authoritative and power-laden images of the non-Western other"(154). Typically, orientalism involves Western representations of non-Westerners as inferior and culturally deficient.

In the Central American–North American dynamic, North American sanctuary workers typically glorified Central Americans as a way of showing their dissatisfaction with their white middle-class cultural values (based on individualism, consumerism, and competition). Ironically, though, as Coutin explains, by idealizing Central Americans, North Americans still reproduced "culturally ingrained Orientalist tendencies to know, define, and create representations of non-Western peoples"(187). Meanwhile, the power differentials between Central Americans and North Americans remained essentially intact.

Jeanine Cohen, who also traveled to Nicaragua for extended periods during the mid-1980s, came to see ethnocentrism as one of the most substantial problems for the movement. Jeanine first got involved in Central America solidarity work in San Francisco through her work with gay and lesbian Latinos who had organized an affinity group in support of Nicaragua. (Her exposure was unlike that of others I interviewed, since her initial interest in Central America was linked to Latino organizing in the United States.) After her first year of traveling in Nicaragua, Jeanine became concerned that North Americans were rarely addressing cross-cultural issues. She began to ask: "What would it require for people to go to Nicaragua with all 'our relative privilege' and provide a service to people without having an arrogant assumption that we were helping people and they needed us?"

Jeanine also asked what it meant when people from the United States became sexually involved with people in Nicaragua. From her perspective, "It was not clean. It was not okay in my book. We need to talk about the implications of what we were doing. What was the effect of women getting involved with Nicaraguan men who were most probably married and had children?" According to Ellen Scott, a sociologist who organized brigades to Nicaragua in the mid-1980s, both heterosexual men and women and lesbians were part of the problem. Some North American women who were working in Nicaragua became involved in relationships with lesbians there. Their affairs caused many problems: Most Nicaraguan lesbians were deeply closeted at that time, and many were often already in other lesbian relationships when they began seeing North American women. In addition, these affairs usually took place in small towns, so the impact of these liaisons was rarely anonymous. Ellen Scott adds, "The North Americans would then, typically, return home, leaving the mess to be picked up by others. In the meantime, they had sexualized and romanticized their work in Nicaragua. They were there for business, doing political activism and community service. They weren't there to get involved with people who would be there for the long haul."[50]

Over time, some feminists who were doing long-term work with Nicaraguans began to include attention to ethnocentrism and the ethics of cross-cultural work in training for those traveling to Nicaragua. For Jeanine, realizing the import of this work began by scrutinizing her own behavior. Sometimes she found herself getting angry with the Nicaraguan organizers. She would assume they did not have proper plans when their plans were merely not apparent to her. She found herself wondering what was "wrong with these people" when they did not do things as she would have. Jeanine believes her attitude, even when unspoken, was apparent in her behavior. "It is arrogant, feeling like it is great, what we are doing, but then in our actual practice, we might have been undermining the very things we were trying to create." From these lessons, Jeanine began doing much more preparatory work with people interested in cross-cultural activism and tried, with others, to openly identify how ethnocentrism among U.S. activists compromised long-term alliances.

"El Salvador Is Spanish for Vietnam"[51]

A third United States–based effort was initiated by activists organizing protests in opposition to the war. The Pledge of Resistance, which began in 1985, organized people to promise to commit civil disobedience if the United States invaded Nicaragua. As the pledge grew, it was able to make a transition from its beginnings as a reactive civil disobedience organization to a preemptive, activist group opposed to U.S. intervention in Central America in general. Although it was a national body, Pledge had a decentralized structure, and its organization varied from city to city. For example, some groups were set up hierarchically, while others relied heavily on affinity groups as the primary method of bringing people together. In Boston, one of the main locations for organizing the pledge, affinity groups were arranged largely by neighborhood and existing social or political networks. Within a year of its inception, the pledge in Boston had organized into 250 affinity groups totaling three thousand people who participated in nonviolence training in preparation for civil disobedience. This training also included attention to homophobia and sexism, two conflicts that arose among those doing civil disobedience.

As was true of the public sanctuary movement in some regions of the country, the pledge had very little contact with United States–based African American or Latino organizing. The coordinating committee in Boston, for example included fifteen members: fourteen white people and one El Salvadoran, Mario Davila.[52] According to Cathy Hoffman, a coordinator of the Pledge of Resistance who was based in Boston, people within the pledge acknowledged to some extent the overwhelming whiteness of the organization.[53] In training, people would bring attention to issues of race, but this attention typically stayed at the level of how race might affect the experience of civil disobedience. For example, some people planning to commit civil disobedience held prejudices against people who were in jail, most of whom were people of color.

Not surprisingly, once people were arrested, their consciousness was often raised considerably about race and class inequities in the criminal justice system. (This experience led a number of people who were first involved in Central America solidarity work to become prison activists.) The nonviolent training also addressed the fact that the few people of color who were arrested during civil disobedience were often treated differently than were the white people. Race was also considered, to the extent that pledge people generally understood that for many Latino immigrants, civil disobedience meant risking scrutiny and deportation. Among pledge participants there was a sense that white U.S. citizens had privileges they needed to use in order to confront the U.S. government.

Beyond that, pledge activists did not have an analysis of what multiracial organizing against U.S. intervention might look like. According to Cathy Hoffman, there were a number of reasons for this limitation. First, the emphasis in pledge was on holding people together despite differing perspectives on tactics and politics. There were some people who wanted to write letters, some who wanted to commit civil disobedience, and some who thought taking over buildings was necessary. There was also a range of political perspectives among pledge resisters, from religious groups who were against abortion to feminists who considered access to abortion a key human right. Cathy Hoffman also believes that people put their attention into forming relationships with people in Nicaragua and El Salvador. About the Pledge of Resistance in Boston, Hoffman says, "While we bridged some international gaps, we didn't do that in our own communities at all. Very few links were made between pledge resisters and the Latino communities in Boston." Although pledge adopted many of the strategies developed in the Civil Rights Movement—attention to process, use of songs and stories, and a valuing of community building—there was no real connection made between pledge groups and African American churches and other organizations. When activists traveled to Nicaragua or El Salvador, the communities they worked with did not tend to ask why the contingents were overwhelmingly white.

By the late 1980s, when Cambridge, Massachusetts, became a sister city with Las Flores in El Salvador, the brigades of people who traveled south became more multiracial. This change, Cathy Hoffman believes, occurred once organizers began working with the Cambridge public schools, particularly with the Latino and African American teachers in that system. Although late in coming, by the end of the decade many sister unions and sister colleges and universities were also established, all of which broadened the racial base of the organizing. These linkages nurtured cultural and political exchanges that countered mainstream media and governmental portrayals of the United States and Central America as enemies.

CISPES was also founded in the early 1980s to put pressure on the U.S. government to stop the war. Like the Pledge of Resistance, CISPES organizers had little experience in building a multiracial base. Suzanne Ross joined CISPES in the mid-1980s, when Ronald Reagan began escalating the U.S. presence in El Salvador initiated by Jimmy Carter. Suzanne remembers, "I saw Vietnam, Vietnam, Vietnam. To me it was a total flashback. I went and offered all my services. I think I wasn't working full time. I had just been fired from my job. I had a legal case. I said 'Listen, I am a former college teacher. I can talk publicly, I have a car. I can go anywhere. My schedule is very flexible. You know, I can pay my own expenses, driving places.' People thought I was a godsend in the movement. I started immediately overnight, working on stuff on El Salvador."

Suzanne began traveling all over the country (with the baby she had recently adopted in tow). Almost from the start she began to see limitations in the organizing. The activists were quite young and all white. The Salvadorans controlled much of the organization, played a leading role, and were very hands-on. Because CISPES was led by Salvadorans, many of the white people "hid behind that." The logic was that since "a group of people of color were leading us, we don't have to deal with anything else. It was a real cop out and jive. . . . So there is nothing magic about Salvadorans coming to this country and leading us, in a racist society, especially since many of them didn't really understand the dynamics of racism in this country."

As Suzanne saw it, this was the essential dilemma: "On the one hand, it is important to accept their leadership about their country and also their worldview about imperialism. On the other hand, their relationship with the Black movement in this country was not strong. And they certainly did not impart that to the people they were leading, who were young." When Suzanne began working intensively with CISPES, the leadership in the organization was already tightly held among Salvadorans and white U.S. activists. In their organizing against the war, Salvadorans had first contacted mainstream white peace organizations, many of which had religious affiliations. U.S. faith communities are among the most racially separate institutions in the country. This racial separation was mirrored in the sanctuary movement in many regions across the country as well.

Because Salvadorans and white organizers did not initially contact African American organizations, CISPES's reputation on the street was as a white organization that worked with Salvadorans. Typically, white people who began working with the Salvadorans did not challenge themselves or the Salvadorans to reach out to communities of color in the United States. According to Suzanne, "No one raised the question about, Why this all-white organization? They had very little understanding of the movement in this country. At various stages I argued that we should follow their leadership completely on the question of El Salvadorans but on the question of how to build a movement in this country, we had the responsibility for fighting racism and building a movement that ultimately contributes to progressive work in this country."

Suzanne's priority, as a national leader for CISPES, was to make sure that African Americans were included and that grassroots communities of color cosponsored events. Although Suzanne believes there was a limited consciousness among some Salvadorans, as well as North Americans, about racism in the United States, as a North American her job was to challenge other white people to think beyond exclusively white organizations. She was outraged to learn that even the CISPES office in Washington, D.C.—a primarily African American city—included *only* white staff. Suzanne and some others in CISPES worked on building alliances with African American activists with the Black United Front, a long-standing group led by Reverend Herbert Daughtry; the House of the Lord church in Brooklyn; Harlem Fight Back, an African American workers' organization; and the *North American Congress on Latin America,* a well-known magazine on Latin America. Suzanne also began working closely with Ben Chavis at the United Church of Christ in New York, along with Dominican groups and Puerto Rican activists. Suzanne explains, "We did outreach to the Black community and I felt very committed. While I wanted to stop the war in El Salvador, to stop U.S. intervention in El Salvador, I also wanted to build a kind of movement that wasn't racist."

During this period (1983–1984), the Rainbow Coalition led by Jesse Jackson came out in solidarity with the people of Central America. Jackson took the same position that CISPES took on most issues. According to Suzanne, "He was very radical on his positions. Some of his staff people pushed it. He would get up and say things we [CISPES] wanted said. He was a national candidate pushing our agenda more than anyone else we had. He spoke about Central America all the time. So, I said, we should endorse him as the candidate for president at the Democratic convention in 1984."[54]

When Suzanne began working closely with the Rainbow Coalition, many people in CISPES took exception to her actions. They thought Suzanne and others who were advocating for multiracial alliances in the United States were trying to get the African Americans to take over CISPES. They accused Suzanne of trying to make a multi-issue organization out of CISPES when it was really a single-issue group. Those who disagreed with her said that she wanted to destroy CISPES and that she was not really committed to the Salvadorans. Many in CISPES argued that if they did endorse the Jackson campaign, they would alienate the rest of the Democratic Party. Many Salvadorans, understandably, wanted to garner as much support from the U.S. population as possible for their opposition to the war. But according to Suzanne, their priority was in developing relationships with mainstream organizations and politicians, which undermined multiracial alliances.

Suzanne laments that CISPES "was willing to support anyone who had much weaker positions on Central America than Jesse Jackson. For crumbs they would kiss the ass of Hart or Mondale. There were all kinds of deals made with the Democratic Party. But people wanted to use Jesse too. 'Can we get Jesse to do this or that?' I would say no. I didn't want to ask him if we weren't willing to support him." From Suzanne's perspective, the issue should not have been only whether Jesse Jackson could draw a crowd for CISPES. The issue was one of principles: "that we are antiracist and we support a Black leader running for president because it is in the interest of Salvadorans, for people all over the world."

According to Suzanne, all these "issues came to a head" at the

CISPES national convention after two years of struggling over questions of race.[55] By that point, Suzanne had worked with Latino, African American, and white activists across the country who saw the endorsement of Jesse Jackson and the politics of CISPES as interconnected. A vote was taken on whether to endorse Jackson and the Rainbow Coalition. About a third of the participants voted to support the endorsement. Suzanne says, "We had everything going against us. Racism within the organization. Inexperience. That we got one-third of the votes is amazing." After two-thirds of the members voted against endorsing Jackson, many who supported him walked out in protest. Most of the dissenters never returned, having come to believe that significant change about antiracism within the organization would never happen. Following this break, CISPES did elect a Chicana from Los Angeles, Angela Sembrano, to be president. Sembrano did work with the Rainbow Coalition, but according to Suzanne, the relationship between CISPES and African American and Latino organizations was generally tenuous.

As often in her life, Suzanne found her positions within CISPES and the Rainbow Coalition requiring her to straddle multiple agendas simultaneously. When Jackson announced his candidacy for president, activists working with Clergy and Laity Concerned asked Suzanne to get involved. African American–Jewish relations were very strained at the time, partly because of Jackson's calling New York "Hymie town." After working with Jackson for about two years, Suzanne was asked to be one of the people to introduce him at the Democratic National Convention in San Francisco in 1984. Suzanne recalls, "He had one gay person. One Palestinian. One Jewish person. I was the Jewish person." The situation however, "became confrontative." On the one hand, "I was supporting the Black movement and communities of color. On the other hand, I would always take on any kind of anti-Semitic comment I heard. That would get me in trouble. I often felt like I would end up having no friends. Jews would hate me, and Black people would hate me, and everyone would be mad at me at the end." While Suzanne was negotiating amid these conflicting perspectives in the Jackson campaign, she tried to maintain complicated political principles in her work with CISPES: respectful of Salvadoran leadership, cognizant of the limits of CISPES in building a multiracial movement, and wary of CISPES's relationship with Jackson and the Rainbow Coalition.

Naomi Jaffe also worked with CISPES and struggled with contradictions embedded in the organization's sense of accountability. The CISPES chapter in upstate New York, like the one in New York City, was primarily white with some Central American male leadership. Two Latinas were also involved, although according to Naomi, "there was no consciousness" that the Central American leadership was male dominated. From her perspective, there was also very little consciousness within the organization about what it meant to be predominantly white.

Eventually there was a struggle within CISPES about the relationship between the Central America solidarity movement and liberation struggles in the United States. Naomi asked, "Are we going to be accountable to the revolutionaries in Central America or to a movement in the United States?" Naomi asserted that CISPES "needed to be accountable to people here, to people of color. To be part of an alliance, a revolutionary set of coalitions in this country. In a way, we were talking about leadership from two different sets of people of color. . . . How much accountability do we really have to leaders in Central America as opposed to in our own communities?" From her perspective, a model that was accountable to Central American activists *and* to communities of color in the United States was the antiracist position. Naomi and her allies lost that struggle. CISPES and several other United States–based groups continued to see themselves as a continuation of the liberation struggle in Central America and did not do substantial coalition work in the United States.

Naomi believes that white people had an easier time holding themselves accountable to Central Americans as an abstract concept than they did working closely with Latinos and African Americans in the United States. This dynamic appeared to exist in much of the sanctuary movement as well. Darlene Nicgorski remembers that, increasingly, it became an issue and priority to have leadership from Central Americans in sanctuary meetings (locally, regionally, and nationally). At no time, however, "do I recall it being an issue about whether sanctuary should be more grounded in domestic communities of color."[56]

At the heart of Naomi's concern was the question about accountability to multiple communities. U.S. activist John Beam writes, in his examination of the contradictions in solidarity organizing in the early 1980s, "Salvadoran solidarity work, expressed primarily as anti-interventionist activity, is undoubtedly the most extensive, broadest-based manifestation of internationalism in the United States at this time. Still, it draws heavily from a disproportionately young, Anglo base of individuals driven by a radical critique of imperialism, some concept of Christian witness, or both. Neither tendency has much concrete connection with the low- and moderate-income mainstream or other groups that might logically be considered potential allies. For instance, CISPES defines its role as organizing North Americans to try to change United States policy. Organizing resident Central Americans is seen as separate activity for some other, in most places non-existent, organization."[57]

Naomi Jaffe and John Beam were dialoguing with Central American solidarity activists about an issue already visited by whites who identified themselves as anti-imperialists in the late 1960s and early 1970s. In retrospect, some of them have asked whether it was enough to have been influenced by the leadership of Che Guevara, Fidel Castro, and other liberation leaders who grew up outside the United States, whether accountability should have also included leaders in U.S. communities of color. Naomi was an activist in the 1960s who had come to an anti-imperialist perspective before she came to understand racism domestically—an ordering in consciousness that by the 1980s she considered limited. By the time Naomi was involved in CISPES, she knew from experience that anti-imperialism and antiracism had to go hand in hand, a perspective still in the minority in the overwhelmingly white organizations that opposed U.S. intervention in Central America.

Take Two, Take Three, Take Four . . .

The impact of the war on Central Americans was devastating. In Nicaragua 30,000 people were killed, 100,000 were killed in El Salvador, and as many as 1.5 million Central Americans were driven from their homes.[58] Although the success of the U.S. peace movement is hard to measure, many believe the activists' initiatives deterred Reagan from escalating the war to the extent that Presidents Johnson and Nixon had in Vietnam. The peace movement made it clear that although Reagan may have wanted to get beyond the "Vietnam syndrome," activists in neither era were willing to lay back and allow war to continue unabated.

The protests, harboring of refugees, and activist trips to Central America all made public a war that the U.S. government hoped to keep "technological, clean and distant."[59] Between its official start in 1982 and its tapering off in 1986, the sanctuary movement provided thousands of refugees with contacts and resources that might have otherwise been unavailable to them. By 1986 the emphasis had shifted to providing legal resources and support for resettlement. In 1987 the Supreme Court ruled that the INS must interpret the 1980 Refugee Act more broadly to include recognition of the fear of persecution as a possible criterion for asylum. Between 1982 and 1986 fewer than 1 percent of all the asylum cases were granted; by the middle of 1987 half of the Salvadoran applications in Arizona had been granted.[60] In 1990 the Justice Department settled a lawsuit brought forward in 1985 by eighty immigrants' rights and church groups against the INS. The settlement granted temporary legal status to Salvadoran refugees. It required the INS to rehear 150,000 cases in which asylum had been denied and to hire new INS agents who would be knowledgeable about conditions in Central America.[61]

Both the public sanctuary movement and Witness for Peace gave concrete examples of people who did not agree with U.S. policy and were willing to put their lives on the line if need be. In that way, those involved broke open the notion of a monolithic U.S. citizen. This break was important for Central Americans, whose images of people in the United States might have otherwise been monopolized by Reagan-supported military men. Protests by people from the United States also raised the consciousness of others who, upon learning from those working with refugees or from those who had traveled south, joined in opposing the war.

The organizing in the United States was the most substantial anti-war effort in twenty years. And yet very little has been written about the ways race, racism, and ethnocentrism limited the movement.[62] For example, to my knowledge, there is no analysis of what made possible as well as hindered connections between the public sanctuary movement and the much larger clandestine absorption of refugees into existing Latino communities. According to Mario Davila, one of the key Salvadoran activists in the 1980s and 1990s, there are many reasons for this gap. First, the overriding mission of the sixty or so Salvadorans living in the United States who provided key leadership in CISPES, the pledge, and other organizations was to ensure that the U.S. government stopped the war in Central America. For the Salvadorans, that goal meant influencing public policy, which required developing a funding base. From the perspective of Salvadorans, white people had the wealth to fund such activism.

Second, many white activists considered the whiteness of the organizations and their lack of multiracial ties unremarkable. Most white people involved in the Pledge of Resistance and sanctuary had very few existing networks with United States–based Latino and African American organizations. Those white activists who saw multiracial ties as crucial ran the risk of being dismissed by other whites or of being thought an impediment, slowing the momentum of the Salvadorans' agenda to stop the war.

A third reality that hindered political alliances between the two responses to Central American refugees is that refugees coming to the United States were not necessarily political people prior to leaving their own countries. In El Salvador and Guatemala people were being persecuted simply because they were church members. According to Mario Davila, their arrival in the United States did not necessarily mean they believed they had a right to political asylum; nor were they necessarily interested in political work. The Salvadoran activists in the struggle to stop the war knew well the risks involved for undocumented refugees who were activists in the United States, and so they were careful about what they asked of them politically.

All the people I interviewed spoke passionately about their work against U.S. involvement and considered collective pressure against the war vital. All, however, saw the work as an uphill climb, most obviously because of the intransigence of the U.S. government and the horrible impact of the war on Central Americans. The struggle was also caused by limited knowledge among activist organizations of what it means to do social justice work that is both cross-cultural and antiracist. Although refugees in the sanctuary movement potentially faced being infantilized by their host communities, Central American activist leaders in CISPES or in Central America ran the risk of being idealized or stretched beyond their capacity in terms of providing "inside" knowledge about political strategies and historical background about their countries. Neither tendency nurtured equal, powerful, cross-cultural political relations.

The Central America peace movement raises questions about solidarity that were taken up in the late 1960s and early 1970s as well. For white activists at that time, "solidarity" often meant being willing to sustain risks similar to those assumed by Black activists. For those who worked closely with Black nationalist groups, this meant risking arrest and possible long-term prison sentences, using access to financial resources to fund the movement, and listening carefully to and learning from Black activists. In that period, what it meant to act in solidarity was shaped in large part by government repression against activists.

In the 1980s many white activists also spoke of standing in solidarity, a position that involved contradictions specific to that particular time. For sanctuary workers on the border between Mexico and Arizona, standing in solidarity meant dodging the border patrol and literally walking and driving alongside refugees. Most white activists were aware, however, of the limits of that shared act. Refugees who were caught crossing the border ran the risk of deportation and possible death upon return to their countries. White activists risked possible arrest and, in a few cases, imprisonment. For CISPES workers, "solidarity" meant being willing to risk arrest for civil disobedience, an act of defiance that largely depended upon having U.S. citizenship. Refugees simply could not afford to commit such acts. They not only had to forfeit their right to civil disobedience, but as refugees, their very existence in the United States was also under threat. For people who traveled to Central America on brigades or with Witness for Peace, standing in solidarity meant making a commitment to take what they learned back to the United States in order to push for changes in foreign policy. Travel to Central America could also mean being in physical danger, although North Americans were generally much less at risk than were Central Americans. Most travelers, however, were aware that the choice to travel to Central America could not be compared with the forced "decision" of hundreds of thousands of Central Americans to travel from their homes to avoid being tortured or killed.

The enormous difference in the risks and costs highlights the limits of solidarity. This does not mean that the actions are not worthy. But damage is done when these differences are not acknowledged openly. In some instances white idealization of Central American culture and religion served as a distraction from dealing with power inequities. The distance between the two cultures kept that idealization intact, which is another reason many white activists in the 1980s seemed more willing to confront poverty and repression in Central America than to confront it as it affects the working class or people of color in the United States.

Many issues remain unresolved about what might have strengthened the Central America peace movement. What might it have taken to make the movement multiracial from the beginning—not just in pockets, as in the Southwest, but nationally? What might it have taken to build organizations in the United States so that CISPES and early brigades going to Central America could have developed and sustained relationships with African American and Latino organizations in the United States?

One lesson that emerges from this and other organizing is how important it is to create multiracial alliances from day one when a new organization begins or a crisis hits and to maintain these alliances across the life span of the organization. Had Witness for Peace and Pledge of Resistance activists worked closely with African American and domestic Latino organizations in the beginning—in 1982 and 1983—who knows how much more powerful a coalition against U.S. intervention might have been formed. In many ways, the racial and class divides evident in the anti–Vietnam War movement manifested themselves again in the 1980s. The anti-imperialist thrust of organizing did not go hand in hand with an antiracist agenda in the United States.

I also wonder whether, if white activists in the 1960s had been better able to respond to the increasingly multiracial composition of activist organizations of that period—the Brown Berets, the American Indian Movement (AIM), Puerto Rican independence activists—white activists might have been better prepared to participate in Latino–African American–white alliances in the 1980s? Sociologist Christian Smith reports that "more than one half of [white] Central American peace activists had participated in civil rights, anti–Vietnam war, environmental and anti-poverty campaigns."[63] These are all locations where lessons might have been learned about the limits of all-white groups and an emphasis on anti-imperialism without commensurate attention to anti-racism in the United States.

The limits of the Central America peace movement are particularly alarming to me given how many women who worked with the Pledge of Resistance and sanctuary were also feminists, and at a time in the feminist movement when attention to race was particularly strong.

Although there is power in a peace movement that mobilized upwards of 100,000 people, there were limits to the organizing from a perspective of antiracism. Ironically, and as had been true of Students for a Democratic Society (SDS) two decades before, the overwhelming whiteness of the organizations seemed to stand in the way of rather than facilitate an awareness of race and racism.

Central America solidarity work also provides example of white activists who struggled with principles of self-determination. They sometimes fell into the trap of trying to do things their way instead of listening to Nicaraguan or Salvadoran leaders, imposing white middle-class attitudes in their evaluations of Central American–based initiatives, and romanticizing Nicaraguan or Guatemalan activists. All these tendencies were also evident in white New Left organizing in the 1960s, perhaps most clearly in SDS's Economic Research and Action Program (ERAP) programs in urban areas. As had been true for white Student Nonviolent Coordinating Committee (SNCC) workers, those white activists who had the closest and longest-standing contact with Central American activists were often those best able to guard against either romanticizing Central Americans or trying to control their agendas.

Parallels between Central America activism and earlier activism also include enduring debates about pacifist versus militant approaches to social change. As had been true in the early Civil Rights Movement and in multiracial feminism, those who worked in the sanctuary movement and with the Pledge of Resistance assumed a pacifist approach to activism and treated their struggle as both a process and a goal (that is, there was much attention to group process, democratic decision making, and nonhierarchical structures). By contrast, a significant portion of CISPES activists believed opposition to U.S. militarism required respect for tactics of self-defense and armed struggle. Like the Black Panther Party, many CISPES activists saw a pacifist stance as unrealistic, given that the United States was funding a war against the people of Nicaragua and El Salvador. These two ideological strains operated simultaneously, as the sometimes bitter exchanges between the two groups reflected.

Since 1990 armed conflict in Central America has died down. The successful United Nations–sponsored El Salvadoran peace accords in 1992, the Guatemalan government's demilitarization, and the end of the contra war in Nicaragua in the late 1980s all contributed to peace in the region. Not surprisingly, though, reasons for close connections between progressive activists in the United States and Central America remain. The increasing power of the International Monetary Fund (IMF) and the World Bank on the region's economy has the potential to bring activists from both regions together again to oppose the neo-colonialism upheld through these agencies' policies and their long-standing ties to the U.S. economic agenda. Among the multiple lessons to be learned from the Central America solidarity work of the 1980s is the need to build a multiracial base in the United States while nurturing ties to progressives movements internationally. Building a progressive multiracial base remains a significant challenge and goal for activists standing up against the World Trade Organization and other international financial centers of power. Not surprisingly, debates about strategy for organizing continue, as do conversations about pacifist versus militant protests and the approaches required to build multiracial alliances that must be, by necessity, increasingly international.

9

Prison Activism: The Vastness of the Sky

To think of roses and gardens inside is bad,
to think of seas and mountains is good.
Read and write without rest,
and I also advise weaving
and making mirrors
I mean, it's not that you can't pass
      ten or fifteen years inside
          and more—
    you can,
      as long as the jewel
        on the left side of your chest doesn't lose its luster!
                Nazim Hikmet, "Some Advice to Those
                Who Will Serve Time in Prison," 1949

It is a war now. That is my sadness that is different than in the sixties and seventies when there was some kind of widespread organizing. It was different. We, as revolutionaries, weren't the majority, we weren't the mainstream. But we weren't from Mars. Our perspective was part of the national agenda.

                            Naomi Jaffe, interview, 1997

In 1971, while in prison herself, Angela Davis offered this definition of a political prisoner: "There is a distinct and qualitative difference between one breaking a law for one's own individual self-interest and violating it in the interest of a class or a people whose oppression is expressed either directly or indirectly through that particular law. The former might be called a criminal (though in many instances he is a victim), but the latter, as a reformist or revolutionary, is interested in universal social change. Captured, he or she is a political prisoner."[1]

Political prisoners include about 150 people who are in federal and state prisons as a result of having opposed inhumane conditions and polices in the United States. Their arrests and convictions reflect a form of retaliation against their activism and a means of stopping them from continuing their work outside of prison.[2] Political prisoners in the United States reflect several categories of activists: African Americans affiliated with political organizations, primarily the Black Panther Party; Puerto Rican *independistas;* Native Americans seeking redress for state acts of genocide; people of Mexican descent seeking political and financial reparations for territories stolen; white people opposed to racism and imperialism; nonviolent opponents of nuclear weapons and militarization; a member of the Irish Republican Army (IRA); and two Virgin Islanders.[3] These political prisoners have provided much of the leadership—both inside and outside of prison—in collective organizing on behalf of health care, education, legal aid, and the right to religious and cultural freedom, and against the beating and sexual abuse of prisoners.

There has always been antiracist activism against prisons in the United States, in part because state punishment has always been racialized. Although the visibility of activism against race and class bias in incarceration rates and sentencing has waxed and waned during different historical periods, prison activists have long understood that inequalities are reflected in their most crystalized form in prisons. State punishment has historically targeted people of color, whether in the form of more than 350 years of slavery; the Black Codes, which gave post-slavery legal justification for the imprisonment of Blacks in the South; convict leasing (through which, from the late 1860s to the late 1920s, the labor of southern Black prisoners was leased out under conditions often worse than those during slavery); Immigration and Naturalization Service (INS) detention of immigrants; internment camps during World War II; or the current drug laws that lead to far lengthier sentences for Blacks and Latinos than for whites.[4]

There are several connections between past and present prison activism. In many ways, current organizing against the escalation of the prison industry is an outgrowth of 1960s activism. Many activists who are now in prison are there because of their political work in the 1960s, serving sentences far out of line with the crimes they were said to have committed.[5] In the late 1960s and 1970s the Black Panther Party considered political mobilization for prisoners a key act and struggled hard for the release of African American, Latino, and white activists.[6] The many African American activists of the 1960s who are continuing prison activism now include Angela Davis, who was imprisoned in the early 1970s and has remained a leading prison activist since;[7] Safiya Bukhari-Alston, who was a political prisoner for nine years and is now a leading activist in Jericho, a national organization in support of political prisoners; Kazi Toure, who was a political prisoner and now works with the American Friends Service Committee project on prisons; and Pam Africa, who is a member of MOVE (a long-standing spiritual community and activist organization in Philadelphia), and a leading activist in the international campaign for a new trial for Mumia Abu-Jamal.

A second historical connection to the 1960s is that the massive growth in prisons is directly tied to deindustrialization, whose roots lie in the post–World War II transition from a manufacturing-based economy (steel, cars, textiles) to a social service–based economy. This transition has been coupled with a shift from a capitalist economy, whose main industries drew on labor in the United States, to an economy that increasingly draws on international labor to increase its profits. Through the North American Free Trade Agreement (NAFTA) and other trade decisions, corporations are being given free reign to decide where they set up shop and with whom they want to do business.[8] The globalization of capital has severely undermined job security for working-class people and sabotaged union organizing, both in the United States and in countries where United States–based corporations have sought their labor forces.

The increase in poverty and economic insecurity this shift has generated has left many poor communities in shambles, a reality that makes them more vulnerable to what Angela Davis terms "criminalization—a race and class ideology that has been used to justify an explosion in incarceration of poor people, people of color in particular. Black people are 7.8 times as likely to be imprisoned as whites."[9] As of 1997, 5.1 million people in the United States were either incarcerated, on parole, or on probation. Between 1980 and 1992 there was a 163 percent increase in incarceration for men and a 276 percent increase for women.[10] The ideology used to support this increase has been based on a fierce and steady campaign to convince people that crime has not only skyrocket-ed but is also what people should most fear. Davis writes, "The fear of crime has attained a status that bears a sinister similarity to the fear of communism as it came to restructure social perceptions during the 1950s and 1960s. The figure of the 'criminal'—the racialized figure of the criminal—has come to represent the most menacing enemy of 'American society.'"[11]

With deindustrialization and corporate flight from the United States, the construction of new prisons and the expansion of old ones has be-come a booming business. In this late-capitalist economy, people are increasingly dependent upon social service jobs—jobs that cannot be deported—to support their families. Prisons provide jobs for men and women, many of whom might have in earlier times worked in manu-facturing industries. The reality that correctional officers are often only one small degree removed economically and educationally from those they guard is a painful example of the way working-class people are pitted against each other while racial divides are heightened. Davis ex-plains that by providing jobs and supporting racial scapegoating, pris-ons "relieve us of the responsibility of dealing with problems of late capitalism, of transnational capital."[12]

An increasing number of businesses see prisons as cheap and re-liable sources of labor, since they are not required to provide benefits or pay close to the minimum wage. (Prison wages range from twenty-five cents to $1.10 per hour.)[13] Corporations are attracted to prisons for cheap labor as they have been attracted to Third World countries; in both locations, strikes and unions are rarely a threat.[14] This underpaid labor then undercuts labor on the outside, since outside workers can-not compete with the virtually free labor available in prison.

Inside Activism: "The Genius of Survival"[15]

For activists in prison, the challenges of organizing inside are myriad. At every turn, attempts to organize collectively can be sabotaged by prison officials, who use any number of reasons to halt prisoner initia-tives. Two of the most common tactics are to transfer activists to other sections of the prison or to other prisons entirely, or to create trumped-up disciplinary charges that are really punishment for organizing. Often this retaliation for activism starts with sentencing and continues from there. For example, David Gilbert was sentenced to seventy-five years to life on a conviction linked to the 1981 Brinks robbery and shoot-out in which a Brinks guard and two policemen were killed.[16] David was sentenced to what is in effect his natural life under New York's Felony Murder Law, which means that even though there were no allegations of his having done any shooting or having had a gun, he bore full legal responsibility for all the deaths.

During his years in prison David has been transferred to the three most repressive prisons (of twenty-nine) in New York state—the three known as the "burn circuit." These punitive transfers have been made despite the fact that David has never received a disciplinary violation. Clearly, prison officials are worried about David as an organizer and as someone known for building cross-race unity. After David and fellow activists got a model peer education program running at Auburn Prison, he was suddenly shipped out. David was one of eight people (and the only white person) to sign a public letter calling attention to beatings of a prisoner at Comstock Prison (where David is currently incarcerated). The other signers were shipped out, but David was kept at Comstock—the most repressive prison, located in an isolated small town in upstate New York. Amid these tremendous stresses, David and other prison activists do find ways to "make a way out of no way," a reality that prison activists on the outside frequently say is what keeps them moving forward.

Political prisoners' activism reflects their experiences prior to being incarcerated as well as what they learn once in prison. For David, prior work with Black Liberation Army (BLA) activists provided an initial model for how the African American and white codefendants worked with each other during the trial. According to David, "Despite media to the contrary, race relations among those arrested were very good, amazingly so, given that, of course, errors had been made, and we all were paying an extremely high price.[17] For the first two years I was in prison [1981–1983], I was either in isolation or jailed with my codefendants. It would be very easy for Blacks or whites to point the finger at each other. Nothing like that happened, that I am aware of. Relations were good; including an ability to have serious and honest discussions of errors without recriminations. The state and media made an effort to create and project a white/Black split in a few ways. The state tried to convince us that we were snitching on each other; the media had presented this dichotomy by portraying the Blacks as thugs while presenting the whites as educated but psychologically deranged. The media also floated stories of how the groups used each other."[18]

Once in prison, David did not know what to expect of racial dynamics. He had heard that in California white and African American prisoners were totally separate. Who was "white" was rigidly defined by the Aryan Brotherhood (a white supremacist organization) so there was little or no biracial activism. He had heard that "Bill Harris, as an antiracist white, couldn't go into either the white or the Black yard."[19] But when David got to prison, "I had no problems from white prisoners, and I was received even more warmly than expected by race-conscious Black men, who treated me with solidarity and respect."[20] When David got to prison at Auburn, "There were a couple of Black Liberation Army prisoners who taught me much about surviving right off the bat. In prison, my relationship to African Americans changed radically, first because my contact was much closer than it had been before prison."

At Columbia University, where David had been an organizer in the late 1960s, "much of the leadership was African American, and certainly Malcolm X was a huge influence on my life, but my day-to-day interactions and organizations were largely among white people. Once in prison, much of my work has been with African Americans, as have been many of my primary friendships. I got to spend much time with Kuwasi Balagoon, one of the Panther Twenty-One and a codefendant in the Brinks trial.[21] We developed a close political relationship as revolutionaries based on two fundamentals: Don't cave in to the pressure to renounce, and do self-criticism so others can learn from your setbacks. It is very hard to do both of these things simultaneously. Through our friendship, we tried to carry out both of these responsibilities."

During David's first six months in prison he got into many arguments with white people about race and racism. "But," he says, "I got crucial advice from Black Liberation Army members. While they commended me for working with white people, they suggested that I work more slowly and try to better understand where the white people were coming from, and that change does not happen in a day. After six months, I cooled down my approach, particularly when there were no contexts for organizing. Still, I tried to be an antiracist pole and a presence among white prisoners."

David quickly saw that racism is much more explicit in prison than it is on the street and in liberal white society. On the other hand, he says, "There is sometimes actual solidarity among prisoners. Over time, I have come to understand more about the socialization of white men and about class as well. My central point is to develop a social base among white people, while maintaining close contact with Black people. I try to create a little more space to be less racist. I don't believe that any of the organizing I do qualifies as 'revolutionary,' but the work still matters. I feel most at home with politically conscious Blacks, but I have made friends among all people and have tried to maintain a social identity as a white person who is antiracist."

One of the realities that has helped David in dealing with other prisoners is that his case was seen as a "heavy" one, since it involved the shooting of a police officer. As a political prisoner, David also has some privileges not afforded to others. "I am granted respect by the other prisoners and, from some of the correctional officers, a begrudging respect because of my education (which is about class privilege) and how I carry myself."[22] David explains, "That means I can be myself—be soft-spoken and a nice guy. Those are qualities that usually get one labeled as 'soft' and leads to your being tested to see if you can be pushed around, but I haven't had any of those hassles."[23] According to David, "A main way that correctional officers make life difficult, especially for young prisoners and for Black prisoners, is to polarize the prisoners' options between either accepting a humiliation or getting trapped in an escalation that leads to more severe punishment. You see it all the time: A young Black prisoner is put up against the wall, aggressively frisked, called 'asshole.' If he says nothing, it can be perceived as accepting an attack on his manhood; if he answers back, it can lead to a keeplock or even a beatdown. Either way he loses. As an older white man, a political prisoner, someone with a lot of self-confidence, I (along with other experienced prisoners) can usually sidestep those kinds of polarized options."[24]

As a white man who has been to college, David also has race and class privileges that have afforded him more access to outside support than is available to most other prisoners. For inmates at Comstock, access to people on the outside is difficult if the visitors do not have a car. David believes that "all the plagues and disintegration of this society have put tremendous burdens on families in Third World and poor communities." For example, friends and families who live in New York City and who do not have cars but who want to visit prisoners at

Comstock must take a bus that leaves the city at 2:30 in the morning in order to reach the prison in time to be processed for morning visits.

For political prisoners, including David, the issues they organize around are a consequence of what they see as the greatest need within prison walls. For David, inequalities of race, class, and sexuality intersect in devastating ways around the way people with AIDS are treated. There is a desperate need for AIDS education among prisoners. "The racial makeup of those in prison and of those who are contracting HIV are both a function of racism. The numbers of white and Black prisoners are about equal; however, the rate of incarceration is about seven times higher among Black people. The rate of new AIDS cases in 1996 was approximately seven times higher among Blacks. This correlation is not just coincidental, since both incarceration and AIDS have similar social causes. Among New York prisoners, AIDS is by far the leading killer. Throughout the 1990s AIDS deaths were running at about 250 annually (in a population of less than 70,000)."[25] A staggering number of prisoners are now dealing with having a close friend or someone in their families—their mothers, lovers, or cousins—who has AIDS.

The fact that David's closest friend, Kuwasi Balagoon, died of AIDS in 1986 in prison was a huge motivating factor in David's decision to do AIDS education. David remembers, "One of the lowest moments in my life was when my father and Kuwasi died within three months of each other. Kuwasi was a man who was incredibly loved by people around him, including me. Circumstances generated by the outpouring of concern of prisoners at Auburn also taught me a heavy lesson about 'revolutionary humility.' Prisoners were constantly coming to me to find out what really happened. Most believed that the state must have purposely injected Kuwasi with AIDS. Given the history of government assassinations of Black militants and that I didn't know that Kuwasi may have been involved in any high-risk practices, the prisoners' concern seemed a possibility. But his attorney got to speak with Kuwasi before he died, and Kuwasi indicated he had some risk factors over six years earlier. Given that, I did not feel I could honestly charge that the state gave Kuwasi AIDS. The 'revolutionary humility' developed because I was very honored that so many prisoners came to me to find out what really happened. Being honored in that way, I felt a lot of pressure to tell people what they so fervently wanted to hear. But being revolutionary isn't about building up one's self-importance. Respecting people means that you gotta tell the truth as you understand it rather than what makes you feel most glorious. This was true for me around the controversy of Kuwasi's health as well as with other issues I have faced in my life."[26]

David turned his great grief over Kuwasi's death into the energy to study AIDS and its connection to intravenous drug use. He has been focusing on AIDS education since. In 1987 at Auburn, David and two other friends of Kuwasi's started Prisoners' Education Project on AIDS (PEPA). David says, "We drew upon the model of peer education in the gay community in San Francisco and adapted it for the prison context. While there were a few earlier efforts at infirmary visitation to inmates with AIDS, PEPA was the first peer education program on AIDS in prison in the country. The administration, however, saw it as a threat in terms of organizing and uniting prisoners. Machiavelli could have come back from his grave and learned something from how Auburn prison officials maneuvered to prevent the formation of PEPA. My approach to working against AIDS, in conjunction with Mujahid Farid, a jailhouse lawyer and respected member of the Muslim community, and Papo Nieves, a leader in the Latino organization with a lot of experience in developing prisoner programs, was based on a commitment to participatory democracy—to get as many people as possible involved in their own education and how this education will take place."

AIDS education in any setting is difficult, and it is especially so in prison. David says, "The project made little headway with the local AIDS service agency, which was unfortunate particularly because there is such a high prevalence of HIV infection among prisoners. We carefully sought outside support through prisoners' rights organizations. Among prisoners, the major barrier initially was homophobia and the myth that AIDS is a gay disease. By insisting that people be dealt with respectfully, we were taking a practical step against homophobia, but we couldn't be as gay-positive as groups in the street."

The model was based on facilitating "educationals" along with individual work: one-on-one peer education. This program is among an increasing number in the country.[27] According to David, "The organization's main priority was to talk with as many groups within prison as possible—the Muslims, Rastas, Five Percenters, Puerto Ricans, Dominicans, Italians, Bikers, etc. We tried to develop educators in each subcommunity within the prison in order to be trusted and to be able to tailor the education to the particular needs of that group."

After the prisoners got PEPA going at Auburn, David was suddenly shipped out in December 1987. He was sent to Clinton Prison in New York, a very repressive and isolated prison. David was unable to get an organization going there, but he did considerable peer education on his own initiative. When he was transferred to Attica in 1989, he helped start a mutual support group for prisoners with AIDS. After being transferred to Comstock in 1990, he was asked by the African Cultural Organization to form a subcommittee on AIDS education. Comstock already had a good mutual support group, and David became the peer counselor. It took four years of persistent effort before he could get the administration to allow him to set up an AIDS education program of any scope.

Over time, David realized he could not effectively do AIDS education while being a visible focal point for work against prison brutality because that struggle is so intense, can result in repression, and is very hard to win. So he decided to focus on AIDS work at Comstock. Two of the highest moments in David's life since he has been in prison were when prisoners conducted a peaceful protest at Attica (on May 26, 1990) and when eleven two-man teams of peer educators recently went into sixteen different classes in prison and led workshops on AIDS. Those workshops involved 320 men and were facilitated by prisoners whom PEPA had trained. In prison, where organizing any event is difficult, this was a huge accomplishment.

Despite his activism, David increasingly faces isolation in prison, a reality that has much to do with the rise in the number of people in prison, increased repression, and his position as an antiracist. The facts that the prison industry is one of the fastest growing in the country and that the government still allows massive use of drugs (and sometimes facilitates their availability in urban communities) has enormous consequences for organizing within prison. According to David, "There has been a change in the code of ethics in the prison over time, which has meant that it is harder and harder to know who to trust and who you can really talk with. The enormous influx of new people—including many youth who never experienced any effective social struggles—and the influence of drugs is whittling away at the basic notion that prisoners need to stick together. It means that I am taking risks when I talk beyond a superficial level with fellow prisoners who I don't know well." The fact that prison officials have consistently separated David from BLA prisoners and other activists certainly has contributed to his isolation. "However," David continues, "in 1996 they did transfer Herman Bell here, and while I'm sorry he got stuck here, it is a pleasure and a great help to get to talk with him from time to time."[28]

The isolation David faces means there are fewer chances to formulate strategy. "One of the things I loved about activism before prison is that there were many people to talk with, to work things out with together, strategically." He describes himself as having "a basically cautious, conservative personality. I have an especially hard time making leadership decisions when I know they may lead people into repression. The isolation makes thinking things through collectively very hard."

The prevailing racism among white prisoners also accentuates the lack of collectivity and leaves David "a little more aloof from day-to-day culture and activities of the majority of prisoners."[29] David also finds little chance to do antisexist, antiheterosexist work. "There are days and days now when I don't have the opportunity for in-depth discussions based on a shared worldview. For example, I rarely have a chance to engage in serious conversation about sexism—an issue that was fought for long and hard by and with women comrades. Being in this profoundly masculine environment drives me crazy, and sometimes I don't fight against sexism hard enough. Men too often look at women as only to be used, even when it isn't sexually. In general, while there is some level of agreement or resonance with broad principles in terms of respecting women, in a way guys here see me like they'd look at a sincere, humane priest. They respect that I am upholding certain morals, but think I am in a kind of other world."[30] On the rare occasions when David does get to talk with BLA comrades, he is able to "have decent conversations about sexism and women since they have political consciousness on these issues."[31]

For David, the easiest form of resistance is writing, since he can do that on his own. For the past five years he has been writing a book-review column, an idea he got from Sundiata Acoli, who is a writer and a New African political prisoner of war.[32] This enables him to engage with political issues in an analytical way. "It is ironic," he says "because now I have more of an appreciation of democracy than before I was in prison, but now I am in an environment whose basic structure is antidemocratic. It is also ironic that the most multiracial organizing that I have participated in has been while in prison."

Marilyn Buck is serving an eighty-year sentence in California for convictions related to her militancy, including a successful initiative to free Assata Shakur, a Black Panther now living in exile in Cuba.[33] For Marilyn, trying to do antiracist work in prison runs the gamut from "just speaking up for a woman when it is pretty clear she is being shunted or messed over because she is Black or Latina," to leading poetry workshops and translating for Spanish-speaking inmates. Like David Gilbert, Marilyn believes that antiracism includes a range of actions, from everyday activities with people whom one might otherwise ignore or avoid to organizing collective resistance around human rights issues.

As is true for David and many other prison activists, Marilyn considers AIDS education central. Two of Marilyn's friends and fellow political prisoners at Dublin Prison, Laura Whitehorn and Linda Evans, have developed a peer education program.[34] Marilyn says, "All of us who are anti-imperialists think this work is key in terms of the education of women and children. The peer education is extremely critical." Central to the success of the program has been careful considerations of who the leaders should be. For example, although Marilyn, Laura, and Linda talk together about AIDS education, Marilyn is not involved directly. She explains, "Wherever I have been, there have been several white women who have been involved in peer education. It becomes an overload not only of political women but of white women as well." From Marilyn's perspective, prison officials have been increasingly controlling in terms of peer education, including trying to make sure the political women are not involved. From the political women's perspective, "What is important is that the work gets done, not that we get credit for it. That is the critical point."

Like David, Marilyn has also seen dramatic changes in the prison population, changes that have implications for organizing. "There are a lot more white women in jail. Most of them are white, working-class women. The class and education level of a number of the Latin and Black women is higher than that of a lot of the white women." Increasingly, Marilyn sees young white women in prison who "find it natural to associate with young Blacks and Latinos. But that doesn't necessarily make them politically conscious. They may treat people nice and work together and eat dinner together, but that only exists on a personal level. To be a serious antiracist, you have to be conscious twenty-four hours a day, seven days a week. That is hard. There are a number of young white women here. They are not white racists. They have grown up around Black people. Most of them have had Black boy-friends or girlfriends. And a number of them have children by a Black father. On one level, that creates a different openness, but it is not the consciousness of fighting the system that oppresses Black people or Latinos or Asians. It doesn't even give them their own women's consciousness. Without antiracist consciousness, white women do not acknowledge the white privilege that they still enjoy even as prisoners."

Describing changes in prison racial politics, Marilyn says, "When I was first in prison, really the only women I could talk with were the Black and Latin women. Dealing with the white women was difficult. Now there are an increasing number of militia-type women, and women from the tax movement. Right-wing white women. Some of them feel kinship with someone like me, in terms of education and being anti-government, specifically because there is a lot of confusion about what that means, until it comes to challenging white racist privilege. There is a woman here who is from the Plowshares. We have had some interesting discussions. All tax resisters are not the same. I say, do you want to align yourself with white racists? They are not the same as the Plowshares who resist war taxes. They have very different goals." For Marilyn, the challenge is to find ways to talk with white women, to try to understand their perspective and then to continue from there. Her poem "To the Woman Standing behind Me in Line Who Asks Me How Long This Black History Month Is Going to Last" speaks powerfully to her commitment to using everyday situations as a chance for consciousness raising and dialogue:

> the whole month
> even if it is the shortest month
> a good time in this prison life
>
> *you stare at me*
> *and ask me why I think*
> *February is so damned fine*
>
> *I take a breath*
> prisoners fight for February
> African voices cross razor wire
> cut through the flim-flam
> of Amerikkan history

call its cruelties out
confirm the genius of survival
creation and
plain ole enduring

a celebration!

. . . . .

the woman drops her gaze
looks away and wishes
she had not asked
confused that white skin did not guarantee
a conversation she wanted to have

she hasn't spoken to me since
I think I'll try to stand
in line with her
again

Marilyn and her fellow political prisoner friends "really fight for Black history month, for Kwanza, for Latin History month, and for Puerto Rican history events." Marilyn also offers poetry workshops, "where I encourage women to get access to their own voices. To find their own voices."[35] She also tutors math and science for women who want to get their GEDs. And she speaks Spanish. "Over the years I have done a lot of translating while trying not to run it or to mediate it." Marilyn believes it is important for English speakers to know other people's languages, since that is often a prerequisite for understanding people's cultural and political perspectives.

Marilyn has also spent much time, in conversation with others and through her studies in psychology, understanding what it means to be a political prisoner for the long haul. She says, "I don't think you can be a political prisoner, period, for a long period of time without being damaged by it. It is like you are battered every day. Whether it is psychologically or physically, you get scarred by it. How do you deal with that assault upon your being? We all do that differently. You never know who will break. It might be the least suspected. Who goes crazy from it and who gets through it. You are not the same person you were. You wouldn't be the same person if life were perfect.

"I get through it because I look at each day as a challenge. I do believe that we go forward as human beings. It is not exactly history as progress. . . . We go backwards. We go forward. We go sideways. But the potential to go forward always exists. I believe in liberation and justice. They are abstract words but are very concrete in terms of what I see and how we could be as human beings and with each other. I try to analyze my own illnesses. Not just on a physical level. I try to be in tune with my paranoia, with my depression. With all these things, I study psychology. I am trying to get a degree in psychology after many years of thinking that revolutionaries don't need psychology. But I think we need it now more than we ever did. We do need to understand colonial illnesses and mental illnesses of advanced capitalism and imperialism. It affects us differently due to gender, race, and class."

Part of the challenge for Marilyn is to try to see the big picture in all that she does, an approach she believes is exemplified by "[the] poet Nazim Hikmet, a Turkish political prisoner and a Communist who wrote some beautiful poems after ten years in prison.[36] One of his poems is about prisoners. Prisoners should not think of roses or love. Prisoners should think about the sea and the vastness of the sky. You have to think about the world. Not to dwell on the small heartaches about what size shoes your child wears. Or whether your mother is taking the right heart medication. You can't worry about those things in quite that way. You have to look more at what is the vastness of what the world is and where we want to go."

From Marilyn's perspective, political prisoners need, at least partly, to be idealists. "You have to believe in something. And you have to believe you are a hearty individual; and that you can survive it all, whether it is only to tell them to kiss your ass and drop dead when you do. That is sometimes what I say. Well, I will be eighty when I get out. If I drop dead after I get out of the gate that is fine. As long as I can tell them to kiss my ass. You did not beat me. That is a very individual response. Some days that is what I have to go with. Some days you go with a bigger response. I read the paper about the man dragged to death in Palestine, Texas. What do I do?[37] How do you understand such depravity? Or I hear about somebody's life here. Sometimes I can't carry more stories because people's stories are war stories; they are very tragic, very sad. We all bring our own crap into how we end up in worse situations than we might have to be in. But the point is that they are all tragic, horrible stories. So it is like trying to keep some sense of balance and not try to put oneself in the middle of everything."

For Marilyn, the greatest danger for prisoners, including political prisoners, is to allow themselves to feel bitter. "You cannot allow bitterness. Once bitterness takes hold, it deforms you. Worse than all the external and internal battering processes that deform us. Part of not being bitter is taking full responsibility for everything you do. Whether it was right or wrong. Whether you are embarrassed about it or proud of it. It is not defending all of it necessarily, but it is about being responsible for it. If we believe in liberation and humanity and all these things, then however much we can be that, as a woman, leaving aside all the times when I was oppressed and didn't speak out, or wasn't as much as I could be, the point is that I am now more than I was then. And so you hold onto that and nurture that. I think we all keep growing. Then, in times of reaction and horrible things, whether it is the Holocaust or crucifixions, or whatever is going on in society, where there are always massacres and murder of people, then you say that the struggle does carry on. There is such a thing as approaching liberation. And approaching justice."

Marilyn believes that everyone has a chance to get a glimpse of justice. "Some days, that glimpse might be seeing someone that doesn't like someone give that person something they need even though that person needs it too. That is an act of humanity. That act of humanity can be translated into breaking through the individualism to where we function more as a collective, where we aren't afraid to be right, to be wrong, to praise someone else's work. When we do construct things, some of it may turn good. Some of it may be rotten and turn to corruption. But we still exist and still go on. Even if it is three more generations down the line."

Marilyn admits that many days it is not easy to find a political and philosophical perspective to get her through. "It gets harder here. We all become more fragile. You are under assault all the time." When the correctional officer and another official walked across the yard to get Marilyn for our interview, one of the men motioned to Marilyn by simply pointing a finger at her. Marilyn said to herself at the time, "I want to write a poem about how I am never never going to respond again to someone when they do this to me. Those little things eat away. But then I have to remind myself that it happens every day in the world. It is like we are in a separate concentrated space but all of the same crap goes on out there. You might find ways to not have to be next to it. You can go to the movies or to the park. But it is not always qualitatively different. It is quantitatively different." Marilyn believes that "antiracists in the street struggle too. They don't necessarily feel part of a group or know who to talk to. Many of the Black people they come in contact with are not necessarily activists or maybe don't want to talk to white people right now. You are left out there. That can be a place of despair—trying to figure out how to get to the next step but not be the one as a white person to set the terms."

It is a daily challenge for Marilyn to make decisions about what she will and will not tolerate. When she faces disrespect, she has to ask herself if the resistance is worth it. "You make your little choices. You have to bite your teeth and make them sometimes. Well, a mother says, 'I have to go to work today. The boss says, You have to come or you will get fired.' You have to say, I am sorry. I have to stay home with my child. They are all terrible choices to be made every day. Ours are just more constrained and controlled. So you have to look inside of some of the control to find freedom."

Taking Cues from the Inside

Bonnie Kerness has been working against the brutality of the prison system for more than twenty years, and the lessons from prisoners have been her guide each step of the way. Since 1977, Bonnie has served as the associate director of the Criminal Justice Program at the American Friends Service Committee in Newark, and she is a board member of the World Organization against Torture/USA. She is also the coordinator of the National Campaign to Stop Control Unit Prisons. In all of these capacities her primary responsibility and commitment has been to be knowledgeable about prisoners' lives so that their testimonies and experiences form the basis of her strategies for action.

Much of her work has been spearheading a campaign to stop control units, prisons within prisons in which inmates are kept in isolation and sensory deprivation for twenty-three to twenty-four hours each day. The development of control units can be traced to the state response to the Civil Rights Movement, the anti–Vietnam War movement, and the prisoners' rights movement.[38] By 1974 both the federal prison in Marion, Illinois, and the California Department of Corrections had designed isolation sections. In 1983 the warden at Marion declared a state of emergency and instituted a prisonwide lockdown that lasted for years. In 1995 the Federal Bureau of Prisons opened an isolation unit at Florence, Colorado. Trenton State Prison has a control unit with ninety-six beds.[39] By 1996 there were forty control units in U.S. prisons, and there were many more facilities under construction that were either to include control units within the prison or were to be "supermax" prisons, which use sensory deprivation strategies throughout the facility. By 1997 Cook County Jail in Chicago had begun subjecting prisoners who had not yet been convicted to lockdown and sensory deprivation. A juvenile facility in New Jersey has also begun using control units.

Bonnie's work at the American Friends Service Committee includes counseling prisoners who are currently in control units, which means being available twenty-four hours a day to take phone calls, since it is often impossible for prisoners to know when they will be granted a fifteen-minute call. This work led her to begin writing and speaking widely about control units to document that "physical and mental torture are common through means such as humiliating anal probes, hogtying, beatings after restraint, enforced idleness, mail tampering, censorship of ethnic or political literature, and use of strip searching."[40]

Although guards' unions claim that isolation units provide them a safe working environment, Bonnie believes that such units also provide guards with a place in which to engage in unwitnessed torture.[41] Those in control units tend to be former members of the Black Panthers, BLA, Islamic militants, Puerto Rican supporters of independence, American Indian Movement (AIM) members, jailhouse lawyers, and prison activists.[42] As Hatari Wa'Haki, a political prisoner in a control unit in New Jersey, wrote, "You are not placed in the Management Control Unit for anything you've done, or are accused of doing, but for what you *might* do, or are *capable* of doing. In fact, under this criterion, prisoners can be placed in the Management Control Unit simply for enjoying a certain degree of respect, or for being held in high esteem by their fellow prisoners."[43] Ojore Nuru Lutalo, who is a New Afrikan anarchist prisoner of war, has been in the management control unit in New Jersey in total isolation since February 1986, and he has yet to receive an explanation for this isolation.[44] Ruchell Magee has been in a control unit for twenty years.[45] Russell Maroon Shoats has been in various control units in Pennsylvania for seventeen years.[46]

One of the most stunning aspects of the control units is that there is no due process used in establishing who is assigned to one. Bonnie writes, "In New Jersey's Management Control, for example, there is no entrance criteria nor is there an exit criteria. In other words, no official reason is given about why you are placed in the isolation unit nor is there any way for you to 'earn' your way out."[47] A Human Rights Watch report concluded that "perhaps the most troubling aspect of the human rights situation in United States prisons is a trend observed that could be labeled 'marionization' . . . Confinement in which inmates may in fact be sentenced twice: once by the courts to a certain period of imprisonment; and the second time by the prison administration, to particularly harsh conditions. . . . This second sentencing is open-ended—limited only by the overall length of an inmate's sentence and imposed without the benefit of counsel."[48]

Doing prison work has deeply influenced Bonnie's life as an activist and her commitment to justice. "The prison work has profoundly affected my struggle with who I am and who I want to be as I grow. Who I want to be like. I have learned so much. I am clearer about my own feelings. When I speak and write . . . I speak from my gut, from what I have seen. This is twenty years, and every day I am astounded at the level of cruelty that we pay for, that society pays for in its prison system."

From working with prisoners, Bonnie has also learned strategies for coping with the ebb and flow of progressive activism. "I picture the sixties and seventies as being crowded with folks like me, and then somewhere I turned around and there wasn't anybody. When I think about the activists I knew who stopped being activists, I couldn't understand it. I think that many folks who were activists in the sixties and seventies melded. They either melded into the middle-class as their economics got better, or they went into the women's movement or went off into the woods of Maine and into communes." That, of course, led Bonnie to understand the attitudes that activists of color may have about white activists. When "white activists get tired, they often go home to their middle-class lives. There is nothing that compels white activists to stay in the struggle. White activists generally don't see it as a protracted thing, whereas activists of color have no choice."

Sometimes Bonnie has fantasies of "selling scarves at Lord and Taylor or something on my bad days. Oh, just stick me behind a perfume counter." In reality, however, she doesn't believe she would know how to be any other way. "What has sustained me has been the sense that I have a responsibility to represent the people inside on the outside. They can't represent themselves. So that I have to be committed. I have to be credible. I have to maintain my credibility. I have to have a certain kind of strength on a daily basis whether or not I want it because I am representing very strong people. I work with people who I generally believe to be the leadership. I work with Sundiata Acoli. I work with Galil Bottom. Ojore Lutalo. Marilyn Buck. I think if I lived to be two hundred years old I could never be what they are in terms of their steadfastness, their principled and intelligent way of looking at things. My spirit comes from theirs."

The strength she is granted through working with prisoners, and her resolve about doing work she believes in, has been coupled with many political lessons about doing prison work as a white woman. Bonnie's early lessons from prisoners included their insistence that she openly deal with what it means for her to be working with Black and Latino prisoners. Although her consciousness about race began on the streets of New York in the late 1950s and continued through her work with civil rights activists in Tennessee in the 1960s, it was not until she started working with prisoners in the 1970s that she was asked to "study my own whiteness and intellectualize my own oppression as a woman." She says, for example, "that it is always difficult, particularly in prison work, for a white woman who is working in a world that is basically Black men. I think there is a sexual tension there." Over the years, Bonnie has learned the best way to deal with it is by being straightforward. "I say, this is what I am about. This is my work. This is my profession. Even if you and I know each other for fifteen years, we don't have a personal relationship. We have a political relationship, unless we choose to make it personal. But I am in this for political reasons."

Much of Bonnie's work comes from the Black prisoners and their families. "As a prison activist I need to be willing to take direction from family members, who are often Black women partners of the prisoners. If tensions between Black and white women that have historically existed come up, we try to deal with them directly. Often the family members and I brainstorm together about approaches to take.

Taking the lead from prisoners and their families is particularly important, since I then speak to white communities including correctional officers, medical workers, and social workers."

Working with prisoners has also forced Bonnie to deal with the harassment and surveillance often directed at prison activists. "Working with the political prisoner issue is itself a startling experience. I can come home and there will be a car parked outside. Obviously watching the house. When I call the police they will say they are on official business. I have taken my foster son in to visit a political prisoner, and all of a sudden his name and address show up on somebody's rap sheet who is the prisoner's brother. I have had a client picked up by the Essex County police and questioned about me and my relationship with prisoners." In response, Bonnie "collects the evidence, the pieces of paper. I fight it where I can." Recently Bonnie learned that the Department of Corrections in California had written a memo to a prisoner's central file including the accusation that she was a front for a Black militant organization. Bonnie contacted Ron Kuby (law partner of the noted human rights attorney Bill Kuntsler), who wrote a letter of protest. "But they are just so sleazy. There is no pinning them down. There is no addressing it. It wasn't a public document."

When I asked Bonnie if she spends her life bracing against the surveillance and harassment, she replied, "In the beginning I did. But what are they going to do, kill me? So then that makes me about as dead as all the other activists who have come before me. That is part of it. I work with revolutionaries, and in some sense I consider myself one. Imprisonment or dying is, you talk about the women who have come before us, well, this is a fact of life. So no, I am not tense about that. I get irritated. I get angry because if that surveillance is what I see, what comes to me, my gosh, imagine what goes on that doesn't come to me."

From Bonnie's perspective, "The opposition is very much different now than it was thirty years ago. Thirty years ago there was overt hatred. There were dogs. There was the whole media circus. I don't think we would ever see that again. I think they would just kill us. Either through genocide or what is going on now, with the Black leadership, who are behind walls or dead. Or neutralize us other ways. I think they are much better organized than they were years ago. I believe that they have very successful experiments in terms of infiltration with the Panthers. Breaking the back of the Movement was a very deliberate thing.

It was in the last fifteen, sixteen, seventeen years that the Left was de-funded, that most organizing throughout the country was stopped, that many levels of activism ceased. There was a terrible backlash. There were many other things that went on. They killed. I sat and would watch television. I would watch the news and I would watch them slaughtering my peers—civil rights activists and Black Panthers. My God. They are killing my peers. My generation. They are killing them. They are either killing them in Vietnam or killing them on the streets or in the inner cities. But killing them they are. Those are people my age that are now dead. That was the leadership. I understood that even in my twenties."

Bonnie believes that in some sense it is naive to talk about a movement now. She asserts, "Whatever aboveground movements we encourage now, we have to understand those will be acceptable to the government, because anything that is not acceptable must go underground. If we have learned nothing else in the past thirty years, we have to see that. They will kill us the second they feel we have become dangerous in any way, shape, or form. They will take care of that."

Although Bonnie is painfully cognizant of the multiple forces that continue to support the prison system, she is encouraged by the up-surge in activism sparked by the international campaign to gain a new trial for Mumia Abu-Jamal, a political prisoner who has been on death row since 1982. His sentence stems from his exposure of police brutality against MOVE, which police bombed in 1985 (in an attack that killed eleven residents and burned sixty homes in Philadelphia's Osage neighborhood). Since Abu-Jamal's trial, in which he was convicted of killing a police officer, lawyers and activists have worked to win him a new trial, based on the facts that he did not receive adequate representation, that the prosecution withheld crucial evidence, and that his political beliefs were used against him in the sentencing phase of the trial. While in prison, Abu-Jamal has become an internationally known writer and activist. Several heads of state, including Nelson Mandela, and many artists, intellectuals, and activists have campaigned for a new trial.[49]

According to Bonnie, "Mumia has had a remarkable impact on organizing. The Mumia campaign has been one of the most unifying initiatives in the history of this country. People from different generations, nationalities, religions, and political backgrounds have come together. Even folks who are not convinced of his innocence are unified in support for a new trial. The campaign has also drawn some badly needed attention to the race and class bias in the death penalty." From Bonnie's perspective, MOVE's work, which is at the center of the organizing, is what has made the campaign so effective. "There aren't many groups or people in this country who wholeheartedly live and breathe what they believe. MOVE does. You can see it in their healthy and politicized children. They reject bias, any bias, and they welcome all people who are willing to work with them. They are also an activist and spiritual group that continues to demonstrate tremendous courage. They are people who have had war waged on them. They lost children when the government bombed their community in 1985. And yet they are still as vocal and courageous as they were before. They are a model for all of us."

Bonnie is also encouraged to see whites being drawn into the work "in a very similar manner to how they were drawn into some of the other movements of the 1960s, including the Civil Rights Movement." As to why so many people have been drawn to Mumia's campaign, Bonnie says, "In addition to becoming a rallying cry because of his innocence, he has become a rallying cry because he is so out there with his writing, and his writings are great and help broaden people's understanding of the whole picture." At the same time, Bonnie is concerned about the opportunism and naïveté she sees among some of Mumia's supporters. The campaign has drawn people whom Bonnie refers to as the "lifestylists": "Folks who are involved as a lifestyle as opposed to a struggle. Have you seen white kids running about with punk hairdos and green hair and rings in their nose? I have had an opportunity to work with some of them, and they are not serious. Not in the least." From Bonnie's perspective, it is easy for some people to think they are part of a movement even when they are doing none of the work. Bonnie asks these people: "'What is your goal? What is your strategy? Who are you changing?' They think that organizing is throwing an event, and it is not. Not even close." From Bonnie's perspective, "Running around and yelling 'smash the state' is not necessarily productive in terms of organizing a mass movement. The young people have so much potential. We really need their long-term commitment."

Bonnie also believes that some groups are "basically in the business of keeping themselves going, of using Mumia." For example, of all the groups working with Mumia, Bonnie trusts the monetary dealings of only one: the MOVE activists. Money raised by MOVE activists goes to Mumia and the Black United Fund in Philadelphia. As for the rest of the groups, Bonnie says, "If you dig a little you cannot believe the amount of money that is not going to Mumia. It is something that aggravates particularly the older prisoners, the activist prisoners. For many of them, the campaign for Mumia Abu-Jamal is a number-one priority, both because he consistently rallies against abuses endemic to prisons and he has remained true to his politics despite the severe repression he has endured."

In addition to the upsurge in energy in support of Mumia Abu-Jamal, Bonnie has been heartened by two other shifts. One is the U.S. Senate's ratification in the early 1990s of two international treaties—the Convention against Torture and the Convention on the Elimination of Racial Discrimination—that take a strong stand against torture. These treaties have subsequently granted agencies inside and outside the United States the right to investigate reports of torture domestically. This monitoring has made more visible both how and why control units are, by their very design, a form of torture. Conceivably, an increase in documentation of abuse may lead certain government officials to at least show some restraint in building new control unit prisons.[50] The tide may be turning about the denial of torture in the United States as international standards continue to force the state to confront the abuse of prisoners. Bonnie believes it is crucial that lawyers who have been dealing with racial, ethnic, and gender discrimination by drawing upon domestic remedies become willing to apply international standards. "There are limits to what domestic approaches can do in the current environment, and the use of international standards can help overcome these barriers."[51]

A second change Bonnie has seen among prison activists is a shift in their ideological rationale for organizing against prisons. For many years activists have argued that prisons do not work: They do not "rehabilitate" those sentenced. Progressive organizations have documented the fact that conditions in prison often work against the support of physical, emotional, and spiritual well-being. But progressives who argue that prisons should be reformed because they do not deter crime are assuming that crime prevention is in fact the actual purpose. Prison activists are increasingly arguing that prisons do, in fact, work as they were designed to work, that although crime is the rationale the state uses to support the increase in the number of prisons, their real purpose is both political and economic. Bonnie writes, "I don't think that it is any accident that the crime rate, according to the Bureau of Justice Statistics, between 1980 and 1990 remained stable while the overall imprisonment rate went up 112 percent. Imprisonment rates for Black people are more than seven times higher than for white folks, with one out of every three males of Afrikan descent under some form of social control."[52] In reality, prisons are a response to deindustrialization and an upsurge of white supremacy, including an attempt to reinstate aspects of the chattel slavery of the nineteenth century. By imprisoning leaders of the Black Panther Party, BLA, AIM, and white dissident groups, prisons separate leaders on the inside from collective struggles on the outside. In the process, many of the characteristics of slavery that were abolished in 1865 are being reproduced, a reality made possible when the Thirteenth Amendment to the U.S. Constitution excluded from its purview people convicted of a crime.[53] Prisoners are not allowed to vote, earn a living wage, or choose freely whom they want to love, whether they want to procreate, and with whom they wish to associate religiously, politically, and culturally. They also currently have little or no recourse to protect themselves from multiple forms of abuse.

Framing the expansion of the prison industry in this way—as having economic and political functions that maintain racism—shifts the conversation from issues of decreasing crime and rehabilitation to questions of how joblessness in an advanced capitalist economy and white supremacy intersect. From that vantage point, control units not only counter civilized notions of how to treat people but also reflect a society founded on slavery and still upholding it, both north and south of the Mason-Dixon Line.

Lessons for the Long Haul

The experience of prison activists working both inside and outside prison suggests a number of important guidelines for white antiracists. First, a process of self-criticism and accountability needs to be embedded in everything activists do. The principles David Gilbert and his close friend Kuwasi Balagoon have tried to practice—"don't cave in to the pressure to renounce and do self-criticism so others can learn from your setbacks"—go to the heart of the constant education that many prison activists see as foundational for doing antiracist work. For David, not caving in while being scrupulous about self-criticism has meant both acknowledging the dogmatism of the Weather Underground and other white militant groups of the late 1960s and early 1970s and seeing how much the attacks from many sides contributed to that dogmatism.[54] He regrets that the codefendants of the Brinks trial were not able to publicly show their compassion for the family and friends of the police officers and Brinks guard who were killed, while he reminds people that one of the activists' allies, Mtayari Shabaka Sundiata, was killed by police within days of the Brinks event.[55] The relevance of this principle of self-criticism to white activists is that it demands grappling with contradictions and encourages people to move away from the either/or dichotomous thinking that undergirds white culture.

A second guiding principle relates to what it means to be an activist for the long haul. According to Bonnie, one of the biggest mistakes she sees white people make is believing that change will happen quickly. "White people," Bonnie says, "tend to get active for about twenty minutes" and then think that they have done the work. For Bonnie, it is one thing to attend a demonstration in front of a prison on a Saturday afternoon, and it is another thing entirely to live in a multicultural neighborhood, to have Black and Latino colleagues and bosses, to take political risks over the long run. For Marilyn and David, to be a person of honor is to be an activist whom people of color can trust, to be there when the going gets tough. One of the ways Bonnie believes it is possible to nurture a long-haul perspective is by linking seasoned activists with activists just starting out, a belief she put into practice through her Prison Activist Mentorship/Resource Program. The logic is that activists, especially beginners, often feel isolated from the rest of the world unless they are part of a supportive community. Prison activists in particular can feel cut off from people around them, who may not understand what drives them to this cause. These partnerships allow people to build political relationships for the long haul.

Another challenge prison activists identify is the need for whites to be committed to working with other whites who may be at very different levels of awareness about racism. Both David and Marilyn speak about lessons they learned while in prison about accepting white people where they are and then moving from there. David learned this lesson from Black activists who said, Slow down, don't come on so strong, try to see other white people's perspectives. For Marilyn, this consciousness is reflected in part in her poem "To the Woman Standing behind Me," whose last stanza reminds the reader that she hopes to stand in line again with the white woman who was resistant to Black History Month. In "Among the Things That Use to Be," poet Willie M. Coleman asks what happened to the energy that "fermented a revolution" when Black women spent hours together waiting at the hairdresser's, before Black women wore Afros and dreadlocks.[56] In another place and time, Marilyn asks if waiting in line can do the same, can be a step in "fermenting a revolution," even among those initially recalcitrant or backlogged in history.

Third, prison activists emphasize that the links between those outside and inside prison have to be strong and constant. Although activists on the outside can do some types of organizing and some getting the word out that those inside cannot, the radical edge in strategy and alliance building consistently comes from those inside prison. After I interviewed Bonnie Kerness, she sent me a packet of material she had put together to give me a sense of the issues she had been involved with in the preceding several months. Included in this packet was a ten-page handwritten letter from political prisoner Laura Whitehorn, in response to a packet of material from the National Campaign to Stop Control Unit Prisons that Bonnie had recently sent to her to review prior to publication.[57] Laura Whitehorn's letter begins, "First, you are all terrific! What a lot of work you accomplish. Thank you." That was followed by an eight-page respectful and thorough critique of the material, a critique that focused on three issues. First, she writes that the bulk of the Campaign to Stop Control Unit Prisons report focused on men's prisons, even though the increase in the number of women in prison is far outpacing the rise in the imprisonment of men. Laura Whitehorn saw the emphasis on men as a "big mistake" because it "ends up marginalizing women, leaves the analysis incomplete and fails to bring up the clearest example of how a control unit campaign can win, since both of the units that have been closed were in women's prisons. There is also an increasing number of women, both in and out of prison, who are organizing against abuses in prison, a reality that certainly makes sense to highlight."

Whitehorn's second critique of the campaign's report focuses on its "tendency to define control units by their conditions as opposed to their purpose." Whitehorn writes, "The prison system as a whole is intended to repress social and political struggle and to be part of carrying out a program of genocide against Third World populations inside the United States. . . . The repression is intended to prevent any kind of rebellion or disorder as well as to serve as a threat against future unrest." Although there are different mechanisms for control in each state and federal prison, "overall, I think that controlling the whole prison population is the point of these units—keeping resistance from growing and spreading." Laura Whitehorn continues, "I know you [Bonnie Kerness] agree with that, but it tends to get lost in some of the discussions of definition and the conditions rather than the purpose of the units."

Laura Whitehorn also cautioned the campaign not to conceptualize control units as primarily about breaking individuals. Although they do have an individual function, they serve a "collective purpose as well: to try to break the spirit of the prison population in general." On these three issues—women's activism, the purpose of control units, and the limits of an individualistic analysis—Laura Whitehorn's perspective clarified and strengthened the campaign's initial arguments. In this and other instances, Bonnie Kerness knows there is no substitute for insider knowledge as the primary means of getting to the heart of political struggle. This principle is important for white activists, since the majority of prisoners are people of color. In other words, recognizing the centrality of prisoners' perspectives not only provides an insider view in general but also maintains a commitment to leadership by people of color both inside and outside of prison.

Another example of the principle of taking cues from the inside comes from Betty and Herman Liveright, who publish a monthly newsletter, "This Just In: A Bulletin for News of Political Prisoners and Prisoners of War." In 1990 Betty and Herman resigned from their work as codirectors of the Berkshire Forum, a discussion center in New York that had been dealing with controversial social and political issues for eighteen years.[58] When they were well into their eighties, Betty and Herman bought a station wagon and drove across the country in order to interview political prisoners in twenty federal and state prisons. When I asked them why they did this work, they said they wanted to send a message to the progressive community that political prisoners need to be high on the progressive agenda. From their perspective, "Political prisoners have been locked up as payment for their social consciousness."[59] After hearing again and again that isolation is the number-one problem for political prisoners, the Liverights were prompted to produce a newsletter. After their trip they also wrote a book that focuses on political prisoners and the "criminal justice system"; the book includes an overview of the system and thirty-nine profiles of the Puerto Rican, African American, and white prisoners Betty and Herman met on their trip.

Since returning, Betty and Herman have stayed in touch with many of the political prisoners. They also speak passionately about the way their thinking has been influenced by this work. About his interview with Ray Luc Levasseur, who had been in the sensory deprivation unit at Florence, Colorado, for many years until his recent transfer to a prison in Georgia, Herman says, "While ideologically and methodologically Ray has not taught me a great deal, he has reinspired me with the potential of the human spirit and his tremendous respect for humanity." Ray was one of the Ohio Seven, who were arrested for their protests against the Vietnam War and racism. The Ohio Seven included people who decided protest must include sabotage and destruction of government property. They took every precaution possible to avoid injuring people when bombing government facilities. (They never injured anyone.) But they did take a definitive stance that violence was necessary, given the power of the state.

Ray's stance on violence "did not exactly sit right" with the Liverights, a divergence that Herman talked about with him at length. Herman remembers a particularly passionate discussion, when Ray was talking about the especially abominable treatment of African Americans during the Vietnam War. When Herman asked about the ethics of violence, Ray answered, "How can you not use violence?" When Herman told this story, his eyes filled with tears—a tribute to the tremendous respect he has for Ray's commitment to stand up for what he believes, even though that has meant long-term imprisonment in solitary confinement.

Regardless of where people come down on the issue of violence as a form of protest, what moved me about this scene was how powerful political exchange can be in helping people see divergent perspectives. In this instance, it was a combination of Betty and Herman Liveright's passionate commitment to travel around the country to learn about prison activism from those who know it best and Ray Luc Levasseur's willingness to spell out his principles, time and time again, that made such an exchange possible. Three people talking, head to head, about justice, accountability, and multiple strategies for achieving them. Ray's interview with me was a twenty-page, single-spaced, handwritten letter answering my questions, written while he was in isolation at Florence.

Although the escalation of the prison industry is unprecedented in U.S. history and support for criminalization and the construction of new prisons continues unabated, prison activists have won some of their struggles. In 1979 BLA members and white anti-imperialists, including Marilyn Buck, freed Assata Shakur from prison, enabling her to flee to Cuba, where she was granted political asylum and has continued to do activist work. In 1990 activists and lawyers were able to win the release of Dhoruba Bin Wahad, after a court-ordered release of FBI documents demonstrated that his 1973 conviction was unlawful on many accounts. In 1997 Geronimo Pratt, also a former Black Panther, was released after twenty-seven years in prison when a judge acknowledged flagrant violations by witnesses and the prosecution during his trial.[60] In 1989, after three years of protests, activists won their fight to close the control unit at the federal prison in Lexington, Kentucky, where women were kept in isolation in cells thirty feet below ground and designed to eliminate all external stimulus, including fresh air, smell, sound, and access to human voices and touch.[61] In 1990 an activist group in Chicago sponsored an international tribunal in New York, where well-known jurists heard the cases of many political prisoners, an action that brought badly needed attention to the struggles of prisoners in general and political prisoners in particular. In 1999 eleven Puerto Rican political activists were released from prison by President Clinton, who acknowledged that their sentences far exceeded their alleged crimes. The campaign to gain a new trial for Mumia Abu-Jamal has garnered much attention in the United States and internationally; the case is on a par with that of Ethel and Julius Rosenberg in terms of its political significance.

Support for political prisoners continues to be one of many activist priorities, along with the struggle against police brutality, race and class bias in sentencing, abuses in prison, and the inequities embedded in the government's war on drugs. Amid the continued growth of prisons and the ideology used to justify it, chronicling the examples of activist victories remains crucial.

10

Power, Power, Who's Got the Power?

One of the biggest challenges for activists in the 1980s and 1990s is to do work—both paid and otherwise—that will further progressive race-conscious social change in a period of significant backlash. A number of people I interviewed who had been involved in unpaid, full-time activism in the 1960s, when they were in their teens and twenties, had families to support by the 1970s and 1980s. These responsibilities persuaded activists to do paid work, primarily in multiracial organizations.[1] Most of these organizations are nonprofits, doing much of what federally and state-funded programs were doing in the 1960s and 1970s. Dawn Gomes, who works with a nonprofit, sees "nonprofits as one of the fronts against the total brutality of the state." Essentially, Dawn explains, "they've taken on the role of the government for half the dollars and with half the resources."

Activist work in multiracial nonprofits creates a number of political challenges in sustaining progressive agendas while trying to keep organizations financially afloat. Funding sources that come with strings attached can put a real crimp in a transformative politic. Those working in multiracial organizations also grapple with issues of representation, namely, how to create and sustain priorities that emerge directly from the communities with which they work. Their struggles also often include identifying how organizations can still feel "white" in terms of assumptions made and priorities held even when racial parity is met.

In his recent reflections on confronting racism within organizations based on his thirty-plus years as an organizer, Si Kahn writes, "Time and again, work forces, memberships, student bodies, faculties, staffs, boards, organizations, institutions, networks, and coalitions are torn apart by conflicts over race and racially related issues. Energy and commitment that could be applied to addressing critical social issues of shared concern is dissipated within internal struggles. Work on critical and difficult divisions such as gender, class, and sexuality are often complicated by racial dynamics."[2] How people deal with power dynamics within organizations is often a window into what undermines their work in communities.

Although those I interviewed enumerate multiple challenges facing multiracial nonprofits—all of which merit in-depth discussion—my first focus in this chapter is on racial power sharing in several nonprofits. My interest in the topic is partly fueled by the emergence of this theme in previous decades. The complications of white leadership arose in the Student Nonviolent Coordinating Committee (SNCC) when white people who worked in white communities had difficulty maintaining close ties with Black SNCC workers in the process. The problem with sharing power manifested itself again in white militant organizations that, though they were ostensibly working in solidarity with Black nationalist groups, often remained only vaguely accountable to Blacks. It manifested itself in the 1960s and '70s when white people gained experience in Black-run activist groups and then took jobs supervising programs in Black communities. It showed up again in Central America solidarity work when activists postponed or de-emphasized the importance of making alliances with African American and domestic Latino groups.

I follow a discussion of power in nonprofits with an analysis of the efficacy of antiracism training as a method of supporting racial justice. My interest here stems from the influence of such training in shaping the discourse about race in a wide range of settings throughout the United States: in the corporate sector, in education, and in nonprofits. As is true of my discussion of racial representation in nonprofits, my focus on antiracism training in the 1980s and 1990s also has historical resonance. Contradictions embedded in this approach to racial justice reflect reoccurring challenges for white antiracists, challenges having to do with white complicity, the efficacy of antiracist initiatives in capitalist settings, and the work required to ensure long-term change.

Multiracial Organizations

Among those I interviewed, most believe that white people should not ultimately be in charge in multiracial contexts, or if it is absolutely necessary that they be in the highest leadership position, it should be only for very limited periods of time. Most of the people I interviewed who work in nonprofits are on the staff but are not the directors. Several have been key members of organizations that made a transition from being white dominated to being multiracial, with either racial parity or Black or Latino leadership in the top positions. The lessons they have learned working in these organizations have been invaluable; many pivot on experiencing what it means to be a key member of an organization but not the boss. Or as Laurie Schecter says, "The point for white people is not to be the leader of a movement for social change but to be an ally."

As a member of several social change organizations over the years, Laurie Schecter is especially enthusiastic about how power was shared at the Haymarket People's Fund, a progressive funding organization in Boston. Laurie believes the organization upheld a structure and process that modeled principles of race and class equity. The funding board, which Laurie was asked to join, consisted entirely of community activists. This board decided which organizations would receive grants but was separate from the donor board, which provided funding but did not have any control over how the money was spent. The first group largely comprised people of color, including straight as well as gay people and people from a range of religious backgrounds. With the Haymarket Fund, Laurie said, "I really felt a part of something. I felt we were all working for something together. The diversity within the group sparked animated conversation and made room for people to talk openly about the hard issues."

Laurie believes that the structure of the fund also encouraged dynamic and intellectually engaging power sharing that nurtured further community alliances. "The money that was being given to the community, the decisions that were being made, were by people who lived in those communities." Organizations that were funded would come to the office and share their knowledge with the board, and board members would go in pairs to organizations, "not to decide if they were doing a good job" but to understand how they did their work. The pairs would then talk with the other board members about what they had learned. Laurie found this process thrilling. She learned about a range of exciting progressive projects in the 1980s. The success of the Haymarket funding board, however, did not come without a struggle. In the late 1980s the board members began to openly confront the fact that even in a multiracial group, "whiteness and white culture still dominated." According to Laurie, this struggle left the board "in a hard transition as they tried to change these dynamics."

The sense of being part of something but not in charge of it was a theme I heard many times from people who work in multiracial organizations. Sarah Stearns has been working with an antiracist training organization, Vigorous Interventions in Ongoing Natural Settings (VISIONS), for twelve years and says working there has been "a huge gift in my life. As a white person working in an organization led by two African American women in a very Afrocentric-based model, it was so challenging for me initially because I came to the group using some of the old tactics I would use in any group to try to establish myself." For example, when Sarah first joined the group, she "wanted to have a lot of voice" and to be recognized for her expertise as a psychotherapist. "I could protect myself, is the way I look at it, if I was the one who was naming what was going on." Other consultants quickly confronted Sarah's approach because "it protected me from being reflected upon and it also kept me from staying really connected to those places where I would get scared, at a loss, or overwhelmed."

As a white person, Sarah had been trained to assume an observer position and to analyze things from the point of view of finding "the critical flaw." This training started in childhood at the dinner table, where Sarah learned she was in a safer position emotionally if she was "the one who commented rather than the one who was commented upon." It was safer for Sarah to be the observer or to be in charge rather than to simply let the conversation unfold. In VISIONS Sarah found herself repeating that pattern. If there was a conflict between two people during a meeting among the consultants, Sarah believed the way to be helpful was to try to point out some aspect of the way they were relating to each other. The demand from the organization, however, was "that I be there from my own experience." Instead of trying to help explain interactions between other people, the group asked Sarah to think about what the exchange made her think or feel about herself.

Her work with VISIONS led Sarah to reflect upon the ways growing up in a white family in a white community had limited her emotionally. "In my family, there was much emotional constriction. The band of what was safe, even the joyful side, like laughing too loud, was labeled self-panicking. . . . I just learned not to be out there." In VISIONS the "flow of emotions can be so intense and move so rapidly between rage and laughter, that they are fully embodied in the conversation." People in the group would ask Sarah to talk about what was hard for her about participating. As Sarah sees it, "One of the contributions of this exchange is that other people in the group who haven't had that cultural level of emotional constriction get a chance to be much more empathic to what it means for me to come out of that more formal or more constricted shell because they watch me do it. That then informs their work with other white people instead of just getting mad at them. It becomes a vehicle for their understanding." That VISIONS was founded and run by African American women and that the organization "affirms emotions" has opened Sarah up to bigger and "more out there" ways of living in the world.

John Capitman, who also works with VISIONS, says that although they have contemplated the possibility of a white person serving as the director of the group, it has never been a real option, given the importance of African American leadership in their approach to training. Both VISION's internal mechanisms for building community within the group and its approach to trainings themselves depend upon a model that is African American led.

For many people I interviewed, the ability of multicultural organizations to move beyond white cultural norms is coupled with the synergism such diversity makes possible. Dawn Gomes gave a good example of this in describing her work with a nonprofit organization that focuses on emergency preparedness. Dawn began doing recovery work through a cultural exchange program after an earthquake in Mexico in 1985. She started learning how communities can prepare for disasters. From day one, when she began working with the Emergency Services Network in northern California, she "loved it. . . . I went to the first meeting and there were eighty people in the room representing all these different agencies and every class and ethnic group. It was just so working-class and diverse and multiracial, and I thought, yes. This is where I want to be." From the beginning, the staff's responsibility was to bring together a range of nonprofit organizations that in one way or another would be needed to provide relief in the event of a natural disaster. This required close collaboration with many language-specific organizations—the Asian Community Center, the Oakland Chinese

Community Council, a Spanish-speaking citizen's foundation—along with disability rights organizations.

Because the organization worked with a range of communities, Dawn and others defined "emergency" broadly to include those caused by environmental disasters, such as earthquakes, fires, and spills, as well as daily personal disasters, such as homelessness and hunger. How the government responds to communities during disasters, and even what is counted as a disaster tend to reflect systemic inequities. Dawn says, "Disasters have been used as a launch pad for some very reactionary laws." For example, the Federal Emergency Management Agency (FEMA) recently passed a "really fascist law" that does not allow any disaster benefits to non-English-speaking people or to undocumented workers. After a recent earthquake in Los Angeles, "hysteria started rising about undocumented people there, immigrants in L.A. who were getting benefits." From Dawn's perspective, "It was really important that nonprofits and community organizations be on the front line as advocates for people to fight for immigrants' rights to emergency services, health care, and education."

The network also helps communities become self-sufficient, which is especially important during environmental disasters, when whole communities run the risk of being ignored by government services or of having any aid they do receive managed without sufficient community input. Dawn and her colleagues create plans to provide emergency quarters ranging from shelter housing to replacement housing. They work on linking clinics with hospitals, and they have a program to train bilingual youth in all aspects of emergency preparedness. After young people design training procedures, they teach their families and communities. The agency also provides internships in emergency-management fields, including emergency medical services and fire fighting, so that diverse groups have skills to care for themselves and their communities. In all these efforts, multiracial and multilingual representation is crucial. A top-down, hierarchical, white-led structure would be antithetical to the network's mission.

The overwhelming majority of people I interviewed believe that doing antiracist work with integrity as a white person requires working in groups in which people of color are fully represented at every level of authority. White people need to be able to work alongside and to take leadership from people of color. Most people I interviewed believe that in a white supremacist society, white people should not occupy the most powerful position in any organization that calls itself multiracial and is about the work of racial justice. A few, however, believe there comes a point in a white activist's development when it would be dishonest and disingenuous to turn down the highest leadership position as long as it is with the support of people of color. A few people I interviewed are executive directors, presidents, or founding directors of multiracial organizations (or are in a position in which all the people above them in the hierarchy are white). They see potential challenges for white people who are in charge of a project that focuses on racial justice. Yet they believe there are various reasons to continue.

Dorothy Stoneman, founder and president of YouthBuild USA, believes it is acceptable for white people to lead organizations if they understand how to share power and if they anticipate how the outside world may try to manipulate the situation. Dorothy founded YouthBuild USA after living in Harlem for twenty years and working in the East Harlem Block Schools. YouthBuild USA functions as a national support center for local YouthBuild programs, partly by raising money from the federal government. As of 1998 it had raised about 158 million dollars, which was distributed to local community-based programs. These programs engage with young people who have dropped out of school by running alternative schools, where they can earn their GEDs or high school diplomas while working half-time on construction sites to rehabilitate housing for homeless people. The program is designed to be governed by young people so that they can learn to be leaders.

In YouthBuild USA, Dorothy has made sure the majority of the board of directors and the staff are people of color at every level, since the majority of the youth are people of color.[3] According to Dorothy, "Probably, we are the only national organization I can think of with white leadership that has a national board of directors and staff that are majority people of color. I have done that as a matter of principle. Since it is an organization designed for young people, they are also on the board of directors and on staff."

At times that principle has been difficult to uphold, particularly when YouthBuild has had to hire quickly. "There may be a department that slipped into being a little more white than people of color. It is also hard because, although we have decentralized hiring, I have had to be sure that other people are maintaining a balanced staff. That is kind of illegal, not at the level of the board but in hiring. We have had to search and keep searching to make sure that our pool includes people of color and be intentional about that. We did not want to just drift into being a predominantly white organization."

Over the years, some people have thought Dorothy should be more cautious about the organization's affirmative-hiring methods. Dorothy believes practicing affirmative action is simply obvious: An organization must reflect the community it serves. In defense of this stance, she says, "If someone is going to take me to court for that, I will made the argument in the court. Take me to the Supreme Court and I will make the argument there. You have a right to form an organization that counteracts centuries of oppression. I don't advertise it. I just do it. And other managers need to just do it also."

As a white leader, Dorothy has to be careful in working with the media to ensure the organization is not misrepresented. Typically, reporters and analysts want to focus attention on Dorothy, a tendency she abhors. "The white world is so desperate to have positive white role models, and they make it seem like a 'good' white person is the reason anything good is going on. The media will make the African American professionals and activists invisible and attribute all good things to the white person as a way of justifying white people's existence." ABC and NBC only want to interview Dorothy, or if they do interview African American activists, only the section about Dorothy is broadcast. "That has a negative effect on what we are trying to do. So we have to lecture the press. Do not feature the white director. Do not feature me."

Dorothy has also learned to anticipate and correct the way the media typically portrays YouthBuild. *Newsweek*'s first article on the organization reported that YouthBuild serves only African Americans and that the organization does not believe in racial mixing. Dorothy immediately wrote a letter protesting this portrayal, explaining, "We are not trying to build an island of Black activists, just because we are majority Black." While stressing that YouthBuild is multiracial, Dorothy also consistently argues for the need for funding for all-Black programs. She has heard national public-policy officials say they favor integration as justification for not funding African American programs or community-based programs in segregated neighborhoods. "They argue that they are only going to fund programs that bring middle-class young people together with low-income young people so they can be integrated. I am saying, You are out of your minds. This is racist.

They are saying integration—and this is the liberals—and they have not learned how inside-out the liberal line is. So it took us three years to establish this public policy that would fund community-based organizations in low-income communities." As to her racial position among policy makers, Dorothy explains, "At this point, I am sort of an infiltrator. I am sort of quick to see where things are off and then I bring it to people's attention."

Although Dorothy believes that most of the people of color she works with have supported her as president of YouthBuild there have been controversies. One example she gives is of a struggle that occurred after she had founded the Youth Action Program in Harlem, the predecessor to YouthBuild. The project had attracted highly political people. She explains, "On our staff we had a Black nationalist, a Communist, a Maoist, a cocounselor, a born-again Christian, a democratic socialist." By accident Dorothy "had attracted a rather difficult group of staff. Two or three of the people began to assert the idea that I shouldn't be there. They didn't say it to me. You know how it goes. It goes underground first. So I began to get calls from people outside of the organization saying, 'Dorothy, are you aware that some of your staff are agitating against your leadership?'" Eventually Dorothy spoke with one of the Black nationalists on staff, the leader of the dissenters. Dorothy said, "'Look, I am not leaving. You can't run me out with this antiwhite stuff. Is there anyone else on this staff whom you think should run this organization?' He said 'No, not really.' So, I said, 'What is the point in driving me out? As soon as there is someone who can run it, I will leave, I will turn it over to them. I don't feel committed to being in charge forever.' I still think it is better if people of color are in charge of their own organizations. . . . I did, unfortunately, fire him because he was doing a pretty poor job." From Dorothy's perspective, there were people—who tended to be politicized Black nationalists— who said Dorothy should not have lasting power. But according to Dorothy, "The regular people who lived in the community, who were politically sophisticated but not politically rigid, were saying, Don't be silly. We have a multiracial context here."

When Dorothy did attempt to turn the organization over to a man of color, the board of directors, all of whom were people of color, would not accept her resignation. The board's position, according to Dorothy, was that she was trying to resign for the wrong reason: because she was white. They argued that Dorothy was more streetwise than the man who would have replaced her and that she had built the organization. Dorothy believed the board members were telling her to "grow up. I sort of grew up. A couple of other people I respect said similar things, and I decided that I am subordinate to the community for a reason. This board is telling me not to do something because I am white."

Dorothy believes that many people with leftist politics, especially women, have an aversion to power, an aversion she believes undermines progressive activism. When the board refused to accept her resignation, she had to be honest about her fear of power. Earlier in her life, when she was working in Harlem, African American and Latino friends took her aside and said, "Don't stay because you are white, and don't leave because you are white. That is the wrong reason to do that." She has taken this advice to heart ever since.

Eric Mann also believes it is acceptable for certain white people to direct multiracial organizations. In his own case he reasons that he has in effect earned the position. Currently he is the director of the Labor/ Community Strategy Center in Los Angeles, which he describes as "a multiracial think tank/act tank committed to building democratic, internationalist, left social movements." For Eric, the issue about white people's position within multiracial organizations largely depends upon their prior experience working with people of color. Eric says he "worked under the leadership of people of color for thirty years." He was one of the only whites in a predominantly Black chapter of Congress of Racial Equality (CORE) in the mid-1960s in New York. "I was brought into the leadership of the Civil Rights Movement at the highest level of leadership of a predominantly Black organization in the Joe Slovo model."[4] He worked under the leadership of the Chicano president of a United Auto Workers Union local for eight years and under the leadership of the African American president of a union at a Ford plant in California.

People of color radicalized Eric as a young activist and have taught him all his life. He believes it makes sense that in his fifties he would be an elected director of a multiracial organization. In addition, he made it clear that the people who chose him for the position were people of color. As Eric understood their logic, he was not being asked to be "the director of a party or a revolution, just the director of one organization." Those who chose him also argued that he "was already playing an important leadership role, so his appointment was not a radical departure from before." And although he has the final say on decisions, he and the staff, which is predominantly people of color, have constant discussions about the little and big decisions involved in running the organization.

Eric says, "Part of the problem with white people—the ongoing debate that is really at the core of the issue—is whether there is a basis for equality among white and Black people." As Eric sees it, "White people oscillate between condescension and servility, arrogance and servility, and very few find their own legs in those relationships." He portrays accepting his role as the director of the Labor/Community Strategy Center as one way of using his legs. Like Dorothy Stoneman, Eric believes this position requires him to be constantly wary of the media's tendency to place disproportionate attention on him.

Several of the people I interviewed took exception to the idea of white people running multiracial organizations over the long haul. Dottye Burt-Markowitz's perspective on this issue comes from lessons she learned from a troubling situation at the Piedmont Peace Project. This organization was founded in 1984 by Linda Stout, a white woman who grew up in the Piedmont region of North Carolina. Stout had become interested in the peace movement and was a board member of SANE/Nuclear Freeze Campaign, a middle-class, white-dominated peace organization. Stout, a working-class woman, wanted to start a community-empowerment organization that would work to help low-income people develop the skills to speak for themselves and their communities.[5] After meeting and working with Stout, Dottye was asked to be on the board of directors of the Piedmont Peace Project, and she worked closely with the project for several years.

While working with the board members, most of whom were African American, and the staff, which was half African American and half white, Dottye came to understand that Stout was having increasing trouble sharing power in the organization. Part of the difficulty revolved around raising funds. Dottye explains, "Linda has always kept issues of fund-raising to herself. So she was the one who had personal relationships with all of these major donors. The staff was really pushing for that to be broadened, for some of the board members to become involved in the fund-raising projects." Stout was unwilling to do that.

Another controversy at Piedmont Peace Project centered around Klan harassment. The organization had put much effort into protecting Stout personally from possible Klan violence and harassment. Over time, Dottye says, "It started feeling to the staff that everything was going to [Linda Stout], not to the organization. . . . She wasn't the only one doing this work in an area that was dangerous." Dottye believes that Stout's "personal trauma from the Klan harassment gave her a way to manipulate the entire organization." From Dottye's perspective, the board and the staff worked diligently for a year and a half, to no avail, to iron out these issues. Finally, the board recommended that Stout resign as executive director.

Despite all the evidence the staff and board members offered for the need for a change in leadership, a small group of white members and donors backed Stout. To Dottye, this response was a stunning and painful example of maintaining white alliances at the expense of constructive across-race work. "I learned a lot about the capacity of white people to betray people of color and my own capacity to be blind to the kinds of racism that were happening because they were masked by what seemed to be a real effort to overcome classism. And [I learned about] the tremendous capacity of people of color to remain allies to people of color despite what I felt was horrendous betrayal." Part of what exacerbated the whole situation was the "incredible power of a charismatic leader." Dottye was shocked at seeing white people who seemed to understand oppression but who, nevertheless, listened to one charismatic white woman instead of listening to many board members, all of whom were low income and most of whom were African American. "For so many of these white middle-class activists, donors, and supporters of the organization to go with that one person was so stark. It was incomprehensible to me."

Despite this major break in the organization, the Piedmont Peace Project survived, although some of the donors left with Linda Stout. Having had time to reflect upon the process, Dottye now feels that any time she "becomes involved in an organization, either paid work or as a volunteer, that is started by one leader—whether charismatic or not—I would want to ask them at the outset, what their plan is for moving themselves out of the leadership position within five to six years. I would at least want to know how they answer that question."

The racial power dynamics that Dottye witnessed at the Piedmont Peace Project do not mean that all white people who head multiracial organizations will be unable to see if they abuse power. The people I interviewed who now head multiracial organizations raise a number of important points about white leadership. Certainly there is no monolithic position among African Americans or Latinos about whether white people can or should have leading authority within organizations. Eric Mann was appointed by people of color, and both he and Dorothy Stoneman have a majority of people of color on their boards and staff. Dorothy may also be correct in her assertion that progressive women often run from power—a reality perhaps fueled by skepticism toward hierarchical organizations in general. Progressive women who assume powerful positions may be in an especially vexed position, considering the deadly female socialization that teaches women to work amid but never in front of others. Eric's and Dorothy's stories also raise the question of whether deciding not to be the director of a multiracial organization—when the group supports such leadership—fails to take seriously the right and power of people of color to make decisions about leadership and the future directions of organizations.

At the same time, sirens go off in my head when I hear people say there were no people of color who could have taken over or that the board of directors would not let a white person resign. Furthermore, the influence executive directors can exert on the makeup of a board, particularly in an organization founded by that director, makes me wonder whether conflicts of interest might weaken a board's autonomy in warning or firing an executive director. I am also wary of a president's power to fire staff—what Dorothy Stoneman eventually did to the man who initially questioned her right to be an authority in a predominantly Black and Latino group. Although the firing may have been legitimate, job performance and politics are necessarily intertwined in multiracial organizations, which may well hinder level-headed decisions about hiring and firing. I wonder, too, about the potential problems when Eric Mann (and other activists) see themselves as having been "chosen" to be in leadership positions. Might there be some problem with the logic of being among the "chosen few," among the "good whites," among the very few whites African Americans were said to trust?

Although there may not be one right answer to the issue of white people's positions within multiracial organizations, a mathematical equation offered by Anne Braden remains instructive about the limits of white leadership: "The way this society is, white people have a limited view of the world. We have to. Our experience is different. We are just incomplete. We can't have a view of the world that you have if you are Black . . . or Latino or Native American. If you don't have that view of the world, things look different and you just can't simulate that. A bunch of white people sitting in a room are likely to be 90 percent wrong on 90 percent of the questions 90 percent of the time. Not because we are stupid but because our life experience is not the key life experience in this society."

Antiracism Training: From the Streets to the Boardrooms

Antiracist training constitutes another area in which several people I interviewed have been working since the 1980s.[6] The extent to which this work serves as a form of activism, however, is complicated. Clearly, it lacks the straightforward activist agenda that emerged out of SNCC, North Carolinians against Racist and Religious Violence, the Committee in Solidarity with the People of El Salvador (CISPES), and other organizations tied directly to social movements. In these organizations, activism was intentional and central. The same cannot be said for antiracism training. In fact, getting into the corporate or nonprofit door in order to do training sometimes requires soft-pedaling, if not totally minimizing, an activist agenda. At the same time, I include attention to this work partly because antiracism training has long been and continues to be one of the few contexts in which many white people deal with issues of racism and inequality. When a corporation such as DuPont or Mobil Oil hires trainers to provide workshops on race and gender equity to employees at all levels of operation, space is opened up for discussion and networking that might otherwise not exist. And as it turns out, mainstream organizations are not the only groups that seek antiracist training. Frequently, progressive organizations that espouse a total commitment to racial equity still tend to be white-heavy at the top. A second reason I focus on training sessions is that, at least in the ideal, they are important components of support for affirmative action in hiring, recruitment, and retention. Historically, affirmative action has been a crucial step in moving toward racial equity in organizations.

Although training about race and racism in organizations date back to the 1940s and 1950s (in the U.S. Army, in police departments, and elsewhere), the growth of this approach to dealing with racism has skyrocketed since the 1960s. To a large extent, the initial impetus for these training sessions came from corporate executives and middle management who recognized the legal imperative to hire more African Americans and white women following the Equal Pay Act of 1963, the Civil Rights Act of 1964, and the Fair Housing Act of 1968.[7] Early antidiscrimination training educated employees about steps required to comply with federal and state laws, including the implementation of affirmative action guidelines, sexual harassment policies, and, later, the Americans with Disabilities Act.

Corporate concern about meeting federal regulations regarding equal opportunity and antidiscrimination laws dovetailed with the late 1960s growth of Black/white encounter groups and attention in the field of social psychology to organizational development. Added to these influences was a growing push in academic settings for multicultural education, which was spearheaded by activist work to institute African American and women's studies programs and departments, and to facilitate education for staff, administrators, and students about affirmative action and sexual harassment. All these efforts were supported by civil rights activism, which refused "business as usual" segregation in health care, corporations, social services, and education. For some of these activists, working for social change included trying to transform institutions from within—their structure, politics, and cultures.[8]

What is important about this chronology is that the origins of antiracism training came from several directions: from corporate heads who saw compliance and antidiscrimination training as insurance against lawsuits; from clinical and academic research in social psychology and in organizational development; from the push for multicultural education in the academy; and from activists with experience in progressive social movements (primarily the Civil Rights Movement and feminism).

Although this range of influences had the potential to facilitate conversation and action about race in many arenas simultaneously, in reality the activist roots of this work have largely been superseded by the emergence of what Chandra Mohanty has called "the race industry": a multimillion dollar industry that "is responsible for the management, commodification, and domestication of race" on college campuses as well as throughout corporate America.[9]

Beginning in the 1980s and increasingly since, the best-funded and farthest-reaching approach uses "diversity training" as an umbrella term to describe what is in effect a business model for "managing diversity." This industry protects corporations and nonprofits from antidiscrimination suits while maximizing corporate profits. With this approach, as Mohanty explains, "managing diversity" is a "semantic gem that suggests that 'diversity' (a euphemism for people of color) will be out of control unless it is managed."[10] Current books and popular exercises for trainers and those attending workshops include *Diversity Bingo Training Kit, We Connect: A Relationship Building Activity,* and *Managing Workplace Diversity: Turning Difference into Competitive Advantage.*[11] Within this model, such language as "cashing in on diversity" and "a systematic overview of diversity measurement" is used unabashedly to describe why corporations should fund consultants to help ensure a smooth-running and legally compliant organization.[12]

Although the exercises and presentations in diversity training celebrate people's many talents and cultural backgrounds, their intention is to diffuse conflict and cover over stark and subtle forms of stratification. According to Patti DeRosa, a critic of this training model, the "cashing in on diversity" consultants not only say diversity is a more evolved form than affirmative action, but they also use the language of diversity to distance themselves from affirmative action. Diversity teams learn quickly that it is the kiss of death to have anything to do with affirmative action officers.[13]

Some diversity teams go so far as to present affirmative action as the cause of racism, a position that completely undermines racial equity. Diversity is typically pitched as a new phenomenon in the United States rather than a new phenomenon for corporations, which have systematically barred people of color from white-collar positions until political activism and civil rights legislation in the 1960s forced them to open their doors (a crack). As Avery Gordon writes, presenting diversity as new "allows the corporation to ignore the fact that it was instrumental in keeping American business more homogeneous than American society. . . . Thus the sudden discovery of diversity is simultaneously the repression of corporate racism, the history of the corporate demand for racial/gender homogeneity and stratification."[14]

Accompanying and in some instances in combination with what Patti DeRosa calls the "cashing in on diversity" approach to training is a psychological model of training. This model includes a "prejudice reduction" approach, which has its roots in reevaluation counseling; a "modeling differences" approach, which recognizes difference as a "fuel for creativity and innovation"; transactional analysis; and neo-Freudian concepts of human development.[15] At its core, the psychological model assumes that getting along in a multicultural world is contingent upon learning to feel comfortable with and to respect each other, a reality made possible when people who are different get to know each other in safe and supportive environments. The idea is that people often come to relationships as adults with scripts formed through early interactions with or socialization about people who are different from them, scripts that get in the way of honest and equal relationships until the old patterns of interaction are recognized and discarded.

Although this model, like the "cashing in on diversity" model, allows people to talk about race, gender, and ethnicity, its concern is not with leading people to collectively confront the capitalist white culture that dominates corporate life. For example, the psychological model leaves little room for a critique of free trade, which undermines collective organizing within companies and universities. Nor is the history of oppression of African Americans, Native Americans, or Chicanos a central aspect of the sessions. As Chandra Mohanty explains, the prejudice-reduction workshops "domesticate race and difference by formulating problems in narrow, interpersonal terms and by rewriting historical contexts as manageable, psychological ones."[16] Those who use the psychological model rarely provide an anticapitalist analysis, and they rarely disrupt the notion that hierarchies within organizations are inevitable.

Like the "cashing in on diversity" model and the psychological model, a third model, the antiracism model, is sometimes used in corporate settings and does draw on social psychology (in its use of small-group interactions, respect for intrapsychic processes, and recognition of connections among intellectual, cognitive, and emotional learning). Unlike the other models, though, its ultimate agenda decidedly centers on racial justice.[17] Trainers typically work in gender-balanced, biracial, or multiracial teams and offer training to schools, foundations, factories, and other businesses interested in creating a positive, multicultural environment. Although there are variations in the models used by antiracism trainers, generally they assume that dealing with the dynamics of oppression means learning not only how oppression works on a cognitive level but also how it is experienced (the feelings connected with being discriminated against or dominating others).

Among the best-known and longest-standing of these organizations are the People's Institute for Survival and Beyond in New Orleans and Challenging White Supremacy in San Francisco. In general these groups recognize that "diversity" is a catchword that is primarily about numbers. In these training organizations, "power," "oppression," and "activism" are key concepts.[18] The emphasis goes beyond promoting diversity to looking at traditional power structures and the ways institutional processes support hierarchy. Among those I interviewed who do training for corporate and nonprofit organizations, all draw upon an antiracist model. Although some see the limits of training sessions, for various reasons they see the work as a piece of the process of moving an antiracist agenda forward.

The theory behind this training is that race consciousness requires talking openly about what hinders cross-race alliances, scrutinizing the way power is distributed within an organization, and creating a more equitable environment. When an organization hires antiracism consultants, trainers work with staff to identify and confront discrepancies between what the organization says it wants to do and what it is actually doing. Dottye Burt-Markowitz offers an example of this through her work with the American Association of University Women (AAUW), a national organization based in Washington, D.C., and committed to women's education and gender equity. AAUW, which had already been through a series of sessions with another training institute, contacted Dottye's organization, whose workshops focus on racism, classism, heterosexism, internalized oppression, and the dynamics of power and leadership in U.S. history. AAUW had been very effective in producing literature that reflects racial and ethnic diversity. The reality, however, according to Dottye, is that the membership is still 95 percent white and the staff leadership is 100 percent white. Although the staff overall has racial parity (50 percent white and 50 percent people of color), the vast majority of the people of color are in the lowest positions in the organization. Dottye explains that AAUW is "in this stage where the rhetoric is there, the desire is there, but they are up against what it really means to create an equitable institution that really serves what their mission statement says: 'all women and girls.'"

For Dottye and her African American cotrainer at AAUW, the challenge has been to realize how difficult it is to change an institution whose culture is so entrenched. Even the women of color who join

AAUW often seek the status and all the trappings of achievement that reinforce the "way things have always been." According to Dottye, during the first training session, "Every woman who walked into the room was in uniform, with one exception. It [the uniform] was a suit, either pants and a jacket or a skirt and a jacket, with the exact appropriate accessories. The one major exception, of course, was the Asian American lesbian who is head of the diversity resource team. She wore jeans and a T-shirt."

In their next session Dottye and her cotrainer designed an exercise to focus on how people come to dress alike. Dottye asked, "How did all of you come to look so much alike in terms of your style? Were you all dressing this way before you got on the board of AAUW, or did you notice that everyone on the board was dressing that way and so you changed the way you dressed? It is such a symbol, such a symbol of the level of conformity. Not just conformity to that particular culture, but conformity to the dominant culture." For Dottye, changing an organization means working on multiple levels simultaneously, including paying attention to how culture is supported and passed on. "At AAUW, the culture is very formal. Very structured. Very task oriented. Very polite. Very defensive of traditions, and not wanting to really look honestly at the racial or class dynamics. Really wanting not to have a conversation that goes beyond the intellectual, theoretical discussion." The power of training is its ability to address the way race is played out in nonverbal and often insidious ways, so that white propertied people remain the norm, even when an organization professes to want it to be different.

Antiracism training also allows consultants to create multiracial communities among themselves that then serve as models for organizations seeking to become multiracial. The success of consulting work is largely dependent upon the ability of the trainers to work as a team. Typically, the long-lived antiracist training organizations are those that plan plenty of time for trainers to deal with the way inequalities manifest themselves within the group. The success of organizations is dependent upon trust and honesty among the trainers. Without that, the training itself will fail. White consultants, as a matter of course, are expected to consistently analyze how white-skin privilege affects interactions among trainers and with those who attend the workshops.

This reality means that trainers often need to sit with each other, often through painful conflicts, as they sort through racial scripts, expectations, and injuries. Dottye tells of an African American woman trainer who commented in a meeting that sometimes she feels so much anger she "could just pick up a gun and shoot white people." One of the white women in the group (who was not a trainer) was very disturbed by this. After the meeting she called other people in the session, who then raised the subject at the following session. The African American woman was devastated. She had thought she was in a group where she could be honest about her feelings, only to learn she had to choose her words carefully so as not to offend a white woman. Dottye interjected that white people committed to antiracist work need to realize that during racial strife, a white antiracist may only be seen as white; some people of color in the group interpreted her comment as suggesting that white people have more to fear in terms of violence than do people of color. Dottye recalls, "It took a long time to work through those dynamics." Within this group, there were also ongoing tensions about class, sexuality, and religion. Dottye sees these intersections as both difficult and crucial to confront.

White trainers emphasize the importance of recognizing racism as it manifests itself within the group. One of the many lessons Sarah Stearns has learned as a white trainer is how important it is not to immediately "move into a personal assessment of whether I caused" the harm or injury a person of color has identified. Through the years, Sarah has seen many interactions around race in which a white person insists the conversation focus on the personal level of the individual relationship. The "white person's openness to try to understand the experience of racism is limited to their own level of accountability." Sarah believes this reduction stymies many conversations across race. "Unless I am willing, as the white person, to feel and hold the rage of the cultural and institutional racism, then I am basically exercising my privilege to bring the conversation back to What does this have to do with me?" For Sarah, recognizing racism on the personal, cultural, and institutional levels—and not getting defensive in hard conversations— is often easier if white people can make a parallel between racism and other oppressions. A lesbian may know in her gut what it is like for a heterosexual to take every comment personally or reduce every interaction to a personal dynamic. A working-class person may know what it is like to have to minimize her class analysis in order to avoid offending wealthy people. Through the internal sessions in antiracist training organizations, people attempt to hash out these analogies, when they work and when they do not.

According to many trainers, community grows among them through regular and intensive sessions during which there is "real and ongoing attention to understanding our own cultural experiences." For John Capitman, that means learning what it is to be a white middle-class Jewish man. The emphasis in VISIONS on people recognizing each other as whole people has also made room for John to deal with the long-term impact of being disabled. (John was hit by a drunk driver many years ago, which left him with four crushed vertebrae.) Although good periods in his life now include being able to ride his bike and walk comfortably, all that is "because of careful attention by a fleet of chiropractors and acupuncturists and pain killers. . . . Because of my injuries, I will be a quad sooner rather than later. I will lose mobility, and I have this sort of tenuous hold on feeling okay in the world." For John, "the culture of antiracism" at VISIONS allows people to collectively understand their multiple identities and how they influence their approaches.

The work that antiracist trainers do internally within their organizations encourages white trainers to confront various ways in which they tend to distance themselves from one another. John explains that by working with VISIONS he has learned much from white people who "want to keep working on their own stuff. . . . You are growing up and continuously peeling away the pieces of your past." Because the training often makes time for people to meet in separate caucus groups (people of color separate from white people; men separate from women), white trainers regularly work closely with other white people while maintaining close accountability to people of color. In VISIONS, these separate caucus groups have been very instructive. When they were first initiated, the white trainers did not know what to do with each other. They basically stared at each other blank-faced, quiet and distant from each other. Time barely ticked by. Meanwhile the people-of-color caucus group was animated and dynamic. Time flew. The noticeable differences revealed how foreign it is for many white people, including activists, to recognize and engage with each other as allies.

Naomi Jaffe, who is skeptical about whether antiracism training can really bring about long-term change, still facilitates them, partly because they push her to learn to work with white people. In the 1980s and 1990s Naomi's community and political alliances were largely with people, mostly women, of color. But she explains, "I can't only do that and be a white antiracist. I have to be able to work with white people. I am beginning to see that I can't separate myself, to not be forced to see myself in other white people. And see other white people in myself. You can't teach any other way. You can't teach from the point of view of being the expert on antiracism." At least theoretically, antiracist trainers start from an understanding that they are not experts and that they, as much as anybody else, have trouble working respectfully with other white people who are trying to confront racism.

The balance trainers must maintain is to be honest about the preparation, often years in the making, that informs their consciousness about race while remembering there is always more to learn. Dottye Burt-Markowitz explains, "Part of the danger in doing this kind of work as a white person is letting yourself get into the view that somehow I am different from all those other white people. The reality is that, all my life, I have been working to get where I am right now. It has taken a lot of effort, and I have the luxury of doing this work [focusing on race] every day, so I get to think about it every day. So it is only natural that I have some level of understanding that most white people in the room are not going to have. That doesn't mean I am a different species or any better in any respect. It just means that, for lots of different reasons, I have had the ability to focus on race a lot more and to understand what it means for me as a white person to be working against racism. I think there are a lot of people who are really defensive who really don't want to change. They are going to, whether consciously or not, hold on to their power to keep things as white as they can. But I think the majority of people who ask us to do work with them really do want change. They really do want personal transformation to happen. But it is really hard for people living in this culture to let the layers of blinders fall off and really see."

Antiracism training offers white activists a location in which to develop mutual working relationships with others who are struggling to go beyond racist socialization and institutions. In the process, white people identify the ways power differences among whites hinder alliances. Based on her years of experience as a trainer and activist, Dottye has come to believe that white people tend to have very little compassion for each other. She believes that gender is a contributing factor. "I can almost always have conversations with white women that feel like real conversations. Even if we don't agree, I have at least felt there was some ability to have a real dialogue. With white men, I just really have a hard time. I run up against a refusal to grapple with the more subtle aspects of racism. The arrogance and rigidity and intellectualizing."

In antiracism sessions, trainers try to keep people focused on race (that is, to not allow the discussion to be about everything and anything under the sun other than race). They also emphasize how and why whiteness is not a monolithic identity. Dottye explains that one of the biggest differences between herself and most of the white people she works with relates to her background: Unlike many whites, who do not think of themselves as "white" until late childhood, Dottye "can't remember not being intensely aware of being white. East St. Louis had a reputation of being one of the most racist cities in the country. It was the site of one of the worst race riots during World War II, in which many Black people were injured and killed in incredibly brutal ways. I grew up in a place where just about everybody I knew said racist things daily." The only escape Dottye found from this barrage of racism was in her family. "It was like living on an island where the people raising me were teaching me racial bigotry was wrong." Although Dottye knew her parents were right, she was a shy child who did not know how to stand up against the bigotry. Her inaction made her feel "horrible guilt," a bind that took years for Dottye to understand.

In antiracism training, Dottye and fellow trainers encourage people to talk about how class and family dynamics contribute to people's silences, knowledge, and activism. From Dottye's perspective, what is most important "for white people to learn is that we need to take some concrete action to be seen as a true antiracist. It requires some risk for white people." Race consciousness has to go beyond words to action. Through their sessions, she and fellow trainers speak about how they moved from thought to action and the mistakes they make along the way, while encouraging those who attend to either speak about their own activism or identify steps for strategic thinking and alliance building.

Along with the promises and potential of antiracist training, there are still several limits to this approach. As Naomi Jaffe explains succinctly, "The dismantling-racism work isn't confronting power to me. Doing workshops to try to change people's lives is not the same as confronting power." Laurie Holmes agrees: "There was a while there when a lot of people I knew started to become diversity consultants and antiracism trainers. Somehow, I don't think that any of it . . . you can never become an antiracist by sitting in workshops." Laurie does not believe that attending workshops qualifies as having "done your work." From her perspective, "The only work is relationships in life, real, long-term relationships. And that doesn't mean adopting a baby from China." For Marilyn Buck, there are big differences between a militant politic and racial sensitization. "Militant," Marilyn says, "is a spirit of resistance about taking on the power structure, or taking on the state, on different levels. I think a lot of folks who do antiracist organizing, the racial sensitization, I think that is good. I know that it includes a lot of Black folks and Latinos. And it is absolutely legitimate. But it is not anticapitalist. It is not anti-imperialist. It assumes everything can work in the system."

Perhaps the most severe limitation of antiracism training is that even when the consulting team itself is multiracial and runs democratically, the sites in which consultants do their training are white dominated. Although trainers may help people work more cooperatively and respectfully within organizations, trainers cannot change the structure themselves. In her critique of corporate culture, Avery Gordon defines liberal racism as "an *antiracist* attitude that exists without support for racial outcomes. It rejects discrimination on the basis of race or class and abhors the subjection of groups or individuals on racial grounds. But it upholds and defends systems that produce racializing effects, often in the name of some matter more urgent than redressing racial subordination, such as rewarding 'merit,' valuing diversity, or enhancing economic competitiveness."[19] Trainers who seek to confront liberal racism must show how it is enforced in corporations and nonprofits and support those within institutions who have been resisting it all along.

As outside consultants, however, their ability to undermine liberal racism is severely limited in the long run. Too often, trainers end up supporting racism by rejecting discrimination in their workshops while having little power to affect "racial outcomes." Furthermore, when the outside trainers eventually leave, those breaking rank inside are left to make the changes, and they are at a considerably greater risk than are the consultants. This asymmetry in exposure and risk taking in the corporate sector parallels the asymmetry in risk taking for Central

American refugees versus those providing sanctuary in the 1980s. Although refugees in need of sanctuary were required to speak openly about unspeakable atrocities done to them and their families, that level of vulnerability and exposure was rarely required of North American sanctuary workers. Similarly, Black and white SNCC workers from the South were required to take risks northern visitors might take temporarily but could leave behind. And although trainers of color and white trainers are all protected in ways that employees are not, the protection that white trainers receive leaves little room for them to model for whites what it means to endure inside an organization over the long haul.

Another bind trainers face is that they are paid by the institutions they are there to critique. Biting the hand that feeds them is an inevitable constraint for organizations that both want to push groups to change themselves and know that their own organizations need further contracts to continue as viable businesses. For many trainers, there is constant tension between believing that intensive work can change an organization and seeing their own complicity when change is not forthcoming. Anne Litwin, who has been doing antiracism training with the NTL Institute since 1980, is aware that speaking out about the intransigence of racism in certain organizations can lose her valuable contracts. After working with one corporation for three years, Anne finally confronted one of the "clients" about his racism. Anne's job, in part, had been to train him to lead antiracist training sessions. Eventually, after many other attempts, Anne confronted him publicly, in a workshop. Almost immediately after that session, the funds for future work disappeared. Anne explains, "So I lost work. I don't regret it. I would do it again. I don't want him out there."

Honest as Anne was, her bind is emblematic of a larger contradiction in which antiracist trainers find themselves because they are in the *business* of teaching about racism. In his article distinguishing between trainers who maintain the status quo (diversity-management consultants) and those who try to challenge and undermine hierarchy, consultant Mark Chesler asks an important question: Can the latter group survive economically and politically using a challenging model? Chesler reports that there is "substantial evidence that major stockholders in current U.S. organizations resist this approach and seek to defend their own and others racial and gender privileges, especially when challenged." Then those who adopt a justice-oriented model have a hard time surviving, "as academicians, or managers or consultants."[20] But as Chesler rightfully points out, "oppressed groups in the United States are also having a hard time surviving right now," with or without trainings. "So, the questions are: Whose survival? Survival at what level of economic and moral comfort or security?" (249).

The many contradictions embedded in antiracism training raise a question as to whether they constitute activism. Certainly, the fact that training organizations are businesses mitigates building political relationships between organizations. John Capitman reports that VISIONS tried for a while to pull antiracism training organizations together so that they could take some political stands collectively and "try to get some attention in Washington." But real differences in models worked against building political alliances among training organizations. He also reported that "it was hard to get folks together. It is a business where people are competing for the same contracts."

Whether trainers themselves see their work as activism also partly depends on which definition of activism they use: Do they see activism as being centered on mass-movement organizing? Do they see the slow and steady work of education as a type of activism? Under the second definition, antiracism training that emphasizes justice seeking may be activism—as slow, painfully slow, as that type of change can be. Seen in this light, antiracism training parallels the work of antiracist faculty who agitate against the assault on affirmative action; oppose student tracking and institutionalized testing; support faculty, staff, and student unions; and offer an activist-inspired curriculum. Is this activism? Maybe in the wee small hours, when activist-educators hope that doing something is better than nothing at all.

Antiracism trainers are one huge step ahead of antiracist academics in that trainers work in multiracial organizations, often founded and led by people of color. With the exception of African American studies departments and Black colleges, few academic settings offer anything close to racial parity at the level of the department, the division, or the campus. If activism includes not only the product of one's labor but also the process required to get there, antiracism training organizations model a process worth celebrating.

Perhaps more important than deciding whether antiracism training qualifies as activism is clarifying what is required to incite genuine long-term change within foundations, educational settings, and businesses. From my perspective, the trainers best able to agitate for change are those who have their feet in several worlds: as trainers and as organizers in their own communities and with long-term connections with social movements. White trainers also need significant experience working with and taking direction from people of color in order to be effective. At the People's Institute for Survival and Beyond, the trainers have to be community activists in order to lead sessions. Ron Chishom says, "The People's Institute has always been committed to being multiracial and antiracist, which means it has always been led by people of color." The white trainers also know that "people of color can't be holding hands with white people unless they are willing to take risks."[21] Activism gives trainers a way to incorporate concrete examples of organizing right into their presentations. So even though they have the luxury to leave the organizations in which they conduct their trainings, they have not had that same luxury elsewhere. Clearly, trainers need examples of personal experience with collective struggle—from union organizing to supporting affirmative action—in order to move discussions from employee "choices" to collective bargaining, from personal satisfaction to political liberation.

Different Models, All Hard Work

At first, I was baffled about how to include such seemingly disparate forms of activism—in prison, nonprofit multiracial organizations, and training groups—in the two chapters on the 1980s and 1990s. I was afraid nothing held these three types of antiracism together except their simultaneity. Upon first reading, I think it is hard to take seriously the political dilemmas faced by antiracism training within corporate settings when compared with the incredible strain involved in organizing to abolish systematic methods of torture in prison. It seems hard to reconcile a model of antiracist activism that works with—in fact depends upon—capitalism in order to sustain itself as a business when prisoners, by definition of their legal status in the United States, have no leverage for earning a living wage or controlling their work environment. It seems hard to take seriously debates about white people's positions within multiracial organizations when in prison work the divide between white guards and Black prisoners is nonnegotiable. During a recent visit with David Gilbert, I saw dozens of prisoners come into the visitors' room in hopes of getting some time with the friends and family who had traveled to see them. All but one of the prisoners was Latino or Black. All the guards were white. What has become a rational discussion about power sharing in multiracial non-profits outside prison remains a rigid racial hierarchy between inmates and correctional officers inside prison. This hierarchy makes the multiracial organizing among prisoners especially remarkable.

In fact, the disparate examples I chronicle speak to differences in models of activism that have existed historically, differences that raise enduring questions about the necessary components of social transformation. Among the activists currently working inside and outside prison, most used the term "revolutionary" to describe themselves in the 1960s, meaning "willing to risk one's life for the struggle," meaning "willing to question the limits of nonviolence when the state is killing one's friends, one's family, one's political community." In the 1980s and 1990s the same people still try to hold onto revolutionary principles, and yet few think of themselves as revolutionaries now. For them, that term, that identity, relates to a movement that does not currently exist. Instead, in the words of David Gilbert, the challenge is to "try to be an antiracist pole, a presence among white people."

For Marilyn Buck, staying active means being willing to stand in line so she can talk with a white woman about racism. Being willing to say, I have no regrets, even though Marilyn will be eighty when she gets out of prison. Capitalism is the enemy. Colonialism is the enemy. A system that allows guards to hog-tie men and women is the enemy. In 1997 Angela Davis "recounted how Black militant activists would define 'radicals' as bourgeois whites who had political critiques and intellectual commitments to opposing racism and economic exploitation but little experiential confrontation with the state; 'revolutionaries,' on the other hand, were those whose philosophical ideals about a just society and democratic state were manifested in their risk-taking political acts against oppressive state apparatuses. Today, few if any U.S. writers qualify as 'revolutionaries.'"[22] Political prisoners may be the one exception.[23]

Antiracism educators and people working in multiracial nonprofits do not typically use the term "revolutionary." Although this group includes many activists first radicalized in the 1960s, few were militants during that period. And yet it is simplistic to say that the first category is more structurally oriented (anticapitalist, antistate) and the second is more reliant upon psychological models for confronting racism. Marilyn Buck and Bonnie Kerness are both women who identify themselves as "revolutionaries" and also draw extensively on their backgrounds in psychology in their organizing. In some ways, Naomi Jaffe represents a bridge between the two models: a member of the Weather Underground in the early 1970s and currently an antiracism trainer and a prison activist. While offering a pithy analysis of the limits of multiracial feminist organizing and antiracism training—that they do not confront power—she still does the training, aware that people need contexts for honest discussions about what makes it hard to work across race, class, and sexuality.

Even Suzanne Ross and David Wellman, who are both skeptical of antiracism training in general, admit that the Left certainly has made little space for people to deal with the emotional underpinnings of living within hierarchies: the loss, fear, anxiety, jealousy, and competition that coincide with living in a race- and class-stratified society. Multiracial organizations, including training groups, tend to make space for people to deal with oppression as a structural and a psychological issue. Patti DeRosa asserts that trainers reach the people who might otherwise vote for initiatives and candidates who support the prison buildup.[24] In that way—and perhaps others—prison activism and antiracist trainings are not so far apart.

In another place and time, the names of the groups were different: CORE, SNCC, the Black Panthers, the American Indian Movement (AIM), the Weather Underground. Debates about self-defense, the intersection between capitalism and racism, and the complexities of accountability reigned then. In the 1980s and 1990s, when there is still no single movement that holds antiracist work together, it is no surprise that many of the same debates remain.

11

"In All Its Incarnations": White Antiracist Culture

During the years I have spent meeting and learning from white activists, I have been grateful for what people have been willing to share with me about history. And I have been moved by people's willingness to place themselves within that history, as contradictory and as flawed as that history has also been. Despite the tremendous diversity among those I interviewed, what has most stayed with me is a similar quality of living among them, a sameness mostly captured between the lines, in the feel of their houses, in the ways they interact with people, in the food they serve, in the music they play, in what's hanging on their living room walls, in whom they call family, and in the values they hope to pass on to the next generation.

I interviewed most people in their homes, with a few important exceptions. Anne Braden allowed me to interview her while she was traveling in Boston. The interview started at ten at night and went until one in the morning—after she had spoken on a panel on affirmative action and attended a lengthy reception—until I begged for mercy and took what turned out to be an eighty-page interview home with me, unable to sleep the rest of the night, too charged up to put my mind to rest. I did an interview with Eric and Lian Mann, staffmembers at the Labor/Community Strategy Center in Los Angeles, on the carpet in a hotel room in Boston, where they were staying on their way to a badly needed vacation right after Eric's father died. I also conducted interviews with people in prison.

With a few other exceptions, I conducted the rest of the interviews in people's homes, often spending a night or two with them, which gave me a chance to meet their families and friends, see where they worked, spend some time in their neighborhoods, feel the emotional and physical architecture of their days. It was during these visits that I started to feel a real sameness about their lives, across generation and geography, a similarity that was uncanny, given that few of them knew each other. Of those I interviewed, Anne Braden made the most specific reference to a community among activists, which she first came to know when she traveled across the country to network with people about her 1954 sedition trial. By that point, the Black Communist leader William Patterson had told her that she did not have to be part of the world of the lynchers, that she could be part of "the other America." Once Anne started organizing against racism she began to see that there was no turning back. She has been part of the other America since. She says that "even now, in the 1990s, if you are part of the other America, I know it the minute I meet you. There is a sixth sense." For Anne and for many people who have had to leave their communities of origin in order to become activists, creating the "other America" is a matter of survival. Anne knows activists who say that "white people need to go back and get your culture. You have to go back and get your culture. You are from Ireland. From somewhere. No such place as white land. I'd say, the culture I came from wasn't just racist. It was fascist. It literally was. The people I grew up with, and I never quit loving them either, really thought that the South was the last stronghold of Anglo-Saxon civilization. They used that term in this country. It was fascist. I can't go back to that. I don't have any roots there. I had to pull those roots up. But I found my roots in the other America and what I call its incarnation in all the movements."

From my visits with people across the country, I began to understand that what I have been seeing and feeling is in fact the makings of a culture: ways of living and loving informed by activists who are taking little and big steps away from white supremacy. During my travels, I witnessed many examples of antiracist culture. I arrive at Stan and Dottye Markowitz's home in Baltimore on a cold rainy day in March to warm, delicious smells of stew that Stan is cooking for the potluck planned for that evening. A group of close friends and activists, African American and white, secular Jews and Protestant ministers, are coming to watch a video of James Earl Jones's stunning performance of a two-act, one-man play on the life of Paul Robeson. Stan does all the cooking and serving during the dinner, not Dottye. While eating and after the video, the white people in the room really listen to their African American friends. The white people are not controlling or domineering or orchestrating the conversation. The body language, easy laughter, and close conversations suggest an intimacy that is hard to find in mixed-race groups. During the evening, an African American religious educator slips over to where I am sitting and says, "Coming to interview Stan and Dottye is well worth your trip. They are special and unique people and well respected in Baltimore."

Other signs of antiracist culture: The Connecticut home of Ali Bey Hassan and Susan Burnett, the first person I interviewed. I and a friend arrive at their house to stay the night on our way to a rally in New York. It is my first time staying there, so I am worried we might cramp their style. That is not really possible, it seems. Ali Bey's aging aunt is with them, dealing with Alzheimer's disease and other confusions. Most of their five grown children are either staying there or stop by while we are there. Every room has a couch or a space that can turn into a bed. Susan tells me their house had always been open to children of movement activists, especially the children of political prisoners, who have ended up moving around a lot. This scene is dramatically different from but in some ways similar to the calm, cool, quiet home of Ruth Frankenberg and her Indian life partner. When I entered, I immediately felt as if I had entered an ashram. It is a home where connections between spiritual work and antiracist work are nurtured. There is a seriousness about both of these spaces. A conscious effort has been made to make these homes an extension of political work, a key place for nurturance and communication—whether of movement children or of the spirit.

Another early sign of antiracist culture: I arrive in New York City to interview Suzanne Ross, who has taken the day off to talk with me, since one of the officials at the high school where she is a psychologist has denied me access to Suzanne at her place of work. The official is afraid I might see too much, I guess. Living in an antiracist culture includes learning which battles to fight. In this case, it is not worth taking the school official on; better to call in sick and do the interview at home. While I am there, Suzanne gets a call from Pam Africa, a member of MOVE and a leading figure among the many people involved in the international struggle to get a new trial for Mumia Abu-Jamal. It seems Pam is coming into town from Philadelphia to talk with a coalition of people that night and is concerned that one of the sectarian groups that support Mumia will try to take over the meeting. Would

Suzanne come and help support her? Suzanne calle Naomi Jaffe, with whom she had planned an overnight visit months earlier. "I know we were going to go to services together tonight and I know we promised we would not do any political work while you were here. For once. Yes, I knew you would agree that if Pam asks for something, we are there for her, no matter what. Yes, we can still catch up around the edges on our way to and from the event. Yes, Pam wants us at the all-day conference tomorrow, too. Gotta go. We'll iron out the details when you come. Bye."

Another sign of antiracist culture: the home of Dawn Gomes in Berkeley, which she shares with a young, white, feminist woman and Dawn's husband, a Cambodian man, Chuon. Dawn originally married him so he could stay in the country, but then they fell in love. Chuon was in the labor camps in Cambodia when he was five years old, during Pol Pot's reign, when a million people were killed. All those with glasses, for example, were killed based on the notion that their glasses meant they were intellectuals. Chuon saw his mother and father taken away. He, and many others, somehow escaped. While I am at their house, two of their guests, both Asian men who helped Chuon get to the United States, are eating breakfast; one in a silk bathrobe is speaking in French to someone on the phone. They get ready to leave to catch a plane to Cuba. On the mantle in the living room stand many amulets— African, Asian, and Native American, which Dawn has collected over the years—and a dazzling Burmese god that Chuon brought when he moved in. I see white California furniture, with a definite northern California feel in the air, sun streaming in, hardwood floors, flowers in the yard and through the windows everywhere, love between the two of them. She, more than twenty years older than he; he, her first male lover after she has been a lesbian for more than twenty years.

Other examples: In the entryway of Bonnie Kerness's small and peaceful apartment in New Jersey there is a whole wall of photographs of family and friends. Photos of her six biological, adopted, and foster children in various stages of growth hang alongside photos of activists Bonnie has worked with for the last four decades. Photos of celebration, commitment, and struggle are hung up in the same apartment a government official periodically surveils from a car parked across the street.

In many homes I visited there were memorable, yet often hard-to-find, political posters on the walls, some taped, some propped up, some carefully framed. In Suzanne Ross's home there were a brilliantly colored print of a Sandinista woman being thrown in the air by some of her jubilant comrades and a poster with the word "Palestine" etched in bold colors across the space; a poster saying, "Hands Off Assata Shakur" is attached to the refrigerator to advertise an upcoming event to protest the headhunt being led by the governor of New Jersey.

In Michael Lawrence-Riddell's room in his mother's house, where he stays during his breaks from college, there is no blank wall or ceiling space available. It is all covered with life-size posters of Martin Luther King Jr. and Malcolm X and Bob Marley and Walter Payton and a framed photograph of Mike's grandfather and himself. On his bookshelf are *Making Face, Making Soul; A History of South Africa;* and *Catch a Fire: The Life of Bob Marley.* Music from KRS One, an African American rapper booms from his speakers. Mike calls himself a humanist and a worker for revolutionary justice. While Mike plays me many of KRS's songs, he tells me he got the term "humanist" from KRS. Mike believes "humanist" makes room for white people, as does "revolutionary," which Mike says he got from his dad, Karl Marx, and Castro. Of the book *Memoir of a Race Traitor* on his book shelf, Mike says he liked the message, only he would call it "Memoir of a Race Loyalist," since white loyalty to antiracism means devotion to dissidence.

In many people's houses there are rows and rows and rows of books. Many of them, now out of print, were handbooks for survival when they were first published and still remain so for people learning this history for the first time. In general, those I interviewed are voracious readers, often passing the books on to the next person in line. Many of the titles are familiar guideposts and ways to remember where people have come from. Common stock, across region and generation, includes *The Langston Hughes Reader, Cuban Women Now, Sula, Wretched of the Earth,* Marx's writing (in dog-eared paperback and hardback editions), *There Is a River, Black Panthers Speak Out, Home Girls: A Black Feminist Anthology, A People's History of the United States,* and *The Miracle of Mindfulness.*[1]

What do these seemingly disparate scenes have in common? A living practice of crossing borders—racial, cultural, and spiritual; a merging of people's political action and personal lives; a certain flexibility that comes from making one's home welcome to fellow travelers; a seriousness, a humor, and a liveliness born of a people on the move; an intimacy between white people and people of color—as friends, colleagues, and comrades—that includes taking race seriously but not belaboring the differences; working hard enough across race so that there are times when race is somehow transcended, not covered over or ignored, but also not necessarily considered the most essential or problematic issue among people.[2] In an antiracist culture, white people see race as an issue even when only white people are present; parenting includes taking seriously the way Black and Latino children are targeted and teaching white children to be potential allies to children of color from preschool on; activism is considered the breath that gives people life.

My interest in teasing out what I have come to call antiracist culture partly comes from believing that everyday life is where much about race and antiracism is negotiated, learned, and passed on. If antiracism is both a promise (a politic) and a way of life, then it is not only about what people are against but also what they are for. The everyday conflicts and interactions also give a glimpse into what it takes to build a movement. I write about culture, too, as my own way of writing against the notion that whiteness itself has to be abolished. In my view, racism needs to be abolished, a reality that necessarily transforms what it means to live with white skin. When people talk about whiteness needing to be abolished, oftentimes that translates into white people thinking they need to be something else—African American, Native American, or Latino. From my perspective, a third option—one that neither celebrates white dominant culture nor considers whiteness itself deserving of annihilation—is what antiracists attempt to practice. It is in the culture that antiracists create that a transformation occurs, in the moments, sometimes milli-moments, when they are able to move beyond white supremacy and into ways of living that are not about hierarchy and exclusivity.

Antiracist culture in the 1990s draws on many political cultures: African American organizing and arts; progressive activism within the Jewish diaspora; Black and Latina feminist culture and politics; the Communist Party and culture, among other political traditions. Although antiracist culture incorporates these varied traditions, its whole is not simply the sum of those parts, nor is this culture ahistorical. For example, the impact of multiracial feminism on progressive politics has moved beyond the tendency in Communist Party culture to consider psychology a "bourgeois" influence or to consider personalities and principles as necessarily separable. The influence of progressive lesbian politics and culture has severely undermined a tendency in 1950s and 1960s activism to sideline issues of sexuality. The impact of organizing among immigrants (Latinos, Asians, people from the Caribbean) in the last thirty years has reinforced the multiracial, rather than biracial, foundation of progressive activist politics. Just as the political perspectives of those I interviewed tend to be more multiracial in the 1980s and 1990s than previously, it was not until this era that their lives also began to reflect the influence of Puerto Rican, Chicano, and Central American culture. The influences are many—in the language, the music, the food, and the ways people entertain—particularly among those who have bicultural families and those who have lived in Central America for extended periods.

Letting the Work Change People

In the 1990s one of the most profound characteristics of antiracist culture is reflected in the work people do. Many people I interviewed have spent most of their lives working in organizations where racial justice is a priority: in the Student Nonviolent Coordinating Committee (SNCC), at Howard University, in multiracial feminist organizations, in Afrocentric educational projects, and in activist groups while in prison. In most of these settings, white people get a chance to participate fully but must be mindful not to be at the center, a reality that upon first exposure can, in the words of Anne Braden, really "turn your world upside down."

Of the way her whole world turned around during her first meeting with SNCC activists, Maggie Nolan Donovan says, "I know that my initial motivation [to get involved with civil rights] was a sense of injustice and outrage and a sense of helping. But I think I also had, but I didn't articulate it to myself, a sense of white leadership. Well-intentioned white people would pull this off and do something about this. That idea was gone by my first thirty minutes in SNCC. I think that's the first idea that just went right out the window. I remember being so struck by the sort of intellectual powerhouse that I had wandered into. That the people in this room, Black and white, were a lot smarter than anyone else I knew and that I had never been involved in that kind of critical analysis, that kind of intellectual vigor and rigor before. So whatever my white beliefs about Black abilities and intelligence, unarticulated to myself but absorbed for sure, were gone pretty fast. Almost before I had time to acknowledge that they were there. I just saw myself as learning enormous amounts from these people around me, many of whom were Black. I had essentially no political analysis. I didn't understand that Vietnam had anything to do with segregation. I didn't understand a capitalist view or a Marxist view. I didn't understand about class. I came to understand all that pretty quickly."

Since her activism in the 1960s, Maggie's political alliances and friendship networks have remained connected with Black activists—those involved in the Civil Rights Movement and in activism since—and with the Cape Verdean community leaders in the town where Maggie lives. Her interest in learning about multicultural teaching has continued through the years. Her most recent effort is to participate in an intensive summer training program led by Native American educators on how to teach about the conquest of Native Americans and about Native American life in grammar schools.

Like Maggie, Anne Braden came to see that undermining white dominance depends upon recognizing and being changed by Black leadership. From her work with the National Association for the Advancement of Colored People (NAACP) and the Militant Church movement in Louisville in the 1950s to her support for SNCC in the 1960s, Anne learned early on that a movement for the liberation of Blacks depended upon white respect for Black leadership. She also learned that as a white woman, her job was to "get with the white people." That focus did not, however, mean practicing dominant white culture in her life. For Anne, "getting with the white people" means knowing that much of her work requires pulling white people in from as many directions as possible: into environmental justice work, into organizing for affirmative action, into struggles for relevant and up-to-date education. Meanwhile, Anne lives in an African American community in Louisville. "Getting with the white people" requires that Anne stay intimately connected to the pulse of African American community organizing. When the Southern Conference Educational Fund (SCEF) came apart in 1973, Anne vowed never again to work in a white-dominated group. For the last quarter century, her main work has been in organizations that are led by people of color—Southern Organizing Committee (SOC) and the Kentucky Alliance against Racist and Political Repression. Working in organizations led by African Americans gives Anne Braden and other white people a chance to be part of the universe but not the center of it. It allows white people to reevaluate ways of being and acting that are simply assumed within dominant white culture.

Stan Markowitz also traces much of his early learning about what he wanted his life to look like directly back to lessons he learned from African American scholars and friends, as well as from white progressive educators. After serving in the army, where he witnessed massive discrimination against Black enlisted men, Stan was mentored by a white man who was passionately interested in history and helped Stan decide to finish college. Stan's first teaching job (1966–1969) was as a teacher of history at Howard University. He listened to and learned from Black students and faculty and began to see how little he knew about African American history. Learning African American history changed his understanding of history in general. Being at Howard University enabled him to fill in the gaps in his own miseducation, learning about African American history and later about Native American history. The first time a student asked him about Native American history prior to colonialism Stan said there wasn't much to tell. He did some reading and has been making up for his ignorance ever since. Of Howard University, Stan writes, "Working at Howard allowed me to dramatically rethink my education and how to be a teacher who provided a relevant, social justice education."

From his years at Howard University and through lessons learned from Stokely Carmichael, Stan came to see that white people need to work with white people. Although he could have stayed at Howard, he moved to Baltimore and began teaching history at a working-class community college with a white student body, where he remained for twenty-five years. He sees teaching as potentially radical work and believes that very few people are teaching a "people's history," in Howard Zinn's terms. Stan has also worked to push the college forward in terms of affirmative action and multicultural education and has conducted workshops on sexual harassment. He has worked with the Piedmont Peace Project, with the Save Our Cities Campaign, with a group that challenges Johns Hopkins Hospital to work with communities, and with an interfaith racial justice project. Stan leads a full life, an active life, a life closely connected to multiple organizations founded and led by African Americans.

"Loving in the War Years"[3]

Many people I interviewed have also been profoundly changed through long-term intimate relationships with people of color—as lovers, close friends, parents, and political comrades. Interracial relationships are no guarantee that white people deal openly and consistently with race. White people's intimate relationships with people of color can never be a credential of antiracist consciousness. At the same time, the interactions, dialogues, negotiations, and confrontations that daily life is made of can dramatically change a white person's understanding of racism. Through close cross-race relationships, white people come to understand race experientially (not just abstractly) and to realize they cannot afford to distance themselves from the realities of racism.

Through long-term interracial relationships, white people can also learn a tremendous amount about bicultural living. Rose Marie Cummins, who has been a nun since she was eighteen, has come a long way from her childhood in segregated Kentucky. Rose Marie taught school in Puerto Rico for many years and for the last decade has worked with the Latino Health Institute, providing legal immigration support for people with AIDS, homeless people, and people seeking political asylum. When talking about the differences between the culture she grew up in and the racially and culturally diverse community she is part of now, Rose Marie says, "There has been a real transition from living life within the lines to taking time with people. People wouldn't know this by looking at my room, but I think I kind of had some sense of order in the way I think. And I think that my rigidity has changed a lot and I see importance in taking time—taking time, you know, and talking to people, and sitting down for a cup of coffee and visiting people. It's not just getting a piece of work done. Those things are just as important in getting the work done. And I think that music and poetry and color and seeing things in nature have definitely widened my world and enriched it." At this stage in her life, Rose Marie's closest friends are a ninety-year-old Cuban woman and an African American woman she has known for many years. From her youth in a town where Jim Crow was practiced in every realm to now, "my world has definitely gotten a lot bigger."

John Capitman has been married to Valerie Batts, a Christian-raised African American woman from the South, for the past twenty years. He and Valerie share a long-term commitment to the multiracial training institute they cofounded, their joint work against racism in the Quaker school their children attend, and their work as parents of two African American children. Their interracial, bicultural life is characterized by constant negotiation and the need to be flexible. John says, "There is a way in which certain things in my life are more complicated than other people's. Passover and Easter this week. I am not a religious Jew, but this is one of the holidays I have sort of taken seriously. So we have these complicated arrangements about figuring out how to be respectful of each tradition. Christmas gets even wilder. Christmas and Kwanza and Hanukkah. You could say this is religion, not race. But there are so many little things, like Worcestershire sauce. We always had Worcestershire sauce in my house when I grew up. That is not so much about Valerie's life. A-1 sauce is. I am teasing, but music is another example. We have had years of struggle over music. The fact that our stereo has been broken now for about a year is probably reflective. It has been challenging and difficult to come up with music that we are both okay with. . . . Our music is really different. I grew up, my parents liked Benny Goodman. Show tunes. Musical comedies. We sort of listen to the contemporary equivalent of that. But we also listen to rap and reggae and soul music. This is obvious, but I live in a household where there are a variety of sounds. We have pretty regular family events that are much more about continuing Valerie's extended, large, loving family, as opposed to my small, disinterested, actively antagonistic one."

Reebee Garafalo, who lives with his partner, a Colombian woman, and her two children, also emphasizes the mosaic of conversations emblematic of what it means to be part of a multiracial family. For example, over the years he has seen a real transformation in his partner's daughter's identity as she moved from seeing herself as a hippie type growing up in Ithaca, New York, to a Latina young woman who lives with her Dominican boyfriend in the downstairs apartment at Reebee's house. The daughter's boyfriend is an avid follower of Louis Farrakhan, "which means we get into some incredible discussions at the dinner table." Reebee's partner "comes to the table with a sort of Buddhist outlook, and I come to the table with a much more social movements' outlook. I mean there are just a lot of very interesting dynamics in all these points of view. In some ways, those family discussions are a microcosm of the political task of the movement right now; it's to figure out how to make that family a family."

For white antiracists in interracial relationships, everyday living is made sweeter when there are shared understandings of politics and culture. For David Wellman, who has been in a relationship with an African American woman for many years, the deep familiarity between them is partly based on their shared involvement in the Civil Rights Movement. Because he grew up among Black Communist friends of the family and Black families in the neighborhood, much about African American life was part of David's life long before he met his partner: his love of jazz, knowledge of African American labor history, enjoyment of southern Black food, friendships, and political alliances. The meeting between him and his partner was one of great reciprocity, their love strong. But their shared political history added a level of pressure to their relationship that David feared even they might not be able to sustain. "There are times when I feel like we are swimming upstream against a very powerful current. And there are times when I think one of us is going to run out of energy. Or both of us. . . . There is so much going on that you are not aware of, and there is so much that you have no control over. Just a regular sexual relationship is difficult enough to negotiate, and then you add race, and even in a relationship like ours, where we have two very supportive families on both sides. I mean her mother treats me like a son and my father treats her like a daughter, and there is deep, deep, love and affection."

"Even so," David continues, "there are times when I know, I feel her say, 'This white guy just doesn't have a clue.' And I have never had that feeling in another relationship. I can't even name what 'that' is. It is not the old-fashioned hostility. It is not people staring at you. It's just a Black woman and a white guy in 1996 and although we came from similar backgrounds, even came from the same city, the same neighborhood, the same high school, we are so different. There are times when we speak the same language, and we don't communicate. We hear different things. We see different things. We feel different things. And we don't always have the language which allows us. . . . I don't know if that is taboo but it is very unnerving. At the same time, it is very invigorating. It is very exciting. It is very challenging. I have experienced love in a way that I have never experienced it before so that I feel like I know the difference between fucking and making love."

David worries, however, that "if my relationship fails, that it would be more than a personal failure. It would feel like I had failed in a much larger sense of the term. It wouldn't be just another failure in a relationship. It is something about my politics and what I am and who I am and where I stand. I mean a white guy and a Black woman in the 1990s and the white guy has been involved in Movement stuff, in civil rights stuff all his life. And the woman has been involved in similar kinds of things. If they can't make it, in a sense it is emblematic of . . . I can't even finish the sentence. So it takes on a lot more importance, and I guess it makes me work harder."

David cannot separate his love for his partner and the symbolism of a long-term interracial relationship from historical and current realities. He says, "I just know that if we were to go our separate ways, people wouldn't say, 'It is too bad. That couple didn't make it.' They'd say, 'See, it doesn't work. If those two people couldn't make it work, it can't work.'. . . I would never say that to [my partner] because it puts more on the relationship than is already there. . . . the relationship of white men to Black women historically is a relationship of exploitation and violation. And it is different historically and symbolically than the relationship of Black men and white women. So there are times when I know, I can feel, the resentment of Black men when I am in the presence of [my partner] and it is clear we are a couple. And I understand. But I am also not going to dissociate myself. That is a strange place to be."

David is not the only one among those I interviewed who identified painful and important lessons they learned through interracial partnerships. Laurie Holmes spoke eloquently about the stresses she and her Puerto Rican partner tried hard to face. She remembers, "Oh my God. Did we struggle. Did we grow. I sometimes describe myself as a Puerto Rican wanna-be. I am in love with Puerto Rican people in a big way. I am so attracted to the food and music and a kind of familiar familiarity with Latino culture. I was drawn to it long before I ever got involved with my partner. I had studied Spanish and had done a bit of traveling. In my relationship, of course, all of that romantic stuff becomes real life. We clashed around issues of race a lot and class." Laurie's partner was raised Catholic and struggled with identifying as a lesbian in ways that Laurie never had. Laurie's partner had grown up in a poor neighborhood with parents who never learned English, her dad worked constantly, and she had suffered as a child—from poverty, racism, and damaging family dynamics. In her love for her partner, Laurie "always felt like that there was absolutely no reason why she should trust me, when I saw what she had been through in her life. I thought that if I just loved her enough and loved her right, then it was going to be all right." In the process, Laurie felt trapped. On the one hand, she knew that many of the race and class issues they fought about were ones Laurie needed to work on. She was learning and trying to deal with her own racism. On the other hand, in retrospect, she believes she was on the receiving end of her partner's anger too often.

The script that Laurie had carried with her all her life—fear that people of color would reject her and that as a white person she did not deserve cross-race friendships—made it hard for her to stand up for herself when her partner's behavior was hurtful. "Whatever was wrong was my responsibility. I was just more than happy to take it on. And white guilt is in there too. I am a white person. White people are fucked up." When Laurie would question whether the dynamic between them was healthy, her partner would counter with, "This is marriage. This is what relationships are like. You come from a fantasy, fairy-tale world. You don't know what it is really like." And Laurie would agree with her partner.

Laurie was also afraid that if she criticized or left the relationship, she would lose contact with her partner's three children, whom she had helped raise. And she feared she would lose friendships with the lesbians of color in their community. "I really believed that if I wasn't with [her], they wouldn't be friends with me. For some people, that was true because I was a white woman." As Laurie remembers it, "In the late 1970s and early 1980s many African American women and, a little bit later, Latinas were pulling together, creating an identity. These were times when politically, it might sound strange now, but these were times when separatism made sense. I really believe that there is a time for any marginalized group to pull together and caucus and do a separatist thing." As a white woman in an interracial relationship during this period, Laurie worried that she would be left out in the cold by African American and Latina women if she could not sustain her interracial relationship, a worry indicative of how political coalitions and home had become one and the same for Laurie. She feared that losing her relationship meant losing her political and cultural community as well.

As it turns out, when Laurie and her partner did separate, the split did not automatically cost Laurie friendships with women of color. In the process of leaving the relationship, Laurie got into therapy and Narcotics Anonymous, which helped her deal with her long-term drug problem. She also began working with a multiracial community center. Eventually she fell in love again, with another Puerto Rican woman who is also a mother; she describes the relationship as one she has died and gone to heaven for. Conflicts around race, language, parenting, and culture still exist, but Laurie and her partner have found mutually supportive ways of working through them.

The differences are dramatic between the culture Laurie grew up in—white bedroom communities in Connecticut—and her life as a member of a bicultural, bilingual, Puerto Rican lesbian family. "The words that come to me are 'rich' and 'intentionally inclusive' and 'diverse.' I think that we, and I say 'we' because when I am talking about family it is a 'we' thing, I think that Elba and I are attracted to otherness. Where I think the culture I grew up in would have been repelled by the unknown, we are much more interested in it. Somebody new? Somebody different? Oh. Let's get together with them. New music. New food. Let's check it out. Just living it. That is what is natural to us. If I compare it to what I grew up with, difference was the most unnatural thing."

For Jeanine Cohen, everything she does—her friendships, political affiliations, film projects, and artistic work—is based on multiracial collaborations. But the connections she makes across race, nation, and language are not always easy. Like many antiracists, Jeanine is careful to clarify that the work of sustaining a multiracial life is never done. Sometimes she feels angry that she needs to constantly question herself and interrogate her motives, the implications of what she says and does. "Sometimes I just get pissed off. I don't want to have to think about everything I do. Every step I take. Every time I open my mouth. It is not quite that bad, but . . ." Jeanine describes boundary crossing as "a constantly uncomfortable experience. Rarely is it an experience where I don't have some level of discomfort. Some dis-ease." Sometimes, she believes that some piece of racism has won, has whittled away at a belief in the possibility of living in a relaxed way. In those moments she is reminded of how important it is for her "to create community—that it is possible to transcend these boundaries in loving, caring ways with people."

When the Young Ones Have Your Heart

Those I interviewed who raised children of color said that nothing taught them more about race and racism than what they learned from interracial parenting.[4] In 1973, after having been involved in civil rights activism for many years, Dottye Burt-Markowitz married a Black man and soon gave birth to a son, Adam. After she and her partner split up, Dottye moved back to East St. Louis, where she had grown up, but this time to the Black side of town. Living in this community worked exceedingly well for Dottye and Adam, both because it was a child-friendly environment and because Dottye did not have to worry about whether Adam would see his reflection in those around him. When she moved to Carbondale, Illinois, to complete a Ph.D. program in physiological psychology, their situation changed dramatically. She had to be much more intentional about bringing Black people into his life. After living in Florida while she did postdoctoral work, they settled in Baltimore in 1982, when Adam was twelve years old. The move was devastating for him. Baltimore is an extremely segregated town with dramatic delineations across race. In the first school Adam attended, which was predominantly Black, the students told him that he talked white and was not really Black. The few white students at the school made no room for him, since he was biracial. Dottye remembers that "white kids would periodically grab him. Throw his books in the creek. Hit him. He tended to try to hang out with the Black kids. Sometimes they would be friends with him one on one. But when the other kids were around, they didn't want to be with him. Literally almost every day he would come home and cry. It was absolutely horrible."

The next year Dottye enrolled him in an integrated school, although that meant he had to live with a relative and could only come home on weekends. During that period, he was accepted at a Quaker school, which he decided not to attend. Even though it might have been better for him racially, at the last minute Adam decided not to go because the school felt too upper-class. He was not willing to cross that divide as a working-class biracial child being raised by a single white mother. The following year, luckily, he got into a fine arts high school that was much more accepting and eclectic, so Adam found a place for himself. He felt at the center and got much positive attention because of his artistic abilities, his personality, and his mixed background.

Through helping Adam to grow up, Dottye learned many lessons about race. First, she believes she should have known a lot more before becoming the mother of a biracial child. "I didn't have a clue about what I was doing when I decided to have him. I was just oblivious. Initially, I met his dad and fell crazy in love with him and was thrilled that we were having a child. I never imagined raising him myself initially." After she left her husband, "There I was, not having much consciousness at all about what it meant to be a white woman raising a Black male, especially." As to what has given her that consciousness over time, Dottye says, "It has been pretty much trial and error and happenstance." Second, she has learned that children of color being raised by white parents try to protect their parents a lot. As an adult, Adam has told Dottye that he often did not tell her about racial harassment because he knew she would get very upset but would not necessarily be able to stop it. Dottye also learned after the fact that Adam had really worried about her safety when they lived in or visited Black communities. This concern had never occurred to Dottye, since she knew the neighborhoods well. It was painful and shocking for Dottye to learn, only after Adam reached adulthood, all that he had carried around through childhood.

Drawing on their own experiences as mothers and on their work as activists, Dottye and an African American woman educator added workshops on parenting and race to other antiracist workshops they provide. Dottye is especially concerned about the defensiveness she sees among many white people who adopt children of color and their unwillingness to recognize that their children struggle against racism even though their parents are white. In workshops, Dottye and her co-trainer emphasize how crucial it is for parents to talk openly about race with children and to be willing to be changed in the process.

The challenge Dottye offers is no small task, particularly given the multiple barriers to justice parents face when rallying for their African American children. Susan Burnett, who helped raise five of her husband's six children, says, "I wouldn't think of parenting as activism. I would say that is part of what you do. I have learned that is part of what a revolutionary does, what a revolutionary lives his/her life to do. Ali Bey's children brought me into the schools. These kids would then be shoved off into special education programs. Then I would go in and fight back. There was no end to what you have to confront in this system. Genocide in the education area. A young Black male child is taught from the time he is in second and third grade he is disabled. This happened with my grandson. He was immediately identified as learning disabled. We finally got them to admit that they thought the disability was because he is Black." When she and her husband enrolled his oldest two children in high school, the teachers said they needed to put them into remedial classrooms. "What I said is that they need to challenge them. In a way, I think this was all part of my education to bring me to where I am now."

For Susan, antiracism has included taking their landlord to court for racial discrimination while rallying for the children in public school. At each step, she believes it has been easier for her than if she were African American. Her class and race privilege "give me a sense of freedom in a way that others who are Black don't have. I also have knowledge that a lot of white folks don't have or a lot of Black folks: what America tells you to strive for is poison. I know because I was born into it and I know how sick it is." Although Susan is fierce about her loyalty to her stepchildren and their right to justice in their lives, she is also aware that white privilege has helped her rally for them.

Susan also bravely articulates her precarious position within the family. "I don't know if this is about Black and white. I don't think it is. I think it is about being an outsider. Maybe it is about Black and white. One of the things that happens in my family is I am always the one that catches the hell. I am the one who gets all of the hostility. I don't know if that is because I am a stepmom. I don't know if it is because I am white. I don't know if this is what happens with women who are strong. I would really be interested in knowing whether white women who are married to white men and have white stepkids get the same kind of . . . I think maybe this is the woman's role. The children never give him the anger they give to the mom. There are times when I have felt very alone in the family. . . . You are just out there and doing it and doing it and doing it and you just wonder why the fuck am I doing this. I don't know how to separate out the gender piece from being white. I don't think it is because I am white. I think it is because I am a woman. I used to think it was about race."

Antiracists in multiracial families often speak with courage and wisdom about the incredible impact these relationships have had on their consciousness, but they also specify the stresses they face along the way. Bonnie Kerness, who raised six children (of African descent and white, both biological and adopted) writes, "Once the children's father left, I re-formed the household into a communal setting. There was this great sense of the kids and I making it together with few 'top down' issues. I never felt that my being their parent or my additional years made me any wiser than they were. Since the household was mixed culturally, racially, and even religiously, there were many 'bumps' and a lot of laughter. And, if I didn't raise activists, I did raise vehemently antiracist people who have this great love of diversity and who are each nurturers. I suppose that alone is enough of a triumph."

At the same time, the model of parenting Bonnie adopted and her antiracist politics made her family anything but the norm in their community or the larger society. "I used to tell my kids that after me having raised them, they would go out into the world and be prepared for absolutely nothing because the world is not what they lived in at home, which was multiracial, multicultural. . . . They grew up with, two of the kids I helped to raise are gay, one male, one female. One of my kids still tells the story of what happened to her when she saw racism and found herself screaming at somebody on the street. You have a different consciousness, and it is not a mainstream consciousness. . . . Unfortunately, I haven't been able to construct my own community, but I think there is a lot of isolation that goes on. I know my kids have felt it at different times. Why can't Mom be like everyone else? When they were going through the whole process of getting engaged and getting married, they would sit me down with this whole list of instructions of what to say and what not to say. Please don't talk politics. Don't make anybody crazy. Just be like a regular person for one day, just while you are meeting the in-laws. But that is isolating."

Another challenge for antiracist parents involves their knowledge of the impact of their activism on their children. Being raised by activist parents provides children with a language to name the injustices around them and gives them daily examples of people who believe discrimination is neither inevitable nor acceptable. Even very young children have real and immediate reactions to damage being done to others. That damage is even worse for children when those whom they are told to respect and rely upon remain inactive in the face of injustice.

Among the few activists I interviewed who were graced with activist parents, all had deep respect for their parents, a respect they felt when they were children and continue to feel since having become activists themselves. The respect and intimacy they shared because of their mutual activism is a far cry from the deep alienation and loneliness identified by people who had to leave their families—both emotionally and physically—in order to become activists in high school or as young adults.

At the same time, growing up in an activist family is not always easy. David Wellman says that one of the reasons he is protective of the term "activist" is because he "has paid such a high price to be the son of people who are activists, for whom nothing is more important than their activism—including their families—which created some resentment from me, toward them." Anne Braden writes, "All of Carl's and my children lived their childhoods under the shadow of the constant attacks on their parents, facing a world that must have seemed to them even more hostile than it did to us; sometimes it seemed that they could not turn on the TV set without seeing their parents depicted as villains. Sometimes they were penalized for who their parents were. For example, in high school our son Jim was rejected for membership in the National Honor Society—although his grades were excellent and he went on to become a Rhodes scholar and win a full tuition scholarship to Harvard Law School. We learned from people close to the process that their rejection was because he was the child of Carl and Anne Braden. We wanted to fight about that one, but Jim asked us not to, saying he would be embarrassed. Also, as I look back, I realize that our household was one where there was almost constant tension, very little relaxation. People have often asked me whether I felt the kind of life we lived affected our children adversely. Of course it did and I don't know how it could have been otherwise. A friend of mine said something some years back that stayed with me. In the 1950s, there was a war you know, she said, it was a war of the U.S. government on its own people. And children of war, no matter what kind of war, bear scars."[5]

For activists in prison, the impact of their activism on their children is especially complicated. The physical distance enforced by incarceration can be extremely hard on children. At the same time, it is risky for prisoners to talk openly about their worries about their children, given the stigma they face of having abandoned their children because of their activism. When I asked Ray Luc Levasseur about the effect that activism has had on his children, he wrote a lengthy answer that identified a catch-22. "Now you're asking me a question my daughters have asked me. Some of us hesitate to fully address the effects publicly on our children because we see it as personal, private, or the cause/effect of a problem that is not so sure and clear. (Lots of youngsters abuse drugs. If an activist's kid abused drugs it is directly related to the activist's choices/consequences.) If I'd left children behind for Vietnam duty and then returned with all sorts of dysfunctional, post–traumatic stress, would I be asked this question by family and strangers? I think probably not. If I'd resisted the Nazi regime in Germany or fought for my people in El Salvador, would I be asked this question? Probably not. Because most people see these struggles as righteous, but they don't view lifting a hand against 'our' government in the same way. I doubt Mandela gets asked this question in a critical way. People would be afraid they'd insult the man, though Mandela has said he's deeply felt the impact of his imprisonment on his children. I'll also get asked this question by the parole board, though they'll call it 'remorse.' If I tell them I feel remorse they'll say I am lying in an effort to get parole. If they say I don't have remorse they'll use it as a reason to deny parole. The proverbial catch-22."

Ray sees his activism as both a statement in support of children, including his own, and as what stopped him from being with his children when they were growing up. He writes, "When I gave my closing statement to the sedition trial jury I asked them what they'd do if a repressive government with extensive outside support came down to Springfield, Massachusetts, and killed a thousand people, mostly youngsters? 'Cause that's what happened in Soweto, South Africa, and Morozon Province, El Salvador. I showed them pictures of the dead and extensive documentation. They acquitted me because they came to understand and empathize. I felt I did the principled thing, what needed to be done, what was morally right and legally right under international law. To feel remorse for that cuts against the grain of my heart and character. However, in retrospect, at that time and place, under those conditions, it was wrong to have children. In my heart I was choosing life, but life has consequences, particularly under those conditions, and continues to impact my daughters in various ways including through my imprisonment. I recently saw my daughters and we discussed this. But rather than regret a decision, I'd rather choose to focus on the affirmation of life and encourage them to do the same. One group that recognizes the special needs of children of political prisoners and activists who pay a steep price for their commitment is the Rosenberg Fund for Children."

Living the High Life

There is also a sensibility among many activists, more among women than men but among some men too, that being an activist for the long haul means taking care of oneself daily, including making space for reflection and regeneration, taking care of one's mind and body, and seeing the health of an individual as tied to the health of the body politic.

Chronic illness is pervasive in the U.S. population, so perhaps the number of people I interviewed who suffer in this way is not disproportionate. But many link their going up against the system on a daily basis and feeling the toll it takes on their bodies. Many people I interviewed have illnesses that are either caused or aggravated by stress: chronic fatigue syndrome, eating problems, multiple sclerosis, ulcers, immune deficiencies, depression. Ruth Frankenberg, for example, sees a connection between dealing with racism and homophobia and her multiple sclerosis. As a university professor who lectures on oppression, Ruth "has dealt with and experienced a lot of fear in talking about racism and homophobia. Those two in particular. With class inequality and sexism too, but especially around racism and homophobia, I feel myself saying things to people that they don't want to believe and hear. And feeling a lot of anger and hatred coming back at me from my audience, especially when I am in a big lecture situation. And I strongly think that was a big contributor to my first big episode of MS. Just having and feeling that and not knowing how to deal with it."

Tony Ward, a Quaker who cofounded the East Harlem Block Schools and has worked with children of color all of his adult life, links antiracist work and stress. According to Tony, doing his work requires living with constant anger. "I have chronic stomach problems, and Quakerism doesn't help you a lot with that. Quakerism is a religion that tends, it shouldn't, but it makes you repress those things rather than express them, so it leads to that kind of stuff. Mine is rage. It enrages me, and the way I always dealt with the rage is by focusing on work. . . . There is a bottomless pit of rage and sadness about what happens to children of color in everything. I chose to focus on schooling as the thing I try to do something about. . . . In New York right now, it is just unspeakable what Giuliani is doing. With police swaggering around essentially able to shoot any person with brown skin and they do it with total immunity—total immunity. I have a series of spasms and irritations that are all stress related that plague me and have to do with sitting on my emotions."

Bonnie Kerness directly links her work and her mental, physical, and spiritual health. "The world I live in second-hand is one of terror and brutality, and there is no way I can pretend that it hasn't affected me. I believe that the prison culture affects everyone who is touched by it. It is tainted and toxic and often the keepers as well as the prisoners suffer from the complete inappropriateness of caging human beings. My everyday world is full of beatings and torture. Words like 'hog-tying,' 'four-point restraints,' and 'cell extractions' fill my days and thought. It is a rare day that I don't share the tears of a loved one of a prisoner or a prisoner themselves. Sometimes, the silence of a control unit is something I can 'hear' and feel, and sometimes the utter chaos of the noise on the punishment units will echo in my ears for hours after I hang the telephone up with a prisoner from there who has called. I have mourned the death of someone who was murdered by the state as surely as their family has. The surveillance has also impacted me enormously, although I have learned to be almost casual because it has been so prevalent in these past few years."[6]

Bonnie draws direct links between witnessing the cruelty of a system she is trying to intervene against and developing chronic fatigue syndrome. She says, "I don't think you turn yourself as an organizer off when you come home. One of the difficult things I have had to work on with the American Friends Service Committee is that even though they want me to work nine to five, there is no way I can do what I do nine to five. I mean I'll get a phone call at ten at night or someone will try to catch me because the only time we can catch one another is seven in the morning. Most of the folks I work with throughout the country don't get paid to be activists. They just simply are activists and get paid to be teachers or whatever else they do. So there is no way I can fit myself into a nine-to-five job. And I think that trying to do that is perhaps what triggered the chronic fatigue. Now that I have stopped trying, I can get up at six in the morning and hit the computer here and work until nine and then rest all afternoon and maybe go into work at night for a meeting. I put in my required seven hours, but very nontraditionally." In the process, Bonnie says, "I am realizing it is very hard work. It is very passionate work. Most of us, no matter what our salaries are, end up giving huge amounts of money where it is needed. So that I don't necessarily have the money. I have the salary to take vacations, but I don't have the money to take vacations. I don't know that we treat ourselves very well. That may be an individual flaw. I don't like to say white guilt but certainly the feeling that the work is compelling and absorbing. I know very often someone will say to me, How do you do it year after year? My thing is, well, if the prisoners can do it, if they can survive and stay healthy, and stay in the struggle, surely I can, with every luxury I have."

Bonnie sees her decision to put her mental and physical health on the front burner as a way to stay "in the struggle" for the long term. "I have pushed myself far too hard and too long. I decided to get into working out and I decided to get into running. I was a smoker and I was a drinker. I stopped drinking and smoking within the past eight years." For Bonnie, these decisions were based on her physical health as well "as a way of releasing myself from a kind of 'American' style of life—i.e., the two-martini lunch as 'sophistication.' Aside from the enhancement of my discipline in stopping, I also felt a sense of freedom from self-destructive consumerism and mainstream values which say this is okay."[7]

Bonnie also attributes her decision about alcohol and smoking to hard lessons learned from activists. "I have been hanging out intellectually through the prison work with revolutionaries very intensively for more than a decade. In that community, even if you read the literature, many of the disasters, many of the mistakes were made, because folks were getting high. Folks were drinking. Folks were in poor physical shape. I think that played a role in changing me. What was it to smoke cigarettes? What was it to drink? Right now, I am very busy becoming less efficient than I was for most of my life. That has been a hard lesson for me to learn."

The questioning of mainstream values about food, alcohol, and consumerism is also reiterated by antiracists who link being vegetarian to their politics. Of those interviewed, Naomi Jaffe may have best articulated how being a vegetarian is a political issue. Naomi writes, "One important part of who I am is my vegetarianism. I became a vegetarian during the Vietnam War, when my rage was the greatest against the pilots who killed from the air, who never had to look in the eye the destruction and suffering they caused. I thought our relationship to our fellow inhabitants of the earth is like that, that we shape them into slices and patties and don't ever have to even think about their existence or pain; later I came more and more to feel that there is no difference between having a hierarchical view of the world of people versus animals—it's self-serving in the same way, a view imposed by force from the top and not shared by those on the receiving end."[8]

Part of living the high life is about recognizing the toll that going up against racism takes and taking steps given this reality. From Dorothy Stoneman's perspective, the basic consequence of doing antiracism is "living with a broken heart. You are all the time aware of what people are going through in a way that you wouldn't have to be if you chose to be numb. So you have to live with a broken heart and you have to live with rage. But that is just real. It doesn't seem like a cost. It seems like protecting yourself from what is false. Having a way to deal with a broken heart, I cry a lot and rage. I am reminded of my daughter, and this is the cocounseling influence. People have often asked me why I didn't burn out through all of those years. I think I didn't burn out because of cocounseling. I tried to make sure that I had an hour or two or three a week when I could just sob. My daughter, when she was three, we asked her to give up a dog we had found in the street, and I asked her how she felt. She said I can stand anything as long as I am allowed to cry about it. I suppose that is part of it. I think that an awful big part of our society doesn't allow itself to cry. Can't bear to feel the pain. I think that is a loss."

So, what do you do if an activist life means living with a broken heart? For many people, an everyday antidote is humor. Like ethnic or gay humor, the humor of many activists is both self-effacing and somehow affirming at the same time—of a politic, a sensibility, and a way of life they create as they go. The heart of their humor beats to a recognition that being an activist requires a willingness to feel deeply, laugh heartily, find what brings joy in life, and then embellish upon it. The humor draws on identity: the macabre of southern humor; the attention to the body in lesbian humor; Jewish humor, a humor born of just barely making ends meet, for many years in a row.

Being raised in the South gave Anne Braden and Mab Segrest access to a rich tradition of treating the grotesque and paradoxical as a potential site for great humor. The title of Segrest's first book, *My Mama's Dead Squirrel,* comes from a story she tells about her mother, who, remembering a dead squirrel on her couch that she had forgotten to clean up before a bridge party, decided it was better to admit to the presence of this smelly being than to try to cover it up. Segrest uses this image metaphorically to explain her realization, come to many times in her life, that it is better to tell the truth about racism than to lie, since the dead squirrel is in fact in the middle of everybody's living room.[9] "In my southern family, much got swept under the rug—dust, arms, feet, skeletons, dead squirrels, whole bodies."[10]

Like Segrest, Anne Braden (who, in her midseventies, still smokes like a chimney) sprinkles her writing and talks with jokes, political puns, and tongue-in-cheek comments. Her humor shows up throughout her new epilogue to the new edition of *The Wall Between*. When she and her husband Carl were charged a second time with sedition, this time for attempting to overthrow the government of Kentucky by working with coal operators in the mountains, Anne remembers, "Carl used to joke that he and I were probably the only two people in the same country who had been charged twice with trying to overthrow the same state government—and that, since the government was still standing, this could prove we were a bit ineffective."[11]

Braden also tells a story of her husband, most of whose books had been confiscated by the government during the 1954 sedition trial. When he finally got them back (a fabulous array of books on Marx, Lenin, the labor movement, Eugene Debs, and any book that had been in his collection with a Russian name on it), Carl Braden put them in a front hall bookcase—rows and rows of books labeled by the government "Dangerous," "Exhibit #482," "Exhibit #483," and the like. Anne writes that for years, "Carl would give a book to people who came to visit as souvenirs, one by one, until most of them were gone."[12]

There was antiracist humor: Betty and Herman Liveright, for New Year's 1998, sent out a greeting—"Here's to 1998; Let's Agitate"—with a color photo of the two of them waving walkers and canes at each other. The following year's card—"Here's to 1999; May the Struggle Continue until We Win"—shows the two of them pushing a huge red ball, one on one side, one on the other, not unlike Sisyphus at eighty-five years old.

Everybody has the potential to be funny. But I put humor in the category of antiracist culture, since it is a humor about a politic so shaped by race. What makes this humor work, what makes it stick, is its basis in incongruity.[13] Incongruity means using the very privilege granted by white supremacy to undermine it. Incongruity means coming to understand that self-love is a real struggle for antiracists in a society in which being conscious about racism means consistently facing up to what white people do. Anne Braden writes, "Even in the long years when I was the object of vicious attack, there were always certain advantages that came to me because I was white. There is a corruption that comes with such advantage that cramps the soul. And I think no white people in such a society founded on racism ever totally free themselves from that prison."[14] Like Toni Morrison, James Baldwin, Lillian Smith, Mab Segrest, and others, Anne Braden sees racism as a death for its victims as well as for those who support it. Toni Morrison writes, "The trauma of racism is, for the racist and the victim, the severe fragmentation of the self, and has always seemed to me a cause (not a symptom) of psychosis, strangely of no interest to psychiatry."[15] Of the damage of racism to white people, James Baldwin writes, "They are dimly, or vividly aware that the history they have fed themselves is mainly a lie, but they do not know how to release themselves from it, and they suffer enormously from the resulting incoherence."[16] Humor is one way people cope with this incoherence, especially when they are conscious that they are part and parcel of the very problem they are trying to resist.

There is another basic incongruity for antiracist activists: the incongruity of needing to work for a world that looks so dramatically different from the one they are living in. The day I went to interview Betty and Herman Liveright, they laid out a delicious spread while they kept talking, full speed, for hours. They served the food on yellow paper placemats with a sidebar in calligraphy that read: "The Berkshire Forum." (The Berkshire Forum was a Highlander Folk School of the north, although more explicitly Marxist, that the Liverights helped operate for twenty years.) Also in calligraphy on the placemats was a line by Barrow Dunham: "Even now, we ourselves are determining the future, not by knowing what it will be but by conceiving of what it can be"; a politic—embossed on yellow paper placemats—of constant incongruity.

Part of the reason humor is so important for antiracists is that doing the work over the long run requires the ability to live with despair. Ironically, the rage and despair that is an inevitable part of understanding the depths of racism also seems to allow people the capacity to feel great joy as well. In a 1987 speech about organizing against the Klan, Mab Segrest spoke about having had a fear since she was a little girl of men in packs. With the Greensboro Klan murders in 1979, "The pack took on a definite identity—within three years there was a Nazi para-military organization within two hours of my home."[17] Ironically, though, Segrest says that "organizing against the Klan and Nazis helped to open up a world beyond fear of death: to turn me from fear to joy."[18] It was pure joy, for Mab, when she heard her daughter-to-be's heartbeat in her partner's womb; pure joy watching the head poke out. And a joy comes from knowing there are others out there who also move through fear into action.

Alongside benefiting from the regenerative power of humor, many people are in intimate partnerships that have sustained them across the decades. Of all those I interviewed, I felt the synergistic power of a political and intimate love most strongly with Betty and Herman Liveright. Since I interviewed them together, I got to catch a glimpse of what has kept them together for more than sixty years. During the in-terview, they were both interested and respectful of each other's stories. They had obviously heard many of each other's stories before, which might lead one to expect them to drift in their attention when the other was speaking. But as they were talking, it felt as if they had both heard each other's stories before *and* were hearing them for the first time. They made room for each other to offer alternate interpretations and details that made the stories more precise. But it was not as if they were filling in the blanks for each other. Rather, they were telling stories while they were continuing to look for their political significance.

My guess is that part of what has enabled them to maintain their activism for so long has been having each other. As they say, "We have sold the *Daily Worker* together on street corners." They joined the Communist Party together in Philadelphia in 1936. In the 1950s they moved to New Orleans, where they were run out of town for trying to integrate a children's television show. In the 1960s Herman was active in campaigns in Philadelphia against police repression. Betty helped bring the first multiracial play to the McCarter Theater in Princeton. At the same time, they raised two children. They lived through a num-ber of huge historical periods: the McCarthy era, the Black Power and anti–Vietnam War movements, and through the passivity and retrench-ment of the 1980s. From 1972 to 1991 they ran the Berkshire Forum, which "Black associates helped them found." They set the twenty years of political agendas for the weekend workshops together through "very lively arguments" and "screaming a lot." They have been sounding boards for each other since they first met.

Now they are living together in a small apartment and working with political prisoners. And they keep reaching forward. While I was there, for example, a friend who works at a local university called. Betty had called to see if this person might have access to funds to support a Cuban political music group, whose music, Betty tells me, "isn't the kind you would normally hear on NPR [National Public Radio]." Even while Betty was talking with me, she was working with her local contacts to help Cuban musicians get access to necessary resources.

Most of those I interviewed are in long-term intimate relationships with politically like-minded partners. Those who are not in partnerships tend to have extensive friendship networks, both locally and nationally. Their partnerships and friendships came up repeatedly as sources of great strength and companionship. Still, isolation was a theme that eventually came up in many of the interviews, although people were hesitant to draw attention to it. As one of the only progressives in Syracuse, New York, elana levy spoke of the loneliness and isolation she feels. People constantly expect her to be the one to bring up race and cultural issues. Horace Seldon lost his wife, who died of an asthma attack while helping organize a school "stayout" in support of Boston's Black educational movement in 1964. Horace, now in his seventies, has never found anyone of her caliber or courage with whom he can share his activist life in an intimate way. David Gilbert faces sleeping alone night after night, trying to make the most out of visits from friends and his twice-yearly trailer visits with his now-grown son. Their losses and loneliness remain even as they continue to try to take principled stands, against the odds. In "Thirteen Springs," Marilyn Buck writes:

> *had you planted a tree*
> *to fill in the deep well*
> *of my absence*
> *that tree would be*
> *thirteen springs high*
> *high enough to relieve*

the relentless sun of incarceration
strong enough to bear
the weight of children
who might have been born
had I not been seized
from your life and plunged
into this acid-washed crypt
of perpetual loss
and high-wired vigilance

but there is no tree
that stands in my place
to harbor birds and changing winds
perhaps someone will plant
a willow a eucalyptus
or even a redwood
any tree that will
in thirteen years more
bear fruit and provide shelter[19]

Of all the themes I tried to explore with those I interviewed, my interest in the long-term costs and consequences of living an activist life was the one most people balked at, tried to avoid, and said they didn't understand. Their overwhelming sentiment was one of deep gratitude for the work they have been able to do and the people they have worked with and loved along the way. And yet my pursuit of what it takes to be and stay healthy both physically and mentally in a racist society remains important to me, partly because I think that people who are not yet activists but who would like to become active often sense that much of the work can be risky. Activists can lose the four "*F*'s": family, friends, funding, and fun, at least initially. In the end, I think it helps when activists are up front about the stress of antiracist living and explicit about the steps they take along the way to care for themselves and those around them.

When Spirituality Is a Verb

The range of religious backgrounds among antiracists makes absurd any attempt to make blanket statements about connections between religion or spirituality and activism. And yet one of the elements of ac-

tivists' lives that is most characteristic of the late 1980s and 1990s is a
renewed interest in spiritual practice—in its myriad forms—as a guide
and support for antiracist activism. In this way, activists in the 1990s
have come full circle with SCLC and other Black-led activism of the
1950s and 1960s that, in the words of Bernice Johnson Reagon, provided a methodology for the Civil Rights Movement.[20]

What makes attention to spirituality in the 1990s different from the
Protestant-based religious practices of the early Civil Rights Movement and the Christian and Jewish religious basis of the sanctuary
movement in the 1980s is that in the 1990s the practices are much less
institutionally based, more influenced by Eastern-based traditions, and
more eclectic. This eclectic range of spiritual practices include, among
others, Marilyn Buck's practice of yoga and meditation in her prison
cell and during recreation, Laurie Holmes's attempts to incorporate
rituals of healing and compassion into staff meetings at a center where
she works with women in transition, Dottye Burt-Markowitz's passion
for solitude and the power of nature, Bill Walsh's trek to Ireland to explore the spiritual and activist roots of Irish culture, Maggie Nolan
Donovan's interest in Catholic saints, Suzanne Ross's attendance at a
synagogue that shares space with a progressive Protestant church in
Manhattan, Ruth Frankenberg's meditation and worship of the Divine,
and elana levy's Passover seder every year with her daughter and ten
other people, most of whom are not Jewish.

Many antiracists have a sense that justice work and spirituality are
deeply connected. One activist I interviewed traces his commitment to
antiracism as a life-time project to a spiritual message. With vivid detail, Horace Seldon describes a gorgeous Sunday morning ten days
after Martin Luther King Jr. was assassinated. As he was driving home
from church, with his windows wide open, after preaching on the connections between Jesus Christ and King, he "suddenly came to a realization that what I must do with the rest of my life is to work on the
white problem. Just as clear as could be. Clear as a bell. I had no idea
what that meant. I don't know how I got across the turnpike. I alternately sang hymns and cried all the way across the turnpike. It was a
very moving experience. A hugely moving thing. It still moves me to
this day. It was something that taught me how I must spend the rest of
my life. I can't rationalize it. I can't explain it. . . . It was an Epiphany.
The light breaking through 'epi' 'phanos.'" It was that summer, in

1968, that Horace organized Community Change, a center committed to racial justice that is currently in its third decade.

Most people did not have an epiphany like Horace's. Rather, they began to seek a spiritual approach to antiracism after having become activists. Susan Burnett says, "Is my justice work spiritually motivated? Yes. Absolutely. I am saving my soul. I don't know how else to put it. It is my life I am saving. I believe it is what I do for me so that I don't become part of the living dead." For Susan, putting words to this connection has been a revelation. "I couldn't say this ten years ago. That is why I am a revolutionary. I know the system doesn't work. I am working to destroy it because we need to come up with a new system. It kills the oppressor too. I know because I am part of the oppressor class." The key step in honoring the spiritual basis of Susan's justice work occurred when she took her health troubles seriously enough to stop working in the corporate sector. Once she began working at home, she was able to better manage her difficulty breathing and to focus almost full-time on political prisoners. Through that, she got more and more involved with the campaign to free Mumia Abu-Jamal, whose spiritual strength has inspired her tremendously.

Many people talked about the ways that having a spiritual practice opened up new and more expansive ways to support racial justice. Dawn Gomes says the biggest transition in her activism in the last decade is that she no longer thinks there are purely political solutions to problems. The solutions are also spiritual. Dawn believes that doing activist work is too "heartbreaking" and "painful" if people do not have a way to "organize around the pain." For Dawn, meditating and going to a twelve-step recovery program has given her skills to nurture compassion, forgiveness, and healing—all capacities that help her tremendously in the nonprofit disaster relief organization where she works.

Ruth Frankenberg has been an antiracist activist in various contexts since young adulthood. Her initial motivation for developing a spiritual practice came from her own and her partner's health crises. Through their emerging spiritual practice, which centers on meditation, she has come to believe that a spiritual practice encompasses but does not erase activism. She says, "The politics are sheltered and protected by spiritual practice and belief."

This sheltering manifests itself in her teaching and writing in several ways. First, she is much more aware than she was previously that she is being guided in her work. She used to think, when she designed a course or wrote an article, that she had done it. Now she believes "it is a process I am not fully in control of." An example of this occurred recently in a university course she taught called Race, Culture, and Society. She was so ill during the quarter that "it was a miracle that I could even be there and be coherent. But the work the students did was extraordinary." There were a couple of students in the class who, Ruth says, "if [white supremacist] Tom Metzger called, would go with him, not with me. But by the end of the term, they were doing exquisite work." One of the students had spent the quarter doing work that was full of white male resentment, rage, and frustration. Ruth was "at the point where I was trying to think what hate speech regulations there might be on campus" that might stop him. Then Ruth asked him to come to office hours and "she asked for guidance" for how to work with him. She says, "I remembered what Thich Nhat Hanh says, that what people want most is to be listened to.[21] I listened to him and I talked with him and really heard him out and explained things to him he didn't understand. As it turns out, his artwork was very moving. His collage demonstrated his confusion and his sense of stereotypes of white people, his sense of hatred and hostility. The collage captured how he felt about the loss of Martin Luther King and how his death really robbed the country of direction. The student's self-image was at the bottom right-hand corner. It was a magazine picture of a young white man with his head in his hands, which was saying, 'I don't know the way forward.'"

Ruth says that is just one of fifteen or twenty stories she could tell showing she is not working alone. She says, "I really don't think I did that. And I don't think he did it by himself." For Ruth, "the task is about stepping aside and being a coauthor instead of feeling like one, I have to do this and two, I have to be in control of what these people think at the end of a class period or the end of a quarter." Having a spiritual practice has also given Ruth "a greater patience about time—all of which I suppose one would get perfectly well without spiritual practice. But it just so happens I do." Her practice is also "about welcoming miracles." And it is seeing what "we do on this planet as a huge experiment where everything is a teacher and an opportunity to learn."

Ruth believes that "we are working through a hugely multifaceted experiment to see whether we can harmonize human consciousness with divine consciousness. And clearly, right now, we aren't doing so good. Clearly, everyone's job is to do their part toward that harmonizing process." As Ruth sees it, "Antiracist work is very much about harmonizing because it is about addressing a really major misconception with really violent consequences. It is the same as doing work against homophobia. It is about really trying to gently and yet forcefully challenge and yet reorient all kinds of disharmonious thinking and action. Obviously, one of the most enormous of these actions is racism." Her role models along the way have included the engaged Buddhist teacher, writer, and peace activist, Thich Nhat Hanh; Gary Schneider, a Zen practitioner and an environmental activist; and many people involved in liberation theology and civil rights. Ruth says that all of them see antiracism and antihatred activism as inseparable from their spiritual practice.

Jeanine Cohen said that a combination of getting older, finding a way to claim a cultural Jewish identity, working with others who are interested in psychological dynamics of identity formation, and "having an integrated spiritual approach" all contributed to a reorientation in the way she does antiracism work. Through the years, she has tried to come to terms with the racial shame she has carried since she was a young girl in South Africa. She eventually discovered that the shame was getting in the way of being compassionate and nonjudgmental of other white people struggling to understand racism. Her own healing awakened compassion for herself and for other white people. "I was able to embrace myself more, to be a more self-loving human being."

Jeanine's spiritual and psychological work led her to identify the incredible cost she and her family paid for living in a racist society. Jeanine came to understand that she carried deep anger and hurt about what it meant to grow up in and then have to leave South Africa as a consequence of her parents' antiracism. This move meant "the loss of home. And the loss of cultural connectedness that I had as a child that I can never have again." Through the years, Jeanine has also realized the limits of her approach to changing the world. As a young person, "I so desperately wanted to change the world. I have come to understand that desperation was really wanting to change what happened to me [incest, racism she witnessed, and exile]. Wanting to make it different. My sense of absolute desperation about injustice links back to abuse issues. I had to work with the desperation." This work does not mean Jeanine takes racism less seriously or is less passionate about racial justice. But the psychological and spiritual healing has given her a long view, a patience to work with white people in various stages of consciousness, and a willingness to approach antiracism from multiple vantage points.

Antiracists who see their work in spiritual terms face a number of challenges. With the explosion of interest in New Age religious practices in the United States, many people have begun to talk in spiritual terms, but they may not have attached that spirituality to work for any collective politics. Their practices quickly can become ahistorical and individualistic. Those who do draw connections between spirituality and activism then come up against the stereotype that spiritual people are flaky, self-centered, and apolitical. Ruth Frankenberg says she would be very skeptical of her own interest in spirituality if she had not already been trying to do antiracist work for a long time. "I don't trust people who only in some liberal way say, We are all equal in God, and then don't have any comprehension of the dirty water in which we are all swimming, by which I mean racism, and the hatred of other oppression. I trust myself on this current part because of what I did earlier."

People who seek spirituality, says elana levy, are often looking for ways to have a meaningful life that is also apolitical. "If we are really going to make a change, we need a political analysis—an anti-imperialist, anticapitalist analysis." For elana and several others, it is a real challenge to find people who are both spiritually minded and activists. For example, she and her grown daughter are the only people in their spirituality group who see themselves as both spiritual and political. "Even the woman I see as my most important teacher I can't look to for how she fits the political with the spiritual." She continues to search for a melding between the two. That search includes resisting the continued tendency in some male leftist circles to dismiss processing, listening, and sharing leadership—all central components of feminist spirituality. She believes that male models of activism have often reinforced a gap between activist and spiritual approaches to justice work.

For activists who came of age in Communist or New Left politics, grappling with spirituality can feel like coming out of a spiritual closet. Reebee Garafalo says, "One of the reasons, frankly, why I am interested in the way young people think about spirituality is that I think we have a lot to learn about the stress of living an activist life. I have gotten bleeding ulcers at one point of my life because my job is so stressful. I chose to teach at a university that serves working-class people, which means there are no resources. The roof of my office leaks. I have to cover my computer with a piece of plastic every night before I go home. There is this little hose in my ceiling that drains the water into a bucket. Every few days after a rainstorm I take the bucket and go empty it in the bathroom. So I have a sense of humor about this, but I suspect that a faculty member teaching at Harvard would not see this as highly desirable." Reebee says that his partner meditates for a half hour every day, but "I couldn't find a half hour to meditate if my life depended on it. But that is a mistake. I would be a more effective activist if I didn't throw my back out every two weeks. If I set aside time to exercise every day."

Over the years, Reebee has had long-standing debates with activists who run themselves into the ground. He urged one friend to slow down long enough to finish his education so that he could earn a steady income. At the time his friend said that organizing was more important than finishing class assignments. Ultimately, Reebee is concerned about "the extent to which the 'Work, work, work, until you die approach' to organizing is just the political version of the Protestant ethic. It is the denial of pleasure, the denial of anything that works to your benefit. It is this goal of selflessness, the goal of giving yourself up." Reebee believes that "activists have to pay more attention to some level of taking care of themselves. Whether it is some measure of job security, some measure of physical exercise, some measure of spirituality, getting your head right." From Reebee's perspective, "nobody in the 1960s knew how to do that." In the 1990s Reebee is still not sure how. But he is looking.

David Gilbert drew a deep connection between antiracism and spirituality. He says, "Sometimes people have asked me what keeps me going in difficult times, and if spirituality has been helpful. I am definitely not religious. In fact, I would say that I am 'anti-religious.' At the same time, I have a spiritual sense of being connected to human beings. Maintaining friendships fuels this spiritual sense for me. My son also gives me great strength. He is sixteen now and has been raised by close friends of mine and his mother's, who was also imprisoned in 1981. Doing antiracist work has given me many gifts. I don't know how people turn their backs or manage to avoid these issues. I have a much broader sense of what it means to be human, thanks to the work I have done."

"In All Its Incarnations"

So why am I intent on showing that there is such a thing as antiracist culture? Why does it matter? In *The Color Purple,* by Alice Walker, Shug says to Celie, "I think it pisses God off if you walk by the color purple in a field somewhere and don't notice it."[22] In this instance, the color purple is the space that white antiracists live in that has been made possible precisely because of the centuries of struggle by African Americans, Native Americans, Latinos, and Asian Americans. There would be no significant white antiracist struggle or cultural practices were it not for the resistance of people of color. This is a point that some people writing about whiteness miss sometimes: There would be no critical whiteness studies without African American and ethnic studies, whose scholars wrote extensively about whiteness long before it was called "critical whiteness studies" by white academics.[23] If there is one message that emerges from listening to antiracists, it is how profoundly they have been and continue to be influenced by communities of color. Naming the existence of antiracist, multiracial culture as experienced by white people is part of acknowledging one of the fruits of antiracist labor that has been nurtured by people of color.

I also want to make transparent the hazards and great gifts involved in living an activist life. One of the reasons there are not more white people, and perhaps young white people in particular, who take racism seriously is that they know, whether consciously or not, that doing so can forever change their lives. Sociologist Cheryl Hyde writes, "I see my white colleagues and students struggle with absorbing new understandings of racist actions of whites, dealing with the accompanying guilt, and worrying about how they will now interact with family and friends."[24] White people need to know there are other people, other ways of being, other sensibilities, other communities that will catch them if they take steps away from the assumptions and lifestyles of dominant white culture.

Some antiracists grew up in families who supported their activism because their parents, themselves, were activists. Others have relatives who did not necessarily understand but who tried to accept when they dropped out of college, changed their major from economics to sociology, moved to El Salvador, joined the Weather Underground, would not visit them when they vacationed in an overwhelmingly white resort, or became an atheist or a Communist. Other people took stands, often beginning early in life, that forever cost them a sense of home with the people who raised them. Many people were not fortunate enough to come of age during a time when there was a vibrant social movement that could nurture them politically and emotionally. Some people had to travel a long way to begin to make sense out of the discontinuity of the white culture in which they grew up. We need to know the stories of people who have sought racial justice and in the process found a life they had not known was available to them. For them it was a "jump off a cliff and find a giant trampoline waiting for you at the bottom" experience.

Why do I believe we need to think about antiracism not only as a specific set of acts, principles, and alliances but also as a way of life? Because antiracism does not stand up to the test of time unless it is fully integrated into people's lives. Laurie Holmes says, "Fighting racism is about living life and having relationships with people. That is really all I think that it is. I don't think you can be antiracist without entering into real-life struggles where people reflect the diversity of the community that works toward something. Whether it is busing or neighborhood improvement or queer activism or stuff around the cops."

Among antiracists there is no one name people use to identify the culture they are creating. There is no town, no city, no region, and no generation that can be located on a map or in time as a place of antiracist culture. Even those surrounded by great support, including others intimately involved in antiracist struggle, still must contend with isolation and loneliness. The small number of antiracists across the country certainly mitigates any sense of an ample community among white antiracists. Bonnie Kerness says, "I don't fit anywhere. I don't fit in the white community at all. I don't fit in the Black community. So I think we tend to construct our own families, and friends become family."

Some people use the term "border" to describe the psychic place they live in: at least two worlds simultaneously and trying to find restfulness in the space in between. David Wellman writes that although "nobody calls me by it, my racial identity finally has a name I can answer to. I realize now that I am a 'border' person."[25] The Detroit neighborhood in which David grew up was a "borderland," as was SNCC. I would add to that list the multiracial community David is part of now in his work and with his friends. About the idea of recognizing this borderland, David writes, "I find the possibility attractive. It makes sense out of my experience. It names my identity. Sociologically speaking, it also makes my experience a lot less exceptional. It turns out, I'm not alone, in a category of my own."[26]

Of her life as an antiracist transplanted from South Africa, Jeanine Cohen says, "I feel very much like I live on the border and I try to traverse different bridges. I feel a sense of constant shifting, of how I understand myself in the world, given the context that I am in."

About border living, Ruth Frankenberg says, "I think there is a reality that, as a white antiracist, one lives in two worlds. One is a white one. The other is a white antiracist one inasmuch as most white people have absolutely no concept of what life is like if you happen not to be white but a person of color. So there is a way in which we are border crossers." For Ruth, that white antiracist world is with her peers who are antiracists, with "those particular persons where I find a deep sense of trust and recognition in the sense that we do know we are speaking the same language. . . . the reality is that the majority of white people do not have the slightest concept about racism and instead have their own apparatus—denial, color evasion, or race hatred. Really that is my job—to keep knocking on doors and asking people to wake up and smell the coffee."

When I asked Susan Burnett if she feels like she lives in a borderland, she replied, "I don't feel like I live in a borderland. My father's people live in a borderland. I live in the real land. My family lived in a privileged compound. Now I live in the real world with everyone else where I don't have sentries at the gate and I don't have the special meats and all the privileges. I am out there living in the big ocean." Susan's unwillingness to concede the center of society to wealthy white people is a position worthy of consideration given the power of naming.

Meanwhile, whether named or not, white antiracists are living lives that are profoundly multiracial—where they work, where they live, who they call family, and who they call in the middle of the night. They are living lives in which white people are not at the center. Otherness is sought and celebrated. A house is more than a home. It is also a hub. Humor helps to keep people warm. Living the high life means living a vulnerable existence, much of the time, humbled by the work ahead, grateful for the work already done.

Epilogue

Longing for Memory

In her latest book, *The Vulnerable Observer*, Ruth Behar writes,

> Loss, mourning, the longing for memory, the desire to enter into the world around you and having no idea how to do it, the fear of observing too coldly or too distractedly or too raggedly, the rage of cowardice, the insight that is always arriving late, as defiant hindsight, a sense of the utter uselessness of writing anything and yet the burning desire to write something, are the stopping places along the way. At the end of the voyage, if you are lucky, you catch a glimpse of a lighthouse, and you are grateful. Life, after all, is bountiful.[1]

At the other end of this project, with many late trains met and my travel done, I stand grateful to have met those I encountered and moved by their struggle to help make life bountiful. In their stories, they have offered many lighthouses.

In addition to being moved by their courage, what has also stayed with me has been their willingness to reassess, regroup, and learn from their own limitations and those of the movements within which they have worked. The light in a lighthouse is always turning, so, much of the time, the rocks, water, and boats are in the dark. The back of the lighthouse is a necessary part of the story: the unwillingness of the Students for a Democratic Society (SDS) to look at the "whiteness" of the organization; the Weather Underground's arrogance and unreconstructed male dominance; the difficulty the white radical women had in taking on white feminism early on so that they could make second-wave feminism their own from the beginning; the inability of Central America peace organizations to make significant connections with United States–based Latino groups; the tendency of antiracist trainers to keep the workshops at the level of individual transformation; and the susceptibility of prison activists to push beyond their own human capabilities due to the urgency of the struggle. These and other limitations in white antiracist consciousness remain with us to learn from.

The power of studying history from the point of view of people's lives is that their stories provide the nuance, detail, and contradictions from which history is made. When I was a young person, history always stuck dead on the page. Facts, dates, battles, and wars meant little to me; they were part of a history that was largely told from the point of view of those in power, what Adrienne Rich has termed "an advertisement for the state."[2] As a child and young adult, I thought history had little to do with me; meanwhile, I had internalized many of the dominant tellings of history, almost through osmosis. Without a radical history to counter the normative version, I had little way to see history as a liberatory tool.

According to Rich, "Historical amnesia *is* starvation of the imagination, nostalgia is the imagination's sugar rush, leaving depression and emptiness in its wake" (145). Historical amnesia is a powerful process that denies everyday people a way into a history that reflects their own experience. It does double damage. People learn much about history in general that is plain wrong. The power of the dominant history is also its ability to convince people to accept a history that runs counter to their own experience.

The power of telling history from the point of view of "the little guy," the unsung heroes, the rank-and-file members of a community, and those who stand up against the powers that be is its ability to contradict historical amnesia, to affirm a version of history that is so often hidden from view. History told from the point of view of the dissidents, the activists, and the social-change agents counters the contortions of normative accounts. The history of white antiracism is an antidote to these contortions on several accounts: White people weren't "kicked out" of the Civil Rights Movement. Some of those in Student Nonviolent Coordinating Committee (SNCC) at the time may have provided votes that helped swing the decision in favor of SNCC's becoming an all Black organization. Whites who felt personally devastated included those who nevertheless saw the utility and purpose of such a decision. The Weather Underground cannot be simply dismissed as a bunch of crazies. Several of its members suffered from an arrogance made worse by male privilege. But many men and women in white solidarity groups were genuinely attempting to grapple with what accountability and solidarity meant when people were being taken down on the street, in cold blood.

As for antidotes to historical amnesia regarding the feminist movement, there are several to be had. As a teacher of feminist theory and the history of feminist movements I spent several years telling a version of that history that rested upon historical amnesia. The version I passed down assumed there were four branches of the feminist movement: radical, liberal, socialist, and women-of-color feminism. I never included white militant women or the Black Power Movement as part of the genealogy. I bought—hook, line, and sinker—the notion that the Black Power Movement was so sexist there was no way women, white or Black, gained from their experience in the movement. I treated women-of-color feminism as simply one brand of feminism. In the version I passed down, I, as a feminist attempting to be antiracist, was nowhere to be seen. Nowadays I start with the Civil Rights and Black Power Movements and lead up to the emergence of multiracial feminism, on the basis of which liberal, socialist, and radical feminism can then be evaluated.

Social history based on the political biographies of activists also offers new readings of Central America solidarity work as well as other activism in the 1980s and 1990s. There were two sanctuary movements operating during the U.S. intervention in Central America. There was a small, above-ground, media-savvy, and self-named sanctuary movement that was predominantly white and middle class. Alongside it was a much larger, largely underground, media-skeptical sanctuary movement made possible by the Latino neighbors and communities who took in and protected tens of thousands of Central American refugees. Those white activists who linked the two sanctuary movements were few and far between, a reality only hardened by continued U.S. refusal to acknowledge and support its multiracial, multilingual roots.

A race-conscious historiography of the two sanctuary movements requires finding ways to uncover the stories that have necessarily been clandestine. This hold true for the Black Power Movement and white solidarity organizations as well. Such a methodology is also crucial for any comprehensive telling of prison activism, since those on the inside are the most knowledgeable and in touch with the strategies necessary both to organize within prison and to dismantle the prison system. Yet their stories continue to be buried by unconstitutional search-and-seizure operations for materials sent into and out of prisons, the denial of prisoners' rights to free and open speech, and the lack of access to the health care needed so that prisoners are strong and healthy enough to keep speaking up. Adequate health care remains a number-one priority for people in prison. AIDS education remains at the top of an antiracist agenda.

Political prisoners continue to provide leadership for this and many other human rights issues. The master historical narrative ties the end of slavery to the Emancipation Proclamation in 1863. Prisoners' rights activists remind us that although the Thirteenth Amendment was passed in 1865, legally abolishing the slavery, it contained a provision that excluded from its protection anyone who was being punished for a crime. This reality—that many of the practices under slavery are now being upheld within a state- and federally sponsored system in which more than two million people, mostly people are color, are currently entangled—explains why, for antiracist activists, prison activism is a number-one priority.

Antiracist Ethics

Writing a social history of antiracist activism allowed me to rethink key moments in movement history; at the same time, it also enabled me to reconsider the underlying ethics developed for social justice movements. One of the most common ethics, associated first with the New Left and civil rights activism and then extended to second-wave feminism, is "The personal is political." In fact, many people consider movement history from the 1960s to the present as personal politics, believing that the New Left, the Civil Rights, and the feminist movements were powered in large part by politics that were personal. As David Wellman writes, "people's personal experience of oppression or their personal opposition to it was the basis of their involvement in the movements. White people fought for freedom because it was the right thing to do. They felt it personally. It wasn't about their commitment to a particular ideology."[3] The feminist movement expanded upon this philosophy by asserting that many issues that had been deemed personal were actually political and that contributing to the feminist movement required identifying the ways in which personal issues in one's life were in fact political.

I actually believe that this reading of history is only part of the story, that there have been two ethics operating simultaneously in the last forty years that might be captured in the slogan Anne Braden once explained to me: "The personal is political, and the political is personal." From what I see, activists prior to the Civil Rights Movement—Communists, perhaps the best case in point—did not think they had a right to "The personal is political." There was not really space for the "personal," especially for those not from "an oppressor group." People in the Communist Party who did not come from working-class roots, for example, learned that they could not base their politics on what had happened to them personally. In fact quite the opposite was true. Plus, there was not much room for psychology, for personal struggles.

The young people of SNCC, the young people of the New Left, and especially early second-wave feminists said, But wait, there are many personal issues that have been rendered domestic, private, off-limits, that are actually deeply political: abortion, sexual abuse, domestic violence, my right to love who I want to in the bedroom, and so on. But I actually do not think that ethic is what drove the best of the movements, the most-effective or most-encompassing of the movements. Although I believe that many Black people got involved in civil rights and Black Power because of their personal subjugation and that white radical feminists got involved in early second-wave protests and consciousness-raising because of their oppression, I think the white activists who were involved in the struggle against racism for the long haul had a politic that went way beyond, even transcended, "The personal is political." Their ethic—that the personal is political and the political is personal—says people need to stand up against injustice even if they were never personally among the subjugated. In fact, only standing up against what one has personally been subjected to is way too narrow a politic.

The interesting twist is that those who stand up for injustice as a matter of principle, not because they have been personally hurt by it, and who keep standing up for it eventually feel those injustices personally because the people who are personally injured are their lovers, friends, children, and close neighbors. The lives of people whose politics are based on "The political is personal" do change so that things that were never personal before become personal because of the people they know, the streets they walk, the jobs they take. This transformation is the ethical basis of the making of antiracist culture.

That is an ethic of accountability which I do not think is integral to "The personal is political." It is a step beyond it. The leftist organizing of the 1940s and '50s had "The political is personal" down to a "*T*" although there was not a lot of space to talk about how those politics affected people's personal lives. The youth of the Civil Rights Movement and white feminism introduced "The personal is political." But the Marilyn Bucks, Anne Bradens, and Naomi Jaffes of the world balked at "The personal is political" as it was framed by white antipatriarchy feminists, and for good reason. The Marilyn Bucks, Anne Bradens, and Naomi Jaffes came around to calling themselves feminists only after women of color rescued feminism from being reduced to issues that were only personal to white middle-class women.

The best of the feminist movement of the 1980s and '90s was when there was an ethic of accountability written into the social contract: White women needed to be accountable to women of color, straight women needed to be accountable to lesbians, whether or not lesbians or women of color were in the room to remind people about their politics. Those who held onto the longer slogan were the ones who had heard and accepted the notion "Hey, you need to know something is wrong and need to be opposed to it even if I am not here to remind you." And people need to live a life that helps them know it personally, a life in which they have known so many women of color and lesbians and poor women that they know what their position might be even if they are not in the room.

Many of the white antiracists in the Civil Rights Movement also balked at "The personal is political" when some white people personalized the transition from civil rights to Black Power. The David Wellmans of the world said, "That is ridiculous" when white New Lefters got defensive and angry for being left out. The Anne Bradens, David Wellmans, Ray Luc Levasseurs, and Maggie Donovans of the world knew that the transition was not about them personally as white people. It was about group rights and about Black people being up against the most powerful government in the world.

I think this pattern—of needing both "The personal is political" and "The political is personal"—holds true in organizing against U.S. intervention in Central America, in lessons learned from the limits of antiracist education, and in organizing against the punishment industry. White activists in all three instances encountered pitfalls when they tried to stay at the level of "the personal is political"—that is, when they said "I am personally oppressed as a lesbian in Nicaragua, so I will make that the central issue while I am picking coffee beans," when antiracist training is ultimately about providing a space for white people to talk about their own anxieties, often at the expense of the people of color. The goals stay at the level of personal transformation and never reach the level of filing a grievance against the CEO for discrimination.

The power of the double ethic—"The personal is political and the political is personal"—is that it encourages people to see everyday issues as well as pivotal historical events as political acts. The ethic takes seriously a culture of antiracism as something worth identifying, scrutinizing, honoring, and embellishing upon. The ethic also puts to rest simplistic attacks on identity politics, which, as first articulated by the Combahee River Collective, are the heart of the two-part principle. Identity politics establishes that the most radical and forward-thinking politics often come from people's own experience. A radical politic for Black women comes from Black women. In this way, identity politics is another way of affirming self-determination as the foundational principle for the struggle for liberation. The beauty of identity politics, as first articulated by Black women, is that it also opened a way for Jewish women, working-class women, lesbians across race, and other identity groups to articulate what they bring to the table: how their own identities shape their visions and priorities.

This is the essence of self-reflection, a practice that is essential if people are to understand how to contribute to other people's struggle and yet not try to control it; to see when they have institutional power and when they do not; and to deal effectively with the historical relations between different identity groups. Identity politics was founded on a valuing of people's personal experience as oppressed people and a recognition of the alliances made possible when other groups do their self-reflective work as well. Identity politics made room for "The personal is political" and "The political is personal."

The ease with which many young people of many different ethnic groups and sexualities came together to oppose the regressive initiatives in California in 1999 and their continued work to oppose police violence was made possible in large part by the thirty-plus years of identity politics—of recognizing individual stories and group rights; of people's multiple and contradictory identities; of the import of standing up for issues that affect the world even if they do not, at this moment, affect the activist. This, to me, is an example of history as progress, and since I do not think we can count too many examples of really moving forward politically since the 1970s, I'll take this one, wholeheartedly.

Riding the Wave

Since starting this project more than six years ago, I have felt like I have been riding a big wave that picked me up on one beach and has now set me down on another, decidely to the left of the beach where I began. This has not been an easy ride, particularly since I have been moving more and more to the left as the country has continued riding its tidal wave to the right—an alienating juxtaposition, to put it mildly. The day I finished the book, I cried elephant tears, had big sad eyes, and I couldn't stop crying. This was not postpartum crying. I had been ready to be done for some time. Rather, as I began to pick myself up, I realized that the little girl in me somehow thought that once I finished the book, my friend David Gilbert would be able to walk out of prison. It was an irrational, unrealistic association, I admit, but one that I now understand I had been holding onto subconsciously for a long time. This God-seeking, spirit-seeking person had become close friends with a man, both atheist and antireligious, whose compassion for humanity continues to amaze me but whose position I fear I have almost no power to change with the written word.

My tears, my reaction to finishing, made me face a worry I have had for a long time. Do people still read long books, especially history books? I used to think there was something potentially politically useful about writing a book. Writing such a book would be my small contribution to a much bigger struggle. But I am not sure anymore. Might I have been better off finding a way to make a film based on white antiracist activists? I still teach many, many books in my courses, but increasingly they are alongside many films, in an age when I think people see the world more though visual imagery than through the printed page, in an age when MTV, e-mail, and the Internet have abbreviated people's attention spans as people want to feel, see, and listen simultaneously. Words on the page, especially nonfiction, seem much less powerful, much less accessible, more arcane than film and music. I worry not only that my writing will do nothing to help people walk out of prison but also that history books are a medium for an earlier generation, a generation that has been left behind by faster and more three-dimensional ways of learning.

I have also lost a certain political optimism I used to have. When I began teaching Derrick Bell's *And We Are Not Saved* in a critical race theory law course in the early 1990s, I would present Bell's analysis of racism as endemic and a permanent feature of U.S. culture and institutions.[4] From Bell's perspective, the constitutional contradiction—that slavery was written into the Constitution and that capitalism trumps democracy in key ways—means that racism is not going to wear itself out. Although I presented his argument, ultimately I would argue against it. I felt an optimism about social change that encouraged me away from his perspective. I feel differently now. I come more closely down on Derrick Bell's side than before, a position that certainly has not stopped Bell from continuing to stand up for racial justice. His commitment is to do the work "as if" it is going to make a difference, even if it will not. The escalation of the prison system, the spread of capitalism into every nook and cranny across the globe, the increasing disparity between the rich and poor, and the increasing poverty of women and children in particular are among the many realities that have led me to the "act as if" philosophy rather than the "act so that in the future" approach to racial justice. This, perhaps, is a less eloquent version of what Antonio Gramsci long ago called pessimism of the intellect, optimism of the will.

I find it hard, however, to articulate this perspective without seeming to be disrespectful of all the work people have done to improve people's lives. In a much-appreciated exchange I had a few years ago with Bob Blauner, a noted sociologist whose work has long focused on antiracism, he took exception to my assertion that "racism has not lessened since the 1960s." Blauner wrote, "Racism is certainly here to stay in America, very pervasive and deep-seated, but to imply that the Civil Rights Movement did not bring significant changes, yes incredible improvement, is an insult to those who gave the best years of their lives, if not their lives, to the struggle."[5]

As I continue to see affirmative action jeopardized and undermined; as I watch Black men in my community snatched up by the prison system; as I spent four years alternately frantic, numb, and on fire about whether my now-twenty-three-year-old goddaughter would win her risky and unprecedented case to stay in the United States and not be deported to Trinidad (a situation so distorted by anti-immigrant policy regarding many Third World countries in the post–civil rights era); and as I explain to my eleven-year-old Black son what DWB (driving while black) means, I realize that my need to stay present and on guard can easily lead to an ahistorical panic on my part. Meanwhile, Bob Blauner's critique of my assertion and the work of many other activists and historians remind me of the danger of falsely equating or comparing different historical periods.

At the same time, riding this wave for the last several years has tempered the optimism I used to have. And although I would still describe myself as a structuralist—believing that there are structures of domination that influence and sometimes determine consciousness—increasingly, I am finding myself wanting to better understand the consciousness part of the equation. In addition to continuing to read Derrick Bell and Angela Davis and Joy James and Howard Zinn and Karl Marx and *The Nation,* I am also reading the Buddhist nun Pema Chödrön, the Vietnamese teacher Thich Nhat Hanh, and the womanist theologian Katie Cannon. I am finding meditation, yoga, and a daily spiritual practice increasingly crucial to deal with the rage that I feel; it is a sense of goodness amid the evil I see. When I lived in Brazil in 1976 as an exchange student, I used to watch people go through the trash at night searching for food. I was aghast and felt disdain for the homeowners on the street who seemed to just let it happen without helping those in need. I now lay in bed on Monday nights, trash night, and hear people from my neighborhood go through the recycling bins on the street, including the bin in front of my house, which I pay for with a mortgage, not rent. It is harder for me to pull joy inside me than it used to be. I am part of the problem, and I feel it daily.

I am also less willing to think of myself as an activist than I was when I began this project. Yes, I wore a nine-foot cardboard baby bottle through the streets of Colorado Springs in 1977 when I was a first-year college student to protest Nestlé's sale of baby formula that was deadly to newborns and infants; yes, I got arrested in the mid-1980s along with more than five hundred other people, all of whom gave the Nicaraguan revolutionary's name "Sandino" when we were being processed so that the police could not easily book us; yes, I helped organize a lively protest in Maine against the acquittal of the four police officers who beat Rodney King, a regional rally for Mumia Abu-Jamal, and other campus-based protests. Yes to these and other acts. But I am not an activist in the Anne Braden, Naomi Jaffe, Bonnie Kerness, Horace Seldon, and Laurie Holmes sense of the word.

I am more aware of my limits, which has been both humbling and a sign of self-acceptance. I think it is very hard to be a writer and a single mother and a full-time teacher and an activist, too. That is not to take away from what I do try to do. It is to recognize the limits of human energy and the amazing work of organizers who devote their whole lives to that endeavor. They are a special breed of people: They have special capacities and special energy and are human, too.

Coming to terms with where I have put the bulk of my energy (into writing) has also freed me to identify the hazards of that type of contribution—a growing awareness of the limits of the written word and an increasing acknowledgment of the loneliness and isolation writing requires. Even though I have met some extraordinary people along the way, all of whom made writing the book possible and some of whom have changed my life, the actual writing required a hibernation and isolation that, particularly toward the end, made me feel like I was dying. Increasingly, I have felt that an academic career has required me to trade in my body parts. Anything below my neck was traded in. I now want those body parts back. I need to figure out ways to write that make room for the mind and body; a structural analysis alongside attention to consciousness (of those interviewed as well as the interviewer); a method that makes room for writing while, in the words of Dorothy Stoneman, living with a "broken heart."

Meanwhile, I am eager to send this book into the world, grateful to the many people who have nurtured it into existence and hoping that somehow I have done justice to the ups and downs of the period in question. May the lighthouses shine brightly.

Toward a Comparative Feminist Movement (Time Line)

Toward a Comparative Feminist Movement

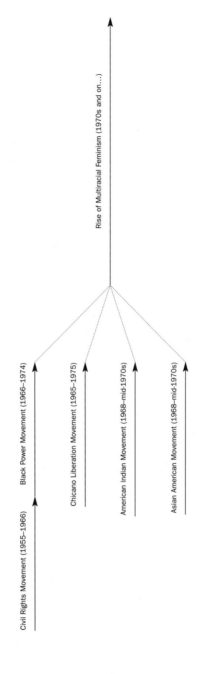

Civil Rights Movement (1955–1966)

Black Power Movement (1966–1974)

Chicano Liberation Movement (1965–1975)

American Indian Movement (1968–mid-1970s)

Asian American Movement (1968–mid-1970s)

Rise of Multiracial Feminism (1970s and on....)

Multiracial Feminism

1959	Cuban Revolution
1960	SNCC founded
1964	Civil Rights Act passed; Immigration and Nationality Act
1965	Johnson signs Affirmative Action executive order; Voting Rights Act
1966	National Welfare Rights Organization founded
1968	Shirley Chisholm elected to Congress; Third World Liberation Front student strikes; American Indian Movement founded
1969	Stonewall uprising; Indians of All Tribes occupation of Alcatraz
1970	*The Black Woman*, Toni Cade; Coalition of 100 Black Women
1971	Attica rebellion; Hijas de Cuauhtemoc Chicana group; Vancouver Indochinese Women's Conference; Asian American Women's Center, Los Angeles; National Conference of Puerto Rico Women founded; National Chicana Conference in Houston, Texas
1972	Angela Davis acquitted of all charges; Trail of Broken Treaties; National Black Feminist Organization; American Indian Movement occupation of Wounded Knee
1973	Coalition of Labor Union Women; Mexican American Women's National Association
1974	Women of All Red Nations founded; Combahee River Collective
1975	*Lilith, Sinister Wisdom,* and *Conditions* founded; U.N. Conference on Women, Mexico City
1976	Anna Mae Aquash killed; National Black Feminist Organization and Sagaris Conference on racism and sexism; Organization of Pan Asian American Women
1977	Combahee River Collective Statement; National Women's Studies Association founded
1978	Bakke Case; Harvey Milk and George Moscone assassinated
1979	Sandinista revolution in Nicaragua; *Conditions: Five, the Black Women's Issue*; Activists killed in Greensboro, N.C.; First National Third World Lesbian and Gay Conference; Assata Shakur freed in New Jersey, in exile in Cuba
1980	Kitchen Table Women of Color Press launched

Height of multiracial feminism (1977–1980)

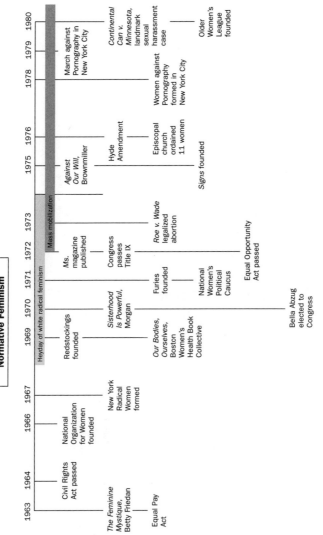

Normative Feminism

| 1963 | 1964 | 1966 | 1967 | 1969 | 1970 | 1971 | 1972 | 1973 | 1975 | 1976 | 1978 | 1979 | 1980 |

Heyday of white radical feminism

Mass mobilization

The Feminine Mystique, Betty Friedan

Civil Rights Act passed

National Organization for Women founded

New York Radical Women formed

Redstockings founded

Sisterhood Is Powerful, Morgan

Ms. magazine published

Against Our Will, Brownmiller

March against Pornography in New York City

Continental Can v. Minnesota, landmark sexual harassment case

Equal Pay Act

Our Bodies, Ourselves, Boston Women's Health Book Collective

Furies founded

Congress passes Title IX

Roe v. Wade legalized abortion

Hyde Amendment

Women against Pornography formed in New York City

Episcopal church ordained 11 women

Older Women's League founded

National Women's Political Caucus

Equal Opportunity Act passed

Signs founded

Bella Abzug elected to Congress

Multiracial Feminism

Timeline years: 1980 1981 1982 1983 1984 1985 1987 1990 1991 1992 1993 1994 1995

Height of multiracial feminism

- Kitchen Table Women of Color Press launched
- But Some of Us Are Brave, Hull, Scott, and Smith
- NY Women against Rape Conference
- Yours in Struggle, Pratt, Bulkin, Smith
- My Mama's Dead Squirrel, Mab Segrest
- National Women's Studies Association at Spelman College
- White Supremacist Beckwith convicted of murdering Medgar Evers

- This Bridge Called My Back, ed. Moraga and Anzaldúa
- Making Waves, Asian Women United of California
- U.N. World Conference on Women, Nairobi
- Bridges founded for Jewish feminists and friends
- Los Angeles rebellion following acquittal of police involved in Rodney King beating
- Protest against U.C. system abolition of affirmative action

- Ain't I a Woman, bell hooks
- A Gathering of Spirit, Beth Brant
- Supreme Court ruling that INS must interpret 1980 Refugee Act more broadly
- African American Women in Defense of Ourselves
- Our Feet Walk the Sky, Women of South Asian Descent Collective
- U.N. World Conference on Women, Beijing

- B. J. Reagon's coalition politics speech
- The Color Purple, Alice Walker
- Wilma Mankiller first principal chief of Cherokee Nation
- Encuentro: Latin American Feminist Meeting, Argentina

- Kitchen Table Women of Color Press
- Third World Women and Feminist Perspectives Conference
- Menavi, South Asian battered women's organization
- Black Women in the Academy Conference, Massachusetts

- National Women's Studies Association Conference, Conn.
- National Black Women's Health Project founded

- Encuentro: Latin American Feminist Meeting, Bogotá

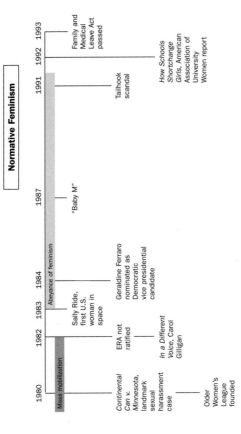

Normative Feminism

1980   1982   1983   1984   1987   1991   1992   1993

Mass mobilization

Abeyance of feminism

Sally Ride, first U.S. woman in space

"Baby M"

Family and Medical Leave Act passed

ERA not ratified

Geraldine Ferraro nominated as Democratic vice presidential candidate

Tailhook scandal

In a Different Voice, Carol Gilligan

How Schools Shortchange Girls, American Association of University Women report

Continental Can v. Minnesota, landmark sexual harassment case

Older Women's League founded

For normative historical periods, see Verta Taylor and Nancy Whittier, "The New Feminist Movement," in *Feminist Frontiers IV*, ed. Richardson et al. (New York: McGraw-Hill, 1997).

Biographical Notes

Here I briefly present biographical data of the people who were interviewed for this book: birth, class, ethnicity, religion, etc.; several of the activist organizations or historical events they link to their activism; and the labels or names they use to identify their antiracist work. With the exception of two people, everyone I interviewed requested that I use their real name.

Jane Ariel (born 1941) grew up in a lower-middle-class, Jewish family in a white, wealthy town in New York. She believes she was born with "eyes that have always looked." She earned her B.A. at Oberlin College, became a professional musician, and then worked as an educational consultant at Harlem Hospital. In the late 1960s her younger brother fell ill with cancer and eventually died, a loss that led Jane to want to do something totally new with her life. She moved to Israel and had two children with her Moroccan Sephardic husband. While living a bicultural life with her husband and his extended family, Jane was the executive director of a research center that focused on the educational and social differences of oppressed groups in Israel. She eventually moved back to the United States, settling in Oakland, California, where her children attended public (primarily Black) schools while Jane earned her doctorate in family therapy. For many years now, Jane has been a lesbian, practiced psychotherapy, and worked as an antiracism trainer with Vigorous Interventions in Ongoing Natural Settings (VISIONS). Her recent interests include community building among women as they age and what it means to be a spiritual Jew. Although she has been an activist at various points in her life, she describes herself as being more interested in recent years in how the psyche is affected by privilege and oppression and how that influence manifests itself in individual and family life.

Anne Braden (born 1924) grew up in Alabama in a family and community that were openly supportive of segregation. After college she became a journalist and then married Carl Braden, her political partner for twenty-seven years (until his death in 1975). In 1954 Anne and Carl purchased a home in a white suburb of Louisville, Kentucky, and sold it to a Black couple. The house was bombed by whites, Carl and Anne were arrested for sedition, and Carl was imprisoned. During the case (1954–1957) Anne and Carl crisscrossed the country several times, meeting with "the cream of the cream" among organizers, who mounted a campaign against the charges. From 1957 to 1973 Anne and Carl worked with the Southern Conference Educational Fund (SCEF), an interracial organization that opposed segregation. In 1975 Anne helped found the Southern Organizing Committee (SOC), a multiracial organization, led by people of color, working against racism, economic injustice, war, and environmental destruction. For twenty years she has also worked closely with the Kentucky Alliance against Racist and Political Repression, which brings people of color together for antiracist action. Anne is the mother of three children and the author of *The Wall Between* (1958), a National Book Award finalist, which chronicles the 1954 sedition trial and the campaign against racist repression. Now in her seventies, Anne continues to work eighteen-hour days as an activist and writer in Louisville, teaches college courses on racism, and speaks widely on antiracism and social justice.

Marilyn Buck (born 1947) was raised in Texas and attended segregated schools. After her father became the minister of the Black Episcopal church, her family lived in east Austin on the Black side of the city. She lived in Chicago as a young adult and worked with SDS. In 1968 she moved to San Francisco, where she worked with Newsreel, a film/propaganda group that showed documentaries about liberation struggles. She supported the Black Panthers and later the Black Liberation Army (BLA). Since 1985 Marilyn has been imprisoned in the federal system. She is currently at Federal Correctional Institute in Dublin, California, where she continues serving an eighty-year sentence for conspiracies to free political prisoners, specifically Assata Shakur, to protest government policies through the use of violence; and to raise funds for Black liberation organizations. She writes poetry, does translation for Spanish-speaking women in prison, tutors in math, and practices meditation and yoga. She recently completed a college degree with a focus in psychology.

Susan Burnett (born 1939, died 1999) was raised in an upper-class, Catholic/Episcopal family in Mexico, Brazil, and the United States. Although she grew up in multicultural environments, her first real learning about racism began through an adolescent friendship with a southern Black woman. This early consciousness led her to the teachings of Malcolm X and Black liberation. As a young adult, after seeing a film about Hitler and learning that Germans in her own family had not opposed the Holocaust, Susan decided to actively resist racism to "save my own soul." She became involved in civil rights activism through the NAACP, SNCC, and the Black Panther Party. She also helped form the first food-package brigade into the prison in Rahway, New Jersey, with the help of Ali Bey Hassan, who at that time was doing time in Rahway Prison. She married Ali Bey Hassan, one of the Panther Twenty-One, and became the stepmother of five now-grown African American children. Several years ago, the combined effects of a physician-botched tracheotomy and asthma left Susan permanently disabled. Although being unable to earn a living outside of her home was frightening financially, eventually it led her to create her own home-based word-processing business. This work both put food on the table and allowed her to work with political prisoners, most visibly on behalf of Mumia Abu-Jamal in conjunction with MOVE (a Black activist organization from Philadelphia). Susan identified herself as a "revolutionary activist and a recovering racist." According to her husband, who has survived her, "Susan struggled daily with her racism more than any person I knew."

Dottye Burt-Markowitz (born 1945) is an antiracism/anti-oppression trainer and community activist who lives in Baltimore with her husband and fellow antiracist Stan Markowitz (q.v.). She is the mother of an adult, biracial son, whom she raised in a Black community during the first years of his life. Dottye grew up in a working-class, Southern Baptist family in a white neighborhood in East St. Louis, Illinois (a city with a substantial Black population), where most of the people she knew, with the exception of her immediate family, were blatant racists. The early turning points in her race consciousness include joining a racially mixed choir in high school and doing community work in a Black community when she was an undergraduate at Texas Christian University; working at the Department of Social Services in New York City during the late 1960s; and raising her son. In the late 1970s Dottye earned a doctorate in physiological psychology. In the 1980s she worked to expand the political agenda of SANE (a nuclear freeze organization) in Washington, D.C., and she worked closely for ten years with the Piedmont Peace Project. Since 1989 she has been self-employed as an antiracism and anti-oppression trainer and is the co-founder of Paso Training and Consulting.

John Capitman (born 1954) was a red-diaper baby born to non-religious, Jewish, upper-middle-class parents who were leaders in the Communist Party in New York City in the late 1940s and early 1950s. Like many Communist families, John's fled during the McCarthy purges to a small town outside the city. As a child, John traveled extensively with his parents while they were conducting marketing research in white and Black communities and speaking on Black/Jewish relationships. His early education about racism included being a white member of the Black Action Society at the University of Pittsburgh and working as a student reporter on civil rights protests in New Orleans. While in graduate school in 1979, John met and married Valerie Batts, an African American woman with whom he cofounded an antiracism training institute, Vigorous Interventions in Ongoing Natural Settings (VISIONS). John has been a trainer with VISIONS since its inception in 1984. Valerie and John have a son and a daughter, both of whom attended an antiracist Quaker school. In the last several years, John has worked at the Heller School at Brandeis University, conducting research on aging, race, ethnicity, and gender in health and health care. Depending on the audience, he describes himself as a "diversity trainer," a "researcher on racism, sexism, classism, ageism," or both.

Jeanine Cohen (born 1953) was raised in a Jewish, middle-class, actively antiapartheid family in Johannesburg, South Africa. Growing up, Jeanine was cared for and stayed with Black South African women, experiences that taught her much about racism. When Jeanine was seven years old, her family moved to London to flee persecution. Her antiracist activism as a young adult and since has included working in the squatters' movement in England; working with a San Francisco–based Black nationalist organization; participating in the battered-women's movement and with Lesbians against Police Violence; and making documentary films/videos on interracial lesbian couples, butch-femme relations, and white racial identity. She is a lesbian, lives in the Bay area, and is a coparent to a Black daughter (whose biological mother is Jeanine's former partner).

Jim Corcoran (born 1954) teaches journalism at Simmons College in Boston and is the author of *Bitter Harvest,* which chronicles contemporary white supremacist organizing. He grew up in North Dakota in a working-class family with populist roots and much regional pride. While working on the railroad during college, he witnessed the management's mistreatment of Black workers. While working as a reporter in North Dakota, he began investigating the life of a white supremacist from that region, a project that eventually led him to write extensively about right-wing organizing. He lives with his partner, a white woman, in a Boston suburb and is currently writing about white supremacist organizing on the Web and internationally.

Rose Marie Cummins (born 1942) was the sixth of eight children raised in an Irish American family in a one-bedroom house in Kentucky during Jim Crow. Her father was in a union, which meant that Rose Marie grew up knowing that "scab" had a double meaning. When she was eighteen years old, Rose Marie joined a Catholic community that has a social justice mission. For Rose Marie, social justice has always been the key to her faith. When she was twenty-four years old, she was sent to Puerto Rico to teach. The lessons she learned from Puerto Rican students and activists taught her much about U.S. imperialism and racism. For the last quarter century Rose Marie has lived in Boston and has been active in several Latino struggles—Witness for Peace in Nicaragua, Centro Presente (an El Salvadoran solidarity organization), in support of people in Chiapas, Mexico—and as a bilingual teacher. In the early 1990s, after earning an M.A. in counseling, she worked with homeless people in Boston. Most recently she has worked at the Latino Health Institute, where she has provided legal support for people who need help with immigration (including people with AIDS, homeless people, and people seeking political asylum).

Maggie Nolan Donovan (born 1944) was raised in a middle-class, Irish Catholic, extended family in Boston. Her parents were pro-union liberals. In her late teens she sought out meetings of the Congress of Racial Equality (CORE) and SNCC on her own and soon became a full-time activist with SNCC. In 1967 she moved to Cape Cod, where she married and had three children. The feminist movement gave her a way to understand her everyday life as political: carpooling, school issues, curriculum-change projects, and support for a multiracial community theater and town library projects. For many years she has taught elementary school and graduate education courses focusing on literacy and multicultural education. She also works with the Cape Verdean community in her town and continues to work closely with civil rights activists. In 1997 Maggie co-organized the Race and Racism in the 1990s: Teaching Social Justice, Living Social Justice conference in Boston. Maggie is the cochair of the Dennis Yarmouth Cultural Diversity Committee and offers workshops on antiracist teaching. She is currently writing a book about studying the Civil Rights Movement with young children.

Ruth Frankenberg (born 1957) was born in Cardiff, Wales. She grew up in a single-mother household outside Manchester, England. She was involved in student politics from high school onward and in feminist and antifascist activism as a student at Cambridge University. When she was twenty-one, she moved to Santa Cruz, California. Her racial awakening as a young adult involved friendships with and mentoring by women of color and learning how race shapes women's experiences. At this point in her life, her critical work in relation to oppression takes place through teaching, research, and writing. She feels that spiritual practice can and perhaps even should be a key aspect of antiracist work. Ruth is the author of *White Women, Race Matters: The Social Construction of Whiteness* (1993) and the editor of *Displacing Whiteness: Essays in Social and Cultural Criticism* (1997). She lives in Oakland, California, with her life partner.

Reebee Garofalo (born 1944) grew up in an Italian, Catholic, middle-class family in New Haven, Connecticut. He considers his involvement in Freedom Summer in 1964 his "political baptism." In the middle to late 1960s he directed an urban youth program before attending graduate school in clinical psychology. In the late 1970s and the 1980s he produced concerts, including the Amandla antiapartheid concert featuring Bob Marley, and he was heavily involved with Rock against Racism in Boston (1980–1987). Music has always been a big part of his life (starting with lessons from his mother, once a member of the all-female 1930s orchestra Evelyn and the Mood Indigo Girls). Reebee is a cultural theorist and professor at the University of Massachusetts at Boston's College of Public and Community Service, whose student body is mostly female, working-class, older students and/or people of color. He lives with his Colombian partner and her two children in a multiethnic Boston neighborhood. He is currently writing books about popular media and culture. He continues to learn much from his wife and stepchildren about self-care and family life and is on the board of Zumix, Inc., a community-based organization that does street-level education through music with young people in East Boston. For relaxation Reebee plays drums and sings with the Blue Suede Boppers, a fifties rock 'n' roll band.

David Gilbert (born 1944) grew up Jewish and middle-class in Brookline, Massachusetts. In his teens David became active in the Civil Rights Movement and in his early twenties with antiwar work, SDS, and later with the Weather Underground, a white militant organization that intended to support Black and Third World struggles. In 1981 David was incarcerated in connection with his work as an ally of the Black Liberation Army, and he is serving a sentence until the year 2056. Currently he is at Comstock Prison in upstate New York, which is considered to be among the "burn circuit" prisons: one of the three most repressive of the twenty-nine in New York State. While in prison his activism has included cofounding peer-led AIDS education projects; peacefully protesting against the beating of prisoners at Attica and elsewhere; and writing book reviews and essays on white accountability in relation to the Black Power Movement, women's rights, AIDS education, and Mumia Abu-Jamal. He is the father of a grown son and has an extensive, multiracial community of friends and family.

Dawn Gomes (born 1944) was raised in a working-class, single-parent family in northern California. In 1968 she moved to San Francisco with her two children. Much of her early learning about antiracism came from her involvement with a Black caucus of a major transportation system in the Bay Area, which spearheaded the first affirmative action plan for the city's transportation system. From 1977 to 1982 Dawn worked extensively with a white group in solidarity with a Black liberation organization. She eventually left the organization, dismayed by their extremism, cult-like rules, internal corruption, and sexism. Over time she began to understand how childhood experiences (of alcoholism and abuse) contributed to her willingness to participate in an organization that she ultimately believed was destructive. In the 1980s Dawn earned a B.A. and M.A. in organizational psychology and worked against U.S. intervention in Central America, with a nonprofit homeless coalition, and with a group opposing violence against women. In the 1990s, Dawn worked with a nonprofit coalition that helps communities prepare for disasters, which enables her to do grassroots organizing and community building with multiple multiracial groups (including people with disabilities and homeless people). Dawn lives in a racially and culturally diverse neighborhood in Oakland, California. After being a lesbian for many years, Dawn recently married a Cambodian man (a survivor of Pol Pot's regime). Over the years her understanding of how racism operates has broadened as her vision has become more multiracial. Dawn now considers spiritual as well as political solutions for social problems.

Laurie Holmes (born 1957) was raised in a "mixed class" (working- and middle-class) family in white suburbs in Massachusetts and Connecticut. At seventeen Laurie moved to Boston. She began driving a school bus during the early years of desegregation of the Boston Public Schools. She considers the seven years she spent as a unionized bus driver "the best schooling" she can imagine for learning about racism and community organizing. Laurie came out as a lesbian in the mid-1970s, got involved in multiracial feminism, and began intentionally integrating her life. In the late 1970s she helped create Lesbians United in Nonnuclear Action, the first lesbian feminist affinity group in Boston, which did civil disobedience against the building of nuclear power plants and challenged the male-dominated hierarchy of the antinuclear Clamshell Alliance. In the late 1980s she worked with a grassroots, neighborhood association where she lived in Egleston Square, a historically Black and Latino neighborhood. In the 1980s Laurie also confronted her long-term drug problem, deciding that she would rather be "awake than asleep during life." In the 1990s she worked at Elizabeth Stone House, a grassroots mental health alternative founded in 1974 by a group of radical social workers and women who were formerly incarcerated on psychiatric wards. She also helped to build the Community Education for Economic Development (CEED) program which treats issues of violence, oppression, and poverty as salient and connected issues in women's lives. In 1998 Laurie was asked to build Harbor Communities Overcoming Violence, which supports survivors of domestic violence north of Boston (including Latina, Asian, Somali, and Bosnian women).

Laurie has three adult Puerto Rican children, whom she coparented with the children's mother (her ex-partner). Laurie is currently in a long-term relationship with a Puerto Rican woman who is a legal advocate and a mother. They live in Jamaica Plain, a multiracial, lesbian-friendly neighborhood in Boston; are involved in community building with neighbors, friends, and family; and spend much time with their children and grandchildren. She is currently involved in two new anti-racist projects. One engages neighborhood residents in dialogue about race, class, and culture. The other promotes a process for "going deeper" to connect across differences in personal relationships, developing self, and groups to organize for revolutionary change.

Naomi Jaffe (born 1943) is the director of Holding Our Own, a multi-racial feminist organization in Albany, New York, and coordinator of the local Free Mumia Committee. She was raised in a Jewish, lower-middle-class family that had a "struggling family farm" in upstate New York. She attended Brandeis University on a scholarship, where she studied Marxism with Herbert Marcuse, met young Communist activists, and heard Malcolm X speak. While in graduate school (1967), she cofounded a chapter of SDS at the New School for Social Research in New York City and joined Women's International Terrorist Conspiracy from Hell (WITCH). By that point she considered herself a "revolutionary," since she saw a Marxist, anti-imperialist analysis as key to social change. In the late 1960s she joined the Weather Underground, despite the organization's antifeminism and homophobia, because she believed that a fundamental redistribution of power and resources in the world would require dramatic action. She went underground from

1970 to 1978. She continues to see a structural analysis—of class, race, and gender—as key to radical politics. She lives with her chiropractor partner and their teenage son in Troy, New York. She is the primary caretaker of her two elderly parents, is involved in confronting racism in the criminal justice system, and is a vegetarian.

Bonnie Kerness (born 1942) was raised in a lower-middle-class, apolitical, Jewish and Catholic family in the Bronx and in Queens. As a teenager she gained early training as an activist through a settlement house in New York City. In her late teens she moved on her own to Tennessee, where she worked with the NAACP and the Highlander Folk School and was trained to be a civil rights activist. Since the 1970s she has worked as an organizer on gay rights and welfare rights campaigns, in support of prisoners' rights, and against the buildup of the punishment industry. She helped raise six African American, mixed-race, and white children (both biologically hers and adopted). Since 1977 she has been the associate director of the American Friends Service Committee Criminal Justice Program in New Jersey. She is also the national coordinator of the National Campaign to Stop Control Unit Prisons and the vice president of the board of the World Organization against Torture/ USA. Bonnie has an M.A. in social work in community organizing and speaks throughout the country on international law and U.S. human rights violations. She identifies herself as a "human rights activist, a prisoner advocate, a mother of Afrikan children, and a child of Afrikan women who befriended and taught me."

Mike Lawrence-Riddell (born 1976) was raised in a progressive, "vaguely Protestant," middle-class family in Northampton, Massachusetts. He became an activist in high school after one of his African American friends was beaten by white classmates. He started a multicultural newspaper in high school, and in high school and college he sought ways to educate young people about racism. He was active in Students in Support of a New Trial for Mumia Abu-Jamal when he was a student at Wesleyan University in Connecticut. He identifies himself as a humanist and a revolutionary justice worker—"revolutionary because I want to change the way society works. To me, revolution includes justice for all humans."

Ray Luc Levasseur (born 1946) was raised in a working-class, French Canadian family in Maine. His family worked in the mills and the shoe factory. Ray joined the army in 1965 and was sent to Vietnam in 1967. His first political activism (1968) was as a member of the Southern Student Organizing Committee (SSOC) in Tennessee (a white, antiracist group that supported Black and white labor organizing, published an alternative paper, and educated whites about racism). In 1969 he was arrested for his political activism and sentenced to the locked-down prison at Brushy Mountain in Tennessee (1969–1971). In 1971 he became Maine's state organizer for Vietnam Vets against the War. He also began working with prisoners and with the Statewide Correctional Alliance for Reform (SCAR), a community-based group whose primary focus was on prison issues (a prison union, a bail fund, and support for Attica). Ray also worked with the Red Star North Bookstore, which provided radical books and literature to prisoners. From 1974 to 1984 he went underground to help build a revolutionary movement, which included supporting the African National Congress, the Pan Africanist Congress, and the Black Consciousness Movement; liberation struggles in Central America; and prison activism in the United States. In 1986 he was convicted in New York of actions carried out by the United Freedom Front (a militant, antiracist organization) and sentenced to forty-five years in prison. In 1989 he represented himself in a sedition trial and was acquitted. He was transferred to Marion Prison (in Illinois) in 1989; to ADX (a sensory deprivation section of the prison) in Florence, Colorado, in 1995; and to the U.S. penitentiary in Atlanta in 1999. Currently, Ray Luc's antiracism includes writing (about poverty; abuse of children caused by war, poverty, and racism; the prison industry; and conditions in control units) and coordinating the unofficial, alternative library to put "radical books into the pipeline for circulation and discussion." His most recent article is "Trouble in Mind: Administrative Maximum—the Fourth Year." Ray Luc has three daughters born while he and his wife were underground from the mid-1970s to mid-1980s.

elana levy (born 1941) is the daughter of Jewish refugees from Nazi Germany; most of her family were murdered in the Holocaust. She explicitly connects her Jewish heritage and her antiracist consciousness, from learning to question authority at an early age to seeing opposition to injustice as an obligation of all people. She is a professor of mathematics at a community college in Syracuse, New York. She has been an activist since the late 1950s. She was involved in Congress of Racial Equality (CORE) in the early 1960s (including arrests and boycotts) and the anti-imperialist wing of the antiwar movement (against U.S. militarism in Vietnam, Nicaragua, and Cuba), participated in Marxist study groups, supported Native American sovereignty, advocated for prisoner rights (beginning with support for the 1971 Attica rebellion), and was one of the organizers of a chapter of the New Jewish Agenda in 1984 in solidarity with Palestinian people. She traveled twice to Israel-Palestine and created a video, *The Intifada: A Jewish Eyewitness*. In the 1990s she organized forums on sexual abuse as a survivor of incest, published poetry about justice, organized trips to Cuba ten times, organized in Syracuse, New York, in support of Mumia Abu-Jamal, supported and visited political prisoners, helped produce a monthly peace newsletter, and is part of a collective that organizes a women's coffee house.

She links the beginning of her work in the feminist movement to the birth of her daughter in 1970. She believes that antiracism is about big and little choices in how people live their lives—from where people buy their books and how they talk with their children about injustice, to the paid work people do, to the demonstrations they organize. She considers antiracism a continuing process, that is, a never-completed act. She describes herself as a "revolutionary feminist" (which she believes also should include opposition to white supremacy, imperialism, male supremacy, anti-Semitism, and heterosexism).

Anne Litwin (born 1947) is a Jewish, middle-class woman who grew up in a rural, white, Christian town in Kansas. Even though some of her relatives were racist, they taught her that Jews have a responsibility to make sure no one is discriminated against. After attending the University of Wisconsin at Madison, she dropped out for seven years in upstate New York, where she lived in a self-sufficient community and did feminist health care organizing. She then moved to New York City, where she worked for the New York Department of Juvenile Justice and the New York City Agency for Child Development, became involved in multiracial feminism, and helped organize a grassroots community group, the West Side Action for Peace and Social Justice. Since 1988 she has been a professional member and faculty of the NTL Institute, a multiracial training organization for corporations, schools, and nonprofit organizations. Anne is also a member of two African American and white women's organizations. She was the partner of an African American man for many years prior to moving to Boston. She now lives with her high school sweetheart (a white man and artist who is also from the Midwest) in a multiracial Boston community. Anne believes self-care is crucial for sustaining antiracist work and that training and leadership organizations should include self-care and community building in their process. Anne considers antiracist work to be as much about personal relationships and small community building as about large-scale institutional change. Currently she is part of a coalition of people working to make Angela Davis's childhood home in Birmingham, Alabama, into a public gathering place and educational institute for progressive social change.

Betty Liveright (born 1913) was raised in a Christian Scientist, middle-class family in a white, politically conservative, Chicago suburb. In her twenties she began her decades-long work in the theater, which included bringing the first multiracial play to the McCarter Theater in Princeton, New Jersey, in 1968. In 1936 she married Herman (see following entry), her husband and political comrade for more than sixty years. In the 1940s they had two children. Betty and Herman joined the Communist Party in New York City in 1936 and remained members for more than twenty years, organizing against police repression, building interracial alliances, and opposing McCarthy-era repression. In 1956, when Herman was harassed by the Subcommittee on Internal Security of the Senate Judiciary Committee headed by Senator James O. Eastland of Mississippi, Betty was forced to leave her job at Tulane University. In 1972 she and Herman founded the Berkshire Forum, which provided a "forum until 1991 for progressively minded people to address social and political issues," including antiracism, Marxism, and feminism. In the 1990s Betty and Herman drove a station wagon across the country to meet political prisoners in state and federal prisons. This trek culminated in their creation of *This Just In: A Bulletin for News of Political Prisoners and POWs,* a nationally distributed monthly newsletter for political prisoners and their supporters. They are currently completing a book on political prisoners, which includes profiles on Puerto Rican, Mexican, Native American, African American, and white prisoners. Betty and Herman have two grown children.

Herman Liveright (born 1912, died 2001) was raised in a Jewish, middle-class family in a suburb of New York City. His early consciousness of anti-Semitism gradually extended to opposing economic oppression and racist bigotry. While attending the University of Wisconsin in the late 1920s, his contact with radical, working-class classmates and his recognition that the Depression was particularly devastating to Blacks were seminal influences in his later affiliation with the Communist Party, which he joined with his wife, Betty (see preceding entry), in 1936. In the 1950s Herman worked in television in New York and New Orleans. In New Orleans he made vigorous attempts, mildly successful, to desegregate the programs. He was eventually called to testify before the Subcommittee on Internal Security of the Senate Judiciary Committee headed by Senator James O. Eastland of Mississippi. He was fired from his job, cited, tried, and convicted for contempt of Congress and spent six years in litigation before his conviction was overturned by a U.S. court of appeals. In 1972 Herman and Betty cofounded the Berkshire Forum. In the 1990s they focused on organizing against the escalation of the punishment industry based on knowledge they gained through their work with political prisoners in the United States. Betty and Herman have two grown children.

Eric Mann (born 1942) is the director of the Labor/Community Strategy Center in Los Angeles, a "multiracial think tank/act tank committed to building democratic, internationalist, left social movements." Eric was raised in a Jewish, middle-class family in New York. His grandmother was a union organizer, and his father was a socialist when young. In the 1960s Eric attended Cornell University and worked in settlement houses in New York City, with Congress of Racial Equality (CORE), and with a Newark antipoverty program. In the 1980s Eric worked with the United Auto Workers Union on an assembly line and helped organize a campaign to keep the GM Van Nuys assembly plant open in Los Angeles (1982–1992). Currently he is helping to organize a "No seat, no fare" protest against overcrowding on Los Angeles buses. He is the author of *Comrade George* (about George Jackson) and *Taking* *on General Motors.* Eric lives in Los Angeles with his wife, Lian Hurst Mann (see following entry), and their children.

Lian Hurst Mann (born 1947) is an architect and writer who grew up in the segregated South in a middle-class, Protestant family with liberal, intellectual parents. Her relatives include people who fought on opposite sides in the Civil War. As a college student at the University of California at Berkeley, Lian participated in the Free Speech and antiwar movements and became involved in lesbian feminism. In the 1980s she served as a shop floor organizer for union democracy in the United Auto Workers Union and was a member of the League of Revolutionary Struggle, a Marxist/Leninist organization. She lives in Los Angeles with her husband and fellow organizer, Eric Mann (see preceding entry), and their children. She is the author of *Reconstructing Architecture: Critical Discourses and Social Practices* and the editor of the bilingual English/Spanish periodical *Ahora Now,* a publication of the Labor/Community Strategy Center, a grassroots, multiracial organization in Los Angeles.

Stan Markowitz (born 1937) was raised in a working-class, Jewish family in a racially mixed but segregated neighborhood in Passaic, New Jersey, until he was thirteen and then in Newark, New Jersey. After high school he joined the army, which began his radicalizing process as he witnessed the racist treatment of the Black enlisted men. From 1966 to 1969 he taught at Howard University, which started him on a lifelong journey to teach African American and Native American history from an inclusive perspective that attempts to demythologize American history and culture. He lives in Baltimore with his wife, Dottye Burt-Markowitz (q.v.), who is also a white antiracist activist. Together they founded Paso Training and Consulting. He worked with the Piedmont Peace Project for ten years and is now working with People's Homesteading Group, Southeast Community Organization, and the Clearing House for a Healthy Community, all of which work for political, economic, and social justice in Baltimore neighborhoods. He retired from teaching history at a community college in Baltimore County in 1997 and now does anti-oppression and social justice training. He is the father of three grown children.

Tom Roderick (born 1942) has been the executive director of Educators for Social Responsibility in the metropolitan area in New York since 1983. He was raised in a suburb of Akron, Ohio, in a white, upper-middle-class, Protestant family. When an undergraduate at Yale University (1960–1964), he got involved in the Northern Student Movement (a civil rights organization) and began reading existentialism, which helped him understand his "responsibility to help make the world more just." After a year with the Northern Student Movement in Philadelphia, Tom earned an M.A. at Bank Street College of Education in New York City, taught third grade for two years in a public school in central Harlem, and then taught at the East Harlem Block Schools, where he worked closely with Puerto Rican and Black activists/parents. In 1982 he joined Educators for Social Responsibility, which was founded by educators concerned about the danger of nuclear war and now focuses on popular education, conflict resolution, and antibias work in the schools. Tom lives with his wife, who manages the magazine *Dissent,* and two daughters in Manhattan and is currently finishing a book on the East Harlem Block Schools.

Suzanne Ross (born 1937), who was born in Belgium to a traditional Jewish family, spent the first years of her life escaping the Nazi Holocaust. Her family spent three of the war years in Mozambique and the last year in Palestine. Suzanne's early consciousness about discrimination was based on her keen awareness of being Jewish in the face of anti-Semitism. As a white child living in Mozambique, she also saw Portuguese domination of Africans. Suzanne's father, unschooled but with a great facility for languages and for working with people, was approached by British and U.S. intelligence while he was working as a bartender in Lourenço Marques (now Maputo). As a result of his work tracking down German and Italian undercover agents in Mozambique, the family was given a visa to the United States. After a delay of a year in Palestine and then months of travel, the family eventually reached New York City in 1945, where Suzanne has lived since.

During the mid-1960s, Suzanne became an activist in opposing the Vietnam War, racism, and U.S. imperialism. She was inspired by SNCC and later the Black Panthers. She also learned a great deal about racism as a young psychologist. She spent five years teaching at Lehman College, the City University of New York campus in the Bronx, and developed her consciousness through her work with students and several radical Black faculty members. For many years Suzanne was not attracted to the feminist movement because she saw it as white-dominated and not militant enough. Only later did her work with Black and Latina feminists lead her to consider revolutionary feminism central to her politics. In the 1980s Suzanne was a national leader with the Committee in Solidarity with the People of El Salvador (CISPES) and with Jesse Jackson's Rainbow Coalition. In the 1990s Suzanne's activism focused on political prisoners and in particular on the International Family and Friends of Mumia Abu-Jamal. She holds a Ph.D. in clinical psychology from Columbia University and has worked as a psychologist in the New York City public schools since the early 1990s. She has been married and divorced twice and lives with her Chilean-born seventeen-year-old daughter, Clara Ana, in Washington Heights in New York.

Laurie Schecter (born 1949) is a wealthy Jewish woman (of Russian and Romanian descent) who grew up in a left-of-liberal, reform Jewish family during Jim Crow times in Florida. While an undergraduate at Wheelock College in Boston, Laurie was peripherally involved in SDS and the anti–Vietnam War movement. As a student teacher in a community-run Boston public school, Laurie saw contradictions in a system that mainly served students of color but whose key administrators and teachers were overwhelmingly white. This experience led her to ask where she could be most useful as a white woman organizer—a question she has come back to many times in her life. After college Laurie worked with a welfare rights organization and with Jobs for Peace, an organization whose goal is to shift money from the military budget into human services. A high in her activism in the 1980s involved serving on the board of the Haymarket People's Fund in Boston. Unlike some other organizations Laurie has worked with, this board was truly multiracial and comprised solely of community organizers. In the early 1990s Laurie and her husband took a backpacking trip for three years in various countries in Africa, South America, and Asia. Since returning, Laurie has worked full-time with the Piedmont Peace Project in North Carolina and most recently helped to found Sparking Powerful Anti-Racist Collaborations (SPARC), a grassroots, Boston-based organization that trains people to do antiracist organizing. Over time Laurie has come to see the importance of activists from wealthy backgrounds doing antiracist work in their own communities. She believes that white people need to be in constant training and to find structured ways to be accountable for the work they do.

Horace Seldon (born 1923) was the founder (in 1968) and until recently the executive director of Community Change, an antiracist organization in downtown Boston. Horace describes Community Change as an organization that is about "networking, resourcing, and catalyzing progressive change." Its library and meeting space provide a "watering hole where people doing justice work can come for energy, rejuvenation, and support." He traces the beginning of his lifelong commitment to antiracist work to an epiphany he had after delivering a sermon on "the white problem"—that is, racism. He was raised in a Protestant, middle-class family in a Boston suburb. After serving in the army during World War II, he attended Amherst College and later the Andover Newton Theological School. His wife, also an activist in the Civil Rights Movement, died unexpectedly in 1964 of an asthma attack while helping to organize a school "stayout" in support of Boston's Black educational movement. Horace raised their two children with the help of his wife's parents, who are also committed to peace and racial justice. Since 1980 Horace has been teaching a History and Development of Racism course at Boston College (which has been completed by nearly two thousand students), and he continues to work with multiple activist organizations in Boston.

Fran Smith (born 1959) was raised in a working-class, Italian American family in Weymouth, a Boston suburb. Fran grew up in an extended family of women who saw struggle as an inevitable part of life. Fran first began to understand racism when she worked on a multiracial regional students' rights group with other high school students from Boston public and suburban schools during the early period of desegregation. By the time Fran began college (first at Franconia College and then at Hampshire College—both alternative schools), activism was already central to her life. Most of Fran's antiracist mentoring while in college came from African American friendships and activist connections, courses in African American studies, and her continued connection to Black activists in Boston. As a student on full scholarship, Fran also saw connections between race and class. In the 1980s she made strong political connections with other white antiracist activists. She has worked with multiple nonprofit and multiracial organizations in Boston, including the Rainbow Coalition with Mel King; Rock against Racism; a multiracial summer camp, Mission Possible; the Hispanic Office of Planning and Evaluation; the Urban League's World of Difference Project; and the Anti-Defamation League. In the 1990s she served as the affirmative action officer for the town of Weymouth. She currently is a parent organizer for the Massachusetts Advocacy Center, working with Boston public schools. She is the single mother of a biracial daughter and lives in a multiracial community in Boston.

Sarah Stearns (born 1951) is an upper-middle-class, lesbian psychotherapist, college teacher, and antiracism consultant. She grew up with four sisters in a liberal family in a small white town in Connecticut. After graduating from Harvard University (where she studied theater and was an activist against the Vietnam War and racism), she studied psychology in Sweden and played in the women's tennis circuit in Europe and in the United States. She earned her Ph.D. in clinical psychology at Duke University, where she met her lifelong friend and political ally Valerie Batts, cofounder of Vigorous Ongoing Interventions in Natural Settings (VISIONS), a training institute on racism and other oppressions. Working with VISIONS has given Sarah a place to learn from and contribute to an Afrocentric model for creating social change. Increasingly, Sarah believes that self-love is key for white people doing antiracist work. She lives in Berkeley, California, and has an extended multiracial family of friends.

Dorothy Stoneman (born 1942) was raised in a white, upper-middle-class town near Boston, joined the Civil Rights Movement in 1964, lived and worked in Harlem for more than twenty years, and now lives in her hometown, where she returned to care for her mother who had Alzheimer's disease. Her mother was a German Presbyterian and her father a Russian Jew. Her mother was disowned by her German parents when she married a Jew in the 1930s. Dorothy was raised Unitarian. While in Harlem, Dorothy was a teacher and executive director of the East Harlem Block Schools and founder and director of the

Youth Action Program. In 1988 she founded and is currently the president of YouthBuild USA, a nonprofit organization that has built a national network of 145 community-based organizations in which low-income young people attend an alternative YouthBuild high school and build homes for homeless people. YouthBuild engages students from all racial groups, in both urban and rural communities, and brings them together in national and regional conferences. Dorothy and her husband, John Bell, who also works at YouthBuild USA, have a white, adult, biological daughter who has returned as a young adult to work in the East Harlem community where she spent her elementary school years; a twelve-year-old adopted indigenous Mapuche son who was born in Chile; and a Puerto Rican godson who grew up with them. They have several other godchildren.

Cooper Thompson (born 1950) was raised in a white, Protestant, middle-class family in a bedroom community in New Jersey. His parents were Republicans, and Cooper grew up hearing explicitly anti-Semitic, classist, and racist comments from many adults. At the time he knew there was something wrong with their prejudices, but he did not see an alternative worldview until after he left home to attend college. His first activity challenging injustice involved leading training sessions about sexism in public schools. He later expanded this work to include attention to homophobia, and he began writing pro–gay and lesbian material for young people. In 1986 he founded and directed the Campaign to End Homophobia. In the 1980s and 1990s he worked as a trainer with diversity projects. He is currently writing about how white privilege and class contributed to inheritance and accumulation of wealth in his own family and what is required for wealthy white people to respond ethically to money made as a result of racism. He is also coauthoring a book (with Emmett Schaefer and Harry Brod) of profiles of white men who challenge racism and sexism. Cooper lives with his partner in Cambridge, Massachusetts, and helped parent her two now-grown children.

Bill Walsh (born 1959) grew up in a working-class, Irish and Polish, Catholic family in Salem, Massachusetts. His parents were "Kennedy liberals," opposed the Vietnam War, and supported Muhammad Ali "even when he boxed an Irish fighter." In law school, as an intern in

Judge Leon Higginbotham's appellate court office in Philadelphia, Bill was mentored by several Black lawyers and witnessed many interracial, progressive alliances. He was also exposed to feminism, an education that has guided his ongoing commitment to gender equity. In the 1990s Bill worked in Washington, D.C., to coordinate Greenpeace's work on toxic issues and environmental racism. He worked nationally with a broad range of Native American, Latino, and African American activists. In the late 1990s he traveled to Ireland, where he learned much about British colonialism, the roots of Irish political radicalism, and the spiritual dimensions of his own activism.

Tony Ward (born 1940) grew up in New York City in an Irish Catholic, upper-middle-class family. At fifteen Tony attended his first Quaker meeting and has been a member of Friends ever since. In 1965 Tony cofounded the East Harlem Block Schools, the first parent-run, publicly funded childcare program in New York City. While living in Harlem, he married a Puerto Rican woman who had four children, whom Tony co-parented. After his marriage broke up (when Tony came out as a gay man), he moved to Europe, where he finished his doctoral work in Germany while participating in Marxist study groups. He returned to New York City in 1976 to start Child Care, Inc., a multiracial umbrella organization for childcare workers and families with children. He served as the executive director of the Task Force on Learning in the Primary Grades at Carnegie Foundation from 1993 to 1997, until he decided to work directly with schoolchildren again. He currently teaches first grade in a high-poverty public school. He lives in Greenwich Village with his partner of nineteen years, Richard Goldstein (who is executive editor of the *Village Voice*). Tony considers the Quaker commitment to egalitarianism the central motivation for his work as an educator: "To say that everybody is absolutely equal leads you to say that color, gender, nationality, and religion are insignificant compared to that basic sameness, oneness, that everybody has a right to."

Lisa Weiner-Mahfuz (born 1972) is a founding member of Sparking Powerful Anti-Racist Collaborations (SPARC), a community-based organization that trains people to organize against racism in white communities. She is the daughter of an Arab (Lebanese) mother and a Jewish father and was raised in a white, Christian town in New Hampshire.

During college Lisa began working closely with women of color to support multicultural education and diversify the student body and faculty. She links her antiracist consciousness to her learning differences and ways she managed to cope with physical disability as a child, to her feminism, and to her increasing consciousness of herself as a young activist from a mixed heritage. She considers herself a mixed-race person with white privilege. Through her work as a community organizer she links racism, anti-Arab racism, and anti-Semitism to other forms of oppression.

David Wellman (born 1940) was raised by longtime Communist parents in a working-class neighborhood in Detroit. Activism against racism and class domination has been central to his life for as long as he can remember. At Wayne State University he got involved in civil rights demonstrations, in which he continued to participate in graduate school at the University of California at Berkeley. He organized against segregation in hotels, restaurants, and auto dealerships; worked with Congress of Racial Equality (CORE), SDS, and SNCC; organized Freedom Schools in Oakland, California, served on the editorial board of *The Movement* newspaper, and participated in the Free Speech movement; and supported the Black Panthers. Currently he is a professor of community studies at the University of California at Santa Cruz and a researcher at the Institute for the Study of Social Change in Berkeley, a multiracial research center. He speaks widely in support of affirmative action and multiracial union organizing and is the author of the classic text *Portraits of White Racism,* as well as *The Union Makes Us Strong* and other scholarly works.

Michael Williams (born 1950) is a clinical social worker who lives and works in Boston, Massachusetts. He grew up in a white, middle-class suburb north of the east-coast city of Durban in the KwaZulu-Natal province of South Africa (one of the most racially diverse areas of the country). The oldest of four children, he grew up in an Episcopalian home, where his mother was outspoken publicly about her opposition to the apartheid government, sometimes embarrassing his father, who held a senior management position in Durban's city government. Michael recalls feeling at odds with the political beliefs and affiliations of his peers and their families while growing up. He uses the term "societal dissociation" to describe his experience of coping with the contradictions of growing up white in apartheid South Africa and coping with his confusion about his sexual orientation. He was enormously relieved upon discovering, when he went to college, other young people who thought and felt as he did, and he was able to join organizations working for social justice. He joined the Black Sash—a group, mostly women, who stand in silence in public to protest apartheid—and supported the squatters' movement. Despite his activism during this period, Michael felt a deep sense of inadequacy that he did not do more to oppose apartheid. This experience was compounded by his undergoing military training, which was compulsory for all young, white men at the time. In 1982 Michael left South Africa, finally settling in the Boston area, where he came out as a gay man. As a social worker, he has worked with a diverse clientele for many years and has been involved in AIDS-related work and more recently in diversity training. A regular visitor to South Africa to see family and friends, Michael has accepted that he will always feel conflicted about his decision not to live in South Africa.

Acknowledgments

This book has been a constant companion for me for six years, and during that time many people opened their hearts and minds to me and the project. I began the research in search of a community of dissent/ descent, a journey that took me into the homes and neighborhoods of many people whose lives form the basis of this book. They are a laughing, kind, intense, overextended, soul-searching, principled, self-reflexive, fire-breathing, never-give-up group. It is an honor to have known and learned from them. My hope is that they believe the book does justice to the depth of their lives. I carry more people in my heart than I did when I started this book; this heart-stretching experience has changed me profoundly.

I want to thank, too, Elly Bulkin. We began this project together, a collaboration that gave the book much of its early backbone. All credit goes to Elly for the principled and loving way she encouraged me to continue with the book even though we would no longer be doing it together. I have also been enormously fortunate to work with Doug Armato, director of the University of Minnesota Press. Three years ago Doug asked me, "What do you need?" I said, "An eye-to-eye, real-live-body conversation over good food." So Doug flew to Boston to have that one-on-one contact, which he followed with a sustained confidence in my work, generous support as I was writing, CDs of Dinah Washington and Bessie Smith, and out-of-print hardback books that inspired me through winter months of writing. Doug is a writer's dream—a true intellectual editor, a rare find.

At his side is Gretchen Asmussen, who has been my friend and confidante at the Press for almost ten years. Amy Unger, Laura Westlund, Kathryn Grimes, and Kathy Delfosse, all at the Press, also put great care into the text and production of the book. Jean Hardisty and Political

Research Associates, a long-standing progressive research group, took me under their wing both financially and politically, and the Simmons Fund for Research helped support some of the early research costs. The librarians at Simmons College—especially Carol Demos, Patti Durisin, Ilze Olmsted, Bernadette Rivard, Ernesto Valencia, and Gianna Gifford—extended themselves constantly, as did the faculty at Simmons who covered for me while I was on leave.

Words to describe days at the desk trying to write: lonely, isolating, exciting, humbling, a luxury, still humbling. Many people held me through the process, especially Sohaila Abdulali; Maggie Nolan Donovan; Yvonne Pappenheim; Diane Harriford; Andrea Doane; Monisha Das Gupta; Sally Abood; Estelle Disch; Lisa Hall; Sangeeta Tyagi; elana levy; Ellen Scott; Kathy Blee; Ashley, Jeff, Rich, and Ginny Onysko; Ruth Frankenberg; Lata Mani; Sohera Syeda; LaMar Delandro; and Marilyn Buck. Thanks to Carolyn Villers, Kristen Dominique, Topaz Terry, Shirlynn Jones, Diane Harrifold, Stefanie Archer, and Kara Smith for making the index an adventure. Thanks especially to Bonnie Kerness for the title of the book and the inspiration you are to so many of us. Thanks, too, to France Winddance Twine for your expansive mind and the synchronicity of our lives.

I was graced with reviews by three scholars (Bob Blauner, T. Sharpley-Whiting, and Howard Winant) who, with respect and affection, asked me hard questions. David Wellman called me, cajoled me, praised me, shared his heart with me, and kept pushing. The epilogue was written with him and Howie in mind. It has been thrilling to be writing about activism while my goddaughter, Khadine Bennett, has been living the life of an activist—and with such flair. The book is dedicated to my grandmother, Beth Fillmore, for her belief in the power of relationships; Susan Kosoff, who heard every word of the book more than once and kissed many tears; and David Gilbert, my spiritual twin, who should be out here with every other prisoner of conscience still behind bars, seeking justice, for the duration.

Notes

Introduction

1. Cherríe Moraga and Gloria Anzaldúa, eds., *This Bridge Called My Back: Writings by Radical Women of Color,* 2nd ed. (New York: Kitchen Table Women of Color Press, 1983).

2. Ibid.

3. Michelle Fine, Lois Weis, Linda Powell, and Mun Wong, eds., *Off White: Readings on Race, Power, and Society* (New York: Routledge, 1997); George Lipsitz, *The Possessive Investment in Whiteness: How White People Profit from Identity Politics* (Philadelphia: Temple University Press, 1998); Mike Hill, ed., *Whiteness: A Critical Reader* (New York: New York University Press, 1997).

4. David Wellman, *Portraits of White Racism,* 2nd ed. (New York: Cambridge University Press, 1993).

5. In personal conversations with the author in 1997, Howard Zinn expressed skepticism about thinking of himself as an "antiracist activist" based on his belief that many have done more than he has to oppose racism. A few of his many books include *A People's History of the United States* (New York: HarperPerennial, 1980), *The Zinn Reader: Writings on Disobedience and Democracy* (New York: Seven Stories Press, 1997), and *You Can't Be Neutral on a Moving Train* (Boston: Beacon Press, 1994).

6. An important exception during this period was the small group of white people who, with members of the Black Liberation Army and Puerto Rican independence activists, went underground during the 1970s. In this instance, the Puerto Ricans, Black Americans, and white people all used the same term— "revolutionary"—to describe their activism.

7. Barbara Smith, ed., *Home Girls: A Black Feminist Anthology* (New York: Kitchen Table Women of Color Press, 1983).

8. Lorraine Bethel, "What Chou Mean 'We,' White Girl?," *Conditions: Five, the Black Women's Issue,* ed. Lorraine Bethel and Barbara Smith, 1979: 86–92.

9. Throughout the book, all unattributed quotations come from the interviews.

10. Toni Morrison, "On Herman Melville," 212; James Baldwin, "White Man's Guilt"; both in *Black on White: Black Writers on What It Means to Be White*, ed. David Roediger (New York: Schocken, 1998).

11. Barbara Flagg, "'Was Blind, but Now I See': White Race Consciousness and the Requirement of Discriminatory Intent," *Michigan Law Review* 91 (March 1993): 953–1017.

12. Ian Haney Lopez, *White by Law: The Legal Construction of Race* (New York: University of New York Press, 1996), 173.

13. For an anthology of selections from this periodical, see Noel Ignatiev and John Garvey, eds., *Race Traitor* (New York: Routledge, 1996).

14. Haney Lopez, *White by Law,* 189.

15. Ibid.

16. Mab Segrest, *Memoir of a Race Traitor* (Boston: South End Press, 1994).

17. David Wellman, "Red and Black in America," in *Names We Call Home: Autobiography on Racial Identity,* ed. Becky Thompson and Sangeeta Tyagi (New York: Routledge, 1996).

18. Ignatiev and Garvey, *Race Traitor,* 2.

19. Howard Winant, *Racial Conditions: Politics, Theory, Practice* (Minneapolis: University of Minnesota Press, 1994).

20. Nancie Caraway, *Segregated Sisterhood: Racism and the Politics of American Feminism* (Knoxville: University of Tennessee Press, 1991), 166.

21. Ruth Frankenberg, *White Women, Race Matters: The Social Construction of Whiteness* (Minneapolis: University of Minnesota Press, 1993); Roediger, *Black on White.*

22. Throughout the book, I refer to those I interviewed first by their full names and subsequently by their first names. Particularly because many people I interviewed are older than I am, I have worried that using their first names might be seen as disrespectful. However, since the intimacy of much of what they shared makes last name references sound too formal and removed, I opted for using first names after first introducing them with full names. In several places in the book, I also refer to written material by those I interviewed— published works, letters they shared, or written additions they made to their interviews.

In addition to conducting in-depth interviews in person, I also conducted a few phone interviews. Since they were not in-depth interviews, I do not include descriptions of these people in the Biographical Notes. Nevertheless, I greatly appreciate their willingness to talk with me on the phone.

23. Although some people's stories appear in more depth and more often than others, everyone who granted me an interview contributed to my understanding of social movement history and antiracism. As is true of qualitative research in general, it is nearly impossible to predict how the montage of interviews will emerge once the data has been collected.

24. They were raised by antireligious Communist parents, now have a Hindu-based spiritual practice, or were raised in mixed religious households by parents who emphasized neither tradition.

25. The number of Jews I interviewed may also be a consequence of having interviewed many people on the East Coast. Had I talked with more people in the South or Northwest, the percentage might have been lower.

26. These writers include Bob Blauner, Howard Winant, Adrienne Rich, David Wellman, Melanie Kaye/Kantrowitz, Karen Brodkin, Elly Bulkin, Ruth Frankenberg, Herbert Aptheker, Howard Zinn, and many others.

27. Abby Ferber, *White Man Falling: Race, Gender, and White Supremacy* (New York: Rowman and Littlefield, 1998).

28. William Pinar, "Notes on Understanding Curriculum as Racial Text," in *Race, Identity, and Representation in Education,* ed. Cameron McCarthy and Warren Chrichlow (New York: Routledge, 1993), 61.

1. Getting Started

1. Bonnie Kerness' interview by the author.

2. Paula Giddings, *When and Where I Enter: The Impact of Black Women on Race and Sex in America* (New York: Bantam Books, 1984), 283.

3. Bonnie Kerness, correspondence with author, August 9, 1996.

4. Harold Cruse, *The Crisis of the Negro Intellectual: A Historical Analysis of the Failure of Black Leadership* (New York: William Morrow, 1967); Robert Allen, *Reluctant Reformers: Racism and Social Reform Movements in the United States* (Washington, D.C.: Howard University Press, 1974); Robin D. G. Kelley, *Race Rebels: Culture, Politics, and the Black Working Class* (New York: Free Press, 1996); Mark Solomon, *The Cry Was Unity: Communists and African Americans, 1917–1936* (Jackson: University of Mississippi, 1998).

5. Richard Wright, "The Initiates: Richard Wright," in *The God That Failed,* ed. Richard Crossman (New York: Harper and Brothers, 1949), 115–162.

6. In 1958, when Anne Braden first published *The Wall Between,* her first-person account of the trial resulting from the Bradens' action to enable a Black family, the Wades, to buy a home in a white suburb of Louisville, Kentucky, in 1954, she did not reveal the name of the person in her childhood who had made that remark, out of "consideration to them when they were living"; Anne Braden, *The Wall Between* (Knoxville: University of Tennessee Press, 1999), 331. In her epilogue to the reissue of the book in 1999, long after her father had died, she connected that pivotal event in her life to her father.

7. Braden, *The Wall Between,* 328.

8. Audre Lorde, *Sister Outsider* (New York: Crossing Press, 1996).

9. Janet E. Helms, ed., *Black and White Racial Identity: Theory, Research, and Practice* (New York: Greenwood Press, 1990).

10. David Wellman, "Red and Black in White America," in *Names We Call Home: Autobiography on Racial Identity,* ed. Becky Thompson and Sangeeta Tyagi (New York: Routledge, 1996), 30.

11. Nelson Mandela, *Long Walk to Freedom* (London: Little, Brown and Company, 1994).

12. Patricia Williams, "The Ethnic Scarring of American Whiteness," in *The House That Race Built: Black Americans, U.S. Terrain,* ed. Wahneema Lubiano (New York: Pantheon, 1997), 263.

13. David Wellman, "Mistaken Identities," in *Red Diapers: Growing Up in the Communist Left,* ed. Judy Kaplan and Linn Shapiro (Chicago: University of Illinois Press, 1998), 174.

14. Adrienne Rich, "Prospective Immigrants Please Note" (1962), in her *The Fact of a Doorframe* (New York: Norton, 1984), 51–52.

15. Ibid.

2. Will the Circle . . .

1. The conference was envisioned by former SNCC activists Bob Zellner, Maggie Nolan Donovan, and Julian Bond along with Susan Kosoff (a teacher at the East Harlem Block Schools in the 1960s and a founder of Boston's Wheelock Family Theatre, a performing arts group with a long-standing multicultural vision). It was attended by many other SNCC activists, including Margaret Burnham, Kathleen Cleaver, Chuck McDew, Joanne Grant, Reggie Robinson, and others. The conference was coordinated by Fran Smith (who is included in this volume). The keynote speakers included Howard Zinn, a long-time radical professor and activist; Katie Cannon, the first Black woman to be ordained as a minister in the Presbyterian church, who grew up in Kannapolis, North Carolina, during the early stages of the Civil Rights Movement; Marilyn Mackel, writer, law professor, and judge in a juvenile court in Los Angeles; and Jacqui Alexander, organizer of the 1992 I Am Your Sister Conference for Audre Lorde and the 1995 Black Nations? Queer Nations? conference on lesbian and gay sexualities in the African diaspora.

2. For a brief history of this song as the signature anthem of the Civil Rights Movement and struggles internationally, see Mary King, *Freedom Song: A Personal History of the 1960s Civil Rights Movement* (New York: William Morrow, 1987), 93–98.

3. For more about Ella Baker's vision and leadership, see Joanne Grant, *Ella Baker: Freedom Bound* (New York: John Wiley and Sons, 1998); Paula Giddings, *When and Where I Enter: The Impact of Black Women on Race and Sex in America* (New York: Bantam Books, 1984), 268–69, 274–75.

4. William H. Chafe, *The Unfinished Journey: America since World War II* (New York: Oxford University Press, 1999), 170.

5. Clayborne Carson, ed., *In Struggle: SNCC and the Black Awakening of the 1960s* (Cambridge, Mass.: Harvard University Press, 1995), 52–54.

6. Howard Zinn, *SNCC: The New Abolitionists* (Boston: Beacon Press, 1964), 181.

7. "I Have a Dream." Address at March on Washington, August 28, 1963.

8. In Cheryl Lynn Greenberg, "SNCC Women and the Stirrings of Feminism," in *A Circle of Trust: Remembering SNCC,* ed. Cheryl Lynn Greenberg (New York: Routledge, 1998), 143.

9. Carson, *In Struggle,* 114.

10. Ibid.; John Lewis, *Walking with the Wind: A Memoir of the Movement* (New York: Simon and Schuster, 1998).

11. John M. Glen, *Highlander: No Ordinary School* (Knoxville: University of Tennessee Press, 1996); Myles Horton with Judith Kohl and Herbert Kohl, *The Long Haul: An Autobiography* (New York: Teachers College Press, 1998).

12. King, *Freedom Song,* 57.

13. Carson, *In Struggle,* 52.

14. Anne Braden, *The Wall Between* (Knoxville: University of Tennessee Press, 1999).

15. For analysis of William Patterson and other Black lawyers' work with the Black liberation movement, see Akinyele Omowale Umoja, "Set Our Warriors Free: The Legacy of the Black Panther Party and Political Prisoners," in *The Black Panther Party Reconsidered,* ed. Charles E. Jones (Baltimore: Black Classic Press, 1998), 420–21.

16. Carson, *In Struggle,* 52.

17. Report by Zellner, May 19, 1962, box 62, folder 3, Braden Papers, SHSW, cited in Carson, *In Struggle,* 53, 313n12.

18. Quoted in untitled manuscript by Anne Braden, box 62, Braden Papers, SHSW cited in Carson, *In Struggle,* 103, 319n15.

19. Carson, *In Struggle,* 118.

20. Ibid., 102–3.

21. Ray Luc Levasseur, *Until All Are Free: The Trial Statement of Ray Luc Levasseur* (London: Attack International, 1989), 13.

22. Carson, *In Struggle,* 103.

23. Among other atrocities, Bob Moses was haunted by the murder, by a white man, E. H. Hurst, of Herbert Lee, a Black farmer who had supported a voter-registration drive Moses had initiated. Another Black man, Lewis Allen, who was willing to come forward to testify about this murder, was killed by whites as well; Chafe, *The Unfinished Journey,* 172–73.

24. Quoted in King, *Freedom Song,* 319.

25. Cited in King, *Freedom Song,* 497.

26. Carson, *In Struggle,* 117.

27. Lewis, *Walking with the Wind*; Chafe, *The Unfinished Journey,* 302–42. Tom Hayden asserts that the government's military assault on Newark citizens following the Newark rebellion in 1967 was the final nail in the coffin of a

nonviolent, integrationist ethic within the movement; Tom Hayden, *Reunion: A Memoir* (New York: Random House, 1988), 162.

28. Carson, *In Struggle,* 105.

29. King, *Freedom Song,* 369.

30. Ibid., 297.

31. Stokely Carmichael (Kwame Toure) and Rap Brown were SNCC leaders who rejected the nonviolent perspective held by earlier SNCC leaders John Lewis and Bob Moses. Lewis and Moses were best known for their leadership in organizing southern voter registration drives and Freedom Summer. Stokely Carmichael was considered a leading architect of the Black Power Movement. With Rap Brown and others, he helped shift SNCC focus from rural to urban areas; see especially "Internal Conflicts" in Carson, *In Struggle,* 229–43.

32. Judy Kaplan and Linn Shapiro explain that "the 1940 Smith Act made it illegal to teach, advocate, or encourage the forcible overthrow of the United States government." In the 1940s and 1950s this act was used to silence and often imprison Communist Party leaders and other labor and antiracist activists. See Judy Kaplan and Linn Shapiro, eds., *Red Diapers: Growing Up in the Communist Left* (Chicago: University of Illinois Press, 1998), 320.

33. Anne Braden, "Epilogue 1999," in her *The Wall Between,* 338.

34. Ibid., 337–38.

35. Carson, *In Struggle,* 229–43.

36. Hayden, *Reunion,* 163–64.

37. Braden, "Epilogue 1999," 340.

38. Giddings, *When and Where I Enter,* 300.

39. In Greenberg, "SNCC Women and the Stirrings of Feminism," 144–45.

40. Sara Evans, *Personal Politics: The Roots of Women's Liberation in the Civil Rights Movement and the New Left* (New York: Vintage Books, 1980).

41. Belinda Robnett, *How Long? How Long? African American Women in the Struggle for Civil Rights* (New York: Oxford University Press, 1997), 115–39.

42. In Greenberg, "SNCC Women and the Stirrings of Feminism," 150.

43. Ibid., 151.

44. Cheryl Lynn Greenberg, introduction to Greenberg, *A Circle of Trust,* 13.

3. . . . Be Unbroken

1. The New Left in the United States includes organizations and ideas associated with the emergence of social justice activism led by young people in SNCC, SDS, the Black Panther Party, feminist organizations, and other progressive groups that emerged in the 1960s. New Left principles include an emphasis on participatory democracy, asserting an individual's right and responsibility to be involved in all political processes; nonhierarchical organizing; the creation of alternative institutions; the sanctity of individual freedom of ex-

pression; and living the principles one professes. The issues most associated with the New Left in the United States in the 1960s included support for voter registration, desegregation, and racial justice in general; opposition to the Vietnam War and to U.S. militarism internationally; promotion of free speech and democratic process in higher education; advocacy of the right to sexual and cultural freedom of expression; opposition to bureaucracy and corporate alienation; and support for women's rights.

The New Left kept "left" in its name because it held onto many Old Left principles, including the struggle for racial and economic justice, an opposition to antidemocratic strategies in government, and support for mass organization as the basis of political mobilization. What made the New Left "new" is that it tended to reject the Old Left's reliance upon hierarchical structures, its more central link to communism and the Soviet Union, and its view that economic inequality is the primary oppression. For an insightful view of the New Left internationally, see George Katsiaficas, *The Imagination of the New Left: A Global Analysis of 1968* (Boston: South End Press, 1987). For scholarship on the New Left in the United States, see Wini Breines, *Community and Organization in the New Left, 1962–1968: The Great Refusal* (New Brunswick, N.J.: Rutgers University Press, 1989); Jack Whelen and Richard Flacks, *Beyond the Barricades: The Sixties Generation Grows Up* (Philadelphia: Temple University Press, 1989).

2. Clayborne Carson, ed., *In Struggle: SNCC and the Black Awakening of the 1960s* (Cambridge, Mass.: Harvard University Press, 1981, 1995), 53.

3. Breines, *Community and Organization,* 11.

4. Todd Gitlin, *The Sixties: Years of Hope, Days of Rage* (New York: Bantam, 1987), 121.

5. Mario Savio, "An End to History," in *Takin' It to the Streets: A '60s Reader,* ed. Alexander Bloom and Wini Breines (New York: Oxford University Press, 1995), 114.

6. Mary King, *Freedom Song: A Personal History of the 1960s Civil Rights Movement* (New York: Morrow, 1987), 285.

7. As critical race law theorists of the late 1980s and since have articulated, proponents of absolutist First Amendment rights fail to take into account the ways racism has historically stopped Black people from being able to speak at all, never mind freely; see Mari Matsuda, Charles Lawrence, Richard Delgado, and Kimberlé Williams Crenshaw, *Words That Wound: Critical Race Theory, Assaultive Speech, and the First Amendment* (Boulder, Colo.: Westview Press, 1993); Charles Lawrence and Mari Matsuda, *We Won't Go Back: Making the Case for Affirmative Action* (New York: Houghton and Mifflin, 1997).

8. Savio, "An End to History," 112.

9. Michael R. Ornelas, *Beyond 1848: Readings in the Modern Chicano Historical Experience* (Dubuque, Iowa: Kendall/Hunt, 1993), 254–60.

10. Breines, *Community and Organization,* 55.

11. Ibid., 97–115.

12. Carl Davidson, "Student Power: A Radical View," in Bloom and Breines, *Takin' It to the Streets,* 132, first cited in Breines, *Community and Organization,* 116.

13. Gitlin, *The Sixties,* 147.

14. Carson, *In Struggle,* 177.

15. Breines, *Community and Organization,* 143.

16. Quoted in Gitlin, *The Sixties,* 167.

17. For an incisive account of the contradictions embedded in the Johnson administration's War on Poverty, see William Chafe, *The Unfinished Journey: America since World War II* (New York: Oxford University Press, 1999), 236–46.

18. Howard Zinn, *A People's History of the United States* (New York: HarperPerennial, 1990), 476, 484.

19. Ray Luc Levasseur, *Until All Are Free: The Trial Statement of Ray Luc Levasseur* (London: Attack International, 1989), 10–11.

20. Chafe, *The Unfinished Journey,* 290.

21. Ibid., 294.

22. SNCC, "The U.S. Government Has Deceived Us," in Bloom and Breines, *Takin' It to the Streets,* 229.

23. Carl Oglesby, "Trapped in a System," in Bloom and Breines, *Takin' It to the Streets,* 223.

24. David Gilbert, correspondence with author, May 5, 1997.

25. Zinn, *A People's History of the United States,* 482.

26. S. Kappor, "Brown Beret: Could This Be a Chicano Peace Brigade?" *Social Alternatives* 16, no. 2 (April 1997): 16; Elizabeth Martínez, ed., *De Colores Means All of Us: Latina Views for a Multi-Colored Century* (Boston: South End Press, 1998), 23.

27. The Left still has a hard time keeping its attention on Puerto Rican independence, which makes little sense given the anti-imperialist, antiracist issues involved. As residents of a U.S. colony, Puerto Ricans cannot vote for the president of the United States, but since the Jones Act passed by Congress in 1917 declared them U.S. citizens, they can be drafted to fight in U.S. wars. They are citizens of the United States, and yet they cannot make basic political and economic decisions. According to activist and journalist Juan Gonzalez, Puerto Ricans remain locked in a subordinate position. The United States, for example, can continue to use Vieques, an island off Puerto Rico, as a military base, while denying Puerto Ricans political power. Admitting Puerto Rico as a state would bring a substantial Latino population into the voting population and would fuel the long-term push by Black activists to recognize the District of Columbia as a state. Gonzalez writes, "The last thing the Republicans want

are two states coming in that would have such huge, poor, non-white, and probably Democratic populations. Puerto Rico right now has a greater population than twenty-four states in the Union"; quoted in David Barsamian, "Juan Gonzalez," *The Progressive* 64, no. 7 (July 2000): 34. Poet Martín Espada asserts that the white left's continued refusal to focus on Puerto Rican independence reflects basic ignorance of Puerto Rican history and that "the cause of Puerto Rican independence is not romantic enough to suit certain North American leftists," adding, "Colonialism in Puerto Rico is an ethical dilemma which the left refuses to see in ethical terms, a crime for which even progressives share responsibility as long as they deny that crime"; Martín Espada, "Viva Vieques," *The Progressive* 64, no. 7 (July 2000): 29.

28. Edward P. Morgan, *The '60s Experience: Hard Lessons about Modern America* (Philadelphia: Temple University Press, 1991), 154–55.

29. Ward Churchill and Jim Vander Wall, *Agents of Repression: The FBI's Secret War against the Black Panther Party and the American Indian Movement* (Boston: South End Press, 1988); Zinn, *A People's History of the United States*, 455.

30. Philip Foner, ed., *The Black Panthers Speak* (New York: De Capo Press, 1995); Charles E. Jones, ed., *The Black Panther Party Reconsidered* (Baltimore: Black Classic Press, 1998).

31. From 1969 to 1971, a coalition organization called Indians of All Tribes occupied Alcatraz Island to call attention to decades-long mistreatment of Native Americans. In 1972 the American Indian Movement organized "the Trail of Broken Treaties" protest in Washington, D.C. The activists occupied the Bureau of Indian Affairs' central headquarters in Washington, D.C., for many days and presented a Twenty Point Program demanding self-determination and sovereignty for Native peoples. See Rebecca Robbins, "Self Determination and Subordination: The Past, Present, and Future of American Governance," 87–121; and Jim Vander Wall, "A Warrior Caged: The Continuing Struggle of Leonard Peltier," 291–310; both in *The State of Native America: Genocide, Colonization, and Resistance*, ed. M. Annette Jaimes (Boston: South End Press, 1992).

32. This strategy built on one SNCC had been developing as early as 1967 when SNCC supported Puerto Rican nationalists by sending Stokely Carmichael to Puerto Rico and when a SNCC delegation signed a treaty with a Hopi leader and activists seeking land the government had stolen in the southwest; Carson, *In Struggle*, 278.

33. This questioning of strategies was indicated in part by changes in where activists turned for intellectual inspiration. In John Lewis's words, "They [the new generation of activists] weren't reading Gandhi or Thoreau. They were reading existentialist philosophers like Camus, and the radical, Black separatist writings of people like Malcolm—*Malcolm X Speaks,* a collection of

Malcolm's more extreme speeches and essays, was particularly popular—and Frantz Fanon, whose book *The Wretched of the Earth* described Algeria under colonial rule and preached the philosophy of violence, justifiable terrorism and an 'eye for an eye'"; John Lewis, *Walking with the Wind: A Memoir of the Movement* (New York: Simon and Schuster, 1998), 349.

34. See especially "Internal Conflict," in Carson, *In Struggle*, 229–43.

35. Seymour Martin Lipset and Everett Carl Ladd, "The Political Future of Activist Generations," in *The New Pilgrims: Youth Protest in Transition*, ed. Philip G. Altbach and Robert Laufer (New York: David McKay, 1972), 63.

36. Breines, *Community and Organization*, 120.

37. Marilyn Buck, David Gilbert, and Laura Whitehorn, *Enemies of the State: A Frank Discussion of Past Political Movements, Victories and Errors, and the Current Political Climate for Revolutionary Struggle within the U.S.A.* (Brooklyn, N.Y.: Resistance in Brooklyn [RnB], 1998), 35. Available through Meyer, c/o WRL, 339 Lafayette St., New York, NY, 10012.

38. See Fredrick D. Miller, "The End of SDS and the Emergence of Weathermen: Demise through Success," in *Waves of Protest*, ed. Jo Freeman and Victoria Johnson (New York: Rowman and Littlefield, 1999) 303–24.

39. Ron Jacobs, *The Way the Wind Blew: A History of the Weather Underground* (New York: Verso, 1997), 5.

40. BLA was a network of armed, clandestine, local collectives active between 1970 and 1981. It included many former members of the Black Panther Party. The Puerto Rican Armed Forces of National Liberation (FALN—Fuerza Armadas de Liberación Nacional Puertorriqueña) "is an armed, underground collective of revolutionary Puerto Ricans living on the U.S. mainland that bombed government, military and corporate buildings from 1974–1983 as part of its strategy to contribute to a people's war to win independence and socialism for Puerto Rico" (81–82). For the above and for more in-depth definitions of these and other terms related to militant organizations, see Buck, Gilbert, and Whitehorn, *Enemies of the State*.

41. For critiques of the Weather Underground by former SDS members, see Tom Hayden, *Reunion: A Memoir* (New York: Random House, 1988); Gitlin, *The Sixties*. For analysis of white leftist characterizations of the Weather Underground, see Wini Breines, "Sixties Stories' Silences: White Feminism, Black Feminism, Black Power," *National Women's Studies Association Journal* 18, no. 3 (Fall 1996): 101–21. Ron Jacobs's book on the Weather Underground offers some helpful analysis of the historical context through which the Weather Underground emerged and why its members considered militancy necessary. However, the book might have been better had Jacobs included interviews with members of the Weather Underground, several of whom are willing to talk critically and analytically about that period in their lives.

42. It is hard for prisoners to get their work widely disseminated, inside or

outside prison. In addition, for some who are currently in prison, writing about their philosophy and affiliation at the time might still be used against them, since their cases are still in the courts.

43. For an expansive anthology of writings by U.S. political prisoners (and lengthy biographical sketches of each of the more than fifty contributors), see Tim Blunk and Raymond Luc Levasseur, eds., *Hauling Up the Morning: Izando la Mañana* (Trenton, N.J.: Red Sea Press, 1990).

44. George Katsiaficas reports about the extraordinary activism of the early 1970s: "During the first six days after the invasion of Cambodia, there was an average of twenty new campuses going on strike every day, and in the days after the slaughter at Kent State on May Fourth [1970], one hundred more colleges joined every day. . . . by the end of the month, at least one-third of the nation's 2827 institutions of higher education were on strike. . . . In the first week [of May] 30 ROTC buildings were burned or bombed. And across the country there were more incidents of arson and bombing (at least 16,995 alone on college campuses) than in any single month in which government records have been kept"; Katsiaficas, *The Imagination of the New Left,* 120.

45. Buck, Gilbert, and Whitehorn, *Enemies of the State,* 39.

46. Ray Luc Levasseur, "Trouble in Mind: ADX—The Fourth Year" (1999), 4. Essay available through December Sixteenth Committee, Box 21073, 2000 SW College, Topeka, Kans., 66621.

47. Levasseur, *Until All Are Free,* 12.

48. The United Freedom Front, a predominantly white organization, worked against apartheid and U.S. involvement in Central America and in support of Puerto Rican independence and prison reform in the United States.

49. Ray Luc Levasseur, "Down with the Struggle," reprint from the Sedition Committee: Ohio Seven on Trial for Sedition Conspiracy (1988), 1.

50. Buck, Gilbert, and Whitehorn, *Enemies of the State.*

51. Todd Gitlin, *Twilight of Common Dreams: Why America Is Wracked by Culture Wars* (New York: Henry Holt, 1996); Michael Tomasky, *Left for Dead: The Life, Death, and Possible Resurrection of Progressive Politics in America* (New York: Free Press, 1996).

52. For an account of another intergenerational conference first inspired by 1960s activists—Mississippi Homecoming 1994—that also pays tribute to young people's insistence on being fully recognized, see Elizabeth Martínez, "On Time in Mississippi," in Martínez, *De Colores Means All of Us,* 153–61.

53. It was not only that many of the young people had scant understanding of labor organizing or the Civil Rights Movement, or that older people knew little about rap, computers, and spirituality in the 1990s. The generations were actually talking across, around, and through each other—not just not knowing but also misunderstanding each other.

4. Black Power and White Accountability

1. Sherna Berger Gluck, "Whose Feminism, Whose History? Reflections on Excavating the History of (the) U.S. Women's Movement(s)" in *Community Activism and Feminist Politics: Organizing across Race, Class, and Gender,* ed. Nancy A. Naples (New York: Routledge, 1998), 34.

2. Ibid., 31. For examples of histories that focus on white feminism, see Sheila Tobias, *Faces of Feminism: An Activist's Reflections on the Women's Movement* (Boulder, Colo.: Westview Press, 1997); Barbara Ryan, *Feminism and the Women's Movement: Dynamics of Change in Social Movement Ideology and Activism* (New York: Routledge, 1992); Alice Echols, *Daring to Be Bad: Radical Feminism in America, 1967–1975* (Minneapolis: University of Minnesota Press, 1989). For histories that counter the "master historical narrative," see Deborah Gray White, *Too Heavy a Load: Black Women in Defense of Themselves* (New York: Norton, 1999); Angela Davis, *The Angela Y. Davis Reader,* ed. Joy James (Malden, Mass.: Blackwell, 1998); Paula Giddings, *When and Where I Enter: The Impact of Black Women on Race and Sex in America* (New York: Bantam, 1984); Rosalind Rosenberg, *Divided Lives: American Women in the Twentieth Century* (New York: Noonday Press, 1992); M. Rivka Polatnick, "Diversity in Women's Liberation Ideology: How a Black and a White Group of the 1960s Viewed Motherhood," *Signs: Journal of Women in Culture and Society* 21, no. 3 (Spring 1996): 679–706.

3. Of these branches of feminism (liberal, socialist, and radical), socialist feminism, which treats sexism and classism as interrelated forms of oppression, may have made the most concerted effort to develop an antiracist agenda in the 1970s. For example, "The Combahee River Collective and Black Feminist Statement" was first published in Zilloh Eisenstein's edited volume *Capitalist Patriarchy and the Case for Socialist Feminism* (New York: Monthly Review Press, 1979), 362–72, before it was published in Barbara Smith's edited volume *Home Girls: A Black Feminist Anthology* (New York: Kitchen Table Women of Color Press, 1983). *Radical America,* a journal begun in 1967 whose contributors and editors included many socialist feminists, consistently publishes articles that examined the relationship between race, class, and gender. The confinement of socialist feminism—in the main—to academic circles, however, limited its effectiveness and visibility as an antiracist presence in early second-wave feminism.

4. Nancy MacLean, "The Hidden History of Affirmative Action: Working Women's Struggles in the 1970s and the Gender of Class," *Feminist Studies* 25, no. 1 (Spring 1999): 47.

5. Barbara Smith, "'Feisty Characters,' and 'Other People's Causes': Memories of White Racism and U.S. Feminism," in *The Feminist Memoir Project: Voices from Women's Liberation,* ed. Rachel Blau DePlessis and Ann Snitow (New York: Three Rivers Press, 1998), 477.

6. Howard Zinn, *A People's History of the United States* (New York: HarperPerennial, 1990), 504–13.

7. For a published version of Flo Kennedy's position on Attica and Naomi Jaffe's perspective, see Smith, "'Feisty Characters,'" 481.

8. For poetry and writing by Marilyn Buck, see "Thirteen Springs" and "No Frills," *Sojourner: The Women's Forum* 29, no. 9 (May 1999): 20; Marilyn Buck, David Gilbert, and Laura Whitehorn, *Enemies of the State: A Frank Discussion of Past Political Movements, Victories and Errors, and the Current Political Climate for Revolutionary Struggle within the U.S.A.* (Brooklyn, N.Y.: Resistance in Brooklyn (RnB), 1998). Available through Meyer, c/o WRL, 339 Lafayette Street, NY, 10012.

9. Kathleen Neal Cleaver, "Racism, Civil Rights, and Feminism," in *Critical Race Feminism: A Reader,* ed. Adrien Katherine Wing (New York: New York University Press, 1997), 37.

10. In their work with the SCEF from 1957 to 1973, Anne Braden and her husband, Carl Braden, refused to dissociate from Communists, a political decision that left them on the edges of mainstream civil rights organizing.

11. The first open letter appeared in the *Southern Patriot* in 1972 and as an educational pamphlet. For a summary of this first letter, see Anne Braden, "A Second Open Letter to Southern White Women," *Southern Exposure* 6, no. 4 (Winter 1977): 50.

12. Ibid.

13. Susan Brownmiller, *Against Our Will: Men, Women, and Rape* (New York: Simon and Schuster, 1975).

14. Braden, "A Second Open Letter" 52.

15. Anne Braden, *The Wall Between* (New York: Monthly Review Press, 1958; Knoxville: University of Tennessee Press, 1999).

16. The primarily East Coast–based groups fighting for independence for Puerto Rico and the Brown Berets on the West Coast were among the Latino groups whose politics were based on self-determination and ethnic nationalism.

17. The term "women of color" (which includes but is not limited to Native American, Asian, African American, Arab, and Latina women) is used for political reasons to underscore unity among women who have historically been colonized, enslaved, and exploited in the United States. The term "Third World" stresses similarities between oppression of women of color in the United States and of women in Third World countries. For analysis of the import and complication of these terms, see Chela Sandoval, "Feminism and Racism: A Report on the 1981 National Women's Studies Association Conference," in *Making Face, Making Soul: Haciendo Caras. Creative and Critical Perspectives by Women of Color,* ed. Gloria Anzaldúa (San Francisco: Aunt Lute Press, 1990), 55–74; Chandra Talpade Mohanty, "Cartographies of Struggle: Third World Women and the Politics of Feminism," 1–50, and "Under Western

Eyes: Feminist Scholarship and Colonial Discourses," 51–80; both in *Third World Women and the Politics of Feminism,* ed. Chandra Talpade Mohanty, Ann Russo, and Lourdes Torres (Bloomington: University of Indiana Press, 1991).

18. Mohanty, "Cartographies of Struggle," 10.

19. A groundbreaking analysis of the consequences of gender socialization that encourages women not to fight back is offered by Melanie Kaye/Kantrowitz. She asks the brave question: Why do women not consider carrying guns to protect themselves against male violence? She ponders the extent to which simplistic notions of women as nonviolent and men as violent stop women from saying, Enough is enough; you come any closer and I will defend myself; Melanie Kaye/Kantrowitz, *The Issue Is Power: Essays on Women, Jews, Violence, and Resistance* (San Francisco: Aunt Lute Press, 1992), 7–74.

20. Kathleen M. Blee, *Women of the Klan: Racism and Gender in the 1920s* (Berkeley and Los Angeles: University of California Press, 1991).

21. Vicki Gabriner, "The Review as Process: Dealing with the Contradictions," in *Feminary* 11, nos. 1–2 (1980): 116–17.

22. See Fran Moira, "Judy Clark: Seventy-Five to Life, but Life Goes On," *off our backs* 14, no. 1 (December 1984): 2–8.

23. Adrienne Rich, *On Lies, Secrets, and Silence* (New York: Norton, 1979), 290.

24. Cherríe Moraga and Gloria Anzaldúa, eds. *This Bridge Called My Back: Writings by Radical Women of Color,* 2nd ed. (New York: Kitchen Table Women of Color Press, 1983).

25. Cherríe Moraga and Gloria Anzaldúa, introduction to Moraga and Anzaldúa, *This Bridge Called My Back,* xxiii–xxiv.

26. Marilyn Buck, "Autobiograph" (unpublished poem). Reprinted with permission.

27. Cherríe Moraga, "A Long Line of Vendidas," in her *Loving in the War Years: Lo que nunca pasó por sus labios* (Boston: South End Press, 1983), 105.

28. White, *Too Heavy a Load,* 219.

29. Ibid., 222–23.

30. Beatriz Pesquera and Denise A. Segura, "There Is No Going Back: Chicanas and Feminism," in *Chicana Critical Issues,* ed. Mujeres Activas en Letras y Cambio Social (Berkeley: Third Woman Press, 1993).

31. Alma Garcia, "The Development of Chicana Feminist Discourse, 1970–1980," in *Unequal Sisters: A Multicultural Reader in U.S. Women's History,* ed. Vicki L. Ruiz and Ellen Carol DuBois (New York: Routledge, 1994), 531–44.

32. Pesquera and Segura, "There Is No Going Back," 102.

33. Moraga, "A Long Line of Vendidas," 103.

34. Aída Hurtado, *The Color of Privilege: Three Blasphemies on Race and Feminism* (Ann Arbor: University of Michigan Press, 1996), 103.

35. Tracye Matthews, "'No One Ever Asks, What a Man's Place in the Revolution Is': Gender and the Politics of the Black Panther Party, 1966–1971," in *The Black Panther Party Reconsidered,* ed. Charles P. Jones (Baltimore: Black Classic Press, 1998), 273.

36. Combahee River Collective, "The Combahee River Collective Statement," in Smith, *Home Girls,* 272–82.

37. Hurtado, *The Color of Privilege,* 107.

38. Paula Gunn Allen, *Sacred Hoop: Recovering the Feminine in American Indian Traditions* (Boston: Beacon Press, 1986); Gluck, "Whose Feminism, Whose History?" 41. See also Rayna Green, "Diary of a Native American Feminist," *Ms.* 11 (July/August 1982): 170–72, 211–13.

39. Angela Davis, "Afro Images: Politics, Fashion, and Nostalgia," in *Names We Call Home: Autobiography on Racial Identity,* ed. Becky Thompson and Sangeeta Tyagi (New York: Routledge, 1996), 87–92. The complications of nationalism as a principle for Black lesbian and gay feminist organizing were the subject of much debate at the historic Black Nations? Queer Nations? conference in New York City in 1995. The conference conveners deliberately set the title with double question marks, cognizant of the power of Black nationalist organizing historically, as well as the damage done in its name to Black gay men and lesbians.

40. For remedies for this marginalization, see Vicki L. Crawford, Jacqueline Anne Rouse, and Barbara Woods, eds., *Women in the Civil Rights Movement: Trailblazers and Torchbearers, 1941–1965* (Bloomington: Indiana University Press, 1993); Belinda Robnett, *How Long? How Long? African American Women in the Struggle for Civil Rights* (New York: Oxford University Press, 1997); White, *Too Heavy a Load;* Davis, *The Angela Y. Davis Reader;* Giddings, *When and Where I Enter.*

For critiques of these silences, see Wini Breines, "Sixties Stories' Silences: White Feminism, Black Feminism, Black Power," *National Women's Studies Association Journal* 18, no. 3 (Fall 1996): 101–17; Cheryl Lynn Greenberg, "SNCC Women and the Stirrings of Feminism," in *A Circle of Trust: Remembering SNCC,* ed. Cheryl Lynn Greenberg (New York: Routledge, 1998), 127–51.

41. Breines, "Sixties Stories' Silences," 109.

42. Ryan, *Feminism and the Women's Movement;* Tobias, *Faces of Feminism;* Jo Freeman, *Women: A Feminist Perspective* (Palo Alto, Calif.: Mayfield, 1975).

43. The historical links these writers make are between the suffrage movement and second-wave feminism—a linkage that downplays the import of Black women's activism in both eras.

44. Echols, *Daring to Be Bad*; Sara Evans, *Personal Politics: The Roots of Women's Liberation in the Civil Rights Movement and the New Left* (New York: Vintage Books, 1979).

45. Smith, "'Feisty Characters,'" 479.

46. Guida West, "Twin-Track Coalitions in the Black Power Movement," in *Interracial Bonds,* ed. Rhoda Goldstein Blumberg and Wendell James Roye (Bayside, N.Y.: General Hall, 1979), 71–87.

5. Multiracial Feminism

1. Chela Sandoval, "Feminism and Racism: A Report on the 1981 National Women's Studies Association Conference," in *Making Face, Making Soul: Haciendo Caras. Creative and Critical Perspectives by Women of Color,* ed. Gloria Anzaldúa (San Francisco: Aunt Lute Press, 1990), 55.

2. Chela Sandoval, "Oppositional Consciousness in the Postmodern World: United States Third World Feminism, Semiotics, and the Methodology of the Oppressed" (Ph.D. diss., University of California at Santa Cruz, 1994).

3. See note 17 in chapter 4 for clarification of the terms "women of color" and "Third World women."

4. Angela Davis, *The Angela Y. Davis Reader,* ed. Joy James (Malden, Mass.: Blackwell, 1998), 15, 314.

5. Sherna Berger Gluck, "Whose Feminism, Whose History? Reflections on Excavating the History of (the) U.S. Women's Movement(s)," in *Community Activism and Feminist Politics: Organizing across Race, Class, and Gender,* ed. Nancy A. Naples (New York: Routledge, 1998), 38–39.

6. Miya Iwataki, "The Asian Women's Movement: A Retrospective," *East Wind,* Spring/Summer 1983, 35–41; Gluck, "Whose Feminism, Whose History?" 39–41.

7. Iwataki, "The Asian Women's Movement," 35–41.

8. Sonia Shah, "Presenting the Blue Goddess: Toward a National Pan-Asian Feminist Agenda," in *The State of Asian America: Activism and Resistance in the 1990s,* ed. Karin Aguilar–San Juan (Boston: South End Press, 1994), 147–58.

9. Iwataki, "The Asian Women's Movement," 41.

10. M. Annette Jaimes with Theresa Halsey, "American Indian Women: At the Center of Indigenous Resistance in Contemporary North America," in *The State of Native America: Genocide, Colonization, and Resistance,* ed. M. Annette Jaimes (Boston: South End Press, 1992), 328–29.

11. Stephanie Autumn, ". . . This Air, This Land, This Water—If We Don't Start Organizing Now, We'll Lose It," *Big Mama Rag* 11, no. 4 (April 1983): 4, 5.

12. For an insightful analysis of the multidimensionality of Black nationalism of the late 1960s and early 1970s, see "Black Nationalism: The '60s and the '90s," in Davis, *The Angela Y. Davis Reader,* 289–96.

13. Deborah Gray White, *Too Heavy a Load: Black Women in Defense of Themselves* (New York: Norton, 1999), 242.

14. Ibid., 242–53.

15. Combahee River Collective, "The Combahee River Collective Statement," in *Home Girls: A Black Feminist Anthology,* ed. Barbara Smith (New York: Kitchen Table Women of Color Press, 1983), 275.

16. In Black womanist theology emerging during this period, the concept of epistemological privilege paralleled this principle. The epistemological privilege is the right and responsibility of those in marginalized positions to name the strategies of resistance and change. See Katie G. Cannon, *Black Womanist Ethics* (Atlanta, Ga.: Scholars Press, 1988).

17. Barbara Smith, "The Boston Murders," in *Life Notes: Personal Writing by Contemporary Black Women,* ed. Patricia Bell-Scott (New York: Norton, 1994), 315.

18. Anna Julia Cooper, "The Status of Women in America," 44–49; Claudia Jones, "An End to the Neglect of the Problems of the Negro Woman!," 108–23; both in *Words of Fire: An Anthology of African-American Feminist Thought,* ed. Beverly Guy-Sheftall (New York: New Press, 1995).

19. Davis, *The Angela Y. Davis Reader,* 313.

20. Barbara Smith, "Racism and Women's Studies," in *All the Women Are White, All the Blacks Are Men, but Some of Us Are Brave: Black Women's Studies,* ed. Gloria T. Hull, Patricia Bell Scott, and Barbara Smith (Old Westbury, N.Y.: Feminist Press, 1982), 49.

21. Patricia Hill Collins, "Feminism in the Twentieth Century," in *Black Women in America: An Historical Encyclopedia,* ed. Darlene Clark Hine (New York: Carlson Publishing, 1993), 418, quoted in Vicki Crawford, "African American Women in the Twenty-First Century: The Continuing Challenge," in *The American Woman, 1999–2000,* ed. Cynthia B. Costello, Shari Miles, and Anne J. Stone (New York: Norton, 1998), 119.

22. Alice Walker, *In Search of Our Mother's Gardens: Womanist Prose* (San Diego, Calif.: Harcourt Brace Jovanovich, 1983).

23. Patricia Zavella, "The Problematic Relationship of Feminism and Chicana Studies," *Women's Studies* 17 (1989): 29; Mujeres Activas en Letras y Cambio Social, eds., *Chicana Critical Issues* (Berkeley: Third Woman Press, 1993).

24. Chela Sandoval, "U.S. Third World Feminism: The Theory and Method of Oppositional Consciousness in Postmodern World" *Genders* 10 (Spring 1991): 5; Gloria Anzaldúa, "La Consciencia de la Mestiza: Towards a New Consciousness," in Anzaldúa, *Making Face, Making Soul,* 377–89; Maxine Hong Kingston, *The Woman Warrior* (New York: Vintage Books, 1977); Audre Lorde, *Sister Outsider* (New York: Crossing Press, 1984).

25. Elizabeth Martínez, "History Makes Us, We Make History," in *The Feminist Memoir Project: Voices from Women's Liberation,* ed. Rachel Blau DuPlessis and Ann Snitow (New York: Three Rivers Press, 1998), 118.

26. Celestine Ware, *Woman Power: The Movement for Women's Liberation* (New York: Tower, 1970). See also Katie King, *Theory in Its Feminist Travels: Conversations in U.S. Women's Movements* (Bloomington: University of Indiana Press, 1994), 126–30, 132–33, 177.

27. Beatriz Pesquera and Denise A. Segura, "There Is No Going Back: Chicanas and Feminism," in *Chicana Critical Issues,* ed. Mujeres Activas en Letras y Cambio Social (Berkeley, Calif.: Third Woman Press), 97.

28. Davis, *The Angela Y. Davis Reader,* 291.

29. Activist organizations of women of color in the 1970s and 1980s included the National Conference of Puerto Rican Women (NaCOPRW, founded in 1972); the Mexican American Women's National Association (MANA, 1974); the Organization of Pan Asian American Women (1976); OHOYO, a national network of American Indian and Alaska Native Women (early 1980s); the National Institute of Women of Color (1981); the National Coalition of One Hundred Black Women (1970); and the Coalition of Labor Union Women (CLUW, 1974). For an excellent multiracial chronicle of second-wave feminist organizations, see Leslie R. Wolfe and Jennifer Tucker, "Feminism Lives: Building a Multiracial Women's Movement in the United States," in *The Challenge of Local Feminisms: Women's Movement in Global Perspective,* ed. Amrita Basu (Boulder, Colo.: Westview, 1995), 435–62.

30. Toni Cade, ed., *The Black Woman: An Anthology* (New York: Signet, 1970); Ntozake Shange, *For Colored Girls Who Have Considered Suicide / When the Rainbow Is Enuf* (New York: Macmillan, 1977); Kingston, *The Woman Warrior; Conditions: Five, the Black Women's Issue,* ed. Lorraine Bethel and Barbara Smith, 1979; Audre Lorde, *The Cancer Journals* (Argyle, N.Y.: Spinsters Ink, 1980).

31. Davis, *The Angela Y. Davis Reader,* 313.

32. Ibid., 313; Cherríe Moraga and Gloria Anzaldúa, eds., *This Bridge Called My Back: Writings by Radical Women of Color,* 2nd ed. (New York: Kitchen Table Women of Color Press, 1983).

33. Gaye Williams, "Anzaldúa and Moraga: Building Bridges," *Sojourner: The Women's Forum* 7, no. 2 (October 1981): 14.

34. Cherríe Moraga, "Refugees of a World on Fire: Foreword to the Second Edition," in Moraga and Anzaldúa, *This Bridge Called My Back,* foreword, no numbered pages.

35. Quoted in Williams, "Anzaldúa and Moraga," 14.

36. Paula Gunn Allen, review of Moraga and Anzaldúa, *This Bridge Called My Back, Conditions: Eight,* 1982: 124.

37. Merle Woo, "Letter to Ma," in Moraga and Anzaldúa, *This Bridge Called My Back,* 140–47.

38. Mitsuye Yamada, "Asian American Women and Feminism" in Moraga and Anzaldúa, *This Bridge Called My Back,* 75.

39. Gloria Anzaldúa, "Speaking in Tongues, in Moraga and Anzaldúa, *This Bridge Called My Back,* 170.

40. Jane Mansbridge, "What Is the Feminist Movement?" in *Feminist Organizations: Harvest of the New Women's Movement,* ed. Myra Marx Ferree and Patricia Yancey Martin (Philadelphia: Temple University Press, 1995), 32.

41. Gluck, "Whose Feminism, Whose History?" 32.

42. Beth Brant, ed. *A Gathering of Spirit: Writing and Art by North American Indian Women* (Rockland, Me.: Sinister Wisdom Books, 1984); Smith, *Home Girls*; Moraga and Anzaldúa, *This Bridge Called My Back.*

43. Cherríe Moraga, preface to Moraga and Anzaldúa, *This Bridge Called My Back,* xiv.

44. Judith Moschkovich, "—But I Know You, American Woman," in Moraga and Anzaldúa, *This Bridge Called My Back,* 80.

45. Adrienne Rich, "Notes Toward Politics of Location," in her *Blood, Bread, and Poetry* (New York: Norton, 1986), 210–32.

46. Sandoval, "Feminism and Racism," 59.

47. James Green, "The Making of Mel King's Rainbow Coalition: Political Changes in Boston, 1963–1983," *Radical America,* double issue: 17, no. 6 (1983) and 18, no. 1 (1984): 18–20.

48. Margaret Cerullo, Marla Erlien, Linda Gordon, and Ann Withorn, "An Interview with Jess Ewing: The Bus Stops Here. Organizing Boston School Bus Drivers," *Radical America* 17, no. 5 (1983): 9.

49. NWRO, which was founded in 1966, was Black led and multiracial (85 percent African American, 5 percent Hispanic). Although NWRO did not explicitly call itself a feminist organization, founder Johnnie Tillmon considered women's liberation "a matter of survival" for poor Black women. See Diane K. Lewis, "A Response to Inequality: Black Women, Racism, and Sexism," in *The Signs Reader: Women, Gender, and Scholarship,* ed. Elizabeth Abel and Emily Abel (Chicago: University of Chicago Press, 1983), 189; White, *Too Heavy a Load,* 212–42; Guida West, *The National Welfare Rights Movement: The Social Protest of Poor Women* (New York: Praeger, 1981); Vicki Crawford, "African American Women in the Twenty-First Century: The Continuing Challenge," in *The American Woman, 1999–2000,* ed. Cynthia B. Costello, Shari Miles, and Anne J. Stone (New York: Norton, 1998), 114–17.

50. Ruth Frankenberg, *White Women, Race Matters: The Social Construction of Whiteness* (Minneapolis: University of Minnesota Press, 1993), 14.

51. Barbara Smith, "'Feisty Characters' and 'Other People's Causes': Memories of White Racism and U.S. Feminism," in DuPlessis and Snitow, *The Feminist Memoir Project,* 480.

52. Ellen Willis, foreword to *Daring to Be Bad: Radical Feminism in America* by Alice Echols (Minneapolis: University of Minnesota Press, 1989), vii.

53. Smith, "'Feisty Characters,'" 480.

54. Ibid., 480.

55. Accounting for race and class disrupts the orthodoxy about stages of early second-wave feminism in other ways as well. For example, Nancy MacLean shows that viewing feminism from the perspective of working-class women "chips away at the orthodoxy" about the post–World War II years as a nadir in feminism, since working-class women made headway in union organizing and pay equity during that period. Nancy MacLean, "The Hidden History of Affirmative Action: Working Women's Struggles in the 1970s and the Gender of Class," *Feminist Studies* 25, no. 1 (Spring 1999): 43–78.

56. Smith, "'Feisty Characters,'" 480.

57. Verta Taylor and Nancy Whittier, "The New Feminist Movement," in *Feminist Frontiers IV,* ed. Laurel Richardson, Verta Taylor, and Nancy Whittier (New York: McGraw-Hill, 1997), 553.

58. From Charlayne Hunter, "Many Blacks Wary of 'Women's Liberation' Movement," *New York Times,* November 17, 1970, 60, quoted in Paula Giddings, *When and Where I Enter: The Impact of Black Women on Race and Sex in America* (New York: Bantam Books, 1984), 305.

6. Seeking a Critical Mass, Ample Work to Be Done

1. Elly Bulkin, "Racism and Writing: Some Implications for White Lesbian Critics," *Sinister Wisdom* 13 (Spring 1980): 3–22. Another early article by a white feminist on racism in women's writing is Margaret A. Simons, "Racism and Feminism: A Schism in the Sisterhood," *Feminist Studies* 5, no. 2 (Summer 1979): 384–401.

2. Adrienne Rich, "Split at the Root: An Essay on Jewish Identity," in her *Blood, Bread, and Poetry,* 10–123.

3. Those who identify with feminism include Jane Ariel, Marilyn Buck, Dottye Burt-Markowitz, Jeanine Cohen, Maggie Nolan Donovan, Ruth Frankenberg, Dawn Gomes, Laurie Holmes, Naomi Jaffe, Bonnie Kerness, elana levy, Anne Litwin, Suzanne Ross, Laurie Schecter, Fran Smith, Sarah Stearns, and Lisa Weiner-Mahfuz. Several men I interviewed also spoke of being influenced by feminism, although for space reasons I do not analyze that here.

4. Faith Rogow, "Why Is This Decade Different from All Other Decades? A Look at the Rise of Jewish Lesbian Feminism," *Bridges: A Journal for Jewish Feminists and Our Friends* 1, no. 1 (Spring 1990): 70.

5. Cherríe Moraga, "Refugees from a World on Fire," in *This Bridge Called My Back: Writings by Radical Women of Color,* 2nd ed., ed. Cherríe Moraga and Gloria Anzaldúa (New York: Kitchen Table Women of Color Press, 1983), iii.

6. Elly Bulkin, "Hard Ground: Jewish Identity, Racism, and Anti-Semitism," in *Yours in Struggle: Three Feminist Perspectives on Anti-Semitism and Racism,* by Elly Bulkin, Minnie Bruce Pratt, and Barbara Smith (Brooklyn, N.Y.: Long Haul Press, 1984), 191.

7. Bernice Johnson Reagon, "Coalition Politics: Turning the Century," in *Home Girls: A Black Feminist Anthology,* ed. Barbara Smith (New York: Kitchen Table Women of Color Press, 1983), 356–69.

8. Beverly Smith with Judith Stein and Priscilla Golding, "'The Possibility of Life between Us:' A Dialogue between Black and Jewish Women," *Conditions: Seven,* 1981: 39.

9. Mab Segrest, *My Mama's Dead Squirrel: Lesbian Essays on Southern Culture* (Ithaca, N.Y.: Firebrand, 1985), 53.

10. Moraga and Anzaldúa, *This Bridge Called My Back.*

11. Lorraine Bethel, "What Chou Mean 'We,' White Girl? Or, the Cullud Lesbian Feminist Declaration of Independence," *Conditions: Five, the Black Women's Issue,* ed. Lorraine Bethel and Barbara Smith, 1979: 86.

12. Wendy Rose, "The Great Pretenders: Further Reflections on Whiteshamanism," in *The State of Native America: Genocide, Colonization, and Resistance,* ed. M. Annette Jaimes (Boston: South End Press, 1992), 403–23.

13. Quoted in Smith, Stein, and Golding, "'The Possibility of Life between Us,'" 36–37.

14. Quoted in Lorraine Sorrel, "This Bridge Moves Feminists," *off our backs* 12, no. 4 (April 1982): 5.

15. Irena Klepfisz, "Resisting and Surviving in America," in *Nice Jewish Girls: A Lesbian Anthology,* ed. Evelyn Torton Beck (Trumansburg, N.Y.: Crossing Press, 1982), 107, as also cited in Rogow, "Why Is This Decade Different?" 68.

16. Elly Bulkin was founder of *Conditions* and Barbara Smith was editor for the fifth issue, on Black women. Both women knew Minnie Bruce Pratt from her work on the journal *Feminary.*

17. For extended analysis of Pratt's essay, see Biddy Martin and Chandra Talpade Mohanty, "Feminist Politics: What's Home Got to Do with It?" in *Feminist Studies/Critical Studies,* ed. Teresa de Lauretis (Bloomington: University of Indiana Press, 1986), 191–212.

18. Minnie Bruce Pratt, "Identity: Skin Blood Heart," in Bulkin, Pratt, and Smith, *Yours in Struggle,* 17.

19. Bulkin, "Hard Ground," 94.

20. Beck, *Nice Jewish Girls;* Melanie Kaye/Kantrowitz and Irena Klepfisz, eds., *The Tribe of Dina: A Jewish Women's Anthology* (Boston: Beacon Press, 1989); Melanie Kaye/Kantrowitz, *The Issue Is Power: Essays on Women, Jews, Violence, and Resistance* (San Francisco: Aunt Lute Foundation Books, 1992); Irena Klepfisz, *Periods of Stress* (Brooklyn, N.Y.: Out and Out Books, 1977), and *Keeper of Accounts* (Watertown, Mass.: Persephone Press, 1982).

21. Paula Gunn Allen, review of Moraga and Anzaldúa, *This Bridge Called My Back,* in *Conditions: Eight,* 1982: 125.

22. Adrienne Rich, *On Lies, Secrets, and Silence* (New York: Norton, 1979), 279.

23. Rogow, "Why Is This Decade Different?" 75.

24. Mab Segrest, "Southern Women Writing: Toward a Literature of Wholeness," *Feminary: A Feminist Journal for the South Emphasizing Lesbian Visions* 10, no. 1 (1978): 28–29. See also: "Southern Women Writing: Toward a Literature of Wholeness," in Segrest, *My Mama's Dead Squirrel,* 20.

25. Cherríe Moraga, "La Güera," in Moraga and Anzaldúa, *This Bridge Called My Back,* 28–29.

26. As of 1993, only 2.2 percent of U.S. marriages were interracial. Statistics on interracial partnerships among lesbians are harder to determine. Aída Hurtado, *The Color of Privilege: Three Blasphemies on Race and Feminism* (Ann Arbor: University of Michigan Press, 1996), 11.

27. Ibid., 23.

28. Adrienne Rich, "Disloyal to Civilization: Feminism, Racism, Gynephobia," in her *On Lies, Secrets, and Silence.*

29. Cherríe Moraga, preface to Moraga and Anzaldúa, *This Bridge Called My Back,* xiv.

30. Joan Gibbs and Sara Bennett, *Top Ranking: A Collection of Articles on Racism and Classism in the Lesbian Community* (New York: Come! Unity Press, 1980).

31. Ruth Frankenberg, *White Women, Race Matters: The Social Construction of Whiteness* (Minneapolis: University of Minnesota Press, 1993); Ruth Frankenberg and Lata Mani, "Crosscurrents, Crosstalk: Race, 'Postcoloniality,' and the Politics of Location," *Cultural Studies* 7, no. 2 (May 1993): 292–310; Lata Mani and Ruth Frankenberg, "The Challenge of Orientalism," *Economy and Society* 14, no. 2 (1985): 174–92; Lata Mani, "Multiple Mediations: Feminist Scholarship in the Age of Multinational Reception," *Feminist Review* 35 (Summer 1990):24–41.

32. Joan Nestle, "'I Lift My Eyes to the Hill: The Life of Mabel Hampton as Told by a White Woman," in her *A Fragile Union: New and Selected Writings by Joan Nestle* (San Francisco: Cleis Press, 1998), 23–48.

33. Cherríe Moraga, review of Gibbs and Bennett, *Top Ranking, Conditions: Seven,* 1981: 141.

34. Pat Parker, "For the White Person Who Wants to Know How To Be My Friend," in *Making Face, Making Soul: Haciendo Caras. Creative and Critical Perspectives by Women of Color,* ed. Gloria Anzaldúa (San Francisco: Aunt Lute Foundation Books, 1990), 297.

35. Rich, *On Lies, Secrets, and Silence,* 299.

36. Adrienne Rich, "Compulsory Heterosexuality and Lesbian Existence," in her *Blood, Bread, and Poetry,* 23–75.

37. Cynthia Washington, "We Started from Different Ends of the Spectrum," *Southern Exposure* 4, no. 4 (Winter 1977): 14–18.

38. Ibid.

39. Joan Nestle, "This Huge Light of Yours," in her *A Restricted Country* (Ithaca, NY: Firebrand, 1987), 49–67.

40. Joan Nestle, "The Will to Remember: The Lesbian Herstory Archives of New York," *Feminist Review,* no. 34 (Spring 1990): 86–95.

41. For foundational research on a genealogy of lesbian feminist activism of U.S. women of color from the 1960s through the 1980s, including their work in publishing, see Lisa Kahaleole Chang Hall, "'Unspeakable Things' Spoken: Toward a Syllabus of Multiple Marginalizations" (Ph.D. diss., University of California at Berkeley, 1997).

42. Myra Marx Ferree and Beth Hess, *Controversy and Coalition: The New Feminist Movement across Three Decades of Change* (New York: Twayne Publishers, 1994), 79, 80.

43. Marta Cotera, "Feminism: The Chicana and Anglo Versions. A Historical Analysis," in *Twice a Minority: Mexican American Women,* ed. Margarita B. Melville (St. Louis, Mo.: C. V. Mosby Company, 1980), 231.

44. Women of color also encouraged men of color to include more writing by women in male-dominated journals. For example, *Bridge: An Asian American Perspective,* a magazine by and for Asian Americans, produced two special issues on Asian American women: 6, no. 4 (Winter 1978–79) and 7, no. 1 (Spring 1979). For a review of these two issues, see Barbara Noda, "Asian American Women, Two Special Issues of *Bridge: An Asian American Perspective,*" in *Conditions: Six,* 1980: 203–11. Mitsuye Yamada's foundational essay "Invisibility Is an Unnatural Disaster"—also well known through its publication in *This Bridge Called My Back*—was first published in *Bridge* 7, no. 1 (Spring 1979): 11–13. *The Black Scholar* included several issues devoted to Black women during the 1970s, including "The Black Woman" (December 1971); "Black Women's Liberation" (March–April 1973); "The Black Woman" (1975); and "The Black Sexism Debate" (May–June 1979). As the 1970s progressed, *De Colores: A Journal of Emerging Raza Philosophies* increased its publication of work by Latinas.

45. Mab Segrest, interviewed by Jean Hardisty, "Writer/Activist Mab Segrest Confronts Racism," *Sojourner: The Women's Forum* 19, no. 12 (August 1994): book section, page 1.

46. Ibid., book section, page 2.

47. Adrienne Rich, interviewed by Elly Bulkin, "Poet(ry) for a Dissenting Movement: An Interview with Poet Adrienne Rich," *Sojourner: The Women's Forum* 24, no. 11 (July 1999): 22.

48. *Chrysalis,* no. 3 (1977), for example, includes Audre Lorde, "Poems Are Not Luxuries," 7–9; June Jordan, "I Must Become a Menace to My Enemies" and "MetaRhetoric," 62–63; and articles by now well known white feminist authors Janice Raymond, Blanche Wiesen Cook, and others.

49. *Chrysalis,* no. 10 (1980): 6–7, for example, includes a letter to the editor by Michelle Cliff regarding what she considers a racist cover of volume 8

by white artist Eleanor Antin. Antin, in her reply, states that Cliff had "mounting hostilities" and was a "white liberal."

50. *Quest: A Feminist Quarterly* 3, no. 4 (Spring 1977). The multiracial editorial collective for *Heresies* 15 (1982) included Vivian Browne, Cynthia Carr, Michele Godwin, hattie gossett, Carole Gregory, Sue Heinemann, Lucy Lippard, May Stevens, Cecilia Vicuna, and Sylvia Witts Vitale. Key articles included Rosario Morales, "The Origins of Racism," 1–5; Alaide Foppa, "Death and Defense: Guatemalan Women," 12–13; May Stevens, "Looking Backward in Order to Look Forward: Memories of a Racist Childhood," 22–23; Pat Parker, "For the White Person Who Wants to Know How to Be My Friend," 59; Jaune Quick-to-See Smith, "Ghost Dance Series" 64; hattie gossett, "Is It True What They Say about Colored Pussy?" 40; and Audre Lorde, "Sister Outsiders," 15.

51. Volume 4, no. 1 (Winter 1979), for example, included Barbara Smith and Beverly Smith, "'I Am Not Meant To Be Alone and without You Who Understand': Letters from Black Feminists, 1972–1978," 62–81; Audre Lorde, "Man Child: A Black Lesbian Feminist's Response," 30–61; Nellie Wong, "Grandmothers," 53–77; and Michelle Cliff's prose poem, "A History of Costume," 100–13.

52. The women who joined *Conditions* included Mirtha Quintanales, a Cuban lesbian feminist anthropologist and essayist; Dorothy Allison, a white working-class novelist from the South; Jewelle Gomez, a Black lesbian poet; Cheryl Clarke, a Black feminist poet; and Carroll Oliver, a Trinidadian writer. See "To Our Readers," *Conditions: Nine,* 1983.

53. Anne Braden, "A Second Open Letter to Southern White Women," *Southern Exposure* 4, no. 4 (Winter 1977): 50–52; Bev Fisher, "Race and Class: Beyond Personal Politics," *Quest* 3, no. 4 (Spring 1977): 2–14; Dorothy Allison, "Confrontation: Black/White," *Quest* 3, no. 4 (Spring 1977): 34–46. See also Margaret Simons, "Racism and Feminism: A Schism in the Sisterhood," *Feminist Studies* 5, no. 2 (Summer 1979): 384–401; Deb Friedman, "Rape, Racism, and Reality," *Quest* 5, no. 1 (Summer 1979): 40–52.

54. The title of the Modern Language Association panel—Transformation of Silence in Language and Action—became the title of one of Audre Lorde's most influential essays: "The Transformation of Silence into Language and Action," in her *Sister Outsider,* 40–44.

55. Rich, "Disloyal to Civilization," 285; Barbara Smith, "Toward a Black Feminist Criticism," 157–75; and the Combahee River Collective, "A Black Feminist Statement," 13–22; both in *All the Women Are White, All the Blacks Are Men, But Some of Us Are Brave,* ed. Gloria T. Hull, Patricia Bell Scott, and Barbara Smith (Old Westbury, N.Y.: Feminist Press, 1982); Toni Cade, ed., *The Black Woman* (New York: Signet, 1970).

56. For example, Adrienne Rich's "Disloyal to Civilization" was first published in *Chrysalis: A Magazine of Woman's Culture,* no. 7 (1979): 9–28. Mab Segrest's "My Mama's Dead Squirrel and Southern Humor" was first pub-

lished in *Feminary: A Feminist Journal for the South Emphasizing Lesbian Visions* 11, no. 3 (1981): 9–25.

57. An important exception to the transition from activist to academic journals is the founding of *Bridges: A Journal for Jewish Feminists and Our Friends* in 1990. Although some of its contributors are academics, most are not. The journal emerged out of activism—the founders knew each other through the New Jewish Agenda—and in response to the "extended wave of conservatism in the 1980s." *Bridges* publishes writing by a range of Jewish feminists as well as "writing of particular relevance to Jewish feminism, by non-Jewish women and by men"; "From the Editors," *Bridges: A Journal for Jewish Feminists and Our Friends* 1, no. 1 (Spring 1990/5750): 3–4.

58. In "Racism and Feminism: A Schism in the Sisterhood," Margaret Simons writes that the 1976 interracial Sagaris-NBFO conference on sexism and racism was a "first practical step in our effort to combat racism within feminism"; *Feminist Studies* 5, no. 2 (Summer 1979): 397.

59. Allison, "Confrontation: Black/White."

60. Ibid.

61. Chela Sandoval, "Feminism and Racism: A Report on the 1981 National Women's Studies Association Conference," in Anzaldúa, *Making Face, Making Soul*, 55–71.

62. Alice Yun Chai, "Toward a Holistic Paradigm for Asian American Women's Studies: A Synthesis of Feminist Scholarship and Women of Color's Feminist Politics," *Women's Studies International Forum* 8, no. 1 (1985): 59–65.

63. Sandoval, "Feminism and Racism," 67.

64. Adrienne Rich, "Disobedience and Women's Studies," in her *Blood, Bread, and Poetry,* 76–84.

65. Loraine Hutchins, "Trouble and Mediation at Yosemite," *off our backs* 11, no. 10 (November 1981): 25.

66. For articles reporting on the protests at the festival, see Barbara Gagliardi, "West Coast Music Festival," *Big Mama Rag* 9, no. 10 (November 1981): 3, 22; Hutchins, "Trouble and Mediation at Yosemite," 12, 13, 25.

67. See Sarie Feld and Sheri Maeda, "Holly Near: Reaching More People with the Speed of Light," *off our backs* 12, no. 11 (December 1982): 20–21.

68. Reagon, "Coalition Politics," 356–69.

69. Ibid., 359.

70. Bernice Johnson Reagon, "The Power of Communal Song," in *Cultures in Contention,* ed. Douglas Kahn and Diane Neumaier (Seattle, Wa.: Real Comet, 1985), 178.

71. Reagon, "Coalition Politics," 362.

72. Estelle Disch, "Common Differences: Third World Women and Feminist Perspectives," *off our backs* 13, no. 7 (July 1983): 4–8; Laura Carlson,

"The Task: Reconstruct Feminism," *Big Mama Rag* 12, no. 1 (January 1984): 12–14, 17.

73. Chandra Talpade Mohanty, Ann Russo, and Lourdes Torres, preface to *Third World Women and the Politics of Feminism* (Bloomington: University of Indiana Press, 1991), ix.

74. Ann Russo, "'We Cannot Live without Our Lives': White Women, Anti-racism, and Feminism," in Mohanty, Russo, and Torres, *Third World Women and the Politics of Feminism*, 297–313.

75. Donna Landerman and Mary McAtee, "Breaking the Racism Barrier: White Anti-Racist Work," *Aegis*, no. 33 (Winter 1982): 19.

76. Griscida A. Haygood, "Combatting Sexual Violence: A Multiracial Perspective," *off our backs* 14, no. 8 (August–September 1984): 23.

77. NYWAR conference brochure. Author's possession.

78. At the time Dawn was involved with a Sicilian Italian woman who "came up with her own brand of Italian nationalism and decided that she wasn't a white woman. . . . She was trying to start this whole frenzy among other Jewish and Italian women canvassers. It was a mess. It was so awful. I thought I was going crazy because I was actually very attached to this woman, of course."

79. Other important conferences of this period include Women against Racism in Iowa City, the annual Women in Print conferences, and the CLUW conferences. See Emily Medvec, "Organizing That Works," *Quest* 1, no. 2 (Fall 1974): 24–34; Fran Moira, "Women in Print," *off our backs* 11, no. 11 (December 1981): 2–3; Alice Henry, "Third World Women Talk at International Book Fair," *off our backs* 14, no. 8, (August–September 1984): 1, 4.

7. Fight the Power, Hold On to Community

1. Chela Sandoval, "U.S. Third World Feminism: The Theory and Method of Opppositional Consciousness in the Postmodern World," *Genders,* no. 10 (Spring 1991): 14.

2. Mab Segrest, *My Mama's Dead Squirrel: Lesbian Essays on Southern Culture* (Ithaca, N.Y.: Firebrand Books, 1985), and *Memoir of a Race Traitor* (Boston: South End Press, 1994).

3. Mab Segrest, "Feminism and Disobedience: Conversations with Barbara Deming," in her *My Mama's Dead Squirrel,* 78–99.

4. Mab Segrest, "Carolina Notebook," in her *My Mama's Dead Squirrel,* 177–226.

5. Segrest, *My Mama's Dead Squirrel,* 167.

6. The book's existence provides another example of the contributions of independent feminist journals of the 1970s and 1980s, including *Feminary,* the southern lesbian feminist journal that Segrest founded and edited for many years. It was in *Feminary* that earlier versions of the essays in *My Mama's Dead Squirrel* were first published—a training ground that facilitated much

interracial dialogue about Segrest's (and many other white women's) writing and politics.

7. Segrest, *My Mama's Dead Squirrel*, 168–69.

8. Segrest, *Memoir of a Race Traitor*, 229.

9. Segrest, *My Mama's Dead Squirrel*, 12.

10. Mab Segrest, interviewed by Jean Hardisty, "Writer/Activist Mab Segrest Confronts Racism," *Sojourner: The Women's Forum* 19, no. 2 (August 1994): book section, page 1.

11. Mab Segrest, "Fear to Joy: Fighting the Klan," *Sojourner: The Women's Forum* 13, no. 13 (November 1987): 20.

12. Ibid.

13. Segrest, *Memoir of a Race Traitor*, 229.

14. Segrest, interviewed by Hardisty, "Writer/Activist," book section, page 1.

15. Segrest, "Fear to Joy," 21.

16. Joy James, *Resisting State Violence: Radicalism, Gender, and Race in U.S. Culture* (Minneapolis: University of Minnesota Press, 1996), 166.

17. Sherna Berger Gluck, "Whose Feminism, Whose History? Reflections on Excavating the History of (the) U.S. Women's Movement(s)," in *Community Activism and Feminist Politics: Organizing across Race, Class, and Gender,* ed. Nancy Naples (New York: Routledge, 1998), 34, 35.

18. Adrienne Rich, *On Lies, Secrets, and Silence* (New York: Norton, 1979), 298.

19. Angela Davis, *The Angela Y. Davis Reader,* ed. Joy James (Malden, Mass.: Blackwell, 1998), 292.

20. Celestine Ware, *Woman Power: The Movement for Women's Liberation* (New York: Tower, 1970). On Shirley Chisholm's campaign, see Paula Giddings, *When and Where I Enter: The Impact of Black Women on Race and Sex in America* (New York: Bantam Books, 1984), 337–40.

21. Cherríe Moraga, preface to *This Bridge Called My Back: Writings by Radical Women of Color,* 2nd ed., ed. Cherríe Moraga and Gloria Anzaldúa (New York: Kitchen Table Women of Color Press, 1983), xix.

22. Cherríe Moraga, "Refugees of a World on Fire," in Moraga and Anzaldúa, *This Bridge Called My Back,* 4.

23. Adrienne Rich, "Disobedience and Women's Studies," in her *Blood, Bread, and Poetry* (New York: Norton, 1986), 83.

24. Kimberly Christensen, "With Whom Do You Believe Your Lot Is Cast? White Feminists and Racism," *Signs: Journal of Women in Culture and Society* 22, no. 3 (1997): 618.

25. Segrest, *My Mama's Dead Squirrel,* 175.

26. Elly Bulkin, "Racism and Writing: Some Implications for White Lesbian Critics," *Sinister Wisdom* 13 (Spring 1980): 4.

27. Adrienne Rich, "Response," *Sinister Wisdom* 14 (Summer 1980): 104.

For support of Elly Bulkin, see Sally Gearhart, 16 (Spring 1981): 80; and for critiques, see H. Patricia Hynes, 15 (Fall 1980): 105–9; Marguerite Fentin, 16 (Spring 1981): 90–93; Louise Mullaley, 16 (Spring 1981): 90; and Andree Collard, 16 (Spring 1981): 93; all in *Sinister Wisdom.*

28. Political Research Associates and North Carolinians against Racist and Religious Violence are two examples of anti-right organizations with significant antiracist feminist leadership. See Jean Hardisty, *Mobilizing Resentment: Conservative Resurgence from the John Birch Society to the Promise Keepers* (Boston: Beacon, 1999); Segrest, *Memoir of a Race Traitor.*

Antiracist Activism in the 1980s and 1990s

1. Joy James, *Resisting State Violence: Radicalism, Gender and Race in U.S. Culture* (Minneapolis: University of Minnesota Press, 1996), 11.

2. Mary Beth Norton, David Katzman, Paul Escott, Howard Chudacoff, Thomas Paterson, and William Tuttle, *A People and a Nation: A History of the United States* (New York: Houghton Mifflin, 1990), 1005.

3. Angela Davis, *The Angela Y. Davis Reader,* ed. Joy James (Malden, Mass.: Blackwell, 1998), 64.

4. Jean Hardisty, *Mobilizing Resentment: Conservative Resurgence from the John Birch Society to the Promise Keepers* (Boston: Beacon, 1999).

5. Susan Lynn, *Progressive Women in Conservative Times: Racial Justice, Peace, and Feminism, 1945 to the 1960s* (New Brunswick, N.J.: Rutgers University Press, 1992).

6. Aldon Morris, *The Origins of the Civil Rights Movement* (New York: Free Press, 1984).

8. Central America Peace Movement

1. William H. Chafe, *The Unfinished Journey: America since World War II* (New York: Oxford, 1999), 476.

2. Renny Golden and Michael McConnell, *Sanctuary: The New Underground Railroad* (Maryknoll, N.Y.: Orbis Books, 1986), 5.

3. Chafe, *The Unfinished Journey,* 477.

4. Martha Thompson, "Repopulated Communities in El Salvador," in *The New Politics of Survival: Grassroots Movements in Central America,* ed. Minor Sinclair (New York: Monthly Review Press, 1995), 109–51.

5. In 1983 the Permanent People's Tribunal concluded that the Guatemalan government actions had constituted genocide, "the systematic killing of a whole people or nation"; Golden and McConnell, *Sanctuary,* 24, 26.

6. Ibid., 27.

7. Howard Zinn documents that the United States used armed force in Nicaragua in 1853 ("to protect American lives and interests during political disturbances"), 1854 ("to avenge an insult to the American Minister to Nicaragua"), 1894 ("to protect American interests at Bluefields following a revolu-

tion"), 1926 ("to counter a revolution which included keeping a U.S. force there for seven years"); Howard Zinn, *A People's History of the United States* (New York: HarperPerennial, 1990) 291, 399. See also Margaret Randall, *Sandino's Daughters Revisited: Feminism in Nicaragua* (New Brunswick, N.J.: Rutgers University Press, 1994), 10.

8. Randall, *Sandino's Daughters Revisited*, 5.

9. Sinclair, *The New Politics of Survival*, 12; Christian Smith, *Resisting Reagan: The U.S. Central America Peace Movement* (Chicago: University of Chicago Press, 1996), 357.

10. Smith, *Resisting Reagan*, 60.

11. Ibid.; Golden and McConnell, *Sanctuary*, 3; Robin Lorentzen, *Women in the Sanctuary Movement* (Philadelphia: Temple University Press, 1991), 14–15.

12. Golden and McConnell, *Sanctuary*, 53, 5, 60.

13. Ibid., 61.

14. Lorentzen, *Women in the Sanctuary Movement*, 15.

15. Golden and McConnell, *Sanctuary*, 48, 60.

16. Ibid., 61; Ann Crittenden, *Sanctuary: A Story of American Conscience and the Law in Collision* (New York: Weidenfeld and Nicolson, 1988).

17. Golden and McConnell, *Sanctuary*, 53.

18. Lorentzen, *Women in the Sanctuary Movement*, 29.

19. Some activists and writers merely treat the public sanctuary movement as the only movement. See, for example, Smith, *Resisting Reagan*, 171. Others, notably Golden and McConnell and Crittenden, are careful to specify that the United States–based Latino response to refugees far outweighed the number of people harbored through churches and synagogues. At the same time, although Golden and McConnell devote an entire chapter to the clandestine movement in Mexico, they do not take the next step and analyze the clandestine movement in the United States. The authors do not analyze a possible relationship between the two forms of sanctuary or the difference that such a relationship might have had on building a multiracial anti-interventionist movement in the United States.

20. Susan Coutin, *The Culture of Protest: Religious Activism in the United States Sanctuary Movement* (Boulder, Colo.: Westview Press, 1993), 223; Adrian Bailey, Richard Wright, Alison Mountz, and Ines Miyares, "Transnational Salvadoran Geographies: Space-Time and the Production of Permanent Temporariness" (paper presented at the American Studies Association Conference, Montreal, Canada, October 30, 1999).

21. For the story of Jim Corbett's background, the events leading up to the first sanctuary church, and the background of John Fife, the minister of the church, see Crittenden, *Sanctuary*, 3–83.

22. Ibid., 26–28.

23. Ibid., 47.

24. Ibid., 78.

25. Darlene Nicgorski, phone interview by the author, November 8, 1999. Unless otherwise noted, all quotations and information about Darlene come from this interview. For a lengthy and sensitive account of Nicgorski's life, see Julia Lieblich, "Daughter of Prophecy: An Activist Takes the Lead," in her *Sisters: Lives of Devotion and Defiance* (New York: Ballantine Books, 1992), 203–81.

26. Crittenden, *Sanctuary,* 120.

27. Ibid., 54.

28. Coutin, *The Culture of Protest,* 11.

29. Golden and McConnell, *Sanctuary,* 77.

30. Crittenden, *Sanctuary,* 22.

31. Ignatius Bau, *This Ground Is Holy: Church Sanctuary and Central American Refugees* (New York: Paulist Press, 1985), 25–26.

32. Golden and McConnell, *Sanctuary,* 165.

33. Ibid., 55.

34. Ibid., 169.

35. Darlene Nicgorski, phone interview by the author, November 8, 1999.

36. For accounts of the trial, see Crittenden, *Sanctuary;* Coutin, *The Culture of Protest,* 131–41.

37. For a description of the eleven defendants and the trial in relation to Darlene Nicgorski's position in particular, see Lieblich, "Daughter of Prophecy," 203–81.

38. Ibid., 233.

39. For an in-depth account of the infiltration of the sanctuary movement by government informants, see Crittenden, *Sanctuary.*

40. Lieblich, "Daughter of Prophecy," 233.

41. For essays and poetry by a white lesbian who was a member of a Witness for Peace delegation that was captured (and released) by the contras in 1985, see Judith McDaniel, *Sanctuary: A Journey* (Ithaca, N.Y.: Firebrand, 1987). For a first-person narrative by a white Jewish lesbian who traveled to Nicaragua with Witness for Peace, see Rebecca Gordon, *Letters from Nicaragua* (San Francisco: Spinsters/Aunt Lute, 1986).

42. M. Jacqui Alexander and Chandra Talpade Mohanty, eds., *Feminist Genealogies, Colonial Legacies, Democratic Futures* (New York: Routledge, 1997); Chandra Talpade Mohanty, Ann Russo, and Lourdes Torres, eds., *Third World Women and the Politics of Feminism* (Bloomington: Indiana University Press, 1991).

43. Audre Lorde, *Sister Outsider* (Freedom, Calif.: Crossing Press, 1984).

44. Randall, *Sandino's Daughters Revisited,* and *Gathering Rage: The Failure of the Twentieth Century Revolutions to Develop a Feminist Agenda* (New

York: Monthly Review Press, 1992); Norma Stoltz Chinchilla, "Feminism, Revolution, and Democratic Transitions in Nicaragua," *The Women's Movement in Latin America,* ed. Jane Jaquette (Boulder, Colo.: Westview Press, 1994); Sinclair, *The New Politics of Survival.*

45. Randall, *Sandino's Daughters Revisited,* 5.

46. Ibid., 12, 87.

47. Randall, *Gathering Rage* and *Sandino's Daughters Revisited*; Karen Kampwirth, "Confronting Adversity with Experience: The Emergence of Feminism in Nicaragua," *Social Politics: International Studies in Gender, State, and Society* 3, nos. 2, 3 (Summer, Fall 1996): 136–58.

48. Although I am highlighting Nicaraguan feminism here, there was significant activist organizing by women in Guatemala and El Savador in the 1980s as well; see Jennifer Schirmer, "The Seeking of Truth and the Gendering of Consciousness: The CoMadres of El Salvador and the CONAVIGUA widows of Guatemala," in *Viva: Women and Popular Protest in Latin America,* ed. Sarah A. Radcliffe and Sallie Westwood (New York: Routledge, 1993), 30–64.

49. Coutin, *The Culture of Protest,* 187.

50. Ellen Scott, analysis based on an oral interview by the author, October 30, 1999.

51. From a bumper sticker in the Manzo office in Tucson, Arizona; see Crittenden, *Sanctuary,* 27.

52. Mario Davila is a specialist in Central American affairs with the American Friends Service Committee in Boston. He was an activist in El Salvador before coming to the United States as a young adult, and he became a leader in the Pledge of Resistance; in establishing sister cities, unions, and universities; and in organizing with Salvadoran activists nationally.

53. This and subsequent information from Cathy Hoffman is from an oral interview by the author, October 25, 1999.

54. Jesse Jackson ran for president in both the 1984 and 1988 elections.

55. For an alternative account of the split in CISPES, see Van Gosse, "'The North American Front': Central American Solidarity in the Reagan Era," in *Reshaping the US Left: Popular Struggles in the 1980s,* ed. Mike Davis and Michael Sprinker (New York: Verso, 1988), 36–39.

56. Darlene Nicgorski, phone interview by the author, November 8, 1999.

57. John Beam, "Solidarity Work and Community Organizing," *Socialist Review* 12, no. 6 (November–December 1982): 45.

58. Sinclair, *The New Politics of Survival,* 12–13.

59. Golden and McConnell, *Sanctuary,* 80.

60. Crittenden, *Sanctuary,* 345, 346, 347.

61. Lieblich, "Daughter of Prophecy," 280.

62. For example, Christian Smith's *Resisting Reagan* offers a comprehensive and well-researched book on the origins, contributions, philosophy, and

limitations of the U.S. peace movement. Smith analyzes important conflicts within the movement, including an overemphasis on antiauthoritarianism, religious and secular divisions, and debates about nonviolence versus tactics of sabotage. Yet Smith does not address conflicts about race and class within the movement, the relationship of white activists to Central Americans, or relations between all white groups and African American and Latino organizations. Smith attributes to the movement a goal to model the kind of world it aspired to create. And yet Smith does not question what might be problematic about considering all-white affinity groups and religious communities as models for the society people hoped to create; Smith, *Resisting Reagan,* 325–47.

63. Smith, *Resisting Reagan,* 175.

9. Prison Activism

The title of this chapter is from Marilyn Buck's interpretation of Nazim Hikmet's poem, "Some Advice to Those Who Will Serve Time in Prison"; see Nazim Hikmet, *Poems of Nazim Hikmet,* trans. Randy Blasing and Mutlu Konuk (New York: Persea Books, 1994), 137–38.

1. Angela Davis, "Political Prisoners, Prisons, and Black Liberation," in *If They Come in the Morning: Voices of Resistance,* ed. Angela Davis and Bettina Aptheker (New York: Signet, 1971), 29–30.

2. For a detailed account of the history of repression against Black leaders and political prisoners who were former members of the Black Panther Party, see: Winston A. Grady-Willis, "The Black Panther Party: State Repression and Political Prisoners," in *The Black Panther Party Reconsidered,* ed. Charles E. Jones (Baltimore: Black Classic Press, 1998), 363–89. For documentation of repression against AIM and the Black Panther Party, see Ward Churchill and Jim Vander Wall, *Agents of Repression: The FBI's Secret War against the Black Panther Party and the American Indian Movement* (Boston: South End Press, 1988).

3. Betty and Herman Liveright, "Their Chance to Speak," unpublished manuscript, 3–4.

4. Angela Davis, "From the Prison of Slavery to the Slavery of Prison: Frederick Douglass and the Convict Lease System," 74–95; and "Racialized Punishment and Prison Abolition," 96–107; both in *The Angela Y. Davis Reader,* ed. Joy James (Malden, Mass.: Blackwell, 1998).

5. In their manuscript on political prisoners, Betty and Herman Liveright write, "We are struck with the relatively trivial sentences and early paroles that radical right extremists receive in contrast to the vindictive sentences and draconian treatment meted out to the militant activists. Linda Evans, a Communist, was sentenced to forty years in prison for using a false I.D. in order to purchase four weapons. Don Black, the KKK Grand Dragon charged with possession of a boatload of munitions to be used to invade a Caribbean island,

was given an eight year sentence. He served two"; Liveright and Liveright, "Their Chance to Speak," 3.

Other examples of this discrepancy: Black Panther political prisoner Romaine Fitzgerald's incarceration "for a single murder was twice as long as that imposed on others charged with the same offense in the state of California," and Timothy Blunk and Susan Rosenberg, two white anti-imperialists, were sentenced to fifty-eight years in a federal prison for the illegal possession of dynamite—the longest sentence in U.S. history for anyone convicted of that offense; see Akinyele Omowole Umoja, "Set Our Warriors Free: The Legacy of the Black Panther Party and Political Prisoners," in Jones, *The Black Panther Party Reconsidered*, 426, 432.

6. Umoja, "Set Our Warriors Free," 420.

7. For a bibliography of Davis's extensive writing on the prison industry, see Davis, *The Angela Y. Davis Reader*, 347–48. For an analysis of Davis's autobiography as activism, see Margo V. Perkins, *Autobiography as Activism: Three Black Women of the Sixties* (Jackson: University Press of Mississippi, 2000).

8. Angela Davis, "Race and Criminalization: Black Americans and the Punishment Industry," in *The House That Race Built: Black Americans, U.S. Terrain*, ed. Wahneema Lubiano (New York: Pantheon, 1997), 271.

9. Ibid., 267.

10. Ibid., 267, 268.

11. Ibid., 270.

12. Ibid., 271.

13. Statistic from the Criminal Justice Program, American Friends Service Committee, Newark, New Jersey, provided by Bonnie Kerness.

14. Davis, "Race and Criminalization," 272–73.

15. From Marilyn Buck's poem "To the Woman Standing behind Me in Line Who Asks Me How Long This Black History Month Is Going to Last" (unpublished poem).

16. According to David, "the purpose of the Brinks action was to acquire funds to build the Black Liberation Army. Funds were needed for such actions as the liberation of Assata Shakur from prison, the day-to-day survival of an underground, and also to support nationalist programs in the community."

17. The following narrative about David Gilbert was first written in the third person, since I was unable to bring a tape recorder into the visitor's area at the prison at Comstock, New York. David and I then worked, by mail, on several major revisions of the interview. During this process, we decided to ready the interview for publication in its entirety, and at that point we decided to change the third-person narrative into a first-person narrative; at that point, much of the writing was his, and the text reads more powerfully in the first person. The direct quotes in the narrative are largely from correspondence that

we added to the original interview, as well as passages David either wrote or said during our initial interview. His and my voice are inevitably slightly blurred, however, because of the initial constraints we faced when doing the interview.

18. David Gilbert, letter to author, May 25, 1997.

19. Bill Harris was a white member of the Symbionese Liberation Army (SLA), the multiracial group that kidnapped Patty Hearst.

20. David Gilbert, letter to author, April 17, 1998.

21. Kuwasi Balagoon was a New Afrikan anarchist political prisoner. For his writing, see Kuwasi Balagoon et al., eds., *Look for Me in the Whirlwind: The Collective Autobiographies of the New York Twenty-One* (New York: Vintage Books, 1971); Tim Blunk and Ray Luc Levasseur, eds., *Hauling Up the Morning: Izando la Mañana* (Trenton, N.J.: Red Sea Press, 1990). For information about Kuwasi Balagoon's activism and 1981 trial, see Umoja, "Set Our Warriors Free," 427–31.

22. David explains that "the exception to this were the correctional officers at Rockland and Orange County jails (where I was before Auburn). They had much more emotional difficulty with my being white than they did with Black defendants in the case. In the back of their minds they could understand why a Black man would rebel. But, the correctional officers' highest aspirations would be to be able to send their sons to a college like Columbia, where I went. In their minds it seems unfathomable how I could have 'gone so wrong.' They saw me as a traitor to my race and privileges."

23. David Gilbert, letter to author, April 17, 1998.

24. Ibid.

25. Ibid.

26. For a poem by David Gilbert about Kuwasi Balagoon's life and death as a freedom fighter, see "Born on Sunday" in Blunk and Levasseur, *Hauling Up the Morning*, 343–45.

27. An early successful program is AIDS Counseling and Education (ACE) at Bedford Hills Prison, the main women's prison in New York, followed by Prisoners' AIDS Counseling and Education, at Eastern Wallkill Prison in New York.

28. David Gilbert, letter to author, April 17, 1998. Herman Bell is a former Black Panther who has been fighting for a new trial since his 1975 conviction for killing two police officers. During his trial, prosecutors suppressed evidence that proved the "alleged weapon could not have been used in the killings"; see Grady-Willis, "The Black Panther Party," 382–83; and Umoja, "Set Our Warriors Free," 424–25.

29. David Gilbert, letter to author, May 25, 1997.

30. David Gilbert, letter to author, May 18, 1997.

31. David Gilbert, letter to author, April 18, 1997.

32. Sundiata Acoli was sentenced to life plus thirty years in connection with a 1973 ambush by New Jersey state troopers of Black activists (including Assata Shakur, Zaya Shakur, and Sundiata Acoli). Acoli was sent to Trenton State Prison, where he was confined to a control unit because of his political background. After the *International Jurist* declared him a political prisoner in 1979, he was shipped to a federal prison in Marion, Illinois—although there were no federal charges against him—where he was kept in lockdown. In 1987 he was transferred to the federal penitentiary at Leavenworth, Kansas. In 1992 he was eligible for parole but was not allowed to attend his own hearing. Although he had an excellent disciplinary record, the parole board denied him parole because of his prior membership in the Black Panther Party and BLA. In 1994 he was transferred to a federal penitentiary in Pennsylvania. In addition to being a writer, he is also a mathematician and a computer analyst. See the National Committee to Free Puerto Rican Prisoners of War and the National Committee to End the Marion Lockdown, eds., *Can't Jail the Spirit: Political Prisoners in the United States* (Chicago: Editorial Coqui Publishers, 1998), 44–46.

33. For background about Assata Shakur, see Assata Shakur, *Assata: An Autobiography* (Chicago: Lawrence Hills Books, 1987); Perkins, *Autobiography as Activism*; Jones, *The Black Panther Party Reconsidered*.

34. Linda Evans is a political prisoner who has been active in SDS, the women's liberation movement, and lesbian politics. She helped support Black and Chicano grassroots organizing against the Klan, forced sterilization, and killer cops. She is serving a forty-year sentence. See the National Committee to Free Puerto Rican Prisoners of War, *Can't Jail the Spirit,* 173. For background on Laura Whitehorn, see note 57 in this chapter.

35. For poetry by Marilyn Buck, see "Thirteen Springs" and "No Frills," both in *Sojourner: The Women's Forum* 24, no. 9 (May 1999): 20; "To Women Who Work," "Remembering a Fifteen-Year-Old Palestinian Woman," and "In Celebration of the Intifadah," all in Blunk and Levasseur, *Hauling Up the Morning,* 59–64; the National Committee to Free Puerto Rican Prisoners of War, *Can't Jail the Spirit.* On Buck's work to free Assata Shakur, see Umoja, "Set Our Warriors Free," 425.

36. Hikmet, "Some Advice," 137–38. For information about Nazim Hikmet's life and translations of his poetry, see www.cs.rpi.edu/~sibel/poetry/nazim_hikmet.html [accessed 11/20/00].

37. James Byrd, an African American living in Palestine, Texas, was murdered in June 1998 by three white men who dragged him from the back of their truck.

38. Early support for control units can be traced in part to a 1961 Federal Bureau of Prisons program that included the symposium Man against Man: Brainwashing. A professor from the Massachusetts Institute of Technology

presented methods of sensory deprivation and solitary confinement based on types of torture Chinese prison guards used on American prisoners of war captured during the Korean conflict. The director of the Federal Bureau of Prisons urged the symposium participants to begin implementing these practices. Liveright and Liveright, "Their Chance to Speak," 12.

39. Bonnie Kerness, "Control Units: Isolation in 1992," unpublished manuscript, 1.

40. Bonnie Kerness, "The History of Control Units" (paper presented at the Northeast Regional Hearings on Control Units, April 27, 1996), 1.

41. Bonnie Kerness, "Turning the Tables on U.S. Abuse of International Human Rights Standards: Exploring Ways to Use International Treaties and Covenants in Domestic Litigation" (paper presented at the National Conference of Black Lawyers, October 8, 1999), 4.

42. Kerness, "The History of Control Units," 3.

43. Hatari Wa'Haki, "Control Units Out of Control" in "Social Control and the Politics of Prisons," packet of speeches, articles, and poems by prison activists. Provided to author by Bonnie Kerness. Hatari Wa'Haki died of medical neglect on July 4, 1999, in the control unit in New Jersey. He was suffering from extreme stomach pain, fever, and other symptoms but was denied proper medical attention. He was in his early forties. The prison officials registered "heat" as the cause of his death. Information about his death provided by Bonnie Kerness.

44. The National Committee to Free Puerto Rican Prisoners of War, *Can't Jail the Spirit,* 91–92.

45. For writing by and about Ruchell Magee, see Robert Kaufman, "Ruchell Magee," 169–74; and "Letters to Angela Y. Davis from Ruchell Magee," 175–80; both in Davis and Aptheker, *If They Come in the Morning.*

46. Russell Maroon Shoats is a New Afrikan political prisoner who has been incarcerated since 1972. He is the father of seven children and was a founding member of the Black Unity Council, which became part of the Black Panther Party in Philadelphia in 1969.

47. Kerness, "The History of Control Units," 1.

48. Human Rights Watch Report, as quoted in Kerness, "The History of Control Units," 2.

49. For Mumia Abu-Jamal's writing, see his *Death Blossoms: Reflections from a Prisoner of Conscience* (Farmington, Pa.: Plough Publishing House, 1997), and *Live from Death Row* (New York: Avon, 1996). See also S. E. Anderson and Tony Medina, eds., *In Defense of Mumia* (New York: Writers and Readers Publishing, 1996); Sohera Syeda and Becky Thompson, "Coalition Politics in Organizing for Mumia Abu-Jamal," in *Feminism and Anti-Racism: International Struggles,* ed. Kathleen M. Blee and France Winddance Twine (New York: New York University Press, forthcoming).

50. On the other hand, as was true of the 1980 Refugee Act, which the United States signed to reduce the discrepancy between international positions on amnesty and U.S. laws, it often takes many years for international pressure to actually reshape U.S. policy.

51. Kerness, "Turning the Tables," 4.

52. Bonnie Kerness, untitled speech given at the Puffin Room, New York, November 2, 1995.

53. Davis, *The Angela Y. Davis Reader*, 75–76, 99.

54. Marilyn Buck, David Gilbert, and Laura Whitehorn, *Enemies of the State: A Frank Discussion of Past Political Movements, Victories and Errors, and the Current Political Climate for Revolutionary Struggle within the U.S.A.* (Brooklyn, N.Y.: Resistance in Brooklyn [RnB], 1998), 39–40. Available through Meyer, c/o WRL, 339 Lafayette St., New York, N.Y., 10012.

55. In another, more personal example, in a letter to me following the interview, David responded at length about an incident I had shared with him in which white colleagues had falsely accused me of being a "reverse racist." David's first question was, "What could you have done differently?" Although I initially bristled at his question, I realized how completely David tries to live by the principle of self-criticism. There is always something I or we could have done better, done differently, done in a way that would have avoided conflict. That does not mean that the accusations leveled at me were justified or that there is such a thing as reverse racism. It does mean that there is always room for refining strategy, knowing how to respond to resistance, realizing the limits of one's own vantage point, and seeking feedback.

56. Willie M. Coleman, "Among the Things That Use to Be," in *Home Girls: A Black Feminist Anthology*, ed. Barbara Smith (New York: Kitchen Table Women of Color Press, 1983), 221–22.

57. Laura Whitehorn is an antiracist white political prisoner who, until she was freed in 1999, had been incarcerated with Marilyn Buck at Dublin Prison in California, serving a twenty-three-year sentence for conspiracy to protest government policies through destruction of government property. During the Vietnam War she helped organize the takeover of a Harvard University building by four hundred women. In the 1970s she helped found a radical art collective. For her writing, see her "From Maximum to Minimum Security," *Sojourner: The Women's Forum* 24, no. 9 (May 1999): 19. See also Buck, Gilbert, and Whitehorn, *Enemies of the State*.

58. Betty and Herman described the Berkshire Forum as similar to the Highlander School in Tennessee in that it provided a place for people to openly discuss relevant political and social issues of the times. The forum sponsored weekend workshops that were facilitated by progressive leaders from throughout the country—Anne Braden, Bettina Aptheker, Johnnetta Cole, Robert Meeropol, Jessica Mitford, Bernie Sanders, and many others. One of the several

differences between Highlander and the Berkshire Forum is that the latter was much more explicit about its ties to a class analysis and Marxism. Highlander did not make such an affiliation part of its mission, which is partly a function of its location in the South.

59. Liveright and Liveright, "Their Chance to Speak," 15.

60. For background and analysis of the cases of Dhoruba Bin Wahad and Geronimo Pratt, see Grady-Willis, "The Black Panther Party," 375–82; Umoja, "Set Our Warriors Free," 422–35.

61. Umoja, "Set Our Warriors Free," 433.

10. Power, Power, Who's Got the Power?

1. People I interviewed worked in a variety of nonprofits in the 1980s and 1990s, including Mission Possible, a multiracial summer camp in Boston; the Piedmont Peace Project, a grassroots group that organizes low-income African Americans and whites to work together for community change; Harbor Communities Overcoming Violence, a grassroots center north of Boston that supports survivors of domestic violence; the Haymarket People's Fund, a multiracial group of activists that works with and funds activist organizations; the Institute for the Study of Social Change, a multiracial research center in Berkeley; Rock against Racism in Boston; and the Latino Health Institute in Boston.

2. Si Kahn, "Multiracial Organizations: Theory and Practice," *Network* 14, no. 2 (Summer 1997): 27.

3. YouthBuild participants are 68 percent African American, 15 percent Latino, 13 percent white, and 4 percent Native American.

4. Joe Slovo was a white Communist member of the African National Congress and a leader in the military arm of the organization. He was widely respected by Black and white antiapartheid activists in South Africa; see: Joshua N. Lazerson, *Against the Tide: Whites in the Struggle against Apartheid* (Boulder, Colo.: Westview Press, 1994).

5. Linda Stout, *Bridging the Class Divide and Other Lessons from Grassroots Organizing* (Boston: Beacon Press, 1996).

6. I want to thank Patti DeRosa, an antiracism educator and activist in Boston, for her many conversations about the politics of training and her patient and generous help with this chapter.

7. Clare C. Swanger, "Perspectives on the History of Ameliorating Oppression and Supporting Diversity in United States Organizations," in *The Promise of Diversity*, ed. Elsie Y. Cross, Judith Katz, Frederick Miller, and Edith Seashore (Chicago: Irwin, 1994), 9–10.

8. For groundbreaking books that mapped out parameters of training as a method for changing racial dynamics and white control within organizations, see Judith Katz, *White Awareness: Handbook for Anti-Racism Training* (Norman: University of Oklahoma Press, 1978); Robert Terry, *For Whites Only* (Grand Rapids, Mich.: William B. Eerdmans, 1970).

9. Chandra Talpade Mohanty, "On Race and Voice: Challenges for Liberal Education in the 1990s," in *Beyond a Dream Deferred: Multicultural Education and the Politics of Excellence,* ed. Becky Thompson and Sangeeta Tyagi (Minneapolis: University of Minnesota Press, 1993), 45.

10. Ibid., 55.

11. These and several hundred other diversity training materials are advertised in the *Workforce Diversity Catalog: Diversity Awareness and Training Products from HR Press.*

12. "Cashing in on diversity" is a phrase used by ethnic and cultural studies researcher Norma Smith in "Expansive Data Collection, Focused Analysis: Combining Oral History and Grounded Theory Procedures as Research Methodology for Studies in Race, Gender, and Class" (paper presented at the 1999 Race, Gender, and Class Project Conference at Southern University of New Orleans).

13. Patti DeRosa, conversation with the author, November 30, 1999.

14. Avery Gordon, "The Work of Corporate Culture," *Social Text* 44, vol. 13, no. 3 (Fall/Winter 1995): 16.

15. Patti DeRosa, "Diversity Training: In Search of Anti-Racism," *PeaceWork: Global Thought and Local Action,* no. 240 (April 1994): 2–3.

16. Mohanty, "On Race and Voice," 55.

17. Two of the training groups that best exemplify a social justice model are the People's Institute for Survival and Beyond (a training institute founded twenty years ago by African American activist Ron Chishom), 1444 North Johnson Street, New Orleans, La., 70116-1767, (504) 944-2354; and Sharon Martinas's, Challenging White Supremacy, 2440 16th Street, P.M.B. #275, San Francisco, Calif., 94103, (415) 647-0921.

18. DeRosa, "Diversity Training," 3.

19. Gordon, "The Work of Corporate Culture," 17–18.

20. Mark Chesler, "Organizational Development Is Not the Same as Multicultural Organizational Development," in Cross et al., *The Promise of Diversity,* 249.

21. Ron Chishom, phone interview with the author, December 10, 1999.

22. Joy James, introduction to *The Angela Y. Davis Reader,* ed. Joy James (Malden, Mass.: Blackwell, 1998), 19–20.

23. Ibid., 20.

24. Patti DeRosa, conversation with the author, November 1999.

11. "In All Its Incarnations"

The title of this chapter is from my interview with Anne Braden.

1. Ray Luc Levasseur's list of books that he smuggles into welcoming hands as the unofficial librarian in prison are equally revealing of an activist life. He writes, "Books I have now gotten into circulation include *The Black Panthers Speak, A Taste of Power, The Struggle: A History of the African*

National Congress, both of George Jackson's books, *Che, Worse Than Slavery, Rasta and Resistance, American Negro Slave Revolts, Cages of Steel, Wretched of the Earth, The Communist Manifesto, Assata, A People's History of the United States,* various periodicals from *The Revolutionary Worker,* and *Prison Legal News.*"

2. Thank you to Patti DeRosa for conversation and clarity on this point.

3. Title from Cherríe Moraga, *Loving in the War Years: Lo que nunca pasó por sus labios* (Boston: South End Press, 1983).

4. For important writing on white parenting of children of color, see Jane Lazarre, *Beyond the Whiteness of Whiteness: Memoir of a White Mother of Black Sons* (Durham, N.C.: Duke University Press, 1996); Maureen Reddy, *Crossing the Color Line: Race, Parenting, and Culture* (New Brunswick, N.J.: Rutgers University Press, 1994); and Maureen Reddy, ed., *Everyday Acts against Racism: Raising Children in a Multiracial World* (Seattle, Wash.: Seal Press, 1996).

5. Anne Braden, epilogue to her *The Wall Between* (Knoxville: University of Tennessee Press, 1999), 329–30.

6. Bonnie Kerness, letter to author, August 9, 1996.

7. Ibid.

8. Naomi Jaffe, letter to author, October 13, 1997.

9. Mab Segrest, *My Mama's Dead Squirrel: Lesbian Essays on Southern Culture* (Ithaca, N.Y.: Firebrand Books, 1985), 56–57.

10. Ibid., 59.

11. Braden, *The Wall Between,* 324.

12. Ibid., 311. This story about the absurdity of antileft censorship parallels, in a frightening way, a scene in a recent Canadian film, *Better Than Chocolate,* about a 1990s lesbian/transgendered community. The feminist bookstore in town—Ten Percent Review—had a batch of books with telltale titles (or so the officials thought) confiscated at the border—*Virtual S and M; Butch Politics, Femme Play; Safe Sex and Other Naughty Acts;* and *Little Red Riding Hood.* Officials admitted, upon really looking at *Little Red Riding Hood*—the children's story—that they had thought it was something else. (I wonder what?) That book, alone, they agreed to release. The U.S. government takes all the books from the Bradens with a "Russian sounding author" in the 1950s, while the Canadian government takes *Little Red Riding Hood* in the 1990s. For this reason, mainly, it is impossible to accept the notion of history as progress.

13. Thanks to Susan Kosoff, producer and playwright, for this point.

14. Braden, *The Wall Between,* 339.

15. Toni Morrison, "On Herman Melville," in *Black on White: Black Writers on What It Means To Be White,* ed. David R. Roediger (New York: Schocken, 1998), 212.

16. James Baldwin, "White Man's Guilt," in Roediger, *Black on White,* 321.

17. Mab Segrest, "Fear to Joy: Fighting the Klan," *Sojourner: The Women's Forum* 17, no. 3 (November 1987): 21.

18. Ibid.

19. Marilyn Buck, "Thirteen Springs," *Sojourner: The Women's Forum* 29, no. 9 (May 1999): 20.

20. Bernice Johnson Reagon, "African Disapora Women: The Making of Cultural Workers," *Feminist Studies* 12, no. 1 (1986): 77.

21. See, for example, Thich Nhat Hanh, *The Miracle of Mindfulness: A Manual of Meditation* (Boston: Beacon, 1987), and *Peace Is Every Step: The Path of Mindfulness in Everyday Life.* (New York: Bantam, 1991).

22. Alice Walker, *The Color Purple* (New York: Harcourt Brace Jovanovich, 1982), 203.

23. Roediger, *Black on White.*

24. Cheryl Hyde, "The Meaning of Whiteness," *Qualitative Sociology* 18, no. 1 (1995): 92.

25. David Wellman, "Red and Black in White America: Discovering Cross-Border Identities and Other Subversive Activities," in *Names We Call Home: Autobiography on Racial Identity,* ed. Becky Thompson and Sangeeta Tyagi (New York: Routledge, 1996), 35.

26. Ibid., 36.

Epilogue

1. Ruth Behar, *The Vulnerable Observer: Anthropology That Breaks Your Heart* (Boston: Beacon Press, 1996), 3.

2. Adrienne Rich, *Blood, Bread, and Poetry* (New York: Norton, 1986), 141.

3. Personal correspondence with the author, June 2000.

4. Derrick Bell, *And We Are Not Saved* (New York: Norton, 1989).

5. For two of Blauner's key works see Robert Blauner, *Racial Oppression in America* (New York: Harper and Row, 1972), and *Black Lives, White Lives: Three Decades of Race Relations in America* (Berkeley and Los Angeles: University of California Press, 1989).

Select Bibliography

Abu-Jamal, Mumia. *Death Blossoms: Reflections from a Prisoner of Conscience*. Farmington, Pa.: Plough Publishing House, 1997.
———. *Live from Death Row*. New York: Avon, 1996.
Aguilar–San Juan, Karin, ed. *The State of Asian America: Activism and Resistance in the 1990s*. Boston: South End Press, 1994.
Alexander, M. Jacqui, and Chandra Talpade Mohanty, eds. *Feminist Genealogies, Colonial Legacies, Democratic Futures*. New York: Routledge, 1997.
Allen, Paula Gunn. *Sacred Hoop: Recovering the Feminine in American Indian Traditions*. Boston: Beacon Press, 1986.
Allen, Robert. *Reluctant Reformers: Racism and Social Reform Movements in the United States*. Washington, D.C.: Howard University Press, 1974.
Anzaldúa, Gloria, ed. *Making Face, Making Soul: Haciendo Caras. Creative and Critical Perspectives by Women of Color*. San Francisco: Aunt Lute Foundation Books, 1990.
Aptheker, Herbert. *Anti-Racism in U.S. History: The First Two Hundred Years*. Westport, Conn.: Praeger, 1993.
Balagoon Kuwasi et al., eds. *Look for Me in the Whirlwind: The Collective Autobiographies of the New York Twenty-One*. New York: Vintage Books, 1971.
Basu, Amrita, ed. *The Challenge of Local Feminisms: Women's Movement in Global Perspective*. Boulder, Colo.: Westview, 1995.
Beck, Evelyn Torton, ed. *Nice Jewish Girls: A Lesbian Anthology*. Trumansburg, N.Y.: The Crossing Press, 1982.
Behar, Ruth. *The Vulnerable Observer: Anthropology That Breaks Your Heart*. Boston: Beacon Press, 1996.
Bell, Derrick. *And We Are Not Saved: The Elusive Quest for Racial Justice*. New York: Basic Books, 1989.
Blauner, Robert. *Black Lives, White Lives: Three Decades of Race Relations in America*. Berkeley and Los Angeles: University of California Press, 1989.
———. *Racial Oppression in America*. New York: Harper and Row, 1972.

Blee, Kathleen M. *Women of the Klan: Racism and Gender in the 1920s.* Berkeley and Los Angeles: University of California Press, 1991.

Blee, Kathleen M., and France Winddance Twine. *Feminisms and Antiracisms: International Struggles for Justice.* New York: New York University Press, forthcoming.

Bloom, Alexander, and Wini Breines, eds. *Takin' It to the Streets: A '60s Reader.* New York: Oxford University Press, 1995.

Blunk, Tim, and Raymond Luc Levasseur, eds. *Hauling Up the Morning: Izando la Mañana.* Trenton, N.J.: Red Sea Press, 1990.

Bowser, Benjamin, ed. *Racism and Anti-Racism in World Perspective.* Beverly Hills, Calif.: Sage, 1995.

Braden, Anne. *The Wall Between.* New York: Monthly Review Press, 1958; reprint Knoxville: University of Tennessee Press, 1999.

Brant, Beth, ed. *A Gathering of Spirit: Writing and Art by North American Indian Women.* Rockland, Me.: Sinister Wisdom Books, 1984.

Breines, Wini. *Community and Organization in the New Left, 1962–1968: The Great Refusal.* New Brunswick, N.J.: Rutgers University Press, 1989.

Bulkin, Elly, Minnie Bruce Pratt, and Barbara Smith. *Yours in Struggle: Three Feminist Perspectives on Anti-Semitism and Racism.* Brooklyn, N.Y.: Long Haul Press, 1984.

Cade, Toni, ed. *The Black Woman: An Anthology.* New York: Signet, 1970.

Cannon, Katie G. *Black Womanist Ethics.* Atlanta, Ga.: Scholars Press, 1988.

Caraway, Nancie. *Segregated Sisterhood: Racism and the Politics of American Feminism.* Knoxville: University of Tennessee Press, 1991.

Carson, Clayborne, ed. *In Struggle: SNCC and the Black Awakening of the 1960s.* Cambridge, Mass.: Harvard University Press, 1981, 1995.

Chafe, William, H. *The Unfinished Journey: America since World War II.* New York: Oxford University Press, 1999.

Churchill, Ward, and Jim Vander Wall. *Agents of Repression: The FBI's Secret War against the Black Panther Party and the American Indian Movement.* Boston: South End Press, 1988.

Coutin, Susan. *The Culture of Protest: Religious Activism in the United States Sanctuary Movement.* Boulder, Colo.: Westview Press, 1993.

Crawford, Vicki L., Jacqueline Anne Rouse, and Barbara Woods, eds. *Women in the Civil Rights Movement: Trailblazers and Torchbearers, 1941–1965.* Bloomington: Indiana University Press, 1993.

Crittenden, Ann. *Sanctuary: A Story of American Conscience and the Law in Collision.* New York: Weidenfeld and Nicolson, 1988.

Cross, Elsie Y., Judith Katz, Frederick Miller, and Edith Seashore, eds. *The Promise of Diversity.* Chicago: Irwin, 1994.

Cruse, Harold. *The Crisis of the Negro Intellectual: A Historical Analysis of the Failure of Black Leadership.* New York: William Morrow, 1967.

Davis, Angela. *Angela Davis: An Autobiography.* New York: Random House, 1974.

———. *The Angela Y. Davis Reader.* Edited by Joy James. Malden, Mass.: Blackwell, 1998.

Davis, Angela, and Bettina Aptheker, eds. *If They Come in the Morning: Voices of Resistance.* New York: Signet, 1971.

DePlessis, Rachel Blau, and Ann Snitow, eds. *The Feminist Memoir Project: Voices from Women's Liberation.* New York: Three Rivers Press, 1998.

Dunbar, Anthony. *Against the Grain: Southern Radicals, 1929–1959.* Charlottesville: University Press of Virginia, 1981.

Echols, Alice. *Daring to Be Bad: Radical Feminism in America, 1967–1975.* Minneapolis: University of Minnesota Press, 1989.

Evans, Sara. *Personal Politics: The Roots of Women's Liberation in the Civil Rights Movement and the New Left.* New York: Vintage Books, 1980.

Ferree, Myra Marx, and Beth B. Hess. *Controversy and Coalition: The New Feminist Movement across Three Decades of Change.* Boston: Twayne Publishers, 1994.

Foner, Philip, ed. *The Black Panthers Speak.* New York: De Capo Press, 1995.

Frankenberg, Ruth. *White Women, Race Matters: The Social Construction of Whiteness.* Minneapolis: University of Minnesota Press, 1993.

Gibbs, Joan, and Sara Bennett. *Top Ranking: A Collection of Articles on Racism and Classism in the Lesbian Community.* New York: Come! Unity Press, 1980.

Giddings, Paula. *When and Where I Enter: The Impact of Black Women on Race and Sex in America.* New York: Bantam Books, 1984.

Gitlin, Todd. *The Sixties: Years of Hope, Days of Rage.* New York: Bantam Books, 1987.

Golden, Renny, and Michael McConnell. *Sanctuary: The New Underground Railroad.* Maryknoll, N.Y.: Orbis Books, 1986.

Greenberg, Cheryl Lynn, ed. *A Circle of Trust: Remembering SNCC.* New York: Routledge, 1998.

Guy-Sheftall, Beverly, ed. *Words of Fire: An Anthology of African-American Feminist Thought.* New York: New Press, 1995.

Hall, Jacqueline Dowd. *Revolt against Chivalry: Jessie Daniel Ames and the Women's Campaign against Lynching.* New York: Columbia University Press, 1993.

Hall, Lisa Kahaleole Chang. "'Unspeakable Things' Spoken: Toward a Syllabus of Multiple Marginalization." Ph.D. diss., University of California at Berkeley, 1997.

Haney Lopez, Ian. *White by Law: The Legal Construction of Race.* New York: University of New York Press, 1996.

Harding, Vincent. *There Is a River: The Black Struggle for Freedom in America.* New York: Random House, 1983.

Hardisty, Jean. *Mobilizing Resentment: Conservative Resurgence from the John Birch Society to the Promise Keepers.* Boston: Beacon, 1999.

Helms, Janet E., ed. *Black and White Racial Identity: Theory, Research, and Practice.* New York: Greenwood Press, 1990.

Hull, Gloria T., Patricia Bell Scott, and Barbara Smith, eds. *All the Women Are White, All the Blacks Are Men, But Some of Us Are Brave: Black Women's Studies.* Old Westbury, N.Y.: Feminist Press, 1982.

Hurtado, Aída. *The Color of Privilege: Three Blasphemies on Race and Feminism.* Ann Arbor: University of Michigan Press, 1996.

Ignatiev, Noel, and John Garvey, eds. *Race Traitor.* New York: Routledge, 1996.

Jacobs, Ron. *The Way the Wind Blew: A History of the Weather Underground.* New York: Verso, 1997.

Jaimes, M. Annette, ed. *The State of Native America: Genocide, Colonization, and Resistance.* Boston: South End Press, 1992.

James, Joy. *Resisting State Violence: Radicalism, Gender, and Race in U.S. Culture.* Minneapolis: University of Minnesota Press, 1996.

Jones, Charles E., ed. *The Black Panther Party Reconsidered.* Baltimore: Black Classic Press, 1998.

Kaplan, Judy, and Linn Shapiro, eds. *Red Diapers: Growing Up in the Communist Left.* Chicago: University of Illinois Press, 1998.

Katz, Judith. *White Awareness: Handbook for Anti-Racism Training.* Norman: University of Oklahoma Press, 1978.

Kaye/Kantrowitz, Melanie. *The Issue Is Power: Essays on Women, Jews, Violence, and Resistance.* San Francisco: Aunt Lute Foundation Books, 1992.

Kelley, Robin D. G. *Race Rebels: Culture, Politics, and the Black Working Class.* New York: Free Press, 1994.

King, Katie. *Theory in Its Feminist Travels: Conversations in U.S. Women's Movements.* Bloomington: University of Indiana Press, 1994.

King, Mary. *Freedom Song: A Personal History of the 1960s Civil Rights Movement.* New York: William Morrow, 1987.

Lazarre, Jane. *Beyond the Whiteness of Whiteness: Memoir of a White Mother of Black Sons.* Durham, N.C.: Duke University Press, 1996.

Lazerson, Joshua N. *Against the Tide: Whites in the Struggle against Apartheid.* Boulder, Colo.: Westview Press, 1997.

Lewis, John. *Walking with the Wind: A Memoir of the Movement.* New York: Simon and Schuster, 1998.

Lieblich, Julia. *Sisters: Lives of Devotion and Defiance.* New York: Ballantine Books, 1992.

Lorde, Audre. *Sister Outsider.* New York: Crossing Press, 1996.

Lorentzen, Robin. *Women in the Sanctuary Movement.* Philadelphia: Temple University Press, 1991.

Lubiano, Wahneema, ed. *The House That Race Built: Black Americans, U.S. Terrain.* New York: Pantheon, 1997.

Lynn, Susan. *Progressive Women in Conservative Times: Racial Justice, Peace, and Feminism, 1945 to the 1960s.* New Brunswick, N.J.: Rutgers University Press, 1992.

Marable, Manning. *How Capitalism Underdeveloped Black America.* Boston: South End Press, 1983.

Martínez, Elizabeth. *De Colores Means All of Us: Latina Views for a Multi-Colored Century.* Boston: South End Press, 1998.

McDaniel, Judith. *Sanctuary: A Journey.* Ithaca, N.Y.: Firebrand, 1987.

McIntosh, Peggy. "White Privilege and Male Privilege: A Personal Account of Coming To See Correspondences through Work in Women's Studies." Working paper no. 189, Center for Research on Women, Wellesley, Mass., 1988.

Mohanty, Chandra Talpade, Ann Russo, and Lourdes Torres, eds. *Third World Women and the Politics of Feminism.* Bloomington: University of Indiana Press, 1991.

Moraga, Cherríe, and Gloria Anzaldúa, eds. *This Bridge Called My Back: Writings by Radical Women of Color.* 2nd ed. New York: Kitchen Table Women of Color Press, 1983.

Morgan, Edward P. *The '60s Experience: Hard Lessons about Modern America.* Philadelphia: Temple University Press, 1991.

Morris, Aldon. *The Origins of the Civil Rights Movement.* New York: Free Press, 1984.

Mujeres Activas en Letras y Cambio Social, eds. *Chicana Critical Issues.* Berkeley, Calif.: Third Woman Press, 1993.

Naples, Nancy A., ed. *Community Activism and Feminist Politics: Organizing Across Race, Class, and Gender.* New York: Routledge, 1998.

The National Committee to Free Puerto Rican Prisoners of War and the National Committee to End the Marion Lockdown, eds. *Can't Jail the Spirit: Political Prisoners in the United States.* Chicago: Editorial Coqui Publishers, 1998.

Nestle, Joan. *A Restricted Country.* Ithaca, N.Y.: Firebrand, 1987.

Nhat Hanh, Thich. *The Miracle of Mindfulness: A Manual of Meditation.* Boston: Beacon, 1987.

Ornelas, Michael R. *Beyond 1848: Readings in the Modern Chicano Historical Experience.* Dubuque, Iowa: Kendall/Hunt, 1993.

Perkins, Margo V. *Autobiography as Activism: Three Black Women of the Sixties.* Jackson: University Press of Mississippi, 2000.

Randall, Margaret. *Sandino's Daughters Revisited: Feminism in Nicaragua.* New Brunswick, N.J.: Rutgers University Press, 1994.

———. *Gathering Rage: The Failure of the Twentieth Century Revolutions to Develop a Feminist Agenda.* New York: Monthly Review Press, 1992.

Reddy, Maureen. *Crossing the Color Line: Race, Parenting, and Culture*. New Brunswick, N.J.: Rutgers University Press, 1994.

———. ed. *Everyday Acts against Racism: Raising Children in a Multiracial World*. Seattle, Wash.: Seal Press, 1996.

Rich, Adrienne. *Blood, Bread, and Poetry*. New York: Norton, 1986.

———. *On Lies, Secrets, and Silence*. New York: Norton, 1979.

Robnett, Belinda. *How Long? How Long? African American Women in the Struggle for Civil Rights*. New York: Oxford University Press, 1997.

Roediger, David, ed. *Black on White: Black Writers on What It Means to Be White*. New York: Schocken, 1998.

Ruiz, Vicki L., and Ellen Carol DuBois, eds. *Unequal Sisters: A Multicultural Reader in U.S. Women's History*. New York: Routledge, 1994.

Ryan, Barbara. *Feminism and the Women's Movement: Dynamics of Change in Social Movement Ideology and Activism*. New York: Routledge, 1992.

Sandoval, Chela. "Oppositional Consciousness in the Postmodern World: United States Third World Feminism, Semiotics, and the Methodology of the Oppressed." Ph.D. diss., University of California at Santa Cruz, 1994.

———. "U.S. Third World Feminism: The Theory and Method of Oppositional Consciousness in the Postmodern World." *Genders* 10 (Spring 1991):1–24.

Segrest, Mab. *Memoir of a Race Traitor*. Boston: South End Press, 1994.

———. *My Mama's Dead Squirrel: Lesbian Essays on Southern Culture*. Ithaca, N.Y.: Firebrand, 1985.

Shakur, Assata. *Assata: An Autobiography*. Chicago: Lawrence Hills Books, 1987.

Sinclair, Minor, ed. *The New Politics of Survival: Grassroots Movements in Central America*. New York: Monthly Review Press, 1995.

Smith, Barbara, ed. *Home Girls: A Black Feminist Anthology*. New York: Kitchen Table Women of Color Press, 1983.

Smith, Christian. *Resisting Reagan: The U.S. Central America Peace Movement*. Chicago: University of Chicago Press, 1996.

Smith, Lillian. *Killers of the Dream*. New York: Norton, 1994.

Terry, Robert. *For Whites Only*. Grand Rapids, Mich.: William B. Eerdmans, 1970.

Thompson, Becky, and Sangeeta Tyagi, eds. *Names We Call Home: Autobiography on Racial Identity*. New York: Routledge, 1996.

Walker, Alice. *The Color Purple*. New York: Harcourt Brace Jovanovich, 1982.

Wellman, David. *Portraits of White Racism*. New York: Cambridge University Press, 1977, 1993.

White, Deborah Gray. *Too Heavy a Load: Black Women in Defense of Themselves*. New York: Norton, 1999.

Winant, Howard. *Racial Conditions: Politics, Theory, Practice*. Minneapolis: University of Minnesota Press, 1994.

Zinn, Howard. *The Zinn Reader: Writings on Disobedience and Democracy*. New York: Seven Stories Press, 1997.

———. *You Can't Be Neutral on a Moving Train*. Boston: Beacon Press, 1994.

———. *A People's History of the United States*. New York: HarperPerennial, 1980.

———. *SNCC: The New Abolitionists*. Boston: Beacon Press, 1964.

Index

120, 130, 132; socialist, 120, 143, 163, 366 420n3
Feminist organizations, multiracial: American Indian and Alaska Native Women, 426n29; Asian Sisters, 145, 146, 192; Coalition of Labor Union Women, 168; Combahee River Collective, 138, 146–49, 154, 168, 171, 184, 192, 197, 220, 370; Dykes against Racism Everywhere, 172, 207; Elizabeth Stone House, 161–62, 391; Feminist Action Network, 156, 184; Harbor Communities Overcoming Violence, 390–91, 446n1; Hijas de Cuauhtemoc, 145, 146; Holding Our Own, 154, 391–92; International Working Women's Day Committee, 213; Kitchen Table Women of Color Press, 189, 196; Lesbians against Police Violence, 188, 207, 387; Mexican American Women's National Association, 426n29; National Black Feminist Organization, 138, 146, 168, 192, 198, 206, 220; National Black Women's Health Project, 220; National Institute of Women of Color, 426n29; National Welfare Rights Organization, 163, 427n49; National Women's Studies Assocation, 158, 172, 189, 192, 199–200, 204, 206; New York Women against Rape (NYWAR), 204, 205, 206; Organization of Pan Asian American Women, 426n29; Third World Women's Alliance, 144, 169, 426n29; Vancouver Indochinese Women's Conference, 145; Women of All Red Nations,

145–146, 168. *See also* Antiracist organizations
Ferber, Abby, xxvi
Firestone, Shulamith, 149
First Amendment and racism, 415n7
Flagg, Barbara, xx
Fonda, Jane, 87
For Colored Girls Who Have Considered Suicide/When the Rainbow Is Enuf, 150
Forman, Jim, 54, 57, 60, 64, 79
Frankenberg, Ruth: antiracist culture, 327, 346; biographical note, 388; multiracial feminism, 162–66; racial identity development, 223; range of activism, xxvii; spirituality, 355, 356–58, 363; *White Women, Race Matters,* xxiii, 167, 189, 223
Freedman's Bureau, 221
Freedom Singers, 45, 72
Freedom Summer, 4, 41, 50, 55–56, 59, 76, 78, 80
Free speech movement, 74, 75–78, 325
Friedan, Betty, 115

Gabriner, Vicki, 131–32
Garofalo, Reebee, 80; antiracist culture, 335–36, 359–60; biographical note, 388–390; range of activism, xxviii; SNCC, 50, 56, 59–60
Garvey, John, xx
Gathering of Spirit: Writing and Art by North American Indian Women, A, 153, 184
Gibbs, Joan, 189
Giddings, Paula, 71
Gilbert, David, 216, 322–323; antiracist culture, 353, 360–61, 371; antiracist ethics, 290–92;

Becky Thompson is associate professor of sociology at Simmons College in Boston, where she teaches courses in African American studies, women's studies, and sociology. Through her social justice work, she has organized in support of Mumia Abu-Jamal, multiracial feminism, multicultural education, and human rights and against apartheid and U.S. intervention in Central America. She is the legal guardian of a son and the godmother of a third-wave feminist activist.

She is author of *Mothering without a Compass: White Mother's Love, Black Son's Courage* (Minnesota, 2000) and *A Hunger So Wide and So Deep: A Multiracial View of Women's Eating Problems* (Minnesota, 1994). She coedited, with Sangeeta Tyagi, *Names We Call Home: Autobiography on Racial Identity* and *Beyond a Dream Deferred: Multicultural Education and the Politics of Excellence* (Minnesota, 1993), which was awarded the Gustavus Myers Award for Outstanding Book on Human Rights in North America.